**CITY OF BIRMINGHAM
POLYTECHNIC LIBRARY**

The Schools Council project Extending Beginning Reading was directed by Vera Southgate. It was based at the School of Education, University of Manchester from September 1973 to December 1977.

In addition to the director there were four research associates who worked as members of the team for the following periods:

| | |
|---|---|
| Helen Arnold | September 1973—March 1977 |
| Elizabeth Burke | September 1973—March 1975 |
| Gerald Keil | May—September 1975 |
| Sandra Johnson | September 1975—December 1977 |

Two reading specialists from the U.S.A. joined the team, on a voluntary basis, for a number of weeks each during 1976:

| | |
|---|---|
| Professor James T. Fleming | State University of New York at Albany |
| Professor Lillian R. Putnam | Kean College, New Jersey |

# Extending Beginning Reading

Vera Southgate, Helen Arnold

and

Sandra Johnson

H·E·B

Published for the Schools Council by
Heinemann Educational Books

Heinemann Educational Books Ltd
22 Bedford Square, London WC1B 3HH
LONDON   EDINBURGH   MELBOURNE   AUCKLAND
HONG KONG   SINGAPORE   KUALA LUMPUR   NEW DELHI
IBADAN   NAIROBI   JOHANNESBURG
EXETER (NH)   KINGSTON   PORT OF SPAIN

ISBN  0 435 10820 4 (cased)
      0 435 10821 2 (paper)

Typeset by the Castlefield Press of Northampton,
and printed and bound in Great Britain by
Biddles Ltd of Guildford

# Contents

# Acknowledgements

The authors of this report would first like to thank all the members of the Consultative Committee who gave so much of their time to advising and supporting them over a four-year period, and also to the members of the Local Committee who were equally helpful during the first two years of the project. At the same time, we wish to record our deepest thanks to Dr. J. Rushton, who so ably chaired both committees throughout the period.

As the major portion of the research in the project Extending Beginning Reading was concerned with on-going school and classroom practices, the co-operation of the staffs of a large number of primary schools formed an essential prerequisite to the many investigations undertaken. Accordingly, we wish to express our gratitude to the headteachers and staffs of the 170 schools who worked so closely with us. Many of the headteachers and class teachers were active members of the Teachers' Reading Research Groups; in other cases the schools were used for general observations, pilot tests, training for classroom observers or as 'intensive study schools' in the third year of the project. The headteachers and staffs of the 12 intensive study schools merit particularly warm thanks, as they suffered all the inconvenience of researchers, testers and observers continually in and out of their classrooms for an entire school year.

A complete list of the schools which participated in the various project activities is given in Appendix 1-A. These schools were drawn from the following 14 Local Education Authorities: Blackburn, Bolton, Bury, Cheshire, Lancashire, Manchester, Oldham, Rochdale, Salford, Stockport, Tameside, Trafford, Warrington and Wigan; and we should like to acknowledge the co-operation of the Chief Education Officers and advisory staff concerned. Our special thanks must go to the following local advisers who worked so closely with us in the preparations for the intensive study, as well as giving us help throughout that whole year:

Mr. J. Islip, District Inspector, Manchester; Miss M. Jee, General Adviser, Trafford; Mr. R.W. Johnson, Primary Phase Specialist, Cheshire; Mr. K. R. Hanham, Senior Adviser, Bolton; Mr. P. Noden, General Adviser for Primary Education, Trafford.

We also wish to acknowledge our indebtedness to all the following people who so willingly gave their help in a variety of ways: Miss D. Ainsworth, Principal Lecturer in Education, Didsbury College of Higher Education; Mr. D. W. Boote, Lecturer in Professional Studies, Didsbury College of Higher Education; Mr. G. Bradley, Principal Lecturer in Special Education, City of Manchester College of Higher Education; Mr. R. W. Doyle, Adviser for Primary Education, St. Helens; Miss L. Lea, former Headteacher; Mrs. B. Percy, Audio-Visual Services, University of Manchester; Mr. D. P. Pumfrey, Senior Lecturer in Education, University of Manchester; Mr. D. Rigby, Education Officer, Somerset; Miss M. Skeffington, Senior Lecturer in Education, University of Manchester; Members of the staff of the Audio-Visual Unit, Didsbury College of Higher Education; Members of the Schools Library Services of Bolton, Cheshire, Manchester and Trafford; Teachers following Advanced Diploma Courses at the University of Manchester and the City of Manchester College of Higher Education; and Post-graduate students at Didsbury College of Higher Education.

Finally, neither the research itself nor the report could have been completed without great support in the form of typing and clerical work, undertaken by Sylvia Davis, Ann Epton and Joyce Levison, to whom we are extremely grateful.

Vera Southgate
Helen Arnold
Sandra Johnson

# PART ONE

## Origin and Scope of the Project

CHAPTER 1

# Background to the Project

## I Historical Background

### A. *Introduction*

Ever since the Education Acts of 1870-1902 established compulsory education, teaching children to read has always been considered by British teachers to be of great importance. Yet, until the 1940s, the task of teaching reading was somehow or other regarded as solely the concern of infant teachers. The general assumption was that, after two or three years in school, the majority of children would have mastered what were then thought of as the rudiments or mechanics of reading. It was assumed that after this stage, with a little help from their teachers — the help usually being envisaged mainly as the provision of increasingly more difficult reading textbooks — children would eventually become efficient adult readers.

The fallacy of this hope was eventually demonstrated by the numbers of adult illiterates discovered in the armed forces during World War II. The result of this discovery was that, for the next 20 years or so, the subject of teaching reading was regarded as being divided into two main areas: the major area was considered to be teaching infants to read, while the subsidiary area was helping older, backward readers.

The concept that learning to read was a developmental process which extended from infancy to adulthood — a concept which had been recognized in the USA for about 30 years — did not begin to percolate into British educational circles until towards the end of the 1960s. This failure to realize that, at each level and stage of reading progress there were more advanced skills to be acquired, was exemplified in four main areas: Ministry or Department of Education policies; initial training of teachers; further education of teachers in the form of lectures, conferences and publications; and in the field of research.

### B. *Ministry and Department of Education's Policies*

The Board of Education's report on Primary Education (1931, reprinted 1952) suggested that: '. . . few children would not have mastered the mechanics of reading by the age of 7.' It made no mention of those developmental aspects of learning to read which need specific teaching after the age of 7. The same is true of the Ministry of Education's (1959) *Primary Education* which, in relation to children aged 7, indicated that: 'Some read fluently and with deep absorption; many can use books to find out what they want to know. All but a very few will have made a start in reading.' The book contains a 16-page section entitled 'Reading and Writing', but this gives no indication of how 7 to 11 year-olds might be helped to increase their skill in reading, other than suggestions relating to the provision of library books for individual reading. The Ministry's concern about 'backward readers' on the other hand was illustrated by its publication *Reading Ability: Some Suggestions for Helping the Backward* (Ministry of Education 1950).

The Department of Education and Science's (1967) report, *Children and Their Primary Schools* (the *Plowden Report*), followed a similar pattern. In this 500-page report, only one page was devoted to the subject of 'Teaching Children to Read' and even this gave no suggestion of reading skills which needed to be acquired by children over the age of 7.

## C. *Initial Training of Teachers*

Throughout the 1950s and well into the 1960s, Colleges of Education courses for the initial training of teachers illustrated the same lack of appreciation of the breadth of the subject of 'Reading'. For example, as late as 1967, a questionnaire completed by College of Education lecturers in one area training organization, indicated that students training to teach 5 to 7 year-olds received on average only 12 hours instruction in the early stages of learning to read, students training to teach 7 to 11 year-olds received only 1-6 hours instruction, while for those planning to teach pupils older than 11 years, instruction in teaching reading was rarely even considered.

However, by the end of the 1960s, in certain Colleges of Education, courses in the teaching of reading had been expanded in a number of ways. The subject matter was extended to include developmental aspects of reading teaching with different age groups, the number of hours of study was increased and additional courses were provided for students preparing to teach both junior and secondary pupils.

## D. *Further Education of Teachers*

Until almost the end of the 1960s courses of in-service training, conferences, and publications for teachers relating to reading were concerned almost exclusively with beginning reading and remedial reading. This was exemplified in the published proceedings of the first conference on reading, sponsored by the United Kingdom Reading Association, at

Oxford in 1964 (Downing 1966). The ten papers presented by well-known British lecturers were equally divided between these two areas of reading. Morris (1967) was among the first to draw attention to the need for a widening of the concept of reading teaching. She pointed out that: '. . . effective reading involves the acquisition of a wide range of skills throughout a child's school career and beyond; . . .' Even so, it was well into the 1970s before such an idea began to be accepted by educationists in general rather than just by those deeply committed to the cause of reading.

## E. *Reading Research*

In any area of the curriculum, the growing points are frequently those which prescient researchers have pursued a few years earlier. Yet Goodacre's (1972) review of reading research, covering the period of the 1950s and 1960s, shows that the research projects were mainly concerned with surveys of reading attainment, the early stages of reading, and teaching older backward readers. In that period, the only important piece of research relating to children aged 7 to 11 years was carried out in Kent from 1954-7 by Morris (1959 and 1966) for the National Foundation for Educational Research. The project was concerned with children in the whole primary school age-range (5 to 11 year-olds), and concentrated on those factors in the school situation which appeared to influence children's reading progress. It provided a detailed account of reading teaching in primary schools and reinforced the fact that, at that time, teachers' main concerns were with beginning readers and backward readers.

In describing reading research undertaken by the Schools Council, Goodacre (1972), after mentioning seven reading projects listed in the Schools Council's 1969/70 report, goes on to say:

> The impression is that the Schools Council is now being directed away from the initial stages of learning to read, and towards exploration of how proficiency in reading skill can be not only maintained but improved, so that children can use it for their own enjoyment and interest.

## II  Basis of the First Proposal

## A. *Limited Conception of Reading Teaching*

The proposal for this reading research project was first submitted in December 1969. It sprang from the knowledge that in England the concept of teaching was narrowly based and, as educationists in general were unfamiliar with the broader view, the proposal commenced with an attempt to outline the total field of reading teaching. The following were the main points made in this connection.

Learning to read is a developmental process extending from infancy to adulthood and it is very closely linked with the other language arts, namely listening, speaking and writing. Moreover, progress towards efficient reading involves, at every level, an ever-expanding mastery of the more advanced skills which make up the total skill of reading. These skills may be grouped in three or four broad categories.

First, there are certain skills of word recognition, among which are the acquisition of a large sight vocabulary, the development of various strategies for deciphering unknown words by means of phonic analysis, structural analysis or contextual clues, and the development of different speeds of reading appropriate for different purposes and different reading materials. Closely related to the word recognition skills is a wide range of skills relating to reading comprehension. These include the extension of vocabulary, the ability to grasp the meaning of passages of increasing length and complexity, to read for different purposes and to evaluate what is read.

Word recognition skills and comprehension skills form the basic skills of reading. Mastery of even the simplest elements of these skills enables the child to begin to read for different purposes, providing he is sufficiently motivated to want to do so. Given strong motivation and guided practice leading to the formation of efficient reading habits, the skills of word recognition and comprehension may be utilized in two broad categories of reading, functional reading and recreational reading, each requiring competence in certain additional techniques. The special techniques required in functional reading are generally termed study skills. They include the ability to find information  for specific purposes by using card indexes, dictionaries, encyclopedias and other reference books; a knowledge of how to locate books in libraries, and the relevant chapters or passages within these books; experience in selecting what is appropriate; and finally, the ability to organize what is read by summarizing or outlining it. The skills of recreational reading include the development of pleasure in reading and the ability to appreciate and evaluate what is read.

Unfortunately, in Britain the emphasis had been placed almost exclusively on beginning reading, and within that narrow field, almost solely on word recognition skills. Consequently, learning to read had tended to be regarded as a subject of concern only to infant teachers and remedial teachers. Yet the average child leaving an infant class with a reading age of $7^6$, who has probably completed a basic infant reading scheme and learned to read a few simple books on his own, has only *begun* to learn to read. If he is ever to achieve an efficient level of adult reading, he must continue to improve and extend his reading skills at every stage of education.

When this present project was proposed, its director also indicated that in the USA the development of intermediate and higher order skills in reading had received a great deal of attention and had been highly systematized in the form of earnest and, in her view, often boring routines of instruction. Such procedures were entirely out of tune with current educational thought in primary schools in Britain and she would not wish to advise adopting them. Therefore, it was proposed that the research project should begin by investigating what was currently taking place in English primary schools before considering how procedures might be developed to extend children's reading proficiency in a manner compatible with discovery methods of learning, without jeopardizing the motivational elements which such methods foster.

## B. *Vital Stage of 7+*

The title of the first proposal was 'Developing Reading Skills Beyond the Infant Stage'. It was suggested that at the level of a reading age of approximately 7, many children reached a plateau of attainment in reading, beyond which their progress slowed or sometimes almost ceased. Possible reasons suggested for this were either that once a child had finished an infant reading scheme his teacher tended to concentrate on the slower children in the class, or perhaps the teacher was not knowledgeable about the stages of reading tuition which should follow. As this was considered a vital stage in the continuing process which should lead the child on to efficient adult reading, it was suggested that the project should concentrate on average readers in the first two years of junior education, i.e. children aged 7 to 9+.

## C. *Proposed Research Procedures*

The proposal stressed the fact that the result of the project should be of practical value to teachers. To this end, two main approaches would be employed. The first would be the involvement of practising teachers, meeting in reading research groups and working with children in their own schools. The second would take the form of extensive observations in schools, accompanied by detailed assessments and recordings of children's reading attainments and activities, as well as their teachers' methods of forwarding the children's reading progress. It was pointed out that as the project was planned as an 'intensive' rather than an 'extensive' piece of research, it was essential that the schools concerned should be within easy access of the research centre. In these circumstances, neither sampling techniques nor standardization of results involving geographically dispersed areas would be appropriate.

## III Acceptance of the Proposal

During the next two years the climate of educational thought in the country changed and reading began to be regarded as of much greater importance. The crucial factor affecting this change was the publication, by the National Foundation for Educational Research in England and

Wales, of *The Trend of Reading Standards* (Start and Wells 1972). This report presented the findings of the latest (1970/1) governmental, national survey of reading comprehension. The results appeared to indicate that, in contrast to previous Ministerial reading surveys undertaken between 1948 and 1964, which had shown a trend of successively higher reading standards for 11 and 15 year-olds, average test scores were now levelling out or falling behind. The shock of this report provoked, not just from educationists, but also from employers, parents and the public at large, angry questions concerning the ways in which children were being taught to read. One result was that the Secretary of State for Education announced the setting up of a special committee of enquiry into reading and the use of English, under the chairmanship of Sir Alan Bullock. In this climate of increasing interest in the teaching of reading, the Schools Council announced acceptance of two reading proposals already before it — the current proposal relating to children of 7 to 9+ and Professor Lunzer's proposal[1] concerning children aged 10 to 15; both proposals being scheduled to commence in September 1973.

---

[1]The findings of this particular research project are given in the published report — Lunzer and Gardner (1979).

CHAPTER 2

# Outline of the Four Years' Project

## I Preliminary Details

The project was based at the University of Manchester, under the direction of Vera Southgate. The research team consisted of the director and two research associates. The project team were supported by two committees, a consultative committee shared with the Nottingham project, 'The Effective Use of Reading', and a local committee consisting of teachers, advisers, lecturers and reading specialists. The research team were grateful for the comments, ideas and support of the members of both these committees, which they found to be extremely valuable.

The schools which participated in the project were all situated within a radius of 30 miles of Manchester and were drawn from 14 local education authorities. The children concerned were classes of first- and second-year juniors, aged 7 to 9+, with a special emphasis on the children of average reading ability within these classes.

The project was originally planned to last for the three years 1973 to 1976. The first year was to be devoted to general observations in schools, pilot studies and work with teachers' reading research groups; the second year was set aside for an intensive study in a small number of schools; while the third year was to be devoted to analyzing data and writing the report. As it turned out, the information gained from the teachers' groups proved so valuable that the project was lengthened by a year. The pattern of the four-year project, which extended from September 1973 to August 1977 was therefore as follows:

*1st Year* – general observations in schools;
      – work with teachers' groups;
      – two pilot studies;
*2nd Year* – further work with teachers' groups;
      – devising and trying out observation schedules and other instruments for use in the intensive study;
      – undertaking a pilot study in preparation for the intensive study;
*3rd Year* – carrying out an intensive study in 12 schools;
*4th Year* – completion on an investigation into the reading environments of 8 of the schools in the intensive study;

— processing and analyzing data;
— beginning to write the report.

## II  Rationale Underlying the Project

The rationale underlying the research has been outlined in Chapter 1. This rationale was responsible for two of the most important features of the project.

First, it was not the kind of research project in which hypotheses were advanced, in order to be confirmed or refuted. In other words, it did not set out to prove anything. So little was known about current classroom practices relating to reading in English schools, and the ways in which children in these age-groups learned and behaved, that the project was essentially a fact-finding investigation. It was based on the belief that a clear insight into what was currently happening in their classes would provide teachers with the most effective basis for considering whether it was either possible or desirable to effect improvements and, if so, how this might best be done. The project was therefore planned as an 'intensive' rather than an 'extensive' study and an important part of the proposal was to study a small number of schools in depth.

Secondly, the project was, from the very beginning, firmly school-based, all the field work being carried out in normal school conditions. The entire project leaned very heavily on the contributions of practising teachers. The two main methods being used, teachers' reading research groups and detailed observations in schools, were complementary to each other and both were wholly dependent upon the co-operation of teachers. The amount of time, patience, tolerance and work demanded from all the teachers who co-operated with the research team in these ways was very great indeed.

While the central basis of the project remained as planned, what was actually done over the four-year period showed certain changes of emphasis. Ideas relating to helping children to read had developed in the years between 1969 and 1977 — the latter being the year in which the field work was completed. For example, the growing interest in psycholinguistics had drawn attention to *the ways in which children learn* in contrast to an earlier emphasis on *what* they had learned. Where changes in anticipated procedures did occur, they were in the nature of extensions to the original plans — developments arising from the growing interest in, and knowledge about, reading.

The focus of the research had never varied. It centred on those children who at 7 years of age had achieved average reading standards, that is, who had mastered the stage of 'beginning reading'; and on what happened to them in their next two years of schooling. The main objectives of the project were as follows:

(i)  to discover exact details of these children's competencies and the ways in which they utilize their reading skills;

(ii) to locate points at which difficulties occur and the strategies the children employ to overcome these difficulties;

(iii) to note the methods their teachers employ to help them to 'extend' their proficiency during their next two years of schooling, as well as the progress the children make during this period;

(iv) and to examine, in the children, habits and attitudes likely to encourage them to utilize fully their reading abilities outside school and when they finally leave school.

## III  Research Procedures

### A.  Teachers' Reading Research Groups

One side of the investigation involved practising teachers, recruited as members of reading research groups, carrying out various reading assessments of children in their own classes and providing the project team with the results, together with other details of their own and the children's reading practices. Teams of teachers who were currently teaching children aged 7 to 9+ years worked with the project team and each was led by the headteacher or the deputy headteacher.

The first Teachers' Reading Research Group, operating during 1973–4, consisted of 440 teachers, working in teams drawn from 119 junior and primary schools in 14 LEAs. The first task which the research team set themselves was to devise a scheme whereby these teachers might have the opportunity of either confirming that the project as planned would produce information of practical value to them or indicate those areas of the project's brief which they would prefer to see emphasized. The manner in which this exercise was undertaken, together with the results obtained, is outlined in Chapter 4, 'Teachers' Preferred Outcomes of the Project'. Teachers in the first Reading Research Group undertook various assessments in first- and second-year junior classes.

The second Reading Research Group of 1974–5 consisted of 258 teachers, working in teams drawn from 64 schools. A proportion of these teachers had been members of the previous year's groups.

The following are among the assignments the teachers carried out:
1. They tested the reading achievement of all the children (some 3,380 of them) in their classes. Even more important, before doing so, they estimated the result which each child would achieve.
2. They estimated the number of errors children would make in reading a passage from a book and then tested to verify the accuracy of their estimates.
3. They prepared individual reading profiles of average children including assessments of:
(a) Recognition of 'look and say' words;
(b) Knowledge of phonic rules;
(c) Number of errors made in reading aloud from a teacher-selected

book, a story book of the child's own choice and an information book of the child's own choice.
4. Children's miscues in oral reading were examined and classified into categories.
5. Children were tested using Cloze procedure (every tenth word being deleted), to investigate how successfully they were utilizing contextual clues in silent reading.

## B. *Observations and Investigations in Schools*

### 1. The first two years
The second main method of investigation was by means of classroom observations and assessments of children's reading abilities, attitudes and interests, made by members of the project team. Investigations in these areas went on continuously throughout the first two years, and involved 750 children, in 20 schools, drawn from 5 LEAs. The immediate aim of all these observations in schools and discussions with headteachers and their staffs was to provide an overall picture of current teaching and learning activities relating to reading. All activities, such as methods of direct reading instruction, reading materials in use, writing and related activities, and the uses made by children of their varying skills in reading and writing were listed. Children were also interviewed individually on an informal basis, questioned about their reading interests and asked to read aloud from their current books.

The long-term aim was to develop instruments, in the form of questionnaires, individual interviewing schedules, logs, various measures of achievement and observation schedules for use in the third year's intensive study in a small number of selected schools. By using such a diverse battery of probing techniques it was hoped that an accurate picture could be created of all those dynamic processes affecting reading progress which constantly occur in schools throughout the day.

### 2. The intensive study year
The intensive study year covered the period of September 1975 to July 1976, but a great deal of preparatory work relating to the selection of schools and the choosing or devising of appropriate observation and assessment instruments had taken place during the preceding year.

### (a) *Preliminary recruitment of the schools*
The need for members of the research team, and the helpers whom they recruited, to be almost continuously in and out of the schools throughout the intensive study year, made it essential that the schools should not be too widely scattered. Accordingly, schools used in the intensive study were drawn from four LEAs within easy travelling distance of Manchester University, namely Bolton, Cheshire, Manchester and

Trafford. Meetings between the primary advisers from these authorities and the research team resulted in the following decisions:—

(i) *Number of Schools* As a final total of 12 schools appeared to be the maximum number to which a team of 3 researchers could give detailed attention, each of the 4 advisers would recruit 4 or 5 suitable and interested schools. Thus, if, after testing, a school was found to have insufficient average readers or it desired to withdraw for any reason, the target of 3 schools in each of the four LEAs might still be maintained.

(ii) *'Willing' Schools* As the demands made on the teachers in the intensive study schools would be extremely heavy and would extend over an entire school year, the first essential was that the schools finally agreed on should be 'willing' schools. A leaflet was prepared, setting out in detail exactly what would be entailed in agreeing to act as an observation school. This information included the amount of time which would be spent on testing and observations, and also the additional work entailed for teachers in keeping records and completing forms and questionnaires. It also indicated that a member of the research team would be willing to go to any school to answer queries and discuss problems which the staff might have.

(iii) *Suitable Schools* In promoting the initial recruitment of possible schools, each adviser would think in terms of 'typical' schools, while still bearing in mind the need for achieving a balance between: junior and all-age primary schools; one-stream and larger schools; schools in different socio-economic areas; and schools with different average reading levels. While it was also important to have schools with a fairly wide range of average reading standards, schools at the extreme ends of the range would need to be excluded, as it was essential that in each age-group there should be sufficient children of 'average' reading attainments. It had been agreed that schools which had collaborated in the first two years of the project could not participate in the intensive study, as their normal teaching practices might, as a result, have been altered. Discussions between advisers and researchers resulted in 14 schools being available by September for the first round of testing.

(b) *Pre-testing and final selection of schools*

The selection of a standardized reading test to be used as an initial screening test posed a few problems. The first requirement was that the test chosen should be simple and speedy to administer so that children of average reading ability could be quickly identified. The second requirement was that the tests should be capable of providing assessments of reading ability at the beginning and end of the year, for as many children as possible. It was found practically impossible to choose one test which satisfied both these requirements. A group test which could be administered speedily, was sufficiently simple to be understood by, and provide information on the limited reading ability of, the poorest reader of 7 years 0 months at the beginning of the school year, was unlikely to be sufficiently probing or to have adequate headroom to measure fully the attainments of the best reader aged nearly 10 years at the end of the school year.

*Southgate Group Reading Test 2* (Southgate 1962) was finally selected as the screening test, in the knowledge that the *Wide-Span Reading Test* (Brimer 1972), which was going to be administered during the first term and at the end of the third term, had plenty of headroom, being designed for use with children aged 7 to 16 years. In the event, *Southgate Group Reading Test 2* proved effective as a screening test, in that testers were easily trained, a whole class could be tested in 20 minutes, nearly all children were able to understand the instructions and complete at least some of the questions, and the scripts were simple and speedy to mark.

It was essential that the initial screening test should be administered as early as possible in September, as the final selection of schools and classes could not be completed until the scripts were marked and the results examined, so many of the schools allowed the testing to begin in the second week of September.

As soon as the scripts were marked, a class list was prepared for every class, the children being divided into three categories of levels of reading attainment. First-year juniors with reading ages $7^1-8^0$ and second-year juniors with reading ages $8^1-9^0$ (using the original norms) were categorized as having 'average' levels of reading attainment. Children whose scores fell above or below these middle bands were considered to have achieved 'above average' and 'below average' levels respectively. The results, summarized in Tables 1 and 2 of Appendix 2-A, suggest that this procedure was reasonably successful in segregating those children in whom the team were particularly interested, i.e. those with average levels of reading proficiency in each age-group. Although in the complete total of children tested, approximately one-third fell into the middle band of children in each age-group, the range of differences in the numbers of average readers in the various schools and classes was very wide. Among first-year juniors the range in the number of 'average' readers in a class was 21-1, while for second-year juniors the figures were 19-0.

The final selection of classes to be used for the intensive study was based on the criterion that there should be a minimum of 5 children in the class who came within the average band. From the summary of the results of the selection procedure shown in the final column of Table 3 in Appendix 2-A, it can be noted that in the 12 schools finally selected, there were 35 classes containing 1,127 children of whom 587 were first-years and 540 were second-year juniors. Details of the number of children in the three categories of reading attainments in selected classes are set out in Appendix 2-B.

It was decided that concentrated investigations would be centred on 4 children from the middle band in each class. These children were chosen randomly, with, as far as possible, 2 boys and 2 girls in each class. A total of 140 children, on whom classroom observations and detailed assessments and interviews could be focussed throughout the year, was selected in this way. One or two 'reserves' in each class were also nominated.

Once the actual classes to be included in the study had been selected, the headteachers of the schools were informed and they and the relevant members of staff were invited to briefing meetings. These meetings allowed the researchers to ensure that the teachers knew exactly what was required, so that uniform procedures would be followed, and also provided opportunities for general questions and discussions about the project. It was not, however, possible for the team to supply details about the tests, forms of assessment and observation schedules, lest this information should lead teachers to alter their usual practices. These details were, however, supplied when the year's work had been completed.

(c) *Selection of battery of assessments*
The breadth of the aims and objectives of the project, as outlined earlier in this chapter, necessitated the selection and assembly of a large battery of probing techniques and instruments. In some cases standardized, published tests were found to be suitable but in other instances tests had to be devised as did the schedules and procedures for classroom observations. In the same way, questionnaires for teachers, interviewing and recording techniques and other means of gathering what was considered to be necessary information had to be developed.

The two standardized reading tests administered at the beginning and end of the year, *Southgate Group Reading Test 2* and Brimer's *Wide-Span Reading Test* have already been noted. The third reading test used — a new diagnostic phonic test — was devised specifically for the project and is described in Chapter 15. In the same way, in order to discover details of the children's reading competencies and the strategies they employ to overcome their difficulties, it was necessary to select and, in many cases, devise appropriate passages of prose on which to employ Cloze Procedure Techniques and to use for miscue analysis based on oral reading. In some cases, it was also necessary to develop new scoring techniques.

As a measurement of general intelligence, Raven's *Coloured Progressive Matrices* (Raven 1949) was chosen on the grounds that research focused on reading required non-verbal assessment of intelligence. This test had the additional advantage of being not only attractive to children, but also simple to administer as a group test to children as young as 7 years.

Of the various techniques of assessment and observation devised for use in the intensive study year, the development of classroom observation schedules for recording teachers' and children's behaviour relating to reading and writing activities was the most demanding, in terms of the time spent and in the number of prototypes which were produced, used in pilot tests, revised and improved. This work, which extended over the first two years of the project, resulted in the production and printing of new observation schedules, which are described in Chapter 10.

(d) *Overall pattern of the intensive study year*
The year of intensive study in schools proved an even more complex logistic exercise than had been anticipated. The team members were sustained and encouraged, however, by the continual support and co-operation of the staffs of the schools.

The main problems encountered during the year related to deviations from expected routines in schools, the deployment of equipment such as tape-recorders and testing materials, and the recruitment, training and transportation of observers. It was found, for example, that even with great goodwill on the part of the teachers, the number of occasions when 'normal school routines' were interrupted was far greater than had been anticipated. The reasons for the changes were varied and will have a familiar ring to all teachers, for example: a school assembly had been extended; preparations for a concert, harvest festival, carol service, sports day or parents' evening were in progress; students were in charge of classes and so on.

The three researchers were engaged in various activities in the 12 selected schools almost continuously throughout the school year from September 1975 to July 1976. The time-tabling of these activities was largely determined by the need for certain of them to take place at specific times. Into this category fell pre-tests which were administered in the first half of the Autumn term and post-tests carried out during the second half of the Summer term. Consequently, other assessments which only needed to be undertaken once were generally fitted into the Spring term. The much more intensive work of using observation schedules and asking teachers to keep daily logs of all reading, writing and language activities was limited to four weeks in the Autumn term and six weeks in the Spring term.

## C. *Summary of Information Obtained*

The intensive study year in 12 schools produced an enormous amount of data about the schools, classes and teachers, as well as a certain amount of developmental data on over 1,100 first- and second-year junior children and more detailed information on approximately 140 average readers. Details of this information are set out in the following notes.

Notes on information obtained from schools during
the 'intensive study' year
1. *Information about the school*

(a) Factual information about the size and general organization of the school.
(b) Further insight into aims and objectives in the school, the emphasis placed on reading and the detailed organization of the school in relation to reading, gained from an informal but extended interview with the headteacher.
(c) General information about the socio-economic background of the school.
(d) Information about the reading books or schemes used in infant classes or infant schools which fed each junior school.
(e) A detailed assessment of the Reading Environment, gained by a whole day's exercise in 8 of the schools, undertaken jointly by the Director of the project, one or more LEA advisers and various county librarians.

## 2. *Information about the classes*
(a) Factual information — numbers of children, organization, etc.
(b) Approximate proportion of time allocated to reading, writing and language development.
(c) Information about reading schemes in use.
(d) Information about supplementary reading materials, library books, etc. in each class of 8 of the schools, obtained from Observation Schedules and Teachers' Logs.

## 3. *Information about the teachers*
(a) Factual information about length and type of teacher training and details of teaching experience, etc.
(b) The teacher's main objective in the teaching of reading and her[1] related plans for teaching and learning activities, as stated by her at the beginning of the school year.
(c) The teacher's daily log sheets completed during the observation weeks in the Autumn and Spring terms provided details of how the teacher's time was spent in reading and writing activities.
(d) Information provided by the teacher about her practices in, for example, reading stories and poems to children, and also about the amount of time set aside for children's personal reading.
(e) Information about each teacher's teaching practices, obtained from Teacher Observation Schedules.
(f) Teacher's own views on the advantages and disadvantages of the method of disposition and uses of all the books in the 'Book Environment', expressed in a group discussion and by the completion of individual forms.
(g) Each teacher's own assessment, at the end of the year, of the extent to which participation in the project has altered her normal pattern of work.

[1] For the sake of clarity, throughout this report the teacher is referred to as 'she' and the pupils as 'he'.

4. *Information about the children*

(a) *Whole Classes*

| | TERMS | | |
|---|---|---|---|
| | 1st | 2nd | 3rd |
| (i) *Reading* | | | |
| Southgate Group Test 2 | √ | | √ |
| Brimer's *Wide-Span Reading Test* | √ | | √ |
| Children's individual records of books read throughout the year. | √ | √ | √ |
| Children's written comments on 'Books I Have Read'. | | | √ |
| (ii) *Intelligence* | | | |
| Raven's *Coloured Progressive Matrices* | | √ | |
| (b) *140 Children of 'Average' Reading Attainments* (The following information is in addition to the items outlined above.) | | | |
| Crichton *Vocabulary Scale* | | √ | |
| A New Phonic Test of 'Nonsense Words'[1] | | √ | √ |
| Oral Reading of a passage – Miscue Analysis | | | √ |
| Cloze Procedure Passage | | | √ |
| Observation Schedules (4 weeks and 6 weeks) | √ | √ | |
| Individual interviews – attitudes to reading, comments on books read, views on reading difficulties, etc. | | √ | |
| 'Thumb-nail sketches' of 4 average readers by each class teacher | | | √ |
| Examples of written work and art work of some of the average readers | | | √ |

[1]*N.B.* The phonic test was administered to 4 'above average' readers and 4 'below average' readers, as well as to 4 'average' readers in each class.

# PART TWO

## The Task

# CHAPTER 3

# Learning to Read — and Reading

## I Introduction

The task of ensuring that children learn to read, and of finding ways of helping them to do so, is one of general concern to all teachers in primary schools. In the context of the research project, Extending Beginning Reading, the specific task with which teachers are faced is that of making certain that average readers of 7+, having mastered the beginning stages of reading, should continue to extend their reading proficiency in the direction of mature, adult reading. Yet the specific task can only be considered, and carried out, in the context of the teacher's general views about reading and learning to read. The reasons are two-fold: the average readers form parts of classes consisting of children of all levels of reading competencies; and, furthermore, even children of average reading ability show great variety in their particular reading competencies as well as in their rates of progress.

An enquiry such as the present one could only be meaningfully undertaken in the light of: first, current knowledge about the act of reading, the manner in which the skill is learned, and the ways in which the process of learning can be facilitated; and secondly, one's answers to certain basic questions. Of the questions which need to be considered and answered by teachers before they can hope to plan effective strategies for helping children to learn to read, the following three are probably of greatest importance.

1. What *is* reading?  *My def:*
2. How do children really learn to read?  *How can I help?*
3. What are the skills used in reading?  *what shd's have I got dev'd?*

Only when teachers have developed their own clear answers to these three questions, will they be in the position to answer a fourth question which is continually in the forefront of their minds, namely:

4. What can we do to improve children's reading?

Trying to discover satisfying answers to the first three questions at the present time is not nearly as easy or straightforward as it would have been 20 years or even 10 years ago. Ten years ago, for instance, Clymer (1968) was stating some of the difficulties encountered in formulating a definition of reading:

The difficulty in formulating a comprehensive and satisfactory definition of reading is also apparent. The areas of perception, psychology of learning, linguistics, social psychology, and language learning are a few of the fields contributing to an understanding of the reading process and the reading program.

More recently, however, Chall (1977), in discussing some of the important developments in the psychology and teaching of reading during the years 1967–77, points out that: 'Much has happened in the field during the decade – probably more than in the preceding 50 years.' So the problem of defining reading becomes yearly *more*, rather than *less*, difficult. Even so, any attempt to answer the fourth question, which is of vital interest to teachers, can only be successful if it is firmly based on answers to the first three questions.

Clymer (1968) also emphasised the dominating role which a definition of reading plays in the teaching of reading, noting that: 'A teacher's definition of reading influences every action he takes in the classroom.' He went on to quote Strang (1967) who has spelt out even more clearly the effect which a teacher's definition of reading is likely to have on her teaching:

> If reading to him is word recognition, he will drill on the basic sight vocabulary and word recognition skills. If he thinks reading is merely reproducing what the author says, he will direct the student's attention to the literal meaning of the passage and check his comprehension of it. If he views reading as a thinking process, he will be concerned with the reader's skill in making interpretations and generalizations, in drawing inferences and conclusions.

## II What is Reading?

### A. *Reading and Thinking*

Definitions of reading are almost as numerous as the many reading experts who have committed their thoughts to paper. The definitions have changed over the years, sometimes as a result of research findings and the gaining of new knowledge, and sometimes at what appear to be the whims of fashion. While this is not the place to provide a potted history of definitions of reading, teachers are strongly recommended to read such accounts in, for example, Strang (1967), Clymer (1968), Jenkinson (1969) or *Reading Today and Tomorrow* (Melnick and Merritt 1972) – one of the Open University's textbooks which provides excerpts from these and other authors. Additional publications which will be found helpful in this respect are: Spache and Spache (1969), Smith (1971 and 1978), Stauffer (1975), Gibson and Levin (1975), Goodman (1977), and Goodman *et al.* (1978).

Briefly, it might be said that the main trend in definitions of reading, throughout this century, has been away from the earlier ideas of reading as a mechanical process towards an acceptance of it as a thoughtful process, requiring the reader not only to understand what the author is endeavouring to communicate but also to contribute his own experiences and thoughts to the problem of understanding.

As far back as 1913, Huey was beginning to formulate such ideas, as can be noted from his frequently quoted words:

> ... until the insidious thought of reading as word pronouncing is well worked out of our heads, it is well to place the emphasis strongly where it really belongs, on reading as thought-getting, independently of expression.

By 1937 Gray was writing:

> ... the reader not only recognizes the essential facts or ideas presented, but also reflects on their significance, evaluates them critically, discovers relationships between them, and clarifies his understanding of the ideas apprehended.

Such ideas about the nature of reading continued to expand so that in 1949, Gray was writing his well-known phrases, indicating that the reader:

> ... does more than understand and contemplate; his emotions are stirred; his attitudes and purposes are modified; indeed, his innermost being is involved.

Many of the foregoing definitions came from American writers but one of the briefest, and perhaps the most telling definition, came from an Englishman, Morris (1963): 'Reading is thinking under the stimulus of the printed word.'

## B. *The Complexity of the Reading Process*

Defining reading as a thinking process, however, is by no means the end of the story, for as Robinson (1966) points out, the nature of thought is extremely complex and is still not fully understood. At the same time, as knowledge about the actual process of learning to read has increased over the years, so have teachers and other educators come to realise that reading is not nearly such a simple task as it was formerly considered to be. As Smith (1971) has indicated: '... fluent reading is more complex than is frequently believed, and learning to read is far more involved.'

The more aware educators become of the complexities involved in the process of reading, the more complex are definitions of reading likely to become.

One additional point relating to problems of defining reading should be mentioned. A number of writers, including Strang (1965), Robinson (1966) and Clymer (1968), among others, have made pleas to differentiate between the separate issues which require consideration. These are:

(a) the reading process — i.e. what actually is happening when children are attempting to read;
(b) the products — i.e. the skills and abilities used in reading;
(c) the procedures — i.e. the techniques used by teachers in their efforts to help children to learn to read.

Clymer (1968) concluded that:

> While these factors are related and interdependent, a distinction among these factors is essential for thoughtful and productive analysis of reading.

It will also be noted that these three factors bear a close relationship to the first three questions which it has been suggested that teachers need to answer. Strang (1965), in fact, added a fourth point which she termed 'pre-requisites' — i.e. the experiences necessary for successful reading.

From a practical point of view, an understanding of the processes in which a child is engaged in his attempts to read, may seem to obviate the need for a definition of reading. It could be that the teacher who ponders on the question of 'What is reading?' is, in fact, asking 'How do children really learn to read?' Put more specifically, teachers basically want to understand the processes in which their pupils — at the particular stages they have reached — are engaged when they attempt to get meaning from the text. This in turn, will help them to plan their own teaching procedures. Consideration of processes, however, will be facilitated if some thought is first given to comprehension.

## C. *Comprehension*

The trend to regard reading as a thinking process has focussed attention on comprehension, its meaning and its importance. Chall (1977) for instance, writes as follows about two different views on comprehension, which were polarized between 1967 and 1977:

> Probably the more far-reaching theoretical question on reading comprehension is whether it is a general skill or ability or whether it is made up of a number of specific identifiable skills.
>
> This debate was launched recently by Robert L. Thorndike (1973—4) who took the position that reading comprehension is a unitary ability composed mainly of verbal reasoning.

She goes on to quote Davis (1971) as holding views on reading comprehension which are at the other extreme. He concluded that:

> ... comprehension is composed of separate skills and abilities, such as understanding word meanings, verbal reasoning, getting the main idea, detecting the author's mood, and discerning word meanings in context.

However, prior to Thorndike's commitment to the belief that reading comprehension was a unitary ability, there had been other reading experts who were coming to the same conclusion. Spache and Spache (1969), for instance, wrote as follows:

> Reading is not a group of separate skills to be practised in isolation and later blended together in the total act. It is rather a total act from the beginning, limited, of course, by the reader's questioning capacities, his experiences and his reading abilities.

More recently, in England, certain of the findings of the Schools Council's research project *The Effective Use of Reading* (Lunzer and Gardner 1979) lend support to the unitary nature of comprehension, when they conclude that: '. . . reading comprehension cannot be broken down into a number of distinct subskills. Instead, the evidence points strongly to a single aptitude.'

Chall (1977) also points out that the decision on the nature of comprehension has important and far-reaching practical consequences when she notes:

> These two theories of reading comprehension can lead to considerably different approaches to testing and teaching. If the specificity concept is accepted, then both tests and instructional materials will pay particular attention to the different comprehension skills. A general concept of reading comprehension will lead to a more global approach to reading improvement, one that tries to develop reasoning ability by reading and other means.

One further aspect of reading comprehension, to which attention has recently been drawn, relates to the realization that it is not a one-way process. For instance, certain earlier definitions of reading comprehension viewed it as understanding the author's meaning. Yet reading comprehension is more of a two-way process, in that what the reader brings to his reading of the text contributes as much to his comprehension of it as does the message the author is aiming to present. Morris (1963) provided an interesting illustration of this when he quoted Kerfoot (1916) who, in the early days of film-making, drew 'an analogy between the work of a reader with the text of an author, and the work of a producer with the film-writer's scenario'. Morris went on to say:

> On Kerfoot's view no story is ever told by the author of the book; the telling is done by the reader who takes the text for his scenario and produces it on the stage of his own imagination with resources furnished by his own experiences of life.

More recently, Robinson (1977) has shown his concern with the problem in an article entitled 'Comprehension: an elusive concept'. After quoting a number of definitions of reading comprehension made by other reading experts, he suggested the following new one:

> . . . reading comprehension is the difference between what someone knew about a topic prior to the reading and what he or she 'winds

up with' or possesses following the reading.

Such a definition, with its emphasis on 'information gain', clearly has important implications for the kind of 'topic work' in which children of 7 to 9 years are frequently engaged. It has even more relevance for so-called 'comprehension tests', in that it is not possible to ascertain what children have learned from reading a passage, without some assessment of their 'pre-knowledge'.

Finally, the most recent definition of reading comprehension by English writers, namely Lunzer and Gardner (1979), reads as follows:

... to penetrate beyond the verbal forms of text to the underlying ideas, to compare these with what one already knows and also with one another, to pick out what is essential and new, to revise one's previous conceptions.

## III  How Children Learn to Read

An attempt to understand how children do learn to read – the mental processes in which they are involved when they endeavour to obtain meaning from printed or written words – should probably be regarded as the most vital question for teachers to consider. If thought is first given to what a number of writers have termed the 'process' of reading, questions of the skills children need, and use, as well as questions of how teachers can help children to learn to read, i.e. the 'pedagogy' of reading, will fall more easily into place.

Strang (1967) provided the following definition of the reading process:

The psychological process of reading includes all that goes on between intake – the stimulus of the printed word – and output – the reader's response in thought, spoken or written words, or action.

Psycholinguistic theories, based on investigations of the process of reading, have greatly increased our knowledge of what goes on between what Strang described as 'input' and 'output'. Both Jenkinson (1969) and Chall (1977) have paid tribute to the work of Chomsky and Goodman in this respect. Jenkinson, for example, noted that:

Goodman (1964), in his insistence on the types of miscues which can lead to major errors in understanding, has indicated one of the most productive ways of furthering our understanding, since it is often by examination of errors made rather than by competence revealed that our knowledge in any field is enhanced.

Without doubt, Goodman's often quoted definition of reading as 'a psycholinguistic guessing game', while it originally occasioned very grave doubts in the minds of many teachers and others in the field of reading, has caused many educationists to re-examine their ideas about the nature of reading. Such a re-examination must inevitably lead to a greater awareness of the complexities of the process of reading and the importance of comprehension. These factors are stressed by Goodman *et al.* (1978) when, after outlining the many strategies used in reading, they go on to say:

> In any case it is the search for meaning, the active continuous attempt to comprehend, that makes all this complex process work. What distinguishes more and less proficient reading is how well integrated it is: how efficiently and effectively cues of all sorts are used, strategies applied, and meaning created.

Yet, despite advances in psycholinguistics, even at the beginning of the 1970s knowledge about the reading process was still limited, as Smith (1971) indicates:

> The process of reading is not very well understood. Researchers do not yet know enough about the developed skills of the fluent reader, the end product of the instructional process, let alone the process of acquiring these skills. But researchers are beginning to realize that reading will not be completely understood until there is an understanding of all the perceptual, cognitive, linguistic and motivational aspects not just of reading, but of living and learning in general.

One great problem about understanding the nature of reading is that being a mental process it is generally a silent one, which makes it even more difficult to investigate. This is where Goodman's work on 'miscues' is of such great value, in that the errors which children make in oral reading can provide teachers with insight into the mental processes in which their pupils are engaged in their attempts to read. (It is for this reason that certain of the investigations undertaken in the current project were concerned with Miscue Analysis – as reported in Chapter 16.)

Investigations into the processes involved in fluent adult reading have also provided useful clues to the processes in which children are engaged in their attempt to comprehend what they are reading. Some of the conclusions drawn may be difficult for teachers to accept and Smith (1971) shows that he is well aware of this:

> . . . fluent reading, and learning to read fluently, require a willingness to 'make mistakes'. And the extent to which a child is prepared to risk mistakes is directly related to the tolerance of the teacher in accepting them.

It was suggested earlier that the two questions 'What is reading?' and 'How do children learn to read?' were very closely linked and that a consideration of the process of reading, (i.e. the second question), would help teachers to formulate their answers to the first question.

One theory of the process of reading, spelt out by Gibson and Levin (1975) in the following terms, is helpful in this respect:

> The reader constructs the meaning for himself as his eyes move over

the page, forms hypotheses about what is to follow, and pauses for a fixation occasionally to confirm what he has been predicting. . . . The emphasis here is on meaning.

They go on to state:

> The first thing to emphasize is that reading is an adaptive process. It is active and flexible, the processing strategies changing to meet the demands of the text and the purpose of the reader.

Levin and Williams' (1970) description of the process of reading also goes a long way towards providing a definition of reading:

> The reader samples the cues on the printed page, and, using these partial cues together with previous knowledge about printed pages and about the world, he forms hypotheses (expectations), which are confirmed or disconfirmed by subsequent sampling.

Both these examples illustrate the distance which current ideas about the nature of reading have advanced from the older conception of a child moving from word to word, in one direction only, as he concentrates on pronouncing each correctly. They also suggest the inadequacy of the older teaching technique of merely prompting the child, by supplying him with the pronunciation of each single word with which he has difficulty or, alternatively, asking him to 'sound it out'.

## IV  What Skills are Used in Reading?

The third question to which it was suggested earlier that teachers wanted an answer was 'What are the skills used in reading?' If this question were put to teachers in primary schools, the majority of them would probably reply by listing those skills which they already do teach children, for example, phonic rules, recognition of frequently used words, vocabulary extension and so on. In doing so, they might be disregarding the skills which the children already possess and which could be built on, as part of the teachers' strategies of helping the children to improve their reading competence. They might also be failing to extend the children's proficiencies because they were relatively unaware of equally important kinds of help of which the children were greatly in need.

Smith (1971), for example, in the following quotation, has drawn attention to relevant skills which children already possess:

> Two things are perhaps surprising about the skills and knowledge that a child brings with him when he is about to learn to read: the sheer quantity and complexity of his ability, and the small credit that he is usually given.

Among the skills which the child already possesses, Smith places first '. . . a rich and fully functioning knowledge of the spoken aspects of his language.' He points out that the manner in which the child has acquired his facility with spoken language, with minimal formal instruction from adults, shows that he has developed many abilities which will be of great use to him in the task of learning to read. For example, he has learned to look for the significant differences between objects, to group objects according to certain of their characteristics, and 'to accumulate new information by "testing hypotheses", trying out possible rules and getting feedback'. Smith also makes another important point when he says: 'What the child does *not* know is *where* to look for the distinctive features of letters; he knows how to look but not what to look for.' Accordingly, he states:

> A child has to discover the distinctive features of written material, the significant differences by which alternative letters, words, and meanings can be differentiated.

The child has then to learn to group letters and words into categories which are meaningful to him. He has to learn how the rules of syntax, of which he is already aware in spoken language, are related to the written form of language. Finally, he has to learn to read with speed, because only by so doing can the meaning of the text be easily understood. The child who reads word by word, and continually stops to sound out words letter by letter, will find it extremely difficult, if not impossible, to comprehend what he is attempting to read – and this is the essence of all reading.

These few brief points, of course, represent only snippets of psycholinguistic findings. They open up new dimensions for teachers of reading, and they are investigated and elaborated later in this book, particularly in Chapters 16 and 17, which refer to the strategies children use in their reading. Much of the original work of such people as Kenneth Goodman and Frank Smith was carried out in the USA and the reports first published there. Consequently, many British teachers may be unfamiliar with their findings. Certain of the discussions in the *Bullock Report* (1975), however, especially those on primary skills and intermediate skills, in Chapter 6, 'The Reading Process', are based on the writings of Goodman and Smith.

One other problem relating to psycholinguistic theories is that the writers concerned have developed a highly technical vocabulary of their own, which could well discourage some teachers from reading their reports. Nevertheless, their writings provide valuable insights into an area hitherto clouded with mystery and one which teachers will find well worth exploring. In particular, the recent paper by Goodman *et al.* (1978) should prove especially helpful to teachers as it provides short, lucid definitions for many of the terms used in psycholinguistics.

One of the dangers associated with an advocacy of psycholinguistic theories about the strategies children use in learning to read, is that they may cause teachers to think that any direct teaching of certain skills which formerly took place is now no longer either valuable or relevant. It is to be hoped that a growing acceptance of the current newer theories — which can undoubtedly be of great help to teachers and pupils — will not be accompanied by a complete abandonment of what went before. The adoption of a new theory can illuminate and improve teaching procedures; it does not necessarily mean wiping the slate clean and starting again.

The newer psycholinguistic theories have led to the conclusion that children will learn to read by reading, and that, if left to do so, they will form their own expectations of what unknown words could or should mean according to their context. In other words they will 'predict' what the unknown words are likely to be. Children will thus grow to formulate their own hypotheses which they will have to test for verification. They will make their predictions by 'guessing'. They will test the accuracy of their reasoning either by the criterion of whether or not it makes sense to them, or alternatively, they may look to their teacher for verification.

However, what is rarely, if ever, stated is that the child's efforts to comprehend what he is reading, by forming reasonable hypotheses about the likely meaning of unknown words, can only take place if, and when, the child already possesses a store of words which he does understand, as well as a knowledge of certain of the phonic regularities in the language. There needs to be *immediate recognition* of a large proportion of the words he encounters in his reading. (The most desirable percentage of such words is a matter of conjecture but is probably about 95%.) If he can read, and this means comprehend, a large percentage of the words in the text, he may be in a position to make fairly good predictions about the remainder. Cues to the unknown words can be gathered from the text — semantic cues from the meaning of the context and syntactic cues from his basic knowledge of the common grammatical patterns of sentence structure. But it should not be forgotten that the third type of cue on which he can draw lies in the visual appearance of the unknown words, i.e. their phonic structures.

Thus, the child who recognizes a large number of words on sight, who has a wide knowledge of the meanings of words and phrases, and is familiar with the main phonic regularities of the language, as well as common 'word families' and certain irregularities, is in a strong position to help himself to make sense of the books he chooses to read, as well as the instructions and forms it is necessary for him to read. The skills of reading, therefore, include many of the skills which teachers already aim to teach; namely phonic skills, immediate recognition of commonly used words, and an ever-increasing familiarity with an extensive and varied vocabulary. In addition, for optimum progress, the child also needs the kind of guidance which will help him to develop the less visible but important skills suggested by Smith and others — which were briefly outlined earlier.

## V What can the Teacher do to Help?

The question of what the teacher can do to help the child to extend his reading proficiency at this particular stage, is the fourth question mentioned at the beginning of this chapter. From the viewpoint of the teacher, it is also the most practical question and it represents the core of this research project. Consequently, references to it, which it is hoped will go a long way towards helping teachers to formulate their own answers, will be found throughout the remainder of this book. Meanwhile, a few comparisons of various writers' views on the pedagogy of teaching reading may form a base-line, against which can be viewed the findings of the current research project and their implications for teachers.

In England, for example, during the past decade, teachers have been bombarded by a series of five Black Papers, the first of which was published in 1969 (Cox and Dyson) while the fifth appeared in 1977. The writers' theme was that the standards in reading, writing and spelling had fallen alarmingly and that the cure was a return to formal teaching, which in the case of teaching reading meant a return to the old-fashioned phonic drill. This was surely a simplistic view expressed mainly by educators who were by no means knowledgeable about the processes involved in learning to read.

In this connection, Resnick and Resnick (1977) have some interesting comments to make about this 'back to the basics' movement. The summary which precedes their article reads as follows:

> From an historical examination of selected European and American models of literacy, they (i.e. the Resnicks) conclude that reading instruction has been aimed at attaining either a low level of literacy for a large number of people or a high level for an elite. Thus, the contemporary expectations — high levels of literacy for the entire population — represents a relatively recent development. From this stance the Resnicks argue that, contrary to the thrust of the 'back to basics' movement, pedagogical practices from the past offer little remedy for reading problems as currently defined.

They go on to conclude that:

> ... Unless we intend to relinquish the criterion of comprehension as the goal of reading instruction, there is little to go back to in terms of pedagogical method, curriculum or school organisation. The old tried and true approaches, which nostalgia prompts us to believe might solve current problems, were designed neither to achieve the literacy standard sought today nor to assure successful literacy for everyone.

Smith, Goodman and Meredith (1976), from a different viewpoint, also stress that there is no one simple pattern of teaching reading which teachers should follow. They say:

> Most of the simple panaceas in reading instruction are not methods

but sets of tactics that emphasize the learner's use of one set of cues or a group of related cues. Phonics, for example, is a set of tactics for handling letter cues. These tactics, if they are based on a sound understanding of letter-sound relationships, can be fitted into a method of reading instruction. But phonics is not a complete method of reading instruction.

Understanding of reading and learning to read is now making it possible for educators to explain, predict, diagnose and prevent or remedy reading difficulties. But this involves not only highly sophisticated application of knowledge from many disciplines, but also teachers who thoroughly understand language, language learning, and the learners themselves. Any strategy of reading instruction based on a single principle or tactic is incomplete, no matter how valid the principle. Reading methods must be based on a complete understanding of the complex reading process.

While the majority, if not all, of those who have made a detailed study of reading agree on the importance of comprehension, not all are agreed on the amount of support and guidance which the teacher should provide for the child in order to help his understanding of what he reads. The Spaches (1969), for example, emphasized the role of the teacher as being more definite than that advocated by most of those who support linguistic theories. Referring to the results of their analyses of the content of reading tests, mentioned earlier in this chapter, they ask:

> What are the implications of these studies for the classroom teacher? The most obvious implication is, of course, the dependence of the development of the child's thinking efforts in reading upon the direction given by teacher demands. As is true of many facets of the reading act, higher types of thinking do not spontaneously appear or develop simply because the pupil progresses in reading levels. In reading, children and adults employ minimal demands imposed on them. If the purposes for reading are superficial or vague, so is the thinking and retention of the readers.

They go on to state:

> There is one further implication of the concept of reading as a thinking process which must be mentioned briefly. This involves the realization that the thinking processes employed in reading by the school-child are those, in effect, that he is taught to use. The kinds of facts he recognizes and can report on, the relationships among ideas that he realizes, are all the direct result of the nature of the instruction he receives. In other words, as we have already implied, the reader learns to think through his reading materials in the ways in which the teacher's questions guide him.

Stauffer (1975), with his emphasis on reading as a thinking process, points out the importance of the role of the teacher when he writes:

> What is done to promote critical reading, regardless of level, is what makes the difference. In other words, children can be trained to be

thinking readers at any level.

Such a view clearly has relevance for the age-groups with which this project has been concerned.

In contrast, Smith (1977) describes the role of the teacher as much less positive than do either the Spaches or Stauffer. Having stated that:

> Children must have two fundamental insights before they can learn to read . . .
> (1) that print is meaningful, and
> (2) that written language is different from speech.

He then suggests that:

> . . . the implications for instruction are that a child learns to read by reading and that the teacher's role is to make reading easy. I do not mean that reading is made easy by the use of simple material, which can indeed be difficult because of its probable irrelevance and un-predictability. Rather, I suggest helping children to understand any written material that interests them – whether the help is provided by the teacher, an aide, another child, or the tape-recorder, or simply by permitting children to make errors and omissions without penalty and without the disruption of unwanted correction. Children seek help when they need it and ignore it when they do not.

Lest such a philosophy might appear alarming to teachers who are unfamiliar with it, one further question from Smith (1971) should be added:

> I have noted on several occasions that the model of the reading process developed in this book is not a conventional one. Readers are not usually regarded as 'predicting' their way through a passage of text, eliminating some alternatives in advance on the basis of their knowledge of the redundancy of language, and acquiring just enough visual information to eliminate the alternatives remaining. It is also unconventional to suggest that most of the information required by beginning readers is not information that teachers can give them directly.
>
> But nothing I have said should start a classroom revolution. There is no suggestion that teachers of reading should throw away their instructional procedures, or their years of experience, and start all over again. As I said in the Preface, no theoretical analysis of the reading process can dictate an instructional method; pedagogy always has to be tested in the classroom. But the type of theoretical analysis outlined in this book will provide insights about why many teaching methods work, and why on occasion all may fail. A clearer understanding of what the skilled reader can do and of what the beginning reader is trying to do, is far more important for the read-ing teacher than any revision of instructional materials.

As has been suggested previously, teachers are eager to have answers to the question of how they can help children to learn to read. A few of other peoples' suggestions of what might not prove profitable, and others which might do so, have been put forward in this chapter. It seems clear that the more that is known about the process of reading, the more likely it is that teachers' help will prove effective. Accordingly, let the final word be with the Goodmans (1977) who conclude their article with the following brief statement: '. . . oral reading miscues are the windows on the reading process at work.'

## VI  Using the Skill of Reading

One of the reasons why teachers are eager to help children to learn to read is that in modern society literacy is essential if only to deal with the necessary completion of forms or reading of directions on equipment and other commodities. It is probable, however, that teachers' main concern in teaching children to read centres on the hope that the children will not only be able to read, but that their reading will develop into a life-long habit. As Southgate (1973) has pointed out '. . . that pupils not only could read but would want to go on reading, is a goal well worth aiming at'.

Unfortunately, certain studies of children's personal reading habits have shown that this goal has not been achieved. A recent study on children's reading habits, sponsored by the Schools Council (Whitehead *et al.*, 1975), found that children of 10+ read on average only 3 books per month, and that this small amount of personal reading decreased with age to 2.2 books per month at 12+ and 1.9 at 14+. Of the 10+ sample of children, 13% had not read a book in the preceding month, at 12+ the figure was 29% and by 14+, 36% of the children had not done any personal reading during that time.

Adults and, one also hopes, children who can read, use their reading for two main purposes. These two types of reading are usually called functional reading and recreational reading. The first is the reading one needs to do, and the second is the reading one wants to do for interest, pleasure or relaxation. The two sorts of reading should not necessarily be equated with non-fiction and fiction. Functional reading is almost invariably non-fiction. Recreational reading, while frequently consisting of fiction, can include any kind of reading matter, for example magazines, comics, newspapers, biography, poetry, history, travel books, cookery books or information books on any subject which interests the reader. It is the purpose which distinguishes the two.

It should be borne in mind that the children with whom this project is concerned, i.e. average readers of 7+, *have* learned to read at a simple level by the time they enter the first junior class. They are capable of reading easy stories or information books on subjects which interest them, for their own pleasure. They are also likely to have had some experience of dipping into simple information and reference books, to find out facts relating to 'topics' in which the whole class or themselves individually were interested. It can then be said that although these children have not by any means mastered all the necessary techniques of reading, they have reached a stage when their command of the skill of reading can be used and they have begun to do so. Accordingly, during the next four years of primary education, and probably of these four years the first two are the most vital, teachers have not only to continue to teach them to read, but also to help them to use their reading.

One of the problems facing teachers of first- and second-year juniors is that until fairly recently they have been given little guidance about what needs to be done or how to set about doing it. Their initial teacher training was unlikely, unless it was very recent, to have included much in this area; nor have many books on the subject been published to help them. Even the *Bullock Report* (DES 1975) has little to say about these vital two years. Having discussed in a fair amount of detail reading in infant classes, there is then a jump to about third- and fourth-year juniors. For example, the report states:

> There is no doubt in all our minds that one of the most important tasks facing the teacher of older juniors and younger secondary pupils is to increase the amount and range of their voluntary reading.

Fortunately, during the past few years, a number of Universities and Colleges of Higher Education have begun to offer to practising teachers courses leading to Advanced Diplomas and Masters' Degrees with reading as a main subject. At the same time, substantial numbers of other teachers have followed the Open University's courses on Reading Development.

If teachers of children aged 7 to 9+ are not only to continue to improve the reading proficiency of their pupils, but also to ensure that their increasing skill is used at every level, there are certain points to which particular attention should be paid. If these children are to move towards the goal of becoming not only children who *can* read, but children who *do* read, teachers will need to devote a great deal of attention to the following points:

(i) the promotion of children's interest in books;
(ii) the supply, deployment and classification of books;
(iii) guidance in the selection of appropriate books;
(iv) training in study skills;
(v) the provision of time in which to read.

These and other techniques for ensuring that children make the best use of their reading abilities are described in Chapter 11 of this book.

## VII Summary

1. Each decade, as our knowledge about reading is enriched by contributions from the psychology of learning, linguistics, language learning and other studies and, consequently, the more the complexity of the process is realized, the more difficult does it become to define reading.

2. Current attempts to define reading tend to regard it as a thinking

process, with attention focused on comprehension. Furthermore, comprehension is no longer regarded as a one-way process, with the reader merely endeavouring to understand the author's meaning, but rather as a two-way process whereby the reader's own background knowledge contributes as much to his understanding of the passage as do the words of the author.

3. Earlier views of reading as a process made up of separate skills have changed, as it has become clearer that comprehension is a total or global act. The reader, as his eyes move across the page, attempts to use his own knowledge to construct for himself the meaning of the passage, forms hypotheses as he goes along and predicts in advance of what he reads. He confirms or rejects his predictions by using all the cues available to him: semantic cues from his immediate recognition of words and his knowledge of their meaning; phonic cues drawn from his knowledge of the sounds of letters; and syntactic cues drawn from his underlying understanding of the grammatical structure of the English language.

4. This global conception of the nature of the process of reading must inevitably lead to a more general approach to the teaching of reading; the teacher encouraging the child's fluency and understanding rather than allowing him to stumble from word to word, with halts at each minor error. Errors made by the child will be regarded by the teacher as miscues which still provide her with insight into the mental processes in which the child is engaged, and so will provide pointers to future help which can be provided.

5. An acceptance of such psycholinguistic theories need not cause teachers to think that all earlier methods of teaching reading should be abandoned. It is rather a question of emphasis. Instant recognition of common sight words, a knowledge of common phonic rules and the possession of a large sight vocabulary of words whose meanings are understood, still represent the basis from which meaning can be extracted from the text. Indeed, unless a large proportion of the words in a passage can be immediately recognized, endeavours to comprehend it will be doomed to failure.

6. At the same time, the more the teacher encourages the child in the direction of fluency and understanding, while lowering her expectancy of absolute accuracy, the more likely is reading to become a thinking process. Thus, to a large extent, children's reading is more likely to continue to improve if they are encouraged to go on reading rather than being halted at every point of uncertainty.

7. Furthermore, the more encouragement and opportunities children are given in school to use their developing reading skills for fluent, thoughtful reading, the more likely are they to become habitual readers as they grow older. The ages between 7 and 10 years would seem to be vital in this respect.

# PART THREE

## The Teachers' Viewpoints

# CHAPTER 4

# Teachers' Preferred Outcomes of the Project

## I Teachers' Ideas Invited

The project 'Extending Beginning Reading' had been so planned as to enable it to lean very heavily on the contributions made by teachers' groups. The large number of teachers joining the first research group provided an opportunity to devise a scheme whereby teachers might, right from the beginning, exert a certain amount of influence on the direction of the work. The group consisted of 440 headteachers and class teachers of children aged 7 to 9+ years. The aims of the project and the general lines along which it was expected to develop were outlined. It was then indicated that, while the main terms of reference of the project must be adhered to, the emphasis could well be altered in the direction of the expressed needs of the teachers. Members of the group were then invited to send in written suggestions of outcomes of the project which they considered would be of practical guidance to teachers.

## II Teachers' Responses

The response to this request was extremely encouraging, in that suggestions were received from 377 members of the group.

### A. *Five General Areas of Interest*

After sifting the pool of suggestions, eliminating repetitions and collating similarities, it became clear that the teachers' suggestions were clustered around the following five major areas of interest.

### 1. The task

The teachers' first concern seemed to be of a general nature relating to the need for further knowledge about this stage of learning to read. The whole question centred on the reading process itself and on its natural course of development in the age range in question. This area of interest, which was given top priority by the teachers, clearly showed that teachers are very conscious of the complexity of the reading process itself and are aware that greater knowledge on their part would provide a sound basis of reference for their own teaching, aimed at helping the development of their pupils' reading abilities.

## 2. The child as a reader

A second defined area of interest, labelled 'the child as a reader', included comments concerning methods of finding out more about the child — his interests, attitudes and motivation, as well as the ways in which he learns to read and how he uses his developing skills.

## 3. The teacher of reading

A third area of interest concerned ways in which teachers can use their knowledge of the reading process in planning a programme of teaching and learning activities to fit the varying needs of their pupils at different stages of reading development.

## 4. Assessment, diagnosis and record keeping

Certain of the teachers' suggestions took the form of requests for guidance on the selection and use of appropriate reading tests and other forms of assessment, on the ways in which such test results might best be recorded, and on the uses which might be made of the results.

## 5. Reading resources

In this area of interest guidance was sought on the choice and classification of all kinds of reading materials, for example, reading schemes and apparatus, story books and information books. The problem of providing appropriate books to match children's interests and reading abilities was clearly in the teachers' minds.


## B. *Teachers' Main Interests*

While many teachers expressed interest in all five of the preceding areas, the one labelled 'the task' was clearly of top priority to them.

The second important point to be noted was the teachers' awareness that not only do children of the same age show different levels of reading ability, but that even those children with apparently similar levels of reading attainment, such as 'average readers' of 7, 8 or 9 years, may have varying needs for reading tuition. In order to cater adequately for these different needs in their pupils, teachers themselves would like to know more about:
(a) assessment, diagnosis and record-keeping;
(b) the grading of reading materials, in order that they can be matched to the reading levels, interests and needs of individual children.

These preferences expressed by practising teachers may well be regarded as a complete endorsement of the whole plan for the research project 'Extending Beginning Reading'. The outcomes which teachers were requesting in 1974 represent the subject matter of the project, and it is hoped that this report contains information and suggestions which will help to answer these kinds of questions which teachers have been asking.

## C. *One Important Area Disregarded*

Whilst many teachers had indicated their desire for further knowledge and guidance in certain important areas of reading for the 7 to 9+ age groups, one other equally vital area was relatively neglected.

Among the teachers' preferred outcomes, the need for further knowledge about phonic skills and comprehension skills was expressed fairly frequently. Word recognition skills and comprehension skills are, however, merely the basic tools to be utilized in two broad types of reading, namely functional reading and recreational reading, each requiring competencies in certain additional techniques. Moreover, if effective adult reading is to be the ultimate goal, it is essential that a firm basis should be laid for both functional and recreational reading between the ages of 7 and 11. A few teachers showed their awareness of the importance of these areas of reading tuition with children aged 7 to 9+ years, describing them as:

'Guidelines on laying foundations which will lead children to become adults who read.'
'Ways of utilising reading in other classroom activities, e.g. topic work.'
'Accounts of strategies for encouraging children's personal pleasure and satisfaction in reading.'
'Suggestions of ways of developing critical reading.'

However, the use of reading for recreational and functional purposes was largely disregarded when teachers were indicating their desire for further knowledge.

It should be remembered that these preferred outcomes of the project were put forward by the teachers concerned in 1974, before the publication of the *Bullock Report* (1975) which laid great emphasis on functional and recreational aspects of reading. It is hoped that this report on the project 'Extending Beginning Reading' will perform a useful function by encouraging teachers' interest in these areas which were insufficiently highlighted and which merit great emphasis by teachers of children in the first two years of junior education.

## III  Responding to Teachers' Requests

Now that the project is completed, it can be noted that during the four years of research, investigations relating to the majority of the needs expressed by teachers in the first Teachers' Reading Research Group, were undertaken and have been reported on. Answers to questions about how teachers might help children to learn are implied or suggested throughout the report.

The second main area of teachers' concern related to: assessment, diagnosis and record keeping; selecting and grading reading materials; planning reading programmes for classes of mixed reading abilities. Although certain segments of this were not among the central objectives of the project, the requests are nevertheless fairly well catered for in reports on a number of investigations undertaken. For example, although the selection of reading tests did not form part of the brief, teachers are referred to two excellent, recently published books on the subject (Pumfrey 1976 and 1977). On the other hand, the assessment and diagnosis of children's reading difficulties was one of the areas investigated. Record-keeping in this context is suggested by the method of converting the often sterile activity of 'hearing' children read into a means of recording and classifying their errors, so as to produce diagnostic pointers. One method by which children might keep their own records of the books they read was used in the project and is described in Chapter 7. In addition, a number of publications on record-keeping are included in the Teachers' Book Lists.

Teachers' great interest in acquiring further information on the selection and grading of books revealed that many of them were unaware of the number of helpful publications already available on this subject. A selected book list on this topic was, therefore, prepared for the teachers' groups and is included in Appendix 9-A. In addition, work was undertaken by teachers in the first Teachers' Group on establishing the levels of difficulty of books for individual children by means of recording the number of errors made by the children when reading aloud a specific passage of the book. Details of this method, based on 'informal reading inventories', are also given in Chapter 9.

Finally, help with planning a reading programme should be gained from the sections entitled 'Implications for Teachers' which are listed at the end of many of the chapters; and, in particular, from Chapter 18 − the concluding chapter of this book − which contains a section devoted entirely to suggestions for planning a new kind of reading approach.

The area of reading improvement which was largely disregarded in the list of teachers' 'preferred outcomes', namely developing the uses of children's reading skills for functional and recreational purposes, is expanded in various parts of the report, but particularly in Chapter 11.

## IV  Summary

When 440 headteachers and class teachers of children aged 7 to 9+, who were members of a reading research group, were offered the opportunity to indicate possible outcomes of the project which would provide practical guidance for them, the results were as follows:

1. There were two main areas of general concern. The teachers first expressed a need for further knowledge about this particular stage of learning to read. They wanted to know more about what average readers of 7 to 9+ needed to learn, how they learn and how teachers may facilitate the learning process.

2. Secondly, the teachers showed awareness that even children who have reached broadly the same level of reading attainment, nevertheless may have varying needs for reading tuition and that, therefore, the teachers needed further information about assessment, diagnosis and record-keeping, as well as about the readability levels of books.

3. While expressing interest in specific skills such as phonics and comprehension the list of teachers' priorities appeared to indicate that only a small minority of teachers appreciated the need to ensure that a firm basis for both functional and recreational reading be laid during the first two years of junior education.

CHAPTER 5

# Teachers' Aims and Objectives

## I Difficulty in Stating Aims and Objectives

Practitioners in any field rarely find it simple to define their aims and objectives. Teachers are no exception to this general statement. They find it easier to describe what they do and how they do it than why they follow certain practices. Yet the information gathered in this project would have lacked balance if it related entirely to teachers' and children's current behaviour without reference to the teachers' general aims, as well as their shorter term objectives, on both of which their current patterns of behaviour are based.

Accordingly, three separate probes were made to discover the rationale underlying current practices in the 12 schools concerned in the intensive study year. One line of enquiry consisted of a question on aims and objectives, which formed part of an interview with each headteacher. The other two probes took the form of requests for statements in writing, from both headteachers and class teachers.

## II Headteachers' Responses

### A. *Interviews with Headteachers*

In the intensive study year, in order to obtain as complete a picture as possible of each of the 12 schools' background, organization, method of work and underlying philosophy, early in the school year, the director arranged an extended interview with each headteacher. This took the form of a structured discussion based on certain specific questions.

In reply to the first question about their general aims and objectives for their schools, three of the headteachers specifically mentioned reading or other language skills. One headteacher who included 'literacy' in his reply to the first general question added that parents wanted their children to be literate. A second headteacher indicated that 'a grounding in the 3Rs' was one of his general objectives in the school, and a third headteacher began her reply to the question as follows:

> If a child can leave the primary school at 11 years of age, having enjoyed his years at school, can read fluently and with understand-

ing, can write and enjoy writing, is articulate and at ease with the people he meets, we shall have achieved one of our main objectives.

Later in the discussion, each headteacher was asked the question, 'What are your aims and objectives for the school as far as reading and language are concerned.' The 12 replies to this question were as follows:

When children leave the primary school they should be able to read with fluency, understanding and enjoyment.

One of the main aims of the school is to develop communication skills — speech, writing, listening and reading. In reading, we are especially concerned with comprehension.

We want children to get interested in books and develop the habit of referring to books. We want them to be sufficiently excited about books to join a library. They should also be able to compare one book with another and one author with another.

With infants we aim at a reasonable ability in basic reading. But I think we should be doing more about reading skills in junior classes — training them at different levels. It is also important to get the children on their feet and able to talk, to make them not afraid to speak in public.

All children should be able to read, write and communicate. No child should leave school unable to read. In fact, here no child is a non-reader when he leaves, although there is no special emphasis on reading in the school. Reading stories to children is very important and the teachers continue to do this right up to Junior 4.

Our aims are to make sure all children are literate when they leave school and to encourage their use of language to the best of their abilities.

We want all children to be fluent readers, reading not just for day to day business but for pleasure. We encourage them to read for pleasure from an early age.

My aim is to get as many children reading as possible — really reading — to extend them. I myself read widely and I want children to learn to do the same. I have encouraged the teachers to try to let children read for pleasure for half an hour every day.

Regarding reading, it is essential that children learn to read as soon as they are emotionally and intellectually ready to start — and for most children this is in the admission class. As for language development, one can't just leave it to happen as a result of providing interesting experiences for children. It has got to be structured — almost mechanically. At the end of each day teachers have to ask themselves how they have extended children's vocabulary. Children must be forced to express themselves.

Parents want their children to be literate and this is one of the general aims of the school.

Unless we can teach children to read, we can't teach them anything. Everything else depends on it. So we place tremendous emphasis on reading. We also place emphasis on spoken language – conversation is important.

I relate my aims and objectives about reading and language to my general aims for the school. [This headteacher had stated that the foundation of his programme as a headteacher was based on the encouragement of the right relationships between himself, the staff and the children. He wished to create an atmosphere in which each child would be able to develop to be the best that he could be.] I want to give each child the opportunity to communicate with others; that is both incoming and outgoing communication. I stress the importance of talk, because many children come from homes in which there is little conversation. Children's written work is also part of their outgoing language, as long as they are writing for someone. So older children read what they've written to younger children. I want children to read for their own enjoyment as well as for information. Children's reading also helps to facilitate discussions with their teachers and others. We also try to provide opportunities for children to read to others.

These 12 replies are interesting, not only in the different ideas they exhibit, but also as comparisons between each headteacher's response to the question asked earlier about their general aims and objectives for the school. Detailed comments about the responses, however, must be viewed against the realization that the headteachers were speaking extemporarily, and had been doing so for perhaps about two hours, against the normal school background of interruptions by children, teachers, parents and various telephone calls. Had the replies been given in writing, in a period of comparative quietness, no doubt many of them would have been expanded.

Viewed in the light of the four main areas of language development, listening, speaking, reading and writing, all headteachers gave high priority to children being able to read. The area ranking next in importance was speech. Listening was mentioned only specifically by two headteachers: in other instances the word 'communication' was used, which must be taken to imply both listening and talking. Writing would seem to come at the bottom of the list of language skills – which forms an interesting comparison with what actually happened in the schools as noted in Chapters 10 and 15.

Looking at what was said about reading, it can be noted that 'pleasure' and 'interest' were frequently mentioned and that, in general, recreational aims were given precedence over functional aims. As regards specific objectives relating to skills to be mastered, of the two basic skills word recognition skills were not mentioned at all but comprehension or understanding were specifically included in two instances. Just as recreational aims were mentioned more frequently than functional aims, so recreational objectives were given priority over functional objectives – the development of pleasure in reading being mentioned most frequently. One headteacher pursued this to the higher level of evaluation when he spoke of wanting children to be able to compare one book and one author with another. On the functional side, the development of study skills was mentioned only once.

## B. *Questionnaires*

Later in the year, as part of a detailed investigation into the 'reading environment' of eight of the schools, the headteachers, class teachers of first- and second-year juniors and school librarians were asked to complete a questionnaire relating to the book resources in the school. The first question asked was, 'Why do you want to surround children with books?' This particular question afforded headteachers the opportunity of taking time to frame their written replies. In nearly all the headteachers' replies an awareness of the need for balance between reading for functional purposes and for recreational purposes can be noted. (It should be noted that, in contrast to the responses of teachers in Chapter 4, the replies quoted in this chapter were provided by teachers in 1976 – *after* the publication of the *Bullock Report* in February 1975.)

## III  Class Teachers' Responses

### A. *Teachers' Objectives*

At the beginning of the intensive study year, each of the 32 class teachers concerned was given a form for completion, which asked the open-ended question, 'What do you see as your main objectives in the teaching of reading with your present class?' The fact that practitioners usually experience difficulty in stating aims and/or objectives is well illustrated by the class teachers' reactions to this particular question. During the year, many questionnaires and other forms had been sent to the teachers and in every other instance the teachers had been extremely reliable about making returns. In this case, even after reminders were sent out responses were received from only 15 teachers.

#### 1. Basic skills

Virtually every teacher mentioned the increase of proficiency in basic skills as an objective in their reading teaching. Many of the comments related to word-recognition and word-attack skills. Two teachers indicated that they would attempt to 'enlarge the children's vocabulary', while these and a number of others aimed also to develop fluency, accuracy and expression in their pupils' oral reading. Many of the comments on basic skills were more generalized than these, and were of the type: 'to enable the children to master the mechanics of reading'; and 'to develop the reading skills of all the children'. Although basic skills were mentioned equally often in some form or other by both year-groups the second-year teachers often related their comments to their poorer readers. Whenever the general comments on developing reading skills occurred it was often first in the list of teaching objectives.

Realization of the importance of the second main component of the basic skills, namely comprehension, was also reflected in the statements of 11 of the teachers.

## 2. Recreational reading

All the teachers who gave written replies to the question stated that at least one of their objectives and, in fact, usually the main one, was the fostering of an interest in books and reading. Many of the comments were similar to the following: 'to encourage the children to enjoy books, through listening and reading.' And 'to encourage children to read for pleasure.' The following statement: '. . . to foster the growth of imaginative and active responses to written words' illustrates an awareness that comprehension extends beyond merely literal understanding. It points the way to the use of the basic skills for recreational reading which provides emotional satisfaction.

## 3. Functional reading

The second main use to which basic reading skills can be put is functional reading; a fact clearly appreciated by one teacher who wrote:

> The main object of teaching reading is to teach the children first to read with understanding. Without this essential skill, the field of their learning would be seriously limited, but once it is acquired, the children are able to follow-up project work, develop their own interests and make greater use of reference books. The mathematics books of today are also dependent on the ability of the child to read.

At the age level of 7 to 9 years, it is clear that the ability to read with understanding is a prerequisite to extracting information from books. Teachers were obviously aware of this and of the importance of trying to develop such study skills in children. Such comments about 'helping children to extract information' occurred equally often in both year-groups.

Teachers also accepted that this is a relatively high-level skill, more appropriate for teaching to the more able readers.

One other aspect of study skills, rarely mentioned in the teachers' statements of their objectives in the teaching of reading, was the effective use of library provision. The only two comments made, in this connection, both came from teachers of second-year classes.

## B. *Reasons for 'Surrounding Children with Books'*

Class teachers' responses to the later question in the 'Reading Environment' exercise, namely 'Why do you want to surround children with books?', suggest that they found this question either more interesting or easier to answer than the earlier one on teaching objectives. Written replies were received from 22 teachers in the 8 schools to this specific question about books. These teachers' comments on their objectives in 'surrounding children with books' were equally as detailed, thoughtful and interesting as those made by the 8 headteachers. The teachers' replies also showed the same balance between functional reading and recreational reading as had the headteachers'.

## IV  Summary

The attempts to find out about teachers' aims and objectives when teaching reading, and their reasons for believing that children should be 'surrounded by books', provided certain valuable insights which are pertinent to the area being investigated in this project. The following are the most important points which emerged.

1. In the headteachers' responses to the question on their aims and objectives relating to reading and language in their schools, the majority concentrated on aims rather than objectives. Furthermore, recreational aims far outnumbered functional aims.

2. In contrast, in replying to the question on reasons for surrounding children with books, headteachers revealed their awareness of the need for achieving a balance between recreational and functional aims and objectives.

3. Class teachers' responses to the question of their objectives in teaching reading to their current classes illustrated a general concern with ensuring that their pupils should gain competence in the basic skills; both word recognition skills and comprehension skills being mentioned by most of them.

4. The specific question concerning 'surrounding children with books' elicited more detailed responses from class teachers than did the general question on objectives.

5. Teachers' replies to both questions also showed very clearly that, almost without exception, the teachers realized the importance of both recreational and functional needs.

6. Although two of the teachers of second-year classes made special mention of library skills, in general among the class teachers there appeared to be a tendency to think of functional objectives mainly in terms of the more advanced readers in their classes.

# PART FOUR

## The Reading Environment

CHAPTER 6

# Growing Importance of the Reading Environment

## I Changes in Book Provision in Thirty Years

The vast numbers and varieties of books currently in use in primary schools, as well as the large 'resource areas' to be found in some of them, are in marked contrast to the book provision in the 1940s. The changes which have occurred do not merely represent the result of advances in the methods of publication, distribution and sale of books — although these have been great — but also marked changes in the educational philosophies underlying different methods of teaching reading and of using books. To some extent, these changes form a contrast with developments in other English-speaking countries, such as the USA and Canada, as well as other European countries — in few of which one would be likely to find primary age children so 'surrounded by books' as in England.

In the wartime period of 1939--45 and for some years afterwards, when there were severe restrictions on the production of non-essential goods, few innovations occurred either in the production of books for children in primary schools, or in the use of books. In contrast, the succeeding thirty or so years have witnessed extensive changes. During the 1930s, and well into the 1940s, the main books to be found in use in junior classes were of three distinct types: a series of four hard-backed 'reading books', one for each class from Standards I—IV; similar series of four text-books for history and geography and occasionally for nature study; and a selection of so-called 'library books'.

As class reading lessons were the norm, schools ordered the graded sets of reading books and subject books in sets of 40, one set for each class. The books were frequently too difficult for at least half the children in the class. Nevertheless, teaching reading was a class exercise, in which individual children were called upon to read aloud while the rest of the class 'followed' the words in their own books. That such practices were still in existence in the period 1954—7 was noted by Morris (1966) who, reporting on 99 second-, third- and fourth-year junior classes in Kent schools, stated that: 'Class reading was taken regularly each week in 49 of the sample children's classes, occasionally in 30 of them and in 12 classes not at all'.

In many instances the library books were not intended to be read in school but to be taken home. The changing of these books in the final lesson every Friday afternoon was an eagerly anticipated event — at least by the fluent readers. The library book period was less enjoyable for the backward readers who were forced to sit quietly looking at the books they had selected, which were almost invariably beyond their reading abilities.

In the majority of junior classrooms during the 1940s and in some cases the 1950s, the only occasions on which books were in evidence were when either reading lessons or subject lessons such as geography or history were in progress. Reading books, subject books and library books were usually stored in the teachers' cupboards, to which children did not have access. Even if children's reading books were kept in their own desks, other books were rarely placed on display in either classrooms or elsewhere. Yet, by 1975, the *Bullock Report* was providing the following description of the 'book environment' of infant schools — a description which could equally well have been applied to many all-age primary schools:

> . . . the wealth of books in many English Infant schools is a delight to experience. In some they are deployed so skilfully as to give the feel that the whole school is a book environment. They are displayed with natural objects and artefacts, surrounded by colour and placed at points where the child is constantly encountering them. Book areas or corners are made inviting by carpeting and a few chairs. In fact, they come to be seen by the child as a natural and necessary part of his daily life.

In the light of the usual slow rate of change in educational practices, how did these vast changes in the provision of books, and attitudes to their use, come about in primary schools in the space of only 30 years?

Among the many contributory factors, developments in educational philosophies, following on the work of such educators as Pestalozzi and Froebel, should probably be ranked first. An emphasis on the individual child and his particular modes of learning led to 'child-centred' education, with its related beliefs in discovery methods of learning and informality of regimes. Child-centred education and heuristic methods of learning could only become effective if children were not only provided with first-hand experiences, but also had access to a wide range of books which would help to satisfy their curiosity and extend their knowledge and interests.

The period during which these newer educational theories were beginning to be put into practice coincided with an unprecedented expansion in the printing and publishing fields. Books were becoming cheaper and more plentiful, as well as more attractive. Nor should it be forgotten that, as noted by Kamm and Taylor (1966):

> The United Kingdom, then, is one of the very few countries in which there is complete freedom for publishers to produce what books for

schools they want, and for teachers to make their own choice of the books they will use and the children receive these advantages at no direct cost to their parents.

These new developments in educational philosophies and practices which germinated in infant schools were generally supported by HMIs, local advisers and College of Education lecturers. Even so, the extension of child-centred and heuristic methods of learning with the essential concomitant of a stock of varied books freely available to children was probably slower than those educators engaged in training or advising teachers would have hoped; and the movement was certainly later in reaching junior classes than infant classes.

In the changes in book provision and reading practices in primary schools, and particularly in the first two junior years on which this project is centred, the influence exerted by developments in infant education were far-reaching. This was not only because, in the long run, the practices accepted in infant classes tended to spread to the teaching of the succeeding two age-groups, but also because the use of books designed originally for infants extended into junior classes — not just for slower readers but sometimes for half or even whole classes.

Between the late 1930s and 1960s, the production of new reading materials for teaching reading in infant classes showed greater changes than did reading books produced specifically for juniors. 'Look-and-Say' methods of teaching reading, with their emphasis on attractiveness to children, as opposed to the older phonic approaches embodying dullness and drudgery in the early stages, transformed beginning reading books by the use of sentences and stories, accompanied by coloured illustrations, all designed to help children to regard learning to read as a pleasurable activity. *The Happy Venture Readers* (Schonell 1938), *Janet and John* (O'Donnell and Munro 1949), *The Happy Trio Reading Scheme* (Gray *et al* 1956), *The McKee Readers* (McKee *et al* 1956) and the *Ladybird Key Words Reading Scheme* (Murray 1964), are all examples of such reading schemes. During the same period, however, there were also published a few reading schemes with a phonic emphasis; for example *Vanguard Readers* (Kettles and MacDonald 1949), *The Beacon Readers* (Grassam revised 1957), *The Royal Road Readers* (Daniels and Diack 1957) and *The Gay Way Series* (Boyce 1959). In each case, efforts were made by means of illustrations or bright covers to make these phonic books more attractive to children than pre-war phonic reading schemes.

Among the innovations in books for teaching reading which occurred during these post-war years, six should be particularly noted.

1. Many of the new reading schemes included small supplementary books, intended to be read by children after each of the basic reading books. *The Happy Venture, Janet and John, The McKee Readers, Beacon Readers* and *Gay Way* reading schemes, for example, all pro-

duced small, slim, soft-backed supplementary books to support the
early stages of the schemes. In some cases, work-books, cards and other
reading materials or equipment were also added.

2. Many publishers introduced separate and sometimes graded series of
soft-backed 'supplementary' story books intended to be read independently of any particular reading schemes. Examples of these are *Dolphin
Books* (Taylor 1958), *Griffin Pirate Series* (McCullagh 1959) and
*Reading with Rhythm* (Taylor and Ingleby 1961). Such sets of books
were quite often used for group-reading lessons in junior classes. Certain
other series of supplementary books were historically or geographically
based.

3. The publication of a number of series of books for older backward
readers showed that the old myth that all children learned to read in
infant classes was beginning to be squarely faced and found to be
unreliable. Examples of such series were *Adventures in Reading* (Keir
1949), *More Adventures in Reading* (Keir 1953) and *Oxford Colour
Readers* (Carver and Stowasser 1963).

4. The fourth kind of new reading materials — representing attempts
to fulfil the needs expressed by remedial teachers and others, who
had found that the pupils in their charge whose initial reading instruction had rested solely on 'Look-and-Say' methods were deficient or
totally lacking in phonic skills — were books and/or apparatus designed
to teach basic phonics. Among such publications of phonic materials
were *Sounds and Words* (Southgate and Havenhand 1959), *Sound
Sense* (Tansley 1961), *A Remedial Reading Method* (Moxon 1962),
*Fun With Phonics* (Reis 1962), *Programmed Reading Kit* (Stott 1962),
*Sounds for Reading* (O'Donnell and Munro 1965), *Some New Remedial
Techniques* (Webster 1965) and *Six Phonic Workbooks* (Grassam
1966). While certain of these publications were used with upper infants,
to supplement 'Look-and-Say' reading schemes, many were used in
junior classes, as well as remedial groups.

5. Once it was acknowledged that not all infants learned to read and
that even those children who were able to read fluently at an infant
level still had much to learn, new series of reading books for normal
junior children began to be published.

While fewer new reading schemes were published during the 1950s
and 1960s for juniors than for infants, the newer junior schemes did
tend to provide more appropriate materials than earlier schemes.
Schonell and Flowerdew (1953) were first in the field with their
graded sets of reading books for juniors — *Wide Range Readers*, intended to follow the infant *Happy Venture Reading Scheme*. The
authors stated that they were 'primarily planned to provide for the
vital reading experiences and practice of pupils in junior schools', and
that they were graded 'by control of vocabulary and sentence structure,
*according to reading age*.' These two parallel series, each of six books —
Blue Books and Green Books — were soon to be seen in use in nearly all
junior classes and, as will be noted in other parts of this report, are still

the reading books in most common use in junior schools today. Books 1–4 were graded by half-yearly reading ages and were, therefore, intended for average first- and second-year juniors. Books 5 and 6 in each colour were at the levels of third- and fourth-year juniors. The *Wide Range Readers* were soon followed by a few other series of graded reading books for juniors, for example the *Look Ahead Readers* (Ridout and Ainsworth 1956). The authors of the *Janet and John* infant scheme also produced hard-backed continuation readers entitled *High On A Hill, Days in the Sun* and *The Five And A Half Club* in 1956, and they began to be used quite widely in upper infant and lower junior classes. But no other junior reading books ever overtook the lead established by *Wide Range*.

6. A sixth innovation in reading books for juniors during this period was a result of a growing emphasis on 'reading for meaning'. Examples of such sets of books, which generally consisted of passages to be read, followed by questions designed to test 'comprehension', are *Reading to Some Purpose* (Flowerdew and Ridout 1954) and *Using Your Reading* (Gagg 1956). The questions to be answered were generally concerned with merely literal comprehension and it seems doubtful whether the books or the manner in which they were frequently utilized did much either to help children to improve their reading proficiency or to appreciate reading.

But the greatest change of all, occurring in books for primary school children during the post-war years, was the increasing provision and display of books other than those meant for teaching reading. Such books might perhaps be described as 'books for using' rather than 'books for teaching reading'. Even so, however dramatic these changes might now appear in retrospect, they were not nearly as all-pervasive as certain educators liked to think. Morris (1966) for example, reporting on a sample of junior schools in 1954–7, found that half of them had no central collection of books and that, whilst all but one of the classes had class libraries, some of these provided only limited facilities. For instance, approximately 22% of the classrooms had no open shelves and in approximately 27% '... the library books were stored only in cupboards, which in some instances were locked when a teacher was not present.'

It would appear that the Ministry of Education (1959) in their book *Primary Education* were painting a rather rosy picture when they wrote of children at the end of the infant stage of education: 'In many primary schools the distinction between "Library books" and other books is gradually disappearing.'

On the other hand, in the same book, it was still considered necessary to provide the following guidance for teachers on the important part which books should play: 'The rudiments of reading mastered, children need a plentiful supply of books of good quality, and time and quiet in which to read them.' and 'Throughout the primary school, the classroom collection of books should include attractive books of as many types as possible, within the interest and reach of the less proficient readers.'

The *Plowden Report* (1966) strongly supported the growing movement towards child-centred education, informality and discovery methods of learning in primary schools. Referring to conditions in primary schools in 1963–6, the report indicated some of the ways in which improvements in book environments had been effected in the intervening years. It stated:

> As the skill of reading is established, it must be used and here a really remarkable change has taken place since the war. The provision of books, which was usually meagre in quantity and quality in the elementary schools is now much improved.

The point is illustrated by the statement that the average number of school and class library books in primary schools in the national survey undertaken by the Committee was 1,800 and that, in junior schools, libraries of 4,000 to 5,000 were quite common. (As these figures, however, are not related to the number of pupils in the schools, it is impossible to abstract from them ratios of books per pupil – as is done later in this project report, in the description of the reading environment in eight schools.)

The *Plowden Report* goes on to present the following picture of what was happening in 'many' schools in 1963–6:

> Among the most welcome changes which have accompanied the growing informality of the primary school has been the move away from categories of books, each confined to a special time and purpose. In many schools there are now no longer class readers, supplementary readers, group readers, text books and library books . . . there are simply books – to be used as and when they are needed.

Some of those people who were working closely with teachers in primary schools, at that time, may well consider that if the words 'a minority' had replaced the word 'many', the quotation might have presented a more accurate picture of the conditions then existing.

Even so, although there is some doubt about where the phrase 'surrounding children with beautiful books' originated, it was certainly on many people's lips in the early 1960s; for instance, Purton's first edition of *Surrounded by Books* was published in 1962. The idea, as well as the practice, of a range of books being always available to primary school children continued to develop throughout the 1960s and 1970s. At first, the development of the principle of discovery methods of learning led to the provision of many reference and information books. This trend was given further emphasis by the introduction of the 'Nuffield' Science projects in the early 1960s. As the *Plowden Report* (1966) suggested: '. . . much of the money that used to be spent on dull and over-generalized geography and nature study books is now available for the purchase of "books of information".'

In many cases, however, although narrative books were being displayed in classrooms, they were frequently outnumbered by the information books. This practice led to certain fears being expressed that insufficient attention was being given to encouraging children to read and enjoy stories. Plowden (1966) reported:

> ... there are still too few books of literary quality in primary schools and too little time is given to reading them. Even in good schools, it is sometimes thought sufficient to allow a weekly library period, when books for reading at home may be changed, but there is little opportunity for guidance or stimulus.

The *Bullock Report* (1975), reporting the findings of the first Government Committee of Inquiry into Reading and the Use of English ever to be set up in England, provides the most up-to-date account of reading practices, including the use of books in schools, as it refers to information collected during 1972–4. The results of a survey undertaken by the Committee on a sample of over 2,000 maintained primary and secondary schools in England is particularly helpful in this respect, as information was not only gathered about the schools themselves, but also about pupils in four different age-groups, one of which was the 9 year-old age-group.

The results indicate a clear movement away from graded sets of junior reading books, towards more individual reading. For example, while 43% of 9 year-old pupils were still using published reading schemes, just over half of them were no longer using such schemes. The figures relating to classes of 9 year-olds were as follows: 6% used one commercial reading scheme; 37% used more than one commercial reading scheme, together with books graded by the teacher; 54% used both graded and non-graded books.

Although the titles of the reading schemes being used had not been asked for, the results of the survey did indicate that 61% of these classes made use of the supplementary books which formed parts of published reading schemes.

The information gathered about the procedures adopted by the teachers of 9 year-olds, for teaching reading, showed how far the movement from class teaching to individual teaching has progressed. Teachers were asked how often individual children read aloud to them in a week, in terms of 'the ablest', 'an average' and 'the poorest' reader in the class. It was found that, as one might expect, the greatest emphasis was on helping the poorest readers: 48% of them reading aloud to their teachers daily, in contrast to 3% of average readers, and 1% of the ablest readers. In addition to reading aloud to the teacher, in 75% of the cases 9 year-olds were expected to spend some time each week on 'reading practice' on their own, which was defined as using graded and supplementary readers or being engaged in phonic practice. Of the 9 year-olds 59% were expected to read daily from these books, 28%

of them read 3 or 4 times a week and the remainder less often. The class time spent on such 'reading practice' was usually up to half-an-hour or one hour per week and in 27% of the cases the children spent some of their optional time in 'reading practice' from their current books.

The amount of time which 9 year-olds spent on 'reading practice' is contrasted with the amount of time they spent in reading stories, (see Table 6-1). In individual reading activities, the percentage of time spent by 9 year-olds on reading practice had decreased to the point when in less than half the classes did it extend for more than half-an-hour. A very similar pattern emerged in respect of time spent in individual reading of stories; in 54% of the classes of 9 year-olds, this kind of reading extended for less than half-an-hour and in 24% of the classes no class time was allowed for such private reading. In addition to class time spent on these two reading activities, children in 27% of the 9 year-old classes spent some of their optional time on reading practice, while 78% of them spent some of their optional time reading stories.

Table 6-1

*Percentages of classes of 9 year-olds spending time on
'reading practice' and individual reading of stories*

| Time Spent (Hours per week) | Reading Practice | Individual Reading of Stories |
|---|---|---|
| 2½ | 1.5 | 0.4 |
| 2–2½ | 4.1 | 2.2 |
| 1½–2 | 5.8 | 4.0 |
| 1–1½ | 11.0 | 11.4 |
| ½–1 | 21.0 | 27.5 |
| ½ | 27.5 | 30.3 |
| 0 | 29.1 | 24.1 |

(Figures extracted from Tables 54 and 55 of the *Bullock Report* 1975)

In the light of the increase in reference and information books in primary schools during the 1960s and 1970s, it is interesting to note the amount of time which children spent in using these books for 'topic' work. In the *Bullock Report,* it was noted that the time spent on 'topics', i.e. reading and writing, mainly based on reference books, by 42% of 9 year-olds, averaged over an hour a week and that in 68% of these classes children also spent some optional time working on 'topics'. Of course, with this sort of activity it would be extremely difficult, as well as unnecessary, to attempt to make a break-down of the time between reading and writing. On the other hand, it is useful to compare the times spent by 9 year-olds on topic work with the amount of time spent on 'free writing' in the form of stories, personal accounts and creative writing. Table 6-2 compares these two types of activity. The comparison shows that despite the recent emphasis on working with reference and information books, classes of 9 year-olds still spent more class time on free writing than on topic work, and that in 20% of the classes no class time was set aside for topic work. The balance was redressed in the children's optional time, when the 68% of children who did topic work as an optional activity compared favourably with the 50% of children who chose to write stories, etc. in their optional time.

Table 6-2

*Percentages of classes of 9 year-olds spending time on 'topic work' and 'free writing'*

| Time Spent (Hours per week) | Topic Work | Free  Writing |
|---|---|---|
| 2½ | 3.8 | 3.0 |
| 2–2½ | 5.4 | 4.6 |
| 1½–2 | 13.2 | 11.9 |
| 1–1½ | 19.2 | 24.9 |
| ½–1 | 23.8 | 39.4 |
| ½ | 14.1 | 10.8 |
| 0 | 20.6 | 5.8 |

(Figures extracted from Tables 52 and 53 of the *Bullock Report* 1975)

Despite the findings of the Bullock Committee that 78% of 9 year-olds chose to spend some of their optional time on reading stories, the *Bullock Report* echoed the *Plowden Report*'s concern that more opportunities to read for pleasure and more time to do so should be provided in schools. It stated:

There is a strong association between voluntary reading and reading attainment. Teachers should devise various ways of extending their pupils' interest in fiction and of increasing the amount and range of their voluntary private reading.

and

The supply of narrative books – particularly good modern fiction – should be increased in primary schools. We believe that narrative is often neglected in favour of 'information books'.

The report also makes the telling point that when people who joined an adult literacy scheme were asked to say why, in their opinion, they had failed to learn to read at school: 'Only one common factor emerges: they did not learn from the process of learning to read that it was something people did for *pleasure.*'

Accordingly, the *Bullock Report* states firmly that: 'The reading habit should be established early and should receive unqualified encouragement from that point onwards.'

In this respect, the survey conducted by the Committee revealed that 95% of the classes containing 9 year-old pupils had classroom libraries and that, in 90% of the cases, the children had access to books elsewhere in the school, in a central library collection, a corridor or another classroom. They were also pleased to note that 93% of the 9 year-olds were allowed to take books home. As they reported: 'This presents a welcome improvement since the Plowden Committee's findings, reported in 1967, that only 65% of the primary schools in its survey allowed children to take books home.'

Even so, despite their report on improvements in the quantity and use of books in primary schools, the Bullock Committee stressed the need for further advancements: 'We believe that schools can make better use of the books and other materials they at present possess, and that many schools are in urgent need of more.'

The categories and quantities of books available, as well as their deployment and use, in certain primary schools in 1975/6 are described later in this report.

## II Need to Investigate the Reading Environment

The preceding brief summary of recent developments in book resources in English primary schools gives some indication of the increasingly important role that published books have come to play in the teaching of reading. Accordingly, in the current project, it was considered essential that this particular aspect of 'extending beginning reading' should be investigated as fully as possible. The broad term 'reading environment' has been chosen to cover certain aspects of the research, in order to indicate that the investigations were not merely concerned with the rather static exercise of listing titles of books being used in first- and second-year junior classes. An environment is rarely a static entity; in this instance a collection of books. One of the main focuses of interest in any environment is usually the ways in which the living creatures existing within it use it, adapt it to their purposes and, in the long run, alter it. Thus, the term 'reading environment' is used to indicate that the investigations were concerned not only with the books and other reading resources available in the schools for the age-groups of children being studied, but also with dynamic questions relating to the deployment of the resources and the ways in which they were being utilized by both teachers and pupils.

Earlier in this chapter a distinction was being made between 'books for teaching reading' and 'books for using'. The former term refers to basic reading schemes and books designed to develop particular skills such as phonic skills or 'comprehension'. In other words, they are books which children use under a teacher's direction and which the teacher regards as the basic tools for teaching children to read and for effecting improvements in their reading proficiency. In contrast, 'books for using' include all those fiction and non-fiction books which children consult or read for information and pleasure. As has been shown, 'books for using' have a much shorter history than 'teaching books'. The distinction between these two types of books has been retained throughout this report, as it seemed necessary to endeavour to form some sort of comparison of the contributions made to the reading programmes of 7 to 9 year-olds by basic reading schemes and such supportive materials and by the many other books which are in evidence in schools. Moreover, the teachers themselves were clearly able to differentiate between the two kinds of books.

The first reason for needing to investigate the reading environment was the dearth of information available about the books currently being used with the age-range 7 to 9 year-olds, and also about the ways in which they are being used. Morris (1966), for example, mentioned the *Wide Range Readers* (Schonell and Flowerdew 1953) and *The Beacon Readers* (Grassam 1922) as being used by second-year juniors in 1954–7. More recent reports, however, for example the *Plowden Report* (1967) and the *Bullock Report* (1975), did find out a certain amount about how both kinds of books were being used. Even so, little enough is known about books and their uses in classes of younger juniors and, consequently, this was seen as an extremely important facet of 'extending beginning reading' with these age groups, and one which it was essential to investigate.

The second reason for needing to investigate the reading environment was that teachers have usually considered the choice of reading books to be a vital factor affecting children's reading progress. This has been particularly true of infant teachers, in respect of the selection of reading schemes; although teachers of lower juniors, and especially those with a proportion of slower readers in their classes, have also tended to regard the choice of a reading scheme as important. Southgate (1968) never considered that a reading scheme played such an important role as teachers believed, especially in the light of the increasing number of other books to which children in primary schools had access. This judgement received confirmation in the results of a small experiment reported by Southgate and Lewis (1973), in which it was found that only 12% of the time in which infants were engaged in reading and writing activities was in any way connected with the reading schemes on which the teachers thought they were basing their reading teaching. The remaining 88% of the time was taken up with other reading and writing activities entirely unrelated to any reading scheme. The same may well be true in lower junior classes but, as the amount of research which had been undertaken into ongoing reading practices in classes of 7 to 11 year-olds was practically negligible, the facts were just not known. Therefore, it was hoped that an examination of 'teaching books' and 'books for using' in younger junior classes would help to clarify for the teachers the roles played by each.

The constant aims of teachers of children of primary school age are to forward their pupils' reading progress and extend their interest in reading. To arrange for the most effective use of the books already in their schools and to make knowledgeable decisions about the ordering of future books, represents a practical step which teachers can take, here and now, to help to further their aims. Therefore, the third reason for considering it essential to investigate the reading environment was that, to have access to information about what other schools were doing in this respect, and to learn of the advantages other teachers saw and the problems they encountered in their different systems of organizing and using books, would be likely to assist teachers of younger juniors in their own planning. For, as Purton (1970) points out:

> ... there are many (teachers) who have not had the opportunity of seeing other school libraries in operation or of discussing library matters with their colleagues in other schools, with whom they can exchange useful ideas.

It was hoped that the various investigations concerned with the reading environments in which 7 to 9 year-olds were being taught to read, and to use their reading skills, would help to provide answers to some of the following questions.

1. Why do teachers consider learning to read to be important?
2. How much do the teachers rely on basic reading schemes?
3. Which schemes do they use?
4. How do they use them?
5. *Why* do teachers want to 'surround children with books'?
6. In which ways do teachers try to promote children's interest in books?
7. How much reading of fiction and non-fiction books do children do on their own?
8. How are the book resources organized and used to further the end of encouraging and helping children to benefit from being 'surrounded by books'?
9. Are there many different systems being used?
10. What advantages and disadvantages do the teachers find in using the different systems?
11. To what extent do teachers' objectives appear to be being achieved?
12. If the teachers' aims of interesting children in books and turning them into habitual readers do not appear to be entirely successful, can the investigations throw light on practices which might lead to greater success?

Some preliminary explorations of the books children were using in younger junior classes were undertaken with the co-operation of the large Teachers' Reading Research Groups during the first two years of the project. In the 'intensive study' of 12 schools in the third year, a more detailed investigation was put into effect. A number of the investigations carried out in schools during the intensive study year, for example teachers' objectives, teachers' daily logs, 'interviews' with children, and both teachers' and children's observation schedules, also provided clues to the answers to some of these questions. However, the main probes into book resources and the uses made of them centred on the following two activities in the intensive study year:

(a) children's records of books read throughout the year, together with their own comments on their preferences and dislikes;

(b) a detailed 'Book Environmental Exercise' undertaken in 8 schools, with supporting information from the headteachers, class teachers and school librarians concerned.

The results of the various probes are reported later in this book, particularly in Chapter 7 and Chapters 8–12.

# Investigating the Reading Environment in Eight Schools

## I How the Exercise was Carried Out

### A. *Obtaining the Schools' Support*

In the twelve schools used in the intensive study, the idea of carrying out a detailed survey of the book environment of each school was put to each headteacher at the conclusion of two 'interviews' undertaken by the project director.

These 'interviews' took the form of structured discussions, based on a series of specific questions designed to elicit detailed information about the school. Each discussion lasted between one and two hours. The first was concerned with gathering general information about the school, the head-teacher's aims and objectives, main interests and contact with parents. The second discussion was centred firstly on the general policy regarding reading teaching and the way in which reading was taught in the school; and secondly, on the school's book resources, the policy for their use and details of the ways in which they were organized and used.

Following these discussions, it was suggested to the headteacher that to have a complete picture of the total book environment of a variety of schools would enrich the project's investigation, supply the school itself with useful information, and provide the primary school teachers, who would eventually read the project report, with valuable ideas relating to the advantages and disadvantages of different methods of organizing books for younger juniors. All the headteachers considered that such information would be useful to their own staff and also to other primary school teachers. In the event, however, due to the time factor, travelling difficulties, and the problems of assembling the necessary team to undertake the task, the exercise was only carried out in eight schools.

### B. *Preliminary Steps*

The first stage of planning the book environment exercise involved discussions with one local authority adviser who was particularly interested in book resources (see Johnson 1976). The discussion centred on the precise area of investigation and the ways in which the exercise might best be carried out. The following were the most important decisions agreed on:

1. Although the reading schemes in use in first- and second-year junior classes would be noted, the exercise would be mainly concerned with books other than reading schemes, i.e. 'books for using'.
2. In all-age primary schools, infant classes and the books they used would be disregarded.
3. Although the main concern of the investigation was with book resources as they affect first- and second-year junior children, it would be necessary to count and note the arrangements of book provision for all children within the junior age range.
4. The distribution of books between main collections, subsidiary collections and books for classroom use would be noted.
5. The number of books on loan from Schools' Library Services would be differentiated from books belonging to the schools.
6. The number of fiction and non-fiction books would be noted separately.
7. Where possible, numbers of non-fiction books in particular subject areas would be recorded.
8. Fiction books in the main collection in each school would be divided into two categories according to whether they were judged suitable for average younger juniors (first- and second-years) or average older juniors (third- and fourth-years).
9. Local advisers and the staffs of Schools' Library Services, from the other three LEAs involved in the intensive study, would be invited to help with the book environment exercise.

The next stage took the form of a pilot exercise in a school not involved with the project. A team of helpers, including teachers, advisers and school librarians was enlisted. The results reported from the pilot study made it possible to draw up detailed plans for the exercise in the intensive-study schools.

The approval and support of the advisers from the remaining three LEAs was sought and enthusiastically given. In every case the adviser not only agreed to recruit members of the Schools' Library Service but also took part in the exercise himself. The size of the teams which undertook the exercise in the various schools ranged from four to eight members, made up as follows: the project director; one or more advisers from the relevant LEA; one or more of the staff of the Schools' Library Service for the LEA; and sometimes one or two advisers from other LEAs.

A few days before the whole-day exercise was to take place, the children in the school were asked to bring from home all the books which had been borrowed from the school or class libraries. These were to be returned to the places where they were normally kept in the school. Books in classrooms or in children's desks or lockers were also to be returned to their normal shelves or cupboards. A plea was made that no reorganization of book resources should be put into force at this point. (In the event, it was usually noticeable, and probably inevitable, that a little tidying up of book corners and library shelves had gone on in the day or so preceding the exercise!)

## C. *The One-Day Exercise*

The major part of the work for the members of the team participating in the book environment exercise was objective in character. It involved counting books, classifying and recording them in various categories, making notes on methods of presentation and organization and of charts or notices on display which gave guidance to children on how to find books. Members of the Schools' Library Services were generally engaged in counting and classifying books in the central library area, while other members of the team examined displays of books in classrooms or other areas.

There were, however, two areas in which subjective judgements needed to be made. The first was in the assessment of the approximate level of difficulty of every fiction book in the main library area, by judging it as suitable for either 'younger' or 'older' juniors of average reading ability. Although this judgement rested mainly on the reading difficulty of the text, the subject matter, vocabulary, length and structure of the sentences, amount of text, size of print, length of the book and the numbers of illustrations were also taken into account. In order to maintain equivalent levels of judgement throughout the schools the task was undertaken in every school by the project director, who had long experience of this kind of work. In the majority of the schools, when the fiction books had been so divided, a second member of the team who was knowledgeable and experienced in this area, checked a one in ten sample of all the fiction books. In nearly every case, the check supported the original assessment. In the few schools in which the fiction books had already been graded according to difficulty by the school librarian or other teachers, there was found to be a very large measure of agreement between the assessors' and the teacher's judgement.

The second subjective assessment concerned the condition of the books, the appropriateness and usefulness of their arrangement and the attractiveness of the displays. Such judgements always represented a consensus of the views of those members of the team who were frequent visitors to schools and experienced in the assessment of children's books, namely local advisers and the project director.

During the course of the day, discussions were held with the headteacher, the school librarian and teachers of first- and second-year classes, to ensure that the system in force in the school for the use of the books was thoroughly understood. In addition, the project director, in an informal meeting with the school librarian and the teachers concerned, had a more detailed discussion of the book system, how the staff and children used the books and any problems encountered. Enquiries were also made regarding time spent on reading stories to children, time set aside for children to do personal reading, training in the use of the library facilities, books taken home by children and other related matters. At the end of this meeting, the project director asked the following questions:

1. Why do you want to surround children with books?
2. What are the advantages of the present system?
3. What are the disadvantages of the present system?
4. How might the system be improved?

The teachers gave independent written answers to these questions. Every headteacher also completed one of these forms.


## II. Summary of the Reading Environment in Eight Schools


### A. *Background Information*

While the eight schools in which the reading environment exercise was carried out cannot be regarded as a random sample of schools containing children aged 7 to 10 years, they were schools considered as 'typical' by the LEA advisers concerned. Furthermore, they exhibited a wide variety of background features, as the following points will show:

1. The schools were drawn from four local education authorities.
2. Three schools were within a very large metropolitan borough, one was on the periphery of a large conurbation, two were on the outskirts of towns, one was in the centre of a town and one was a city centre school, in an Educational Priority Area.
3. The families from which the pupils were drawn showed a wide range of socio-economic factors.
4. Four of the schools were all-age primary schools and four were junior schools.
5. The dates of the school buildings varied from the early nineteenth century through 1905, 1909, 1935, to more recent ones built between 1966 and 1969.
6. The numbers of children in the schools ranged from 235 to 430. If only children of junior age are counted, the range was 106 to 430.
7. The approximate average levels of intelligence of first year juniors in the eight schools extended from 91 to 112.
8. The range of average reading ages of first-year juniors at the beginning of the school year was 6 years 11 months to 8 years 4 months.

Examples of types of school which are not to be found in this list of eight schools include those with large proportions of immigrant children, small village schools, purpose-built open plan schools and schools in which vertical-grouping existed in junior classes.

# B. *Book Resources*

## 1. Deployment of books

The deployment of books in primary schools, and particularly the division of books between class libraries and central collections, is frequently the subject of discussion among primary school teachers, as well as engaging the attention of authors concerned with primary school book resources, for example, Kamm and Taylor (1966), School Library Association (1966), Osborne (1970), Purton (1970), *Bullock Report* (1975) and McKenzie and Warlow (1977). It is rarely a question of settling on either a central library or class libraries, as a general consensus appears to have been reached that for children aged 7 to 11 years, both kinds of library provision are necessary. The School Library Association (1966), for instance, states:

> Generally speaking we recommend as the kind of library suited to the primary school a system of classroom libraries, linked at any rate in junior schools, with a central collection adequately housed.

The *Bullock Report* (1975) also indicates that:

> Every primary school classroom should therefore have a book corner, partly enclosed and occupying the quietest area of the room.

and

> This localized source should be supplemented by a central collection, which might include non-print material of various kinds.

Teachers in the eight schools concerned were in agreement with these views, in that every school had a central collection of books, as well as class libraries. That the central collection should be 'adequately housed' was not so easy to achieve, as the teachers themselves would be the first to admit, for as Purton (1970) points out:

> There are many primary schools which suffer from lack of space, even those recently built, for when the Department of Education and Science (then the Ministry of Education) in 1950 recommended a separate library room in secondary schools, no such recommendation was extended to primary school buildings.

In only one school was there a purpose-built library — a very large, open area onto which most of the junior classrooms opened. Even so, the remaining schools had all contrived library areas where central collections of books could be housed. Two schools had small rooms used solely as libraries but each was only large enough to accommodate a few children at a time. In a further two schools other areas had been furnished as libraries; in one case an entrance hall and in the other a working bay. These areas, while somewhat larger, suffered the disadvantage of disturbances when individuals or classes had to use them as passage-ways. Two other schools housed their central collections of library books in moveable book cases, which had to be closed up when the areas were used for different purposes. In one case the area was the entrance hall which was used by whole classes viewing television programmes. The second of these schools kept the moveable book cases in the dining room which was also used as a television room. The eighth school, in which one of the buildings had originally been a secondary school, had inherited a spacious library room, with attractive, built-in wooden book shelves covering two walls. Unfortunately, as the school was overcrowded, this library room had to be used as a classroom. So, although a proportion of the library books were kept in it, others were placed on book cases in corridors, so that children could have more frequent access to them.

The picture which emerged of library accommodation in these schools was of headteachers and their staffs eager to provide children with central library areas and, with one exception, being handicapped by the limitations of the buildings. Even so, despite the limitations of space, care and thought, as well as a great deal of ingenuity and hard work, had gone into the provision of central libraries. In some cases, the efforts of the teachers had been supported by Parent-Teachers' Associations, who had raised money for shelving, furniture and additional books.

In every school, each class also had some kind of class library; the books being displayed on open shelves, book racks or book cases. These classroom collections of library books showed great variations, not only between schools but between classes within schools, in the numbers, quality and appropriateness of the books, as well as in their organization and display.

## 2. Numbers of books in collections

First, it should be noted that the actual numbers of books quoted in the following tables can be misleading. In practically every classroom and central library, even when many of the books were attractive and appropriate, a proportion of them were usually old, damaged, unattractive or unsuitable. Teachers, eager to build up class libraries, are understandably reluctant to discard books which just *might* be useful to somebody at some future time, especially in times when the cost of books is soaring. Teachers' reluctance to prune book resources can result in substantial arrays of books which would be better discarded, even though shelves were left relatively empty. Accordingly, in the following tables it should be borne in mind that the numbers of books likely to be used by children were always less than the totals shown; in some cases slightly less but in the majority of cases considerably less.

The division of books between central collections and class libraries in the eight schools is shown in Table 7-1.

Table 7-1

*Allocation of books between main library areas and classrooms*

| School | Numbers of Books | | | % of books in Library |
| --- | --- | --- | --- | --- |
| | Main Library | Classrooms | Total | |
| 4/Z | 3,507 | 1,609 | 5,116 | 69 |
| 9/X | 1,204 | 688 | 1,892 | 64 |
| 2/Z | 1,627 | 1,421 | 3,048 | 53 |
| 3/Z | 1,730 | 1,770 | 3,500 | 49 |
| 7/Y | 1,302 | 1,933 | 3,235 | 40 |
| 5/Y | 1,569 | 2,433 | 4,002 | 39 |
| 12/W | 2,502 | 4,769 | 7,271 | 34 |
| 8/Y | 878 | 2,803 | 3,681 | 24 |

At first glance the large variations in the proportions of the schools'
book resources in central collections, i.e. a range of 69% to 24%, might
suggest different policies in the schools about the allocation and use of
books. This was not necessarily the case. In the first place, none of the
schools involved had ever undertaken an exercise on the scale of this
particular investigation. Indeed, it must be rare for the staff of any
primary school to have the time to carry out such an exercise. Consequently, while the staff of each school were no doubt aware of
whether the balance of books lay in classrooms or central areas, none
was likely to know the exact proportions. Secondly, the numbers of
older, less attractive books found in many classrooms and central
collections are likely to have produced a distorting effect on the figures.
Even so, certain clear patterns can be noted. For example, School 4/Z,
in which 69% of the books were on display in the central library, was
the school with the large resources area, to which classes concerned had
easy access. The flow of children, teachers and classes in and out of
this particular area went on continuously throughout every day, so that
the resources were in constant use. In other schools, where access to
central libraries was less easy, more books were likely to be kept in
classrooms or corridors.

The numbers of books in different classes in the same school also
showed wide variations. Sometimes this had happened almost by
chance. A teacher might have inherited a large stock of library books
from a previous teacher who had carefully built up a class library
over many years. In contrast, a newly established class might have a
very small number of books. Such differences were frequently illustrations of how teachers, with the interests of their own pupils at
heart, almost inevitably become, to a certain extent, possessive about

'their' library books. In schools in which class teachers personally selected new library books for their own classes, as many of them did, it must be extremely difficult not to become rather possessive about them. The important and personal links between a teacher, her pupils and the books in the classroom are noted in the following quotation (McKenzie and Warlow 1977):

> However well-equipped and well-used the school library may be, it does not replace a good collection of books in a primary school classroom, for it is in the classroom that the teacher is aware of and in control of the total learning situation. It is there, too, that good stories are readily available, with immediate opportunity to establish which books are their favourites, which authors they like, which stories and poems they are fond of . . .

Even so, it was noted that in many classrooms there were books which were clearly too difficult for the children in the class and, consequently, were seldom, if ever, used. The retention of such books certainly hinders the flexibility in the use of book resources which is now so often advocated. As the School Library Association (1966) states in its publication *The Library in the Primary School*:

> The aim should be to make interchange between classroom and central collection easy, so that all the books may be available as far as possible to children and staff at any time; for a book lying unused in either place may be just the book that is needed elsewhere.

The general impression gained from the book environment exercise was that collections of books in different areas of schools were quite often fairly static. Even when in theory flexibility and interchangeability of books between classes, and between central and classroom collections, was aimed at, common practices rarely tended to follow this pattern.

## 3. Ratios of books per pupil

The total numbers of books shown in Table 7-1 as being on display in various areas need to be related to the number of pupils in each school. Accordingly in Table 7-2 the numbers of books in each school have been divided by the number of junior-aged pupils, in order to arrive at a ratio of books per pupil.

Table 7-2

*Ratios of books per pupil*

| School | Fiction | Non-Fiction | Total |
|--------|---------|-------------|-------|
| 4/Z | 11.7 | 9.6 | 21.3 |
| 3/Z | 10.2 | 10.6 | 20.8 |
| 12/W | 7.7 | 10.0 | 17.7 |
| 8/Y | 5.4 | 10.2 | 15.6 |
| 5/Y | 5.7 | 8.0 | 13.7 |
| 2/Z | 5.4 | 6.4 | 11.8 |
| 7/Y | 3.9 | 7.1 | 11.0 |
| 9/X | 3.3 | 5.7 | 9.0 |

This table again highlights the large differences between schools in their provision of resource books for children and the relatively small ratio of books per pupil in some of the schools. In this respect it is interesting to note that McKenzie and Warlow (1977) suggest: 'Perhaps a rule of thumb might be that there should be ten books per child in a classroom collection, to cover some of the needs for reading stories and getting information.'

Certain of the classrooms in the eight schools did not achieve this suggested ratio and, if the unsuitable books found in many classrooms had been subtracted from the totals, many classroom collections of books would have been well below the suggested figure.

## 4. Fiction and non-fiction books
A division of the numbers of 'books for using' into fiction and non-fiction throws up some interesting variations in the eight schools. Details are set out in Table 7-3.

One of the most noticeable features of Table 7-3, a point also to be seen in Table 7-2, is the preponderance of non-fiction over fiction books, which illustrates quite clearly the emphasis in primary schools over the past ten years or so on heuristic methods of learning. The figures also support the Bullock Committee's conclusion that: 'The indications are that narrative books are substantially outnumbered by non-fiction in most primary schools.' As can be seen from Table 7-3, in only one of the eight schools was the balance of books in favour of fiction, i.e. 55% of the total. In two schools only 35% of the total number of books in the school were fiction.

Table 7-3

*Fiction and non-fiction books in eight schools*

## NUMBERS OF BOOKS ON DISPLAY

| School | Main Collection | | | | Classrooms | | | | Totals | | | |
|---|---|---|---|---|---|---|---|---|---|---|---|---|
| | Fiction | Non-fiction | Total | % of fiction | Fiction | Non-Fiction | Total | % of fiction | Fiction | Non-fiction | Total | % of fiction |
| 2/Z | 338 | 1,239 | 1,627 | 21 | 1,054 | 367 | 1,421 | 74 | 1,392 | 1,656 | 3,048 | 46 |
| 3/Z | 375 | 1,355 | 1,730 | 22 | 1,344 | 426 | 1,770 | 76 | 1,719 | 1,781 | 3,500 | 49 |
| 4/Z | 1,718 | 1,789 | 3,507 | 49 | 1,098 | 511 | 1,609 | 68 | 2,816 | 2,300 | 5,116 | 55 |
| 5/Y | 583 | 986 | 1,569 | 37 | 1,075 | 1,358 | 2,433 | 44 | 1,658 | 2,344 | 4,002 | 41 |
| 7/Y | 460 | 842 | 1,302 | 35 | 682 | 1,251 | 1,933 | 35 | 1,142 | 2,093 | 3,235 | 35 |
| 8/Y | 274 | 604 | 878 | 31 | 1,000 | 1,803 | 2,803 | 36 | 1,274 | 2,407 | 3,681 | 35 |
| 9/X | 512 | 692 | 1,204 | 43 | 185 | 503 | 688 | 27 | 697 | 1,195 | 1,892 | 37 |
| 12/W | 1,035 | 1,467 | 2,502 | 41 | 2,124 | 2,645 | 4,769 | 45 | 3,159 | 4,112 | 7,271 | 43 |

Of the books in central libraries, in every school the total numbers of non-fiction books exceeded the total of fiction books. The school with the most even balance of books in the library had a ratio of 49% fiction books to 51% non-fiction: the remaining seven schools ranged from 43% to only 21% of fiction books. In six of the schools the balance was redressed in favour of fiction books in the classrooms, with the percentages of fiction books ranging from 76% to 36%. Of the remaining two schools, in one 35% of the books in the classroom were fiction — the same percentage as in the library. In the remaining school only 27% of the classroom books were fiction, in contrast to 43% of the books in the main library. These average figures for fiction and non-fiction books in classrooms disguise the fact that there were wide variations between classes.

Not only were there fewer fiction books in every library than non-fiction books but, as Table 7-4 shows, the balance of the fiction books was usually in favour of older juniors rather than younger juniors.

Table 7-4

*'Older' and 'Younger' fiction books in main library*

| School | Numbers of Books | | | % of younger books |
|--------|-------|---------|-------|---------------------|
|        | Older | Younger | Total |                     |
| 8/Y    | 112   | 162     | 274   | 59 |
| 3/Z    | 190   | 185     | 375   | 49 |
| 2/Z    | 201   | 137     | 338   | 41 |
| 4/Z    | 1,062 | 656     | 1,718 | 38 |
| 7/Y    | 288   | 172     | 460   | 37 |
| 12/W   | 673   | 362     | 1,035 | 35 |
| 9/X    | 392   | 120     | 512   | 23 |
| 5/Y    | 470   | 113     | 583   | 19 |

(N.B. 'Older' books were those considered suitable for average readers in 3rd and 4th year junior classes, while 'younger' books were those considered to be at the level of average 1st and 2nd year juniors.)

In only one of the eight schools did the number of fiction books in the main library, at the level of average readers in younger classes, exceed the total of books for older pupils. Bearing in mind the proportions of first- and second-year children whose reading ability is inevitably below average, the position revealed is that many school libraries lack sufficient easy fiction books to encourage quite large proportions of first- and second-year juniors to attempt to read them, or to enjoy the experience if they do attempt it.

Although the task of judging the difficulty levels of fiction books in classrooms was not undertaken, the general impression gained was that the situation was similar to that in the main libraries, namely a tendency for the majority of the fiction books in classrooms to be too difficult to afford much pleasure to fairly large proportions of the children in the classes. The members of the staffs of Schools' Library Services who formed part of the teams in these investigations of school book environments were particularly interested in this finding. After discussion, it was decided that teachers in primary schools would welcome suggestions of suitable books for younger juniors, and members of two Schools' Library Services agreed to produce such lists.

As the non-fiction books were almost invariably more difficult than the fiction books, the position was that, of all the books on the shelves of central libraries, there were comparatively few that average and below average readers aged 7 to 9 years would be able to read easily. Such a situation, which exists in so many primary schools, must be a cause for concern to the majority of teachers whose stated aims are to interest children in books and tempt them to read them. As it is the slower readers who require most encouragement, a junior school library might perhaps be considered better balanced if it contained more books at easier levels than at advanced levels.

## 5. Sources of supply of books

The main sources from which the eight schools obtained books for class and central libraries were as follows:
(a)  Money set aside from the 'capitation allowance';
(b)  Schools' Library Services — which included the long-term loan of fiction and non-fiction books and, in some cases, the loan of special 'project boxes' containing books and other resources on particular topics;
(c)  The loan of books from local branches of County or Municipal libraries;
(d)  Money to purchase books and library equipment from the School Funds, which could include money raised by Parent-Teachers' Associations or by the school itself from Book Fairs, Book Exhibitions, profits from Book Clubs and other money-raising events;
(e)  Gifts of new or second-hand books made by parents and children.

Some of the schools drew on practically all these sources of supply, while others seemed to have fewer sources available to them.

In recent years, local education authorities, through their Schools' Library Services, have given increasing support to schools in their task of expanding their reading resources. The *Bullock Report*, for example, found that 87% of the schools from which the 9 year-olds in their sample were drawn obtained books from Schools' Library Services. In undertaking the book counts in the eight schools, books on loan from LEAs were counted separately from the books belonging to the schools. The comparative figures are set out in Table 7-5.

Table 7-5

*Books on loan compared with school's own books*

| School | Numbers of Books | | | % of Books on Loan |
| | On Loan | School's Books | Total | |
| --- | --- | --- | --- | --- |
| 2/Z | 537 | 2,511 | 3,048 | 18 |
| 3/Z | 250 | 3,250 | 3,500 | 7 |
| 4/Z | 250 | 4,444 | 5,116 | 13 |
| 5/Y | 672 | 3,086 | 4,002 | 23 |
| 7/Y | 910 | 2,646 | 3,235 | 18 |
| 8/Y | 140 | 3,541 | 3,681 | 4 |
| 9/X | — | 1,892 | 1,892 | — |
| 12/W | 910 | 6,361 | 7,271 | 13 |

The support available in the form of long-term loan of books, while it differed from one local authority to another, was greatly valued by the seven schools in which it operated. Even so, it could be noted that different schools within the same LEA did not always have proportionately equal provision of book resources drawn from those sources locally available to them. This might suggest that the provision of resources by Schools' Library Services, County and Municipal Libraries for schools is a joint venture, depending not only on the generosity and interest of the providers of such lending services but also partly on the enthusiastic and informed requests made by the borrowers.

In certain schools the books lent by the Schools' Library Services were all placed in the central library, while in other cases all or part of these books were used to enrich the class libraries. These books were generally among the most attractive and appropriate books of all the book resources in the schools. They were always in good condition, and usually had colourful dust-jackets, protected by transparent plastic sleeves. The quality of the paper, the illustrations and the general presentation of the books was invariably high. These books made a noticeable and very worthwhile addition to the schools' own book resources.

Money raised by the schools themselves and by Parent-Teacher Associations went a long way towards increasing the provision of book resources in some schools. The socio-economic area in which the school was situated no doubt has some effect on this, in that more well-to-do parents were likely to respond more generously to money-raising events. Yet, again it seemed that a strong drive centred on book provision in schools in areas of lower socio-economic status could draw equally strong responses from poorer parents. The danger is, of course, that constant invitations to money-raising events may deter parents in straitened circumstances from attending school functions. Schools which operated Book Clubs for children, and especially when Book Fairs or Exhibitions were annual events, managed to raise additional funds for books, while at the same time encouraging children to spend their own pocket money on the purchase of books.

Occasionally, the parents of a child leaving the school donated a book to the library and in some schools children gave to the school library books which they had outgrown. The danger of this latter practice is that books donated may be unsuitable or in poor condition, yet refusal to incorporate them in the library could cause distress.

## 6. Selection of books

The selection of books to swell a school's book resources should reflect the total book policy of the school – a policy which has been discussed and agreed on by all members of staff. The *Bullock Report* stated this in the following words:

> Whenever any school buys or borrows a book it has a reason for doing so, but that in itself will not ensure that the stock does not grow by a process of random accretion. What is required is a book policy which reflects a set of objectives understood and accepted by the staff.

The report also recognized that such a book policy does not always exist: 'The building up of book resources is often something of a piece-meal process rather than a planned response to defined objectives.' In the eight schools investigated, although the staffs were invariably eager to optimize the book provision for children in the school, it seemed probable that they, like many other schools, did not always reach those high objectives regarding a school book policy envisaged by the Bullock Committee. One example of this is shown in the relatively low proportions of both fiction and non-fiction books suitable for younger readers or backward readers – a fact commented on by the relevant teachers in most of the schools. Other examples include, in certain schools, gaps in the provision of non-fiction books covering particular subject areas and low provision of high quality modern fiction.

Arrangements for the selection of new books differed in the eight schools, but it was usual for both the school librarian and the head-teacher to play an important role in the selection procedure. In certain schools, class teachers made suggestions of books required to the school librarian, while in other schools class teachers were able to select a number of books for their own classrooms and/or the library. When discussing the advantages and disadvantages of the book policy in their schools, it was evident that teachers greatly appreciated the opportunity of personally selecting books. This important point needs to be balanced against the problem that teachers are likely to feel more possessive about books they have personally chosen for their own classes and the result might be a loss of flexibility in the deployment of books. What came over very clearly was that enthusiasm for improving library resources increased with the personal involvement of all members of staff in the selection, deployment and use of the books.

One other interesting point was noted. When a central library was more heavily weighted in favour of books at the difficulty and interest levels of older juniors, as opposed to younger juniors and slower readers, this was sometimes associated with the headteacher and/or school librarian who taught upper juniors having a large share in the selection of books for the central library. Such a balance could soon be redressed by encouraging teachers of lower juniors and remedial teachers to play a larger role in the selection of books for central collections — both the books purchased and those borrowed.

## C. *The Organization and Use of Books*

In discussing the organization and use of the book resources in a school, the *Bullock Report* indicated that:

> A book policy implies that the school should have a record of all that it possesses. The ideal situation is where any book in the school can be obtained by any child at any time, but in practice this is not always easy to fulfil.

No doubt the majority of teachers of junior-aged children would agree with this statement — and would wholeheartedly endorse the final phrase! The report also supported the conclusions of the School Library Association and many other writers that in a primary school both classroom libraries and a central collection of books are essential. In addition, in advocating the importance of a changing supply of books in classrooms and relating this to the central collection of books, it suggested that:

> The ebb and flow of books into and out of this collection will be a continuous process. The important thing is that there should be a clear and recognized system of organization which allows everyone to know what are the school's resources and how they are dispersed.

While few primary school teachers are likely to disagree with this suggestion they, and more particularly, the school librarians, are only too aware of the problems involved in achieving these ideals.

The organization and use of books in the central collection in schools catering for children aged 7 to 11 is governed by a variety of factors, both ideological and practical. The former include the aims and objectives of the staff in teaching children to read, their desire to stimulate children's interest in books and the strengths of their beliefs in the importance of providing children with maximum access to attractive and appropriate books. The book policy of a school is formulated on the basis of such beliefs. Practical aspects include the limitations imposed by the buildings, the available resources, the expertise of the staff and the time available to them in relation to the time demanded by other school activities and areas of the curriculum.

## 1. Physical conditions

In many primary schools the size and lay-out of the buildings tend to hinder rather than aid the optimum organization and use of books. The majority of the buildings have not been designed around the concept of book resources being of central importance to learning. Consequently aims and objectives have frequently to be adjusted because of accommodation problems. For instance, in only one of the eight schools examined was there a purpose-built central library area. Nevertheless, in the remaining seven schools, it was evident that much thought and trouble had been taken to overcome the difficulties of unsuitable accommodation, in attempts to provide facilities which approached as closely as possible to the teachers' ideals.

The compromise solutions arrived at demonstrated the ingenuity exercised by teachers in the face of far from ideal circumstances. Central library areas of some kind were provided in every school, even though they were sometimes rather small, were not adjacent to the classes concerned, or were used as circulation areas and/or for other purposes. The teachers, when asked about the advantages and disadvantages of their school's system of organizing and using books, were clearly aware of the limiting conditions imposed by the buildings, yet they continued to search for and suggest possible ways of improving the systems in force.

## 2. School librarians

In the task of optimizing and facilitating the use of book resources in the schools, and particularly in central collections, the school librarians were key figures. Their expertise, enthusiasm and energy were vital. The fact that in all eight schools the librarians held posts of special responsibility (Scale 2 or 3) showed the value headteachers placed on librarians' work. The librarians all took their responsibilities very seriously, while at the same time viewing the work as a privilege and a pleasure.

One of the biggest handicaps to the work of librarians in primary schools is that they are nearly always in full-time charge of classes, and consequently have only limited time to spend on library facilities. In most schools the headteacher had tried to arrange for the librarians to have a few free periods for library work. Whilst this was appreciated, it still meant that librarians spent many additional hours, at lunchtimes and after school, in the organization and care of a collection of books. In some schools, child librarians had been trained to help the school librarians. Nevertheless, there were many tasks, for example, classifying and grading books, which only the librarian could undertake.

### 3. The organization and arrangement of books

One of the most important aspects of the librarian's task is the setting up of a system of classification and arrangement of books in the central library which will not only help children to find the books they want as easily as possible, but will also provide records of borrowed books which might need recalling. The listing, card indexing, cataloguing and classifying of books in any library is a time-consuming job. To ensure that such a system is not only effective but is also readily understandable and easily usable by young children poses certain additional problems for the librarians. The school librarians in this study were extremely helpful in explaining the systems they had set up, even in some cases going to the lengths of providing written reports. What was evident was that there was no perfect system; each had both strengths and drawbacks. In the end, in any primary school a compromise must be reached which takes account, as far as possible, of conditions in the school, the views of the librarian and the needs and wishes of the class teachers.

The schools usually separated fiction from non-fiction books in the central collections. In two schools the non-fiction books were divided into a small number of subject categories; the books in the categories being differentiated by coloured stickers on the spines. In four schools simplified Dewey systems of classification were used. In three schools a simple form of colour-coding was used instead of, or in addition to, Dewey figures to indicate general subject classifications. In those schools in which non-fiction books were categorized according to subject areas, charts or lists, giving details of the classification systems, designed to guide children to the books they required were usually displayed on the walls.

Arrangements for organizing and displaying fiction books appeared somewhat less clear-cut in certain of the schools. In two of the eight schools colour coding was used to indicate the levels of reading difficulty of fiction books in the main library. In each case it was interesting to note that the librarian's decisions regarding books at the difficulty levels of upper and lower juniors was in almost complete agreement with the independent assessor's judgement. Fiction books with the same coloured labels were usually shelved together, to help children to select books they were likely to be capable of reading. Arrangements of the fiction books in other schools varied. In some cases large books with many illustrations were shelved separately. In a few cases there were separate collections of books of poems and rhymes. In other cases, the fiction books were arranged alphabetically, according to authors. Certain schools drew attention to new additions by arranging special displays but in other cases, shortage of space or the use of the library area for other purposes limited these possibilities. Pressure of time, from the librarian's and other teachers' points of view, was also probably responsible for the fact that eye-catching notices and displays, drawing attention to fiction books and related materials concerning current interest or designed to stimulate new interests, were not always in evidence.

## 4. Training and supervision of children in the use of the library

The task of introducing young juniors, and especially children straight from infant classes, to the arrangement of the books in the central collections, helping them to choose suitable books, initiating them into the procedures for borrowing and returning books and generally training them to use the available facilities were matters of great concern to the teachers. Group discussions between the interviewer, the school librarian and the teachers highlighted the difficulties and showed how teachers, while attempting to solve these important problems, generally regarded the solutions adopted to be, inevitably, compromises.

The teachers and/or the librarians usually tried to take first-year juniors into the library area fairly early in the school year, in order to explain the system to them. However, in order to become familiar with a system, repeated and supervised practice in its use is essential. This was rarely possible, except in a school in which the central library was sufficiently spacious to allow its use by a whole class together. Even the changing of the library books to be taken home by children, once a week, was usually a complicated business, entailing teachers supervising a class in one part of the school, while trying to keep an eye on groups of children sent to change library books in another part of the school.

The problems of training young children to locate, in central libraries, the relevant reference books, relating to topics or projects on which they were currently working, and, even more difficult, supervising their working with these books in areas not adjacent to their own classroom, were very great indeed. Although these teachers did what they could, few of them were entirely satisfied with the results. There was a certain amelioration of the situation in those schools in which older pupils were on hand in the library to help the younger ones. Despite the difficulties in some cases teachers considered that by the end of their second year a proportion of the children were using the library facilities confidently and fairly efficiently. The general conclusion drawn was that for teachers to be able to help young children to maximize their use of the increasing supplies of 'books for using', the siting and physical conditions of resource areas in many primary schools will need to be radically improved. Teachers themselves mentioned that the current decline in the birthrate might soon release a spare classroom or two in primary schools which could be utilized as a book resource area.

## D. *Fostering Children's Interest in Books*

The use of the book resources in any school is closely bound up with two important facets of the total reading environment; namely, the ways in which the individual teachers endeavour to promote children's interest in books and the amount of time which is set aside by each teacher for children to read personally selected books. The practices adopted by the teachers in the eight schools concerned are amalgamated in Chapter 11 with those followed by a wide range of teachers.

## E. *Other Reading Resources*

Many recent publications have been concerned with 'resource centres' rather than with merely 'books' or 'libraries'; for example *Not By Books Alone* (Waite and Colebourn 1975), *School Resource Centres* (Beswick 1972), *Organizing Resources* (Beswick 1975) and the *Bullock Report* (1975). This last report, for instance, cited the evidence given by two witnesses to the Committee, as follows:

> ... One asked that we should 'counter a persistent bias towards books as the exclusive medium of learning'.

> The day has come when educationists should seriously question the extent to which the printed and spoken word should predominate in education to the exclusion of the image.

The Bullock Committee, however, reiterated their belief in the importance of the printed word: '... we argued that the medium of print occupies, and will continue to occupy, a position of the highest importance in the education process.' The detailed investigation of the reading environment in eight schools, in this project, as well as visits to many other primary schools would certainly confirm that, as far as teaching reading to first- and second-year junior classes is concerned, reading resources are overwhelmingly in the form of books.

The *Bullock Report,* although emphasizing the importance of books, went on to suggest additional resources for improving reading and language.

> Resource centres acknowledge that books should be supplemented by other media to give the maximum support for learning situations. These will include a wide variety of audio-visual aids, so that the pupil is able not only to look up books and other print material but also to study slides and film loops and listen to tapes and cassettes. ... All these enrich the possibilities open to the teacher but the resource centre is effective in proportion to the ease with which the pupils themselves can use it.

In one of the eight schools investigated, the librarian had assembled an extensive collection of resources but this was exceptional and represented a great deal of zeal and time spent on the part of the librarian, which is not always a practical possibility for all teachers in primary schools.

Certain of the schools had used tape-recorders to record stories from radio or television programmes. One school used a tape-recorder for reading games produced by the teacher, while another school made use of commercial tapes designed to encourage children to read popular children's books and children's classics. One further school mentioned the use of cassette recorders and earphones. In other schools commercial apparatus for teaching reading was in use, e.g. Stott's *Programmed Reading Kit* (Stott 1962). In most cases such aids were used by remedial teachers or with slower readers in normal classes. On the other hand, seven of the schools possessed one or more of the *S.R.A. Reading Laboratories* (Parker and Scannell 1963) which they used in junior classes; sometimes according to the authors' suggestions and in other cases following the teachers' ideas. Television programmes designed to improve reading were frequently followed. For example, in five of the eight schools, first- and second-year classes were regularly following the television programme 'Look and Read' which was being featured at that time.

To summarize the reading resources in the eight schools, it could be said that while the main resources were books, in every school there could be noted the beginnings of a movement to extend the resources to include certain of the additional resources mentioned in the *Bullock Report*.

## III Implications for Teachers

1. In all eight schools in which the book resources were closely examined a tendency was noted for books which were old, dilapidated or otherwise unsuitable to be retained in both classroom and central libraries. Such books were more likely to deter than tempt children to read. The implications are that if teachers in other schools were to undertake rigorous pruning of their book resources by ruthlessly discarding tattered, out-of-date and unattractive books those retained on display in classrooms, central libraries and other areas would probably prove doubly attractive and useful to the children concerned.

2. In every school there were wide variations in the numbers of 'books for using' to be found in different classrooms. This suggests that in many schools the pruning of books already suggested might well be followed by a consideration of the re-allocation of certain books. The first step could be for every teacher to put on one side all those books which were clearly too difficult for the children in the class — and practically every class is certain to have such books. These could then be re-allocated to classes of older children who *could* read them. A similar process, but in reverse, could be used for books too easy for children in a class, although the numbers would be very much smaller

than the preceding category. A ratio of 'books for using' per pupil, in each class, could then be calculated so that the available books could be more fairly distributed. As the effect of moving more difficult books to older classes would be to denude younger classes of books, future money available for the purchase of books for class libraries should be divided between those classes at the bottom of the ratio table, rather than every class having equal shares of it. In the meantime, facilities for borrowing books, for example from Schools' Library Services, should be utilized, as far as possible, to fill the gaps.

3. The proportions of narrative and non-fiction books in both central and class libraries should be checked in other schools, and the lower proportion of narrative books likely to be noted should be redressed.

4. It was found in seven out of eight schools investigated that more fiction books in the central library were suitable for older juniors than younger juniors. The proportions of all books in classrooms appeared similar: and this applied particularly to non-fiction books. Again, teachers in other schools would be well advised to check their own stocks with this in mind and then try to redress the future balance in favour of easier books. This is especially important in that, if the habit of reading is not established in the first two years of the junior school, owing to a dearth of books which the children can read with ease, it is less and less likely to develop as the children grow older. One method of ensuring that adequate supplies of books at a simpler level were available in the central library would be to offer teachers of lower juniors and remedial teachers opportunities to play a larger role in the selection of its books. A second method would be to adopt some simple systems of grading and colour-coding the books in the library according to their levels of difficulty. (This subject is discussed in Chapter 9 and a reference list of useful publications is provided in Appendix 9-A.)

5. Training children to make the best use of available library resources by guiding them to locate and select books of interest to them, and which they will be able to read and understand, is facilitated by the adoption of a simplified form of Dewey classification for non-fiction books and author classification of fiction books, together with a broad form of grading according to levels of difficulty.

6. It was found that even within the same authority or town, schools varied in the amount of help they received in the form of loans of books from Schools' Library Services and local libraries. It is, therefore, suggested that all schools should explore *all* the facilities available to them and make the maximum use of them.

7. Staff meetings, devoted entirely to discussions of the most advantageous ways of deploying, classifying, arranging and borrowing books might be one way of initiating improvements in library facilities, as

might visits to other schools where innovations have taken place.

8. Even so, all members of staff need to appreciate that the post of school librarian in a primary school is particularly onerous because he or she is invariably in charge of a class and, consequently, even when free periods are arranged for this work, the time is never sufficient. It follows that other members of staff who are eager to see a well-organized, efficient use of the book resources of the school, need to offer the school librarian as much help and support as possible. Only by good team-work can the central library facilities develop into flourishing resource centres.

# PART FIVE

## Teachers of Reading

# CHAPTER 8

# Teachers' Estimates of Children's Reading Ability

## I Estimating Before Testing

In planning reading activities or selecting books for their pupils, teachers are continually making subjective judgements on the level of reading they think individual children have reached. The better the judgements the more appropriate the teachers' planning will be. The first Teachers' Reading Research Group afforded an opportunity to appraise these judgements. Of the 440 members, 119 were headteachers and 321 were class teachers of first- and second-year juniors. The assessments the class teachers were going to undertake during the year had to be preceded by the administration of a standardized reading test. *Schonell's Graded Word Reading Test* (1948)[1], an individually administered oral word recognition test, was selected for this purpose, on the grounds that all the teachers had access to it. The original norms, based on ten words per year for ages 5 to 15, were adhered to.

The class teachers were asked, before undertaking the testing, to estimate the results which would be achieved by the children in their classes whose chronological ages fell between $7^9-8^3$ (first-years) or $8^9-9^3$ (second-years). This age restriction served to exclude children who had spent either more or less than the average amount of time in infant classes. The estimates were to be based on the teacher's knowledge of the child's work over the previous six months and on any previous test results they might have available. The teachers were asked to place each child in categories of six months in terms of reading age, rather than attempt an exact estimate. Teachers worked in pairs, each estimating the performance of her own pupils before the other teacher administered the actual test.

## II Responses from Teachers

239 lists, comprising results for 3,381 children, were returned on the

---

[1] It should be emphasized that *Schonell's Graded Word Reading Test* was used because, in the light of the unexpectedly large number of teachers in the research group, all with access to this test, it ensured speed in the necessary preliminary testing. Normally reading tests in the form of prose are preferable and two were used later in the project.

forms provided. The information given indicated that approximately 90% of first-year teachers and 80% of second-year teachers had access to the results of previous reading tests. The earlier testing had usually taken place at the beginning of the school year (six months earlier) and the test used had in the vast majority of cases been either *Schonell's Graded Word Reading Test* (1948) or Burt's (*Rearranged*) *Word Reading Test* (1954).

Certain of the class lists could not be included in the following analysis of data, as they concerned children in classes of mixed age-groups, contained fewer than four children of either or both sexes, or, if the estimates were based on preceding test results, the test was other than the two just mentioned. As a result, the analysis was based on 134 lists from 67 first-year and 67 second-year classes. These included teachers who had access to the results of one or other of the above tests as well as certain teachers with no earlier reading test results available to them. Table 8-1 shows the number of teachers falling into each category.

Table 8-1

*Numbers of teachers with or without previous test information available*

| Class Taught | No. of Teachers | | | |
|---|---|---|---|---|
| | With earlier test results | | No earlier results | Total |
| | Burt | Schonell | | |
| 1st year | 30 | 29 | 8 | 67 |
| 2nd year | 29 | 24 | 14 | 67 |
| | 59 | 53 | 22 | 134 |

In order that the sexes should be represented equally in subsequent analyses, whenever a class list included unequal numbers of children in the two sexes, then children were randomly selected from the over-represented sex and eliminated, until the sexes were matched in number for analysis. This procedure resulted in a total of 1,638 children (806 first-years and 832 second-years) divided equally between the sexes.

## III  Results of the Investigation

### A. *Reading Ages in Year Groups*

As was to be expected, the range of reading ages of the children concerned was extremely wide, despite the fact that within each age group the span of chronological ages was only six months. The reading ages in each age-group ranged from $5^0$ to $14^0$. The average reading age for first-years was $8^5$ and for second years $9^6$.

## B. *Teachers' Ability to Estimate*

The main questions being asked in this investigation were:

How realistic are teachers in general when estimating their pupils' reading ages (i.e. children's performances on a reading test)?

How precisely are individual children's reading ages estimated?

How, if at all, does information about previous reading test results affect the teacher's estimates?

Are teachers' estimates related in any way to the ages and/or sexes of their pupils?

### 1. General pattern of estimations

In order to investigate the characteristics of the teachers, in general, as estimators, each of the 134 teachers was classified as an over-estimator, an under-estimator or an inconsistent estimator. A teacher was classified as an over-estimator if more than three-quarters of her pupil's performances on the test had been in any way over-estimated. Similarly, a teacher was classified as an under-estimator if at least three-quarters of her pupils' results had been underestimated in any way. An inconsistent estimator was a teacher whose estimates of the children's reading ages were about equally under- and over-estimates. The proportion of teachers falling into each of these categories is shown in Table 8-2.

The general pattern of teachers' estimates in Table 8-2 can be seen in the final column which indicates that, when all the teachers were considered together, almost half of them (48%) were inconsistent estimators, who over-estimated about half of their pupils' performances, while under-estimating the rest. Of the remaining 52% of the teachers, about two-thirds were under-estimators, the rest being over-estimators. If the two age-groups are considered separately, it can be seen that first-year teachers more frequently under-estimated their pupils' performances, while second-year teachers more frequently over-estimated.

### 2. 'Correctness' of teachers' estimations

The question of how near to the children's actual results on the test a teacher's estimates should be, if that teacher is to be considered a 'good' estimator, is certainly a debatable one. One would have to consider the general question of how near an estimate should be to the actual result to be counted as 'correct'; for example, whether an estimate within three months or six months of the result would be

Table 8-2

*Teachers as estimators*

| Category of Estimator | 1st year Teachers | | | 2nd year Teachers | | | Teachers | | |
| --- | --- | --- | --- | --- | --- | --- | --- | --- | --- |
| | No test results | Burt | Schonell | No test results | Burt | Schonell | 1st year | 2nd year | Total |
| Over-estimator | 4 | 4 | 1 | 4 | 8 | 4 | 9 | 16 | 25 |
| Under-estimator | – | 13 | 12 | 5 | 8 | 7 | 25 | 20 | 45 |
| Inconsistent | 4 | 13 | 16 | 5 | 13 | 13 | 33 | 31 | 64 |
| No. of teachers | 8 | 30 | 29 | 14 | 29 | 24 | 67 | 67 | 134 |

sufficiently accurate. The proportion of a teacher's pupils whose results were 'correctly' forecast would also need to be considered in relation to a definition of an acceptable level of estimation.

One teacher in the analysis, for example, could certainly be classed as a very good estimator, in that she estimated the current reading ages of all the pupils on her list to within ± three months. The class was a second-year class, and the teacher had access to her pupils' previous test results on Schonell's *Graded Word Reading Test*. A further three teachers, all first-year teachers with previous test results available on the Burt test, managed to estimate each reading age on the Schonell test correct to within six months. But these examples were exceptions. To demand as a criterion that good estimators should be able to estimate the reading performance of *all* their pupils to within a specified few months, would be to exclude those teachers whose estimations for only one, or a few of their pupils were wide of the mark.

A clearer idea of the end result of the teachers' estimations can be gained by examining the percentages of the 1,638 pupils concerned, who fell into various categories of over-estimation and under-estimation. The proportion of children falling into various categories are set out in Table 8-3.

It can be noted from Table 8-3 that when a teacher's estimate for a child was within ± three months of the actual test result, this was counted as a 'correct' estimate. The remainder of the categories of increasingly large under-estimates and over-estimates are set out at three-monthly intervals of distance from the actual test result. Regarded in this way it can be seen that the test scores achieved by 36% of all the children were correctly forecast by their teachers. If the category of 'correctness' of estimation is broadened to include estimates within six months of the test scores achieved, 64% of the children would be included in this category. Thus one can state that the teachers were able to assess the current reading proficiency of approximately two-thirds of their pupils with an acceptable degree of accuracy.

Table 8-3 also reaffirms the pattern of underestimates of performance exceeding over-estimates. While nearly 36% of the children's performances were under-estimated by more than three months, only 28% were over-estimated by this amount. If the broader category of six months is employed, the figures still bear the same relationship, 22% of children's results being under-estimated but only 14% being over-estimated.

## 3. Examples of extreme over- and under-estimating

The data presented in Table 8-3, indicating that the performance of 4.5% of all children was over-estimated by more than one year, while 6.6% of all children's results were under-estimated by more than one year, suggests that in some cases teachers' estimates were seriously in error. Yet these categories of thirteen months or more of over- or

Table 8-3

*Percentages of children in various categories of estimates*

| | 1st Years | | | | | | 2nd Years | | | | | | | | | | |
|---|---|---|---|---|---|---|---|---|---|---|---|---|---|---|---|---|---|
| | No prior results | | Burt Results | | Schonell Results | | No prior results | | Burt Results | | Schonell Results | | 1st years | 2nd years | Boys | Girls | All |
| | Boys | Girls | Boys | Girls | Boys | Girls | Boys | Girls | Boys | Girls | Boys | Girls | | | Boys | Girls | |
| *Over-estimation* | | | | | | | | | | | | | | | | | |
| by more than 12 months | 8.3 | 12.5 | 5.7 | 2.3 | — | — | 7.9 | 7.9 | 5.6 | 9.6 | 3.1 | 2.5 | 3.2 | 5.8 | 4.4 | 4.6 | 4.5 |
| by 10 to 12 months | 14.6 | 10.4 | 3.4 | 4.0 | 2.8 | 2.8 | 7.9 | 10.5 | 7.3 | 5.1 | 3.1 | 1.8 | 4.3 | 5.3 | 5.1 | 4.5 | 4.8 |
| by 7 to 9 months | 6.3 | 10.4 | 14.3 | 14.3 | 9.4 | 16.1 | 7.9 | 13.2 | 9.0 | 15.7 | 15.4 | 16.7 | 14.8 | 13.5 | 12.3 | 15.9 | 14.1 |
| Correct to within 3 months | 27.1 | 27.1 | 36.0 | 30.3 | 40.1 | 43.9 | 22.4 | 25.0 | 36.0 | 31.5 | 35.2 | 51.9 | 36.4 | 35.7 | 34.9 | 37.1 | 36.0 |
| *Under-estimation* | | | | | | | | | | | | | | | | | |
| by 4 to 6 months | 6.3 | 10.4 | 16.0 | 20.0 | 16.7 | 12.8 | 11.8 | 9.2 | 10.0 | 10.1 | 21.6 | 8.0 | 15.4 | 12.9 | 15.9 | 12.3 | 14.1 |
| by 7 to 9 months | 10.4 | 6.3 | 10.9 | 13.1 | 10.0 | 9.4 | 14.5 | 10.5 | 9.4 | 11.8 | 8.0 | 7.4 | 10.5 | 9.7 | 10.0 | 10.3 | 10.1 |
| by 10 to 12 months | — | — | 3.4 | 4.0 | 10.0 | 7.2 | 7.9 | 3.9 | 6.7 | 3.4 | 4.3 | 3.7 | 5.5 | 4.8 | 6.0 | 4.3 | 5.1 |
| by more than 12 months | — | — | 7.4 | 6.3 | 7.8 | 2.8 | 13.2 | 17.1 | 6.2 | 6.2 | 7.4 | 4.3 | 5.5 | 7.7 | 7.4 | 5.7 | 6.6 |
| Nos. of Children | 48 | 48 | 175 | 175 | 180 | 180 | 76 | 76 | 178 | 178 | 162 | 162 | 806 | 832 | 819 | 819 | 1,638 |

under-estimates disguise even greater discrepancies on the part of a minority of teachers. The range of individual errors, as can be noted in Table 8-4, extended from an over-estimate of three years and six months to an under-estimate of three years.

Table 8-4

*Individual teachers' greatest discrepancies in estimating reading ages*

| Group of Pupils | | Teacher's Over-Estimate | Teacher's Under-Estimate |
|---|---|---|---|
| 8 year-olds | Boys | + 2yr. 3m. | – 3yr. 0m. |
| | Girls | + 2yr. 1m. | – 2yr. 8m. |
| 9 year-olds | Boys | + 2yr. 5m. | – 2yr. 9m. |
| | Girls | + 3yr. 6m. | – 2yr. 5m. |

A few specific examples of what is entailed when teachers' estimates are so extremely different from children's performances are given in Table 8-5.

Table 8-5

*Examples of discrepancies in estimations*

| Example | Child's Actual Reading Age | Teacher's Estimate | Discrepancy |
|---|---|---|---|
| 1. 1st year girl | 7yr. 7m. | 10yr. 0m. | Over-estimate 2yr. 9m. |
| 2. 2nd year girl | 8yr. 0m. | 11yr. 6m. | Over-estimate 3yr. 6m. |
| 3. 1st year boy | 10yr. 5m. | 12yr. 8m. | Over-estimate 2yr. 3m. |
| 4. 2nd year boy | 11yr. 2m. | 8yr. 6m. | Under-estimate 2yr. 8m. |

The implications of these extreme examples of over-estimating and under-estimating are certainly disturbing to contemplate. One wonders what level of book and what kind of reading teaching a teacher would be providing for a girl whose reading age was only eight years, but whom she considered to be such a good reader as to have a reading age of 11 years 6 months. Inevitably this girl must have been struggling desperately with the books she was expected to read, and was unlikely to regard reading as a pleasurable activity. In contrast, the boy with a reading age of over 11 years, whose teacher regarded him as having a reading age of only 8½ years, was more than likely to have been completely bored with a 'teaching book' at about the level of *Wide Range*

*Book 3* (Schonell and Flowerdew 1953) when he could easily have been racing ahead, reading practically any book in the school library which took his fancy. Fortunately, these were some of the extreme examples, although errors in estimating of more or less two years must still be regarded seriously.

## 4. Influence of previous test results on estimations

It might have been expected that teachers with knowledge of their pupils' performances on the same or another reading test administered within the preceding six months, would be more accurate at estimating their pupils' current reading standards than teachers who lacked this information. Certain indications that such expectations were to some extent justified can be observed in both Tables 8-2 and 8-3. For example, the data in Table 8-2 showed a significant overall difference in the proportion of teachers in the three categories of estimators, depending on whether or not they had access to the results of previous reading tests ($\chi^2$ = 8.2 with 4 d.f.). It seems to have made little difference to which of the two reading tests the teachers had access. The greatest difference occurred for the first-year teachers, where teachers with no previous reading test results for their pupils tended to be over-estimators more often than those who had such results available to them. However, as there were only eight teachers here who had no previous information, this result should probably be treated with caution.

Firmer confirmation, however, about the improvement in teachers' accuracy of estimation when they have some knowledge of their pupils' previous test results can be noted in the data in Table 8-3. Not surprisingly, in this case, the best estimators were those teachers who had access to the results of prior testing using Schonell's *Graded Word Reading Test*, although those with previous results on the Burt test were almost as good. For example, in the category of 'correct' estimations it can be noted that for both boys and girls, in each age-group, the percentages increase from no previous test results, to previous Burt results, and on to the largest number of correct estimates based on earlier Schonell results. One other effect of knowledge of previous test scores was to reduce the incidence of extreme mis-estimation, and this effect was significant for both age-groups ($\chi^2$ = 81.9 for first-years and 56.8 for second-years, each with 16 d.f., $p \leqslant 0.001$.)

## 5. Effect of children's ages on teachers' estimates

Certain information about differences in the general patterns of estimating made by teachers of first-year classes and second-year classes, can be gathered from the data in Table 8-2. Although almost equal proportions of teachers of each age-group fall into the category of inconsistent estimators, it can be seen that, if all second-year teachers are considered together, a higher proportion of them were over-estimators, compared with first-year teachers, and the opposite was the case for underestimations.

## 6. Effect of children's sex on teachers' estimates

It is interesting to note from the information provided in Table 8-3 that teachers did not, in general, appear markedly to favour one sex of pupil more than the other. In fact, detailed scrutiny of the results for each of the 134 teachers showed that only one teacher had over-estimated boys, while one other had over-estimated girls.

However, when the percentages of children in various categories of estimates were examined in Table 8-3, it became apparent that there was an overall sex difference in the accuracy of the estimations ($\chi^2 = 17.1$ with 8 d.f., $p \leqslant 0.05$). This had the effect of more girls being slightly over-estimated than boys, and rather more boys being under-estimated than girls. It is also true that a higher proportion of boys than girls appeared in the category of 'under-estimated by more than one year'.

## IV Summary

1. Teachers in the first Teachers' Reading Research Group were very willing to co-operate in forecasting their pupils' performances on Schonell's *Graded Word Reading Test,* and to forward these estimates, alongside the actual test results, to the project director. Lists were obtained from 291 classes, referring to 3,381 first- and second-year junior pupils.

2. The reading ages scored on the test, in each year group, ranged from $5^0$ to $14^0$.

3. The general pattern of teachers' estimations was as follows:
(a) Almost half of all teachers were classified as 'inconsistent' esti-mators, as they over-estimated the reading proficiency of about half their pupils, and under-estimated the remaining half.
(b) Similar proportions of teachers were categorized as inconsistent in the two age-groups (just under 50% in each case). Of the remaining teachers, more of those in the first year tended to be under-estimators than those in the second year.

4. When the results of the estimates were examined in the light of the percentages of pupils falling into various categories of over- and under-estimations, it was found that the test scores achieved by 36% of all the pupils were correctly forecast by their teachers to within three months. If this category is extended to include estimates within six months of the actual reading age, it would include 64% of the pupils − which would seem to represent an acceptable degree of accuracy.

5. The figures for percentages of pupils in different categories re-affirmed that children's scores on the test were more often under-estimated than over-estimated.

6. The teachers who were least successful in estimating their pupils' reading performances showed errors ranging from an over-estimate of 3 years 6 months to an under-estimate of 3 years.

7. Not surprisingly, there were certain indications that teachers who had based their estimates on previous reading test results were some-what better at estimating their pupils' reading proficiency than teachers without such results available.

8. The results obtained by children in the second junior year were more frequently over-estimated, while those of first-year juniors were more often under-estimated.

9. It was also noted that teachers showed a slight tendency to over-estimate the reading proficiency of girls and to under-estimate that of boys.

## V  Implications for Teachers

1. As the range of reading ages for both first- and second-year juniors extended from $5^0$ to $14^0$, it follows that teachers of these two age groups need to ask themselves whether they provide a variety of reading programmes which are sufficiently differentiated to cater for the various groups of children in their classes who may well span a nine years' difference in reading attainments.

2. As it has been shown that the reading proficiency of children was more often under-estimated than over-estimated by their teachers, all teachers should give serious consideration to the question of whether or not they are 'stretching' their pupils sufficiently. For example, one of the questions to be asked about every child might be: 'Is this child being expected to work with a relatively simple reading book, when his reading ability is such that he could enjoy much more advanced books?'

3. The fact that a minority of teachers were quite seriously in error when estimating their pupils' performances on a well-known reading test, must surely cause all teachers to re-examine their own procedures for monitoring children's reading progress.

4. The teachers in this study who had access to previous reading test results had been asked to base their estimates of children's current reading performance on their knowledge of the earlier results – and they proved more accurate estimators than teachers who lacked earlier test results. This finding might well cause those teachers who tend to

regard testing as a waste of time to reconsider the prognostic value of prior test results. Alternatively, teachers who have available earlier test results resting unnoticed in drawers or record books might well consider the value of referring more frequently to such records.

5. The finding that the reading proficiency of second-year children was more often over-estimated, while that of first-years tended to be under-estimated, certainly merits discussion. What are the reasons for this? If certain first-years' reading proficiency is under-estimated, is it likely that teachers fail to 'stretch' them? Might this account for the fact that certain second-years are not as good at reading as their teachers expect or assume them to be? Alternatively, do second-year teachers sometimes assume that their pupils are more proficient than they are, because they themselves have failed to diagnose the strengths and weaknesses of individual children?

6. The slight tendency for the reading performance of boys to be under-estimated while the proficiency of girls was somewhat over-estimated, is a point which other teachers are bound to want to discuss. They are likely to wonder not only whether they themselves act similarly, but also how such a situation arises and what effect it might have on the children's progress. For example, it has long been known that a pupil's performance is frequently related to his teacher's expectations for him. Accordingly, might the fact that boys' scores on a reading test are often below those of girls' of similar ages be related to their teachers' different expectations?

The slight sex bias discovered in this exercise may also lead teachers to give further thought to those boys who appear particularly restless in reading periods. May the reason be that too little is being asked of them? If their reading standards are two or three years more advanced than the levels of the books they are supposed to be quietly reading, might they not be more likely to become absorbed in more advanced, and probably more exciting books?

What about those girls whose reading proficiency was over-estimated? Could it be that in some cases their relative docility disguised the fact that they were not coping too well with the reading tasks being set them?

In the case of both boys whose performance has been under-estimated, and girls whose performance has been over-estimated, it would seem that closer monitoring of reading progress is called for.

# CHAPTER 9

# The Books Teachers Use for Teaching Reading

## I Use of Basic Reading Schemes

The *Plowden Report* (1967) presented the following picture of what was happening in 'many' schools in relation to the books children were reading, in 1963–6.

> Among the most welcome changes which have accompanied the growing informality of the primary school has been the move away from categories of books, each confined to a special time and purpose. In many schools there are now no longer class readers, supplementary readers, group readers, text books and library books. ... There are simply books – to be used as and when they are needed.

This description appears to indicate a marked decline in the use of basic reading schemes as a major component in teaching children to read.

Yet, approximately ten years later, comments in the *Bullock Report* (1975) relating to common practices in primary schools in 1972–4 would seem to suggest that this trend away from reading schemes had not been as rapid as Plowden had envisaged. Referring to reading schemes, Bullock states: 'We are certainly not advocating that the school should necessarily use one, and we welcome the enterprise of the schools which have successfully planned the teaching of reading without the use of a graded series.' Certainly, as far as the current project was concerned, the majority of teachers of children aged 7 to 9, in the schools visited, in the teachers' research groups, and in the schools participating in the intensive study year, found no difficulty in naming the basic reading scheme or schemes they used. Accordingly, as the majority of teachers do make a distinction between 'teaching books' and 'books for using', these phrases are retained throughout this report.

## II Paucity of Information on Junior Reading Books

Throughout this project it was found that in first- and second-year junior classes, teachers relied almost entirely on reading schemes and other books as the medium for teaching reading. With few exceptions, aids to teaching reading other than teacher-made materials were rarely employed. The exceptions were that some schools utilized *S.R.A. Reading Laboratories* (Parker and Scannell 1963) and many classes regularly watched TV programmes on reading.

As the normal means of trying to extend the reading proficiency of average 7 to 9 year-olds is through books, and usually by means of reading schemes, the lack of information available about the actual books used is rather surprising. Little, if any, information is available in this area, although a number of investigations into the reading schemes used with infants have been reported. Their findings are of interest in this context, as teachers in junior schools frequently continue to use books from infant schemes with their slower, and even average, readers.

Morris (1959), for example, reporting on information collected in 1954 in 60 primary schools in Kent found that the most popular infant reading schemes were *Happy Venture* (Schonell 1938), *Janet and John* (O'Donnell and Munro 1949) and *The Beacon Readers* (Grassam 1957) – in that order, but that in each of the 60 schools the main scheme was supplemented by other reading books. 12 of the 60 schools were junior schools, where these schemes were used for the slower readers. In a later report of a follow-up study carried out during 1954–7, Morris (1966) provided a list of books used by second-year juniors, which include the two reading schemes, *The Beacon Readers* (Grassam 1957) and *The Wide Range Readers* (Schonell and Flowerdew 1953).

A more recent report of reading schemes used with infants comes from Goodacre (1969), who found that infant teachers were using more reading schemes than in her earlier report (Goodacre (1967) based on information collected in 1959). Teachers tended to use several schemes rather than one and many were the same schemes as those used in 1959. Of the six schemes most frequently used, *Janet and John* (O'Donnell and Munro 1949) was used by 81% of the infant schools, while the remaining five schemes were each mentioned as in use in approximately one-third of the schools (ranging from 38%–31%). The majority of the schemes mentioned were mainly 'Look and Say' schemes, based on the principle of vocabulary control.

The questionnaire on which the survey undertaken by the Bullock Committee in 1972 was based provided little useful information about reading schemes in junior classes, as teachers were not asked to record the titles of the reading schemes they used. In fact, up-to-date information about books used for teaching or 'extending' reading in junior classes in England would still be hard to find. This lack of available information on junior reading books probably reflects the dearth of published reading schemes for juniors.

## III   Levels of Difficulty of Books

### A. *Teachers' Interest in Grading Books*

In contrast to normal practices in certain other countries, teachers in English schools have usually been allowed freedom in their choice of books for teaching reading, and in their ways of using them. The teachers have always cherished this freedom which gave them great flexibility and generally resulted in the use of more than one reading scheme, supported by supplementary books from many other series. Yet practices which can provide flexibility for experienced teachers can raise problems for less experienced teachers. One of the findings of this research project is that junior teachers are not very confident about their ability to assess the levels of difficulty of books and are anxious to increase their knowledge in this area.

The question of assessing the readability levels of texts is one which has exercised educators and researchers in the USA for at least 30 or 40 years. Interest in the subject has centred on the levels of difficulty of reading materials, with a view to matching difficulty of text with the reader's competence. Methods of assessing the readability levels of children's books have ranged from subjective judgements by teachers, through trial runs on children whose reading levels have been assessed by standardized tests, to the application of readability formulae to the text by the teacher, and the completion of Cloze passages from the text by the children concerned.

Interest in the assessment of the levels of difficulty of children's books in the UK, however, does not have such a long history. Indeed it was only during the 1970s that a marked interest in this topic began to be expressed by class teachers, although remedial teachers and teachers of backward children have recognised the problem and tried to find practical solutions to it for over 20 years. For example, the remedial services in Worcester and West Bromwich were among the first to produce, about 1953, duplicated lists of reading books, graded according to their difficulty, for the use of class teachers within their local education authorities. One reading centre which has become well known, both nationally and internationally, for its helpful lists of publications relating to reading resources for normal as well as retarded readers is the Centre for the Teaching of Reading at the University of Reading.

Yet despite the increase in availability of graded book lists, many class teachers of first- and second-year juniors who were involved in this project were found to be largely unaware of their existence. For instance, when the teachers in the first Teachers' Reading Research Group were asked to place 45 of their 'preferred outcomes' of the project in rank order, the grading of reading material was placed fifth. Accordingly, a list of such publications was prepared and distributed to teachers in both the first and second Teachers' Reading Research

Groups, and is included in Appendix 9-A.

## B. *Graded Book Lists*

The first publication of this nature, *A Survey of Books for Backward Readers* by Pascoe, appeared in 1956 and a revised version, entitled *A Second Survey of Books for Backward Readers*, was published in 1962. This survey reviewed and graded 147 books and/or series of books, divided into the categories of Reading Schemes, Graded Series, Supplementary Reading Books, English Books and Books for Other Subjects. A large proportion of these books can still be seen in use in junior classrooms today. The reviews were based on descriptions and assessments made by experienced teacher-reviewers and committee members who had used the books with children. In addition to a detailed appraisal, each book reviewed was given an interest age and a reading age. The reading ages provided were the result of trying out the books with children whose reading ages had been ascertained by standardized tests. Although information is not provided about the criteria of judgement, for example, in terms of error counts, the suggested reading ages are nevertheless valuable, particularly in providing a hierarchy of difficulty for all the books reviewed.

The West Bromwich Child Psychology Service have continued, since 1953, to revise and enlarge their graded book lists; the most recent list, *Reading Schemes for Slow Learners* (West Bromwich Child Psychology Service), being published in 1973. As it covers books 'designed to inculcate reading skills', it consists of 'Reading Schemes, Graded Series and Supplementary Readers up to a Readability Age of 10 Years'. It thus provides teachers with an extremely useful guide to books intended for teaching reading. The books have been assessed by their structure, appeal and content. Interest ages and reading ages are also provided for each book. The latest development in the grading of reading materials designed to forward the process of teaching reading, can be seen in the two following books, both published by the Centre for the Teaching of Reading at the University of Reading: *Reading Resources* – A Catalogue of Games, Audio-Visual Aids, Language Kits, Laboratories and All Other Support Materials; and *Reading Skill Acquisition* (Raban 1973) – Comparative Lists of Reading Games and Support Materials. Three additional graded book lists which class teachers of lower juniors will also find useful are Goodacre (1972), Atkinson and Gains (1973) and Moon (1973 – revised 1979). Atkinson and Gains, as well as Goodacre, give reading ages for the books listed. Moon, on the other hand, groups a large variety of books into 13 progressive stages. He also states that: '. . . if a permissible error rate of one word in twenty-five is used as a rule of thumb, the book should be about the right readability level for the child . . .'

## C. *Readability Formulae*

While studies of readability and the production of readability formulae designed to assess the levels of difficulty of reading materials have a long history in the USA, they have only fairly recently begun to interest British teachers. The *Bullock Report* (1975), for instance, stated that: '. . . a particularly important teaching skill is that of assessing the level of difficulty of books by applying measures of readability'. Gilliland (1972), in his book entitled *Readability*, lists a variety of methods of assessing readability, including the use of readability formulae. He describes readability formulae as follows:

> The application of a formula usually involves the selection of a sample from a text, the counting of some easily identifiable characteristics, such as the average number of words per sentence or the proportion of polysyllabic words in the sample, and then performing a calculation to produce a score.

He then goes on to describe various American readability formulae. Harrison (1977), in a paper entitled 'Assessing the Readability of School Texts', also comments on the advantages and disadvantages of a variety of readability formulae. The teacher of children aged 7 to 9 years will, on reading these descriptions, be struck by the fact that so many of them appear to be both complicated and time-consuming to apply. (The simplest one, *SMOG Grading* (McLaughlin 1969), takes 9 minutes to apply.) Gilliland suggests that teachers will look for measures which are 'easy to apply, easy to mark, easy to calculate and accurate'. He then adds a cautionary note to the effect that, 'Very often, the accuracy of a measure decreases with its ease of application'.

Both Harrison and Gilliland indicate another difficulty faced by teachers who wish to use readability formulae; namely that, depending on the elements in the text which were measured, different formulae produce different results.

A third question relating to readability formulae is also important. Gilliland defines 'readability' as the matching of reader and text. Such a definition immediately alerts one to the fact that the levels of difficulty of texts, considered in isolation, are insufficient. What the reader brings with him, in attempting to read the text, is equally important. His interest, motivation and relevant background knowledge will all affect his ability to understand the text. As Gilliland points out: '. . . as they are conventionally used, readability formulae deal with only one side of the matching exercise, namely the book.' Graded book lists and the use of readability formulae are thus both concerned with general levels of difficulty of texts, and are unrelated to the knowledge which an individual child may bring to the text to aid his comprehension of it.

Chall (1977) has recently sounded a further note of caution about readability formulae, when she stated:

> It should be noted that none of the objective readability measures
> tells how difficult reading material should be. . . . The concern
> should go, it seems, not only to books that may be too difficult
> but to those that may be too easy. Of even greater importance
> is that we study what constitutes optimal challenge at all
> levels . . .

Two additional ways of assessing readability, the use of Cloze
procedure and informal reading inventories, are concerned with an
individual's performance on a text, rather than on a general level of
difficulty. In both cases, a pupil's comprehension of a particular passage
can be assessed.

## D. *Cloze Procedure*

Cloze procedure involves the insertion, by the child, of words into a
passage of prose from which certain words have been deleted. Such a
test has frequently been used to provide an assessment of a child's
comprehension of the passage. Taylor (1953), Bormuth (1966), Klare
(1963) and others have also used Cloze procedure as a measure of the
readability of texts. This method of assessing readability was not
used in the current project, but teachers who are interested can find
accounts of it in Moyle (1971), Gilliland (1972) and Harrison (1977).
Although Gilliland suggests how this method might be utilized to
advantage by teachers, Harrison concludes:

> Lastly, one would suggest that although it offers an attractive win-
> dow into the reader's response, the use of Cloze tests as a measure
> of readability still requires a fair amount of fundamental research.

In the current research project, Cloze procedure was used solely as a
means of probing the strategies which children employ in their reading (Chapter 16).

## E. *Informal Reading Inventories*

Informal reading inventories were originally developed in the USA by
Betts (1946) and have frequently been modified by other American
authors since then. One of the basic purposes of an informal reading
inventory is to discover whether the book which the child is reading
or the one the teacher wishes him to read is too easy, too difficult or
about right for him. A second purpose is to discover the book level
at which the child can best be instructed in reading. Informal reading
inventories can, however, if used flexibly, provide an opportunity for
the teacher to assess much more than the readability level of particular
books in relation to a child's reading skill. As Strang (1969) observed,
they can 'combine the diagnostic values of oral reading and observation'.

The *Bullock Report* (1975) recommended the use of informal reading inventories in the following terms:

> If a teacher is to plan individual instruction to meet specific needs her first task is to assess the attainment level of every child and provide each with reading material of the right level of readability. This sounds obvious, but it is not common to find the process carried out with the necessary precision. A simple and effective means of approaching the task of matching child and material is the use of informal reading inventories, which are in effect structured observations of reading performance.

Descriptions of informal reading inventories are provided by many American authors, e.g. Betts (1946 and 1957), Johnson and Kress (1967), McCracken (1969), Strang (1969 and 1972) and Harris and Sipay (1975), yet at the time when the *Bullock Report* was written, few British teachers were either acquainted with them or had used them. A description of informal reading inventories can, however, now be found in Pumfrey (1976).

Briefly, an informal reading inventory is conducted as follows: passages from books at increasingly more difficult levels, (e.g. basic reading schemes), are selected by the teacher and a child is asked to read them silently and orally while the class is engaged in other work. During the oral reading the teacher records all errors.[1] After reading each selection the child's comprehension is checked by asking him to retell the story and/or answer questions about it. The reading achievement of the child is then calculated at every book level, as falling into three reading levels. McCracken (1969) describes these as follows.

> The *independent reading level* is the highest book level at which a child can read without assistance. His comprehension is excellent, his reading is fluent, and he is completely comfortable when reading.

> The *instructional level* is the book level (usually levels) at which the child can profit from and needs instruction from a teacher.

> *Frustration level* is the lowest book level at which the child cannot be expected to read even with excellent instruction.

The criteria for assessing children's reading levels, based on word recognition and comprehension, has varied from author to author, but the figures have usually fallen within the ranges shown in Table 9.1.

---

[1] Merely to count the number of errors is the simplest way of conducting an informal reading inventory, in order to find appropriate levels of books. More information about the child's reading performance can be obtained by using the assessment diagnostically, for example classifying the errors, noting the speed of reading and so on.

Table 9-1

*Generally accepted ranges of achievements in informal reading inventories*

| Reading Level | Word Recognition | Comprehension |
|---|---|---|
| Independent | 99–100% | 90–100% |
| Instructional | 95–98% | 70–89% |
| Frustration | Less than 95% | Less than 70% |

It should be noted, however, that Powell (1970), suspecting that word-recognition at the instructional level could be lower than 95%, reported an experiment which supports this view for children in grades 1–6 (i.e. 6–13 years-old). Even more interestingly, he reports that: 'The data clearly indicate that pupils in grades one and two could tolerate *on the average* an 85% word recognition score and still maintain 70% comprehension.'

Two of the exercises undertaken by the first Teachers' Reading Research Group in this project related to error-counting, as used in informal reading inventories, although no assessments of comprehension were made. That English teachers were unfamiliar with informal reading inventories at that time (1974), was well illustrated by the fact that not one member of the group of over 400 teachers had either heard of them or used them. In the first exercise, teachers were provided with details of McCracken's system of scoring errors. They were then asked to test their pupils in first- and second-year juniors, whose reading ages had previously been assessed on Schonell's *Graded Word Reading Test* (1948), by having them read aloud a selected passage of 200 words from *Wide Range Readers* Blue Book 3 (Schonell and Flowerdew 1953), intended as a teaching book for average children of 8–8½ years, while they recorded the errors made. The number of errors made by 115 children aged 8 years and 9 years, with reading ages of $8^0$ ± 3 months, are set out in Table 9-2.

The first interesting point to note in Table 9-2 is that of the two age-groups with identical reading ages, the children aged $9^0$ were making more errors in oral reading of the same passage than children aged $8^0$. This suggests that the older children, who were below average readers, were probably less confident in their reading than the younger children who were of average reading ability for their age-group. It could also be that the older children had developed faulty reading strategies which were hindering their progress. Individual diagnosis of the nature of the errors would be required in order to pinpoint the negative strategies which were causing these children to read less well than children one year younger.

Secondly, that 50% of all the children were making only 4 or less

Table 9-2

*Error rates in oral reading* * *of first-year juniors (c.a. $8^0$) & second-year juniors (c.a. $9^0$) whose reading ages were all $8^0$*

| No. of Errors per 100 Words | % of Children | | Overall % of Children |
|---|---|---|---|
| | c.a. $8^0$ | c.a. $9^0$ | |
| 0–4 | 57 | 39 | 50 |
| 5–9 | 36 | 44 | 39 |
| 10–14 | 7 | 16 | 11 |
| Nos. of Children | 72 | 43 | 115 |

(*N.B. Both age-groups were reading the same passage of prose from Schonell's *Wide Range Readers* – Blue Book 3.)

errors per 100 words, and the error rate of an additional 39% was between 5 and 9, in reading aloud from a book which the majority of English teachers would consider to be at an appropriate level for them, supports Powell (1970) in suspecting that word-recognition at the instructional level could probably be lower than 95%.

## IV  Teaching Books in Current Use

In the course of the research project, a number of enquiries were made into the current use of teaching books in schools. During the first two years, information on reading books in use was accumulated on visits to a variety of primary schools and through work with the Teachers' Reading Research Groups. During the third and fourth years, further information was gained in the intensive study and in the investigation into the reading environments in eight schools. The information gathered in these different ways was mutually supportive, so that a very clear picture was formed of the teaching books in current use.

## A.  *Information from Teachers' Reading Research Groups*

### 1.  Selection of children

As already described, each teacher in the first Reading Research Group had identified a group of her own pupils for special study. The selected children in the first-year of the junior school were all aged $8^0$ ± 2 months and had reading ages of $8^0$ ± 2 m on *Schonell's Graded Word Reading Test* (1948) (using the original norms). Second-years' chronological ages were $9^0$ ± 2 months and reading ages of $9^0$ ± 2 m. Each year-group of children was thus of average chronological age and reading ability. These selected groups of children were given a battery of individual assessments by their class teachers, of which only one item, termed 'reading from books', is relevant in this context. 57 schools completed and returned these 'individual reading profiles' for 197 children, of whom 121 children were first-year juniors and 76 were second-year juniors.

## 2. Testing procedure for oral reading

For the three items comprising the exercise of 'Reading from Books', the teacher listened to each child reading orally a passage of 300 words from the following three books: his current reading book which he was using with his teacher; a story book of his own choice; an information book of his own choice. Only the first item is of relevance here. The remaining two items, relating to books chosen by the children, are discussed in Chapter 14.

Teachers were given the following guidance on testing the child on his current reading book. The book, of which the title had to be recorded, was to be the one the child was currently reading *under the teacher's guidance*. The selected story was to be the next one in the book, that is, one which the child had not previously read aloud to the teacher and on which no preparatory work had been done. The child was to read aloud the first 300 words while the teacher scored the number of words the child failed to read correctly. If the same error occurred more than once it was only to be counted as one error.

## 3. Reading books selected by teachers

The list of teacher-selected reading books which the children were using at that time is set out in Table 9-3, apart from a very small number of titles which the research team were unable to identify.

A number of interesting facts, which may be summarized as follows, emerged from the 144 identifiable titles.

(a) Teachers of first-years were using 43 different teaching books while 21 different titles were being used by teachers of second-year children. Of the titles listed, 13 were being used by both first- and second-years, despite the fact that their levels of reading ability differed by one year.

(b) At least 6 of the 8 year-olds, although of average reading ability, were being taught to read by means of books from the earliest stages (i.e. Books 1 and 2) of infant reading schemes.

(c) One noticeable feature of the list of titles is that children of the same age and stage of reading attainment were being taught from reading books which varied greatly in difficulty. For example, the following contrasting standards of reading books were being used by 8 year-old children, all of whom had reading ages of $8^0$:

Table 9-3

*Teacher-selected reading books in use by 144 'average readers' in 1st and 2nd year junior classes*

| Books in use by 1st YEAR CHILDREN ONLY | No. of 1st yrs. | Books in use by *both* 1st & 2nd YEAR CHILDREN | No. of 1st yrs. | No. of 2nd yrs. | Books in use by 2nd YEAR CHILDREN ONLY | No. of 2nd yrs. |
|---|---|---|---|---|---|---|
| Happy Venture Book 2 | 1 | Wide Range Book 1 (Blue or Green) | 10 | 4 | Through the Rainbow Book 6 | 1 |
| Happy Venture Book 3 | 2 | Wide Range Book 2 | 9 | 5 | Beacon – William Tell | 5 |
| Sound Sense Book 1a | 1 | Wide Range Book 3 | 9 | 11 | Beacon – Careful Hans | 1 |
| Ready to Read 1 | 1 | Wide Range Book 4 | 5 | 5 | Beacon – Briar Rose | 1 |
| Radiant Reading 2 | 1 | Wide Range Book 5 | 4 | 4 | Blue Nippers | 2 |
| Griffin Scheme | 5 | Wide Range Book 6 | 4 | 3 | Pleasure and Progress Book 4 | 1 |
| New Interest 4 | 1 | Wide Range Interest Book 2 | 4 | 1 | Reading in Red Book 2 | 1 |
| Racing to Read 9 | 1 | Through the Rainbow Book 4 | 1 | 1 | Sparkling Gems Book 3 | 1 |
| Understanding Through Interest | 1 | Beacon Book 5 | 1 | 2 | | |
| Downing Transfer Book | 1 | Beacon Book 6 | 2 | 1 | | |
| Ladybird Book 5a | 1 | Ladybird Book 5a | 4 | 1 | | |
| Ladybird Book 6a | 1 | Ladybird Book 12a | 1 | 1 | | |
| Ladybird Book 7a | 1 | Royal Road Book 9 | 1 | 1 | | |
| Ladybird Book 7b | 1 | Look Ahead Book 7 | 1 | 1 | | |
| Ladybird Book 8b | 1 | | | | | |
| Ladybird Book 9a | 1 | | | | | |
| Ladybird Book 10a | 1 | | | | | |
| Wide Range Interest Book 1 | 1 | | | | | |
| Wide Range Interest Book 4 | 1 | | | | | |
| Over The Rainbow Book 3 | 2 | | | | | |
| Over The Rainbow Book 4 | 1 | | | | | |
| Over The Rainbow Book 5 | 2 | | | | | |
| Over The Rainbow Book 6 | 1 | | | | | |
| Good Company Book 1 | 3 | | | | | |
| Happy Trio Book 2 | 1 | | | | | |
| Janet and John – Once Upon a Time | 3 | | | | | |
| Janet and John – Magic Everywhere | 2 | | | | | |
| Janet and John – High on A Hill | 3 | | | | | |
| Janet and John – I know A Story | 1 | | | | | |
| Beacon Book 3 | 1 | | | | | |
| Beacon Book 4 | 1 | | | | | |
| Mike and Mandy Book 9 | 1 | | | | | |

|              |                     |
|--------------|---------------------|
| Easy Books   | Happy Venture Book 2 |
|              | Happy Trio Book 2   |
| Difficult Books | Wide Range Book 6 |
|              | Ladybird 12A        |

The first two titles might well be considered appropriate for average readers of 5½–6 years, while the remaining two books are at about the level of average readers of 10+.

(d) The most widely used reading books, in both years, were from the *Wide Range Readers* (Schonell and Flowerdew 1953); 52% of the 8 year-olds and 62% of the 9 year-olds using the first six books in this series. These figures provide a further illustration of the different levels of difficulty of books selected by teachers as appropriate for children with identical levels of reading ability. Book 1 was intended by the authors to be suitable for average readers of 7–7½ years. It was being used by ten 8 year-olds with reading ages of 8 years 0 months and four 9 year-olds with reading ages of 9 years 0 months. At the same time, Book 6, regarded by the authors as at a 10 to 11 year-old level, was the main teaching book with four children with reading ages of 8 years and three children with reading ages of 9 years.

## 4. Levels of difficulty of teacher-selected reading books

An analysis of the number of errors made by children in reading aloud from their current reading books confirmed the wide differences in the levels of difficulty of reading materials which teachers considered appropriate for their pupils. The percentage of errors made by first-years ranged from 0 to 8, while for second-years the errors ranged from 0 to 6.

That many more children were reading, with their teachers, books that were too easy for them rather than books that were too difficult can be seen from Table 9-4.

Table 9-4

*Percentage of errors in children's oral reading from their current reading books*

| No. of Errors per 100 words | Level of Reading Difficulty (According to McCracken) | Percentage of Pupils | |
|---|---|---|---|
| | | 1st year Juniors | 2nd year Juniors |
| 0–1 | Independent Level | 50 | 64 |
| 2–3 | Instructional Level | 38 | 31 |
| 4–5 | Instructional Level (Questionable) | 10 | 3 |
| 6 and over | Frustration Level | 2 | 3 |

The levels of reading difficulty used in Table 9-4 are those suggested by McCracken (1969) and mentioned earlier in this chapter. Briefly, 0—1 errors per 100 words is an acceptable level of difficulty for a book which a child is to read on his own, without help from his teacher. 2—3 errors per 100 words is the level of book which a child can be expected to read with help from his teacher. When the difficulty level rises to 4—5 errors per 100 words, it is doubtful whether the child can profit from reading the book even with the teacher's help. It is suggested that if the child makes 6 or more errors per 100 words he is trying to read at an impossible level of difficulty and is likely to become so frustrated that he will abandon the attempt.

Using McCracken's levels of difficulty, the most striking results in Tables 9-4 are that 50% of first-years and 64% of second-years were able to read these particular books at an independent level. Yet these books which had been chosen by teachers as the major teaching materials, intended to improve and extend children's reading prowess, were so easy that the children concerned were capable of reading them without a teacher's guidance or instruction. It can also be noted from Table 9-4 that only 38% of the children were reading at the instructional level, 10% had books which were probably too difficult for them to read profitably even with help from their teachers, and that for 2% of the children the books were so difficult as to be at frustration level.

## B. *Information from Intensive Study*

In the intensive study year, information on the books for teaching reading came from three sources: classroom observations, teachers' records and children's records of books read.

### 1. Observations and teachers' records
General observations on reading books in use were made by members of the research team during their frequent visits to schools and were confirmed by discussions with the teachers and by information obtained in the reading environment exercise. Books in use were also recorded by observers using the observation schedules, and this information was collaborated by the teachers' own logs of reading activities. (Observation schedules and teachers' logs are described in Chapter 10.)

All such information supported the information already gathered on books for teaching reading. The most popular reading scheme was *Wide Range* (Schonell and Flowerdew 1953), followed closely by *Through The Rainbow* (Bradburne 1965), *Beacon Reading Scheme* (Grassam 1957), *Janet and John* (O'Donnell and Munro 1949), *Griffin Pirate Stories* (McCullough 1959), and *Dragon Pirate Stories* (McCullough 1963). Two classes in one school used the infant reading scheme *Happy Venture* (Schonell and Sergeant 1938).

## 2. Children's records of books read

(a) *Details of the exercise*
Teachers in the 12 schools in the intensive study agreed to a proposal that every child in their classes would keep records of the books they read in school during the year. Exact details of the exercise were explained at the beginning of the year at a briefing meeting and teachers were also provided with duplicated notes of the procedure to be adopted.

Titles of books read were to be recorded in three categories:
(a)  Books I have read with my teacher;
(b)  Books I have read by myself;
(c)  Books I have consulted.
The title of each book read, together with the date it was completed, was to be recorded by the child, although it was accepted that younger children and poorer readers would need help from the teacher. The entries were to be checked at intervals, by the teacher.

Only the first category of books, i.e. 'teaching books', is considered in this chapter. The following quotation, taken from the notes of guidance for teachers, describes the kind of book to be included in this category.

> The first category, 'Books I have read with my teacher,' will usually refer to any book which the teacher has selected as being at an appropriate level for the child and which the child has read right through with such help and guidance as the teacher considered necessary. The teacher will generally have listened to the child reading aloud certain passages of the book but not necessarily every page or story. The teacher will have usually determined the rate at which the book was read, will be satisfied that the child has read and understood it and will regard it as a means whereby the child's mastery of reading has been forwarded.

Discussion at the meeting provided further clarification.

One point ought to be noted about the children's own records of the books they had read. It was never anticipated that they could be regarded as absolutely accurate records, but rather as providing general guidelines on the titles and numbers of books children read. However, observations in schools suggested that the records of books the children had read with their teachers were likely to be the most accurate of the three categories of books to be recorded, as completing a 'teaching book' was generally regarded as a highlight for both the teacher and pupil, and the process of recording it gave satisfaction to both. The recording of the books children had read by themselves was likely to receive less supervision and so be less accurate. Errors would be of two kinds; over-estimates, if children had recorded books they had only glanced at, or under-estimates, if they had forgotten to write down titles of books as they finished them. Experience suggested that the latter error happened most frequently. Regarding the records of books consulted, this item was included purely on an exploratory basis. As was expected, first-year juniors and slower readers in the second year found this difficult and recorded little, if anything. On the other hand, many average and above average readers in both age-groups recorded some interesting items, including not only book titles but other sources such as daily newspapers and colour supplements of Sunday newspapers.

Special notebooks for keeping these records, one for each child in the class, were provided. A colour coding system made it possible at the end of the year to differentiate between above average, average and below average readers. Although the supervision of children's record keeping for an entire school year represented an additional chore for teachers already heavily committed, completed notebooks were received at the end of the year from 26 classes in 10 schools. One interesting point arising as a result of this exercise was that, although only one or two teachers had previously had children keep records of books they had read, nearly all said that they had found it to be of great value and that they planned to continue the practice, and possibly adapt it in various ways.

(b) *Reading schemes in use*[1]
The children's records of the books they had read with the help of their teachers supported and extended the evidence available from other sources about the use of reading schemes. In 17 of the 26 classes, the 'teaching books' in use were books drawn from more than one reading scheme. In 7 of the remaining 9 classes, however, one scheme was used exclusively as follows: *Wide Range* (Schonell and Flowerdew 1953) in four second-year classes; *Through the Rainbow* (Bradburne 1965) in the two first-year classes; *Ladybird Key Words Reading Scheme* (Murray 1964) in one first-year class.

The 'teaching books' used in the remaining two classes were quite different. In one first-year class, at the beginning of the school year, all the children were started on the infant reading scheme, *Happy Venture* (Schonell and Sergeant 1938). Children of below average reading ability started with the Introductory Book in the scheme, average readers began with Book 1 and above average readers with Book 3. By the end of the school year, 9 children — 5 of average reading ability and 4 with below average reading ability at the beginning of the year — had progressed to rather more difficult books from other reading schemes.

Finally, in one second-year class, an entirely different pattern of books read with the help of the teacher was noted. At the beginning of the school year, only about half of the children were using books

[1] Acknowledgement and thanks are due to David Rigby for the detailed examination and analyses which he carried out on some 800 children's record books.

from a reading scheme — *Through The Rainbow* (Bradburne 1965); the remainder were reading a wide variety of books, most of which did not form part of any scheme. By the end of the school year, nearly all the children were reading with the help of their teachers, all kinds of books of different titles, which looked as though they might have been child-selected titles from well-stocked library shelves. The records of this particular class were exceptional, in that very rarely did a child from any other school mention reading, with the help of the teacher, a book outside the schemes or series listed.

Details of the number of classes in which the most popular reading schemes or series of books were being used are set out in Table 9-5. These titles include practically all the books listed as having been read by the children, with the help of their teachers, throughout the school year.

Table 9-5

*Classes in which well-known reading schemes were in use*

| Reading Scheme or Series | Numbers of Classes | | |
|---|---|---|---|
| | 1st years | 2nd years | Total |
| Wide Range Scheme | 10 | 10 | 20 |
| Through The Rainbow Scheme | 8 | 5 | 13 |
| Dragon and Griffin Pirate Stories | 5 | 4 | 9 |
| Beacon Scheme (later books) | 3 | 2 | 5 |
| Janet and John (extension books) | 1 | 3 | 4 |
| Racing to Read Scheme | 4 | — | 4 |
| Ladybird Key Words Scheme | 3 | — | 3 |

(NB: 1st year classes = 13, 2nd year classes = 13, TOTAL = 26.)

*Wide Range Readers,* the only reading scheme written specifically for juniors, was the most popular scheme, being used exclusively in 6 classes and alongside other schemes in 14 classes, i.e. in 20 out of the 26 classes. The authors intended this scheme to provide for children aged 7 to 11 years; Book 6, the final book, being meant for the 10 to 11 age group. In the West Bromwich list, however, Books 5 and 6 are graded as being equivalent to reading ages of $9^3-9^6$. The next most popular scheme, *Through The Rainbow*, was used by half of the classes — 8 first-year classes and 5 second-year classes. This is an infant reading scheme which, in the West Bromwich list, is graded as being equivalent to a reading age of $8^5$ in the final two books. It is difficult to refrain from speculating about whether a staple diet consisting mainly of these two reading schemes, as was the case in a large majority of the classes, is likely to stretch even the children of average reading attainments, much less the above average readers.

The children's records of books read with their teachers' help, supported another point noted in the information gathered from the Teachers' Reading Research Groups. Infant reading schemes were being used not only by children of below average reading ability in first-year classes, but also in some cases by average and above average readers. Occasionally the use of infant reading schemes was even continued with second-year children of average and above average reading ability.

### (c) Numbers of books read

The number of books recorded by each child as having been read with the help of his teacher was counted and the distribution of scores examined separately in the two age-groups.

In each year group the distribution was skewed, with a long tail extending in the direction of individual children who had read many more books than the majority of their classmates. The recorded numbers of books read by first-year children ranged from 1 to 27, while for second-years the range was wider, with between 1 and 58 books being recorded for individual children. The majority of first-years, though, read 3 or 4 books with the help of their teachers, while most second-years were reading 2 or 3 books in this way. Table 9-6 illustrates the substantial numbers of children in each age-group who progressed through only a few 'teaching books' during the school year. (One second-year class, in which the children listed no books in this category, but a substantial number of books they had read on their own, has been excluded from Table 9-6.)

Table 9-6

*Numbers of children completing five or fewer 'teaching books' in one year*

| No. of Books | No. of Children | |
| --- | --- | --- |
| | 1st Years (n = 400) | 2nd Years (n = 390) |
| 1 | 6 | 21 |
| 2 | 24 | 74 |
| 3 | 62 | 67 |
| 4 | 67 | 37 |
| 5 | 35 | 26 |

No figures on books read can be fairly interpreted without reference to the actual book titles given, backed by the experience of having talked with the teachers and observed classroom practices. From the book titles recorded, there appeared to be different reasons for substantial numbers of children in the two age-groups progressing through only a small number of 'teaching books'. In the older age group, when a child had read the final book in a reading scheme with the help of a teacher, it was frequently the practice to allow him to have 'free-choice' books to read on his own. In such cases, for example, a child might have noted only *Wide Range Books* 5 and 6 in his list of books read with the help of his teacher, and so had completed his reading scheme. Then, as the dates showed, his reading which followed belonged to the category of 'Books I have Read By Myself'. Nevertheless, this was not always the case: a proportion of the second-years in Table 9-6 had not reached this stage and the figures represented very slow progress being made with 'books for teaching'.

Some of the factors which affected both the wide variations between the numbers of books read by different children, and the fact that the majority of the children got through so few teaching books in a year, are as follows:

(i) Books used as teaching books with the 7 to 9 year-old age groups vary considerably in size, from a substantial book in the *Wide Range Readers*, made up of 208 well-filled pages, to a slim book such as *Roderick The Red*, the first book in the *Griffin Pirate Series* which consists of 16 pages, each with only two or three short sentences. Even so, it must be remembered that in 20 of the 26 classes *Wide Range Readers* were used as one of the basic schemes. These can be classed as 'substantial' books; as can *Through the Rainbow* (Silver and Gold Books) — used in 13 classes; *Beacon Scheme* (later books) — used in 5 classes; and *Janet and John Extension Readers* (i.e. *High On A Hill*) — used in 4 classes. Accordingly, it is fair to say that in the majority of cases the average and above average readers were reading, with their teachers, books of substantial size.

(ii) Teachers differed in their judgements of appropriate difficulty levels of teaching books in relation to their pupils' reading attainments. So that children in different classes, with the same levels of reading ability, were being taught by means of books of widely different levels of difficulty — as noted earlier in this chapter, from information received from the Teachers' Reading Research Groups. Consequently, a child who progressed through 10 or 20 easy books might only have completed 1 or 2 had they been more difficult.

(iii) Teachers have very different teaching styles. Some teachers followed the practice of listening to the child reading aloud to them every word of the text, while others preferred to listen to a few paragraphs or a page and then allow the child to read the remainder of the story to himself. These different paces of progress through books for teaching could be seen quite clearly in the ranges of numbers of books read in different classes. For example, in one first-year class, the number of books read with the teacher ranged from 2 to 5, while in another it was 5 to 27. Second-year classes showed similar differences: in one, the number of books read ranged from 1 to 4, while in another class it was 6 to 58.

(d) *Time spent on one teaching book*

As the children had recorded the date on which they had completed each reading book, their records provide evidence of the time taken to read the 'substantial' books which formed the bulk of their teaching books. For example, in both first- and second-years, there were one or more children who only read one teaching book in the school year. When the average numbers of books read were considered, it was found that the majority of children in the first-year spent about three months on each teaching book, while the corresponding figure for the second-year children was nearer six months. In fact, a glance at the children's individual records confirmed these assumptions, and provided such examples as the following:

(i) A second-year child of below average reading ability spent over 6 months reading *Wide Range Book 4*;

(ii) A second-year child of above average reading ability spent 6 months reading *Wide Range Book 5*;

(iii) A first-year child of average reading ability spent over 3 months reading *Happy Venture Book 1*.

One cannot refrain from wondering what the effect of such experiences might be on the children's attitudes to reading, and their eventual reading habits – particularly the children of 7 years, with a reading age of 7+, who spent three months with the first book of an infant reading scheme.

## V  Summary

1.   There is a lack of recently published basic reading schemes, in the UK, which are intended to cover the whole junior age-range; the only one in common use, *Wide Range Readers* (Schonell and Flowerdew), having been published in 1953.

2.   Although the vast majority of teachers in first- and second-year junior classes base their reading teaching on a reading scheme or schemes, there has been a great lack of up-to-date information on the actual books used in these age-groups, as well as the ways in which they are being used.

3.   Teachers in the first Teachers' Reading Research Group in this project expressed their need to know more about possible ways of grading books according to levels of difficulty. Four methods of discovering the approximate levels of difficulty of books have, therefore, been mentioned and references given to further reading in each area. It has been suggested that the application of readability formulae would be likely to prove too time-consuming for class teachers at the lower end of the primary school to utilize regularly. The use of Cloze procedure as a means of assessing readability also appears to pose a number of problems. Accordingly, the two methods most likely to prove

practicable for teachers of children aged 7 to 9 years are the use of graded book lists and informal reading inventories.

4.   A list of publications which suggest gradings for books has been provided, and teachers would find it helpful to become familiar with these lists. If these publications were available in a school, they could provide a preliminary grading in the form of a hierarchy of difficulty of the books already in the school. They would also provide suggestions of books at appropriate levels which might be purchased to fill gaps which might be discovered in the provision of books at particular levels of difficulty.

5.   To go further than this, by matching individual children with appropriate books, could be achieved by experimenting with the use of informal reading inventories. Such a procedure would be in line with suggestions for diagnostic investigations which are made elsewhere in this report. They would form part of what the Americans term individual 'conferences' with children, which would consist of longer periods of contact with each child, but at less frequent intervals than now occur in reading periods.

6.   During the course of this research project, a number of probes were made into the teaching books in current use in the first two years of the junior school. These investigations were mutually supportive and so contributed to the provision of a clear picture of current practices.

7.   It was found that different teachers provided children of the same ages and levels of reading attainment with very different levels of teaching books. For example, average readers of 8 years might be provided with books as far apart as *Happy Venture Book 1* or *Wide Range Book 6*, (i.e. a reading level of $5^0-5^6$ at one end and approximately $10^0-10^{11}$ at the other end).

8.   In general, many more children were found to be reading with the help of their teacher, books that were too easy for them rather than too difficult. In one case of the exercises undertaken with the help of practising teachers, 50% of first-years and 64% of second-years were reading with their teachers, books which they could have read perfectly easily on their own.

9.   In the majority of classes more than one reading scheme was used, and these were usually supplemented by other series of slimmer books.

10. The reading scheme most commonly used was *Wide Range Readers*, published in 1953. It was followed in popularity by *Through The Rainbow*, published in 1965.

11. The number of teaching books read by children in one school

year ranged from 1 to 27 in first-year classes and 1 to 58 in second-year classes. In general, first-year children read about 3 or 4 books with the help of their teachers, with second-year children reading 2 or 3 books in this way.

12. Many children spent three or four months reading one book with their teachers, while a few spent the whole school year on one teaching book.

13. Teachers found it helpful to follow the suggested practice of having children record the titles of all the books they read throughout the school year.

## VI  Implications for Teachers

The results of these various investigations into the teaching books in use in first- and second-year junior classes must inevitably cause teachers to ask themselves many questions which could well result in a reconsideration of current practices. The following are among the questions likely to be raised.

1. If the books which many of the children are reading under the teacher's guidance are sufficiently easy for them to read on their own, is this a profitable use of the teacher's time?

2. If these same books are not sufficiently difficult to afford teachers opportunities to help children to read gradually more and more difficult materials, does their total teaching programme include other activities designed to enlarge and improve children's reading skills?

3. Are the basic reading schemes being used the ideal reading materials either to grip the children's interest or to increase their reading ability and fluency? Are these schemes such as to convince children that reading is a desirable pursuit?

4. If children spend a whole year, or even three or four months, laboriously ploughing their way through one reading book with the help of their teacher, is this likely to encourage them to develop the habit of reading for pleasure?

5. Is there any good reason for relying so heavily on the reading schemes currently available, with their disjointed collections of short stories and other items? Might it not be better to grade the majority of all the books in the school, as simply and speedily as possible, and then allow children to select their own books, at particular levels, according to their own interests? Would not children then be likely to read their books more fluently and more speedily, as well as with pleasure? And would not such a procedure be much more likely to guide them towards permanent habits of reading?

# CHAPTER 10

# Teachers' Methods of Teaching Children To Read

## I Introduction

Many activities engaged in by members of the team during the first two years of the project, such as visits to schools, pilot studies, and work with teachers' reading research groups, formed part of the preparation for the intensive study in a small number of schools in the third year. The aim was to develop a diverse battery of probing techniques which would, as far as possible, enable the team to observe, assess and record all those dynamic processes affecting children's reading progress which form a constantly recurring pattern throughout the school year. The objective was to find out which aspects of reading teachers believed to be relevant and in need of development with children aged 7 to 9 years, and which activities they regarded as appropriate to this end. This was considered to be an extremely important part of the project, particularly in the light of the absence of any recent, similar reports — a fact given a degree of emphasis by Morrison and McIntyre (1969) in *Teachers and Teaching*.

The various instruments of assessment which were selected or developed and used in the intensive study are listed in Chapter 2. Those most directly concerned with teachers' classroom practices relating to the teaching of reading are examined in the current chapter. The two most important of the probing techniques were classroom observations, made by trained observers and based on the use of observation schedules; and daily logs kept by the teachers of all activities connected with reading and other areas of language development, undertaken throughout the day.

The detailed information provided here of the practices in which the teachers were engaged in their efforts to forward children's reading progress, is based solely on evidence gained in 33 classrooms in the 12 schools involved in the intensive study year. These did not comprise a national or even locally representative sample of schools. On the other hand, the schools had been selected by experienced local advisers as schools which could be regarded as 'typical'. Furthermore, the team's visits to many other schools, as well as discussions with other teachers and with frequent visitors to schools, such as advisers and University and College lecturers, confirmed that the practices described here are prevalent in the majority of primary schools. The members of the research team believe that large numbers of teachers will recognize their own practices in the descriptions given.

## II  Teachers in the Intensive Study

The teachers in the intensive study had all completed forms giving personal details of their age-group, training, teaching experience and usual teaching practices. The information provided in this way confirmed that these teachers could be considered as a typical cross-section of primary school teachers. The teachers' lengths of service in their current schools ranged from one year to forty years. Approximately half the teachers in each year-group held posts of responsibility. Eighteen of the teachers were currently attached to first-year junior classes, fifteen were teachers of second-year classes, and all professed to use a combination of individual/group/class approaches in their teaching.

At the end of their year with the project, these teachers were asked whether, and to what extent, involvement in the project had caused them to alter their normal practices in reading and language work. Half of them stated that they had not altered their practices at all, while the remaining half considered that involvement in the project had only marginally affected them. In general, the nature of the effect was to increase their awareness of the techniques available, and the problems involved in reading instruction. A number of teachers noted that as a result of keeping daily logs, they had become more aware of the substantial incidence of reading and writing activities across the curriculum. Only three teachers admitted to laying greater emphasis in practice on language work in the classroom. It is assumed, therefore, that any information given in this chapter on the teaching practices of these thirty-three teachers is acceptable as valid in this context.

## III  Teachers' Daily Logs

### A. *Keeping the Logs*

At a briefing meeting held prior to the commencement of the intensive study year, teachers were introduced to the method to be used in recording data on the log sheets, and were provided with supplies of the sheets, together with notes of guidance about completing them. A copy of a log sheet and the related notes is included in Appendix 10-A. Briefly, the exercise involved teachers in keeping daily records of all the various activities relating to reading, in which they or their pupils had been engaged, together with the approximate duration of each activity and the number of children involved collectively or the names of individual children. The logs were open-ended to ensure, as far as possible, that the teachers' normal practices would not be influenced by assumed expectations arising from headings printed on the log sheets. The log sheets were intended to be kept beside the teachers and filled in at intervals as the various activities occurred throughout each day.

The logs were kept for a total period of ten weeks; four weeks during October/November 1975, and six weeks from January to March 1976. The keeping of these logs was the most arduous task asked of the teachers in the intensive study schools. Yet, despite the great work-load imposed on them by this particular task, the teachers kept their records good-naturedly, with only a few unavoidable gaps. When the log sheets were finally collected and examined, it was interesting to remember that they had originally been planned as back-up material to the observation schedules; with the aim of affording teachers the opportunity of recording all the reading and writing activities which went on when observers were *not* in the classroom. In the event, although the observation schedules provided invaluable information, which could not have been obtained in any other way, the teachers' log sheets supplied a wealth of details of the teachers' daily practices aimed at or related to improving children's reading ability, and also furnished insights into general patterns of behavioural differences between teachers. The findings of the whole project would certainly have been the poorer had the teachers concerned not been willing to co-operate as fully as they did, in this way.

## B. *Analysis of the Data*

The demanding nature of the task of keeping the daily logs, as well as the desire to make them open-ended, resulted in a number of in-evitable characteristics in the entries, which had to be taken into consideration in deciding on the method of data analysis. For example, total accuracy of recording could not be expected for, as one or two of the teachers did admit, they sometimes completed a log from memory at the end of the day, on occasions when they had been too involved with the children to stop to complete it during the day. Also, as the logs were open-ended, it was to be expected that some teachers would include more detail than others about the type of activity listed and that certain teachers might fail to record activities which to them were of questionable relevance to reading development, for example reading stories to the class, or watching television programmes. Again, in some cases, both recording and analysis were further complicated by the structure of the teaching programme, particularly where integrated study periods featured strongly. These reasons, together with general problems of definition and classification, precluded the precise quantification of the log data for the purposes of activity breakdown comparisons between different teachers.

The logs were, in fact, analyzed by systematically cataloguing the day to day activity in each classroom into a number of categories of practice — these being determined empirically after an initial review of the log information. The categories used were as follows:

Listening to children reading
Reading to the class
Children's personal reading
Phonic instruction
Vocabulary work (including spelling)
Grammar work
Comprehension tasks
TV or radio periods
TV or radio follow-up work
Handwriting practice
Free-writing sessions
Written work, following discussion
Topic work
Review and discussion (of and about books)
Miscellaneous (related drama, etc.)

Naturally, problems of definition and classification arose during this systematic summarization, particularly when integrated sessions, (noted in one school — four classes), or undetailed 'Reading Workshop' or 'Reading and Study' sessions were prevalent (recorded in two schools — eight classes). Often also, some activity sessions would include components of others. Television follow-up work, for instance, was generally of this nature, sometimes consisting of phonic revision and often of television-stimulated free-writing or topic work. Many activities would occur simultaneously, particularly the various forms of basic skill instruction, and it was not always clear what proportion of the class was engaged in which specific activity for whatever period. For these reasons, and those previously stated, only an approximate time-allocation for each activity on a day-to-day basis was attempted; and this was done simply to provide an impression of the emphasis placed on the various activities, by different teachers, in relation to their stated objectives, to their teaching resources and to each other.

## C. *Information Obtained From Teachers' Logs*

### 1. Hearing children read

The predominant activity in which most of the teachers were engaged for much of their time was listening to children reading; most teachers being involved in this for anything between 20 and 40 minutes, and occasionally 60 to 100 minutes, per day. This was equally true for both year-groups. In fact, listening to individual children reading was clearly regarded by all teachers as the backbone of their teaching and monitoring of reading, a finding which was reiterated again and again throughout this research project.

A questionnaire to the teachers during the year asked, among other things, how often they chose their children's basic reading books for them and how often it was their practice to listen to an above-average, an average and a below-average reader reading from these books. There appeared to be no discernible difference in the response patterns of the two age groups. Only one teacher professed never to choose the teaching books for the children; all others agreed to this as normal procedure.

As for the frequency with which the teachers said they listened to the three grades of readers reading aloud to them, there was usually an increase in frequency from above-average to below-average, although two first-year teachers stated that all their children were heard daily. Only two teachers claimed never to listen to their above-average readers, all others stated that they heard them at least once a week. Average readers were said to be heard two to three times a week, while approximately half the teachers thought they listened to their below average readers daily; the remainder regarded two to three times per week appropriate also for this ability level. The pattern of teachers' responses to this particular question was similar to those reported in the *Bullock Report* (1975). There appeared to be no evidence, either from the questionnaire responses or from the daily logs, that a teacher adopted a particular strategy to match the ability spread of any specific class.

It cannot be surprising that the teachers' statements of intent or actual practice did not always correspond with their records of daily activities. The existence of remedial sessions (two schools — nine classes) would obviously lessen the need for the class teacher to listen to poorer readers as often as might otherwise be thought the case. However, in practice the strategy may often have differed from the intention because the latter had been inappropriate in the context of the teacher's current class. For example, most classes did not have equal distribution of children across the three reading ability bands, and when there were large numbers of below average readers, time spent with each had to be reduced.

The teachers' logs indicated that children were usually heard reading individually for anything between one and fifteen minutes at any one time — the norm being two to three minutes per child. (These figures, however, are much higher than those recorded from the observation schedules — see explanation later in this chapter.) Listening to children's oral reading was done at any time during the day and during any type of lesson. Two-thirds of the 18 first-year teachers and all but two of the 15 second-year teachers listened to children reading solely on an individual basis. The remainder used both individual and group approaches; usually group activity for the better readers and individual attention for the poorer ones. Group size varied between two and ten children, but was generally four to six children, and usually 10 to

15 minutes once each week were spent on hearing the collective members of a group reading. In fact, the children, whether individually or in groups, were generally heard at least once a week, often apparently on a rota basis. Only one teacher demonstrated a contrasting pattern of behaviour to the usual group formation, in that her only group consisted of the four poorest readers who were then heard about three times in any week, while the remaining children were heard individually once a week for about 10 minutes each.

Apart from these grouping arrangements, many teachers did consciously alter the emphasis placed on oral reading for the three ability levels, either by hearing better readers less often than poorer ones or even not at all, or by hearing them for shorter periods at any session, or both. Only seven teachers treated all children similarly regardless of ability level, while two teachers from the same school heard the better readers more often than the poorer ones, though in every case individual sessions lasted only one or two minutes.

The books from which the children read aloud to their teachers were almost invariably the teacher-selected 'teaching books'. Only rarely were children asked to read to their teachers from books they had selected for their own personal reading. The teachers' logs confirmed what has already been discussed in Chapter 9, that the teaching books usually formed part of a basic reading scheme and that *Wide Range Readers* (Schonell and Flowerdew 1953) headed the list, with *Through the Rainbow* (Bradburne 1965) taking second place.

## 2. Instruction in basic skills

As was to be expected, different teachers, no doubt depending on their objectives and on their pupils' assumed competencies in these areas, placed different emphases on such aspects of the basic skills of reading as increasing children's sight vocabulary, improving their phonic skills or helping their comprehension. For instance, while most first-year teachers placed much emphasis on phonic tuition, most teachers of second-years appeared to regard their pupils as beyond the need for this, and instead spent more time on general vocabulary extension, comprehension and written work.

### (a) *Increasing children's sight vocabulary*

The methods which teachers reported in their logs as employing to extend children's vocabulary were many and varied. Although no teacher recorded any work on such British lists of commonly used words, as *Key Words to Literacy* (McNally and Murray 1962), in one school the American list of *Basic Sight Vocabulary of 220 Words* (Dolch 1945) was used for the purpose of checking on and extending children's sight vocabulary. Numerous word games which allow play with familiar words were, however, in evidence; for example, 'Hangman', crossword puzzles, composition of other words from the letters of longer words, and play with rhyming words, as well as commercial packages such as *Programmed Reading Kit* (Stott 1962).

One very common practice was to have the children copying incomplete sentences from the blackboard, and then attempting to fill in any missing words. Also popular was a communal effort at thinking of appropriate words to use either specifically in sentences describing a picture, friend or object, or more generally in subsequent writing often as a television follow-up. Word meanings were usually discussed whenever new words were introduced as spelling lists or when difficult words were met in the children's reading or the teacher's story-telling. Interesting variations were the practice of searching for different ways of starting sentences, using, for example 'as', 'when', 'today', and 'soon', and also searching for synonyms or antonyms to specific words. Weekly dictionary exercises were also recorded in five of the first-year and seven of the second-year classes.

Finally, it should be noted that a good deal of vocabulary work was linked to other areas of the curriculum, particularly with regard to the explanation of terms needed in mathematics and science.

(b) *Improving children's phonic skills*
The phonic teaching which occurred in first year classes was frequently a class lesson, as a follow-up to the BBC television programmes 'Look and Read'. Some phonic work was also based on series of books such as *Sound Sense* (Tansley 1961) and sometimes flash cards were used.

Teaching practices in one other area of the curriculum, which must have contributed towards the effects of phonic instruction, was the teaching of spelling which occurred in virtually every class in both the first and second-years. A common practice seemed to be to provide lists of twenty to thirty new words per week to be learned and followed by a spelling test. On other occasions in spelling lessons teachers were drawing the attention of their classes to similar sounding words with different spellings, for example 'right' and 'write', or unusual spellings such as 'laugh' were highlighted. Phonic tuition was also found combined with vocabulary extension in such tasks as searching for words containing certain letter combinations, or the 'I Spy' game which was frequently mentioned.

(c) *Improving children's comprehension*
Every teacher included in her log sheets records of time set aside for comprehension exercises of various types; as well as a certain amount of work on grammar, such as sentence construction, tenses and word-endings. Most of the comprehension exercises were at an elementary level, which required the children to have sufficient understanding of both text and question to enable them to find a simple word or phrase in the text which would answer a factual question.

It is interesting to note here that much comprehension work was often carried out in lessons other than reading and English lessons.

Many teachers not only helped the children with specialist vocabulary for mathematics and science work, as already mentioned, but they also spent some time helping poorer readers with the written instructions and questions. Another broader sphere in which comprehension skills were developed seemed to be in history, geography and nature lessons.

During reading and English lessons, every teacher but two organized the class on a group basis, with different groups working on phonics, vocabulary, grammar or comprehension exercises. Usually the teacher would give attention to each group for a certain amount of time and also find some time for listening to children reading from their basic reading books.

In addition to this universal approach to language work, four first-year teachers also used in this group work one of the *S.R.A.'s Reading Laboratories* (Parker and Scannell 1963). It was used as the authors intended, that is for a concentrated period of about three months. Three of the teachers used the laboratory almost on a daily basis throughout the Autumn term only. The fourth teacher used it in this way during the Spring term, which was appropriate timing in this case, as the average age of the children in the class was relatively low in comparison with all other first-year classes.

(d) *Written work*
Weekly 30 minute periods of handwriting practice were engaged in by 14 first-year and 10 second-year classes.

'Free' or 'creative' writing was almost a universal practice, although recorded to greater or lesser degrees by different teachers. Two common practices were to have the children complete a half-hour's 'week-end diary' every Monday morning; and secondly, to ask the children to re-write in their own words a story previously heard in class. Free writing designed specifically to improve the children's descriptive powers was often based on familiar objects or situations such as 'My Pet' or 'My Favourite Television Programme', while free writing intended to encourage children's imagination was generally based on a story title or hypothetical situation.

Writing with the aid of reference materials, such as information books or word cards, featured strongly in both years, although to a lesser degree during the first term for first-year juniors. Such writing was often preceded by a lengthy class discussion of the subject matter, and by the second-year had often become work on topics in a subject area such as history, geography or science. (A very interesting discussion on the variety and nature of writing in the primary classroom is given by Rosen and Rosen (1973) in their book *The Language of Primary School Children*, where they also comment on the appropriateness of certain types of writing for children of different abilities.)

Much writing of both main types, that is both with or without reference materials, was inspired initially by a television or radio programme which the class had previously watched or listened to. This comment particularly applies to the programmes 'Merry-Go-Round' and 'Springboard' which were mentioned by approximately one-quarter of first-year teachers and one-third of second-year teachers. The programmes 'Picture Box' and 'Nature' were watched by two first-year and three second-year classes respectively; two of these classes watching both programmes. These programmes were usually followed by a class discussion on the content, and often by relevant vocabulary work. Often, also, some form of writing would follow the discussion. Sometimes the writing was based on blackboard notes or accompanying pamphlets and sometimes additional reference materials were used.

Again, even more so than for the group work on basic skills, all of these class writing periods were used by the teachers, as much for hearing individual children read from their reading books as for giving direct help and instruction in aspects of the main class activity.

## IV  Observation Schedules

### A. *Classroom Observation Techniques*

Although classroom observation is now a fairly well-established technique in the field of educational research, most of the reported studies are American in origin. Many of these studies have involved the recording of the number and type of verbal interactions between the teacher and pupils. A common aim has often been to attempt some clarification of the relationship between pupils' learning and teacher characteristics and/or behaviour. The observation schedules employed in such studies have generally been modified versions of the Interaction Analysis Schedule developed originally by Flanders (1964 and 1970) for use in his own study of verbal interaction in secondary classrooms. Reviews of such investigations with their variety of observation instruments are given by Simon and Boyer (1970) and by Rosenshine (1971), while Bealing (1973) outlines some of the problems associated with observational classroom research in general.

Although a number of British researchers have conducted classroom observations of teachers' and/or children's behaviour in junior schools, for example, Hilsum and Cane (1971), Resnick (1972), Garner and Bing (1973), and Boydell (1974 and 1975), the project team failed to find reports of exercises involving specifically reading and writing activities. The observation schedules used in this research project were, therefore, devised for this purpose.

### B. *The New Observation Schedules*

After extensive trials and revisions during the first two years of the project, two observation schedules, one referring to the teacher and one to the pupil, were finally produced and printed for use in the intensive study year. The schedules were intended to be used in normal classroom situations and were designed as records of all reading and writing activities engaged in by the individual under observation. A time-sampling technique involved recording behaviour at 30-second intervals. A portable cassette recorder was used as a time-keeper.

As voluntary observers were to use the schedules, and as these observers would receive only minimal training, it was essential that the types of behaviour categorized should be sufficiently clearly defined as to allow rapid and objective recognition. The categories finally isolated, as given in Tables 10-1(a) and (b), were the minimum number of categories which were found to cover, adequately and unambiguously, all possible and easily defined teacher or pupil behaviour connected with reading and writing. They were intended to be exhaustive and mutually exclusive so that only one category would need to be recorded at any time-signal. As can be seen from the two tables, the range of activities could well be found in any junior classroom.

Tables 10-1(a) and 10-1(b)
*Behaviour categories in observation schedules*

*Table 10-1(a) — teacher categories*

1. Gives direct instruction related to reading or writing
2. Recounts or reads from a book
3. Explains or expands book content
4. Organizes or supervises reading or writing activity
5. Listens to oral reading
6. Supplies a word or spelling
7. Directs copying or literal recall
8. Requires pupils' ideas on reading or writing
9. Comments on reading or writing activity, i.e. provides feed-back
10. Engaged in other teaching activity — not related to reading or writing
11. Engaged in activities not directly related to teaching-behaviour

*Table 10-1(b) — child categories*

1. Listens to teacher (or media) reading or giving instruction in reading
2. Listens to another child reading
3. Reads assigned book
4. Reads self-selected book
5. Writes, while referring to a book or other printed materials
6. Writes without reference to book or other materials
7. Engaged in other tasks where reading or writing is not involved
8. Asks a question about reading or writing activity
9. Answers a question on reading or writing activity
10. Volunteers an answer
11. Spontaneous contribution on reading or writing activity
12. Non-orientated activity

Copies of both printed observation schedules, together with notes of guidance for the observers, are included in Appendix 10-B.

Both teacher and child schedules made provision for a brief description of the lesson content, with a record of the type of organization and reading materials employed. In addition, the teacher's schedule provided for a record of the number of times the teacher switched attention from one child or group to another during the period of observation.

## C. *Using the Observation Schedule*

The observers used in the study were either B.Ed. students in their final year at a College of Education, or practising teachers following a University Diploma course. Two training sessions based on video-tape recordings were followed by two 'live' practice sessions in class-rooms. On the second live occasion, for the purpose of a simple reliability investigation, the observers worked in classrooms in pairs, observing simultaneously either the teacher or the same child. The overall inter-observer reliability estimates were derived by the usual analysis of variance method on the separate category cumulated scores for 12 observed sessions. The coefficients were found to be 0.93 for child observations and 0.64 for teacher observations.

The relatively low value for teacher observation reliability reflects the difficulty experienced by some of the observers in distinguishing between categories 4 and 7 ('organizes/supervises reading or writing activity' and 'directs copying or literal recall' respectively), and between categories 1 and 9 ('gives direct instruction' and 'comments on reading or writing activity'). These particular points of confusion were thoroughly discussed with the observers after this training period and supplementary notes, designed to clarify the differences between the categories, were added to the instructions for using the schedules. As a result of these improvements, the reliability of the final observation records referred to in this chapter can be assumed to be higher than 0.64 (unfortunately, additional time could not be devoted to further reliability studies). However, as junior teachers generally move around the classroom a great deal, which results in conversational content being less clearly audible to the stationary observer, and as this is associated with a high rate of activity change compared with a pupil, the reliability of teacher-observations cannot be expected to reach that for observations of the children. In fact, the figures quoted above agree very closely with those given by Boydell (1974 and 1975), whose observations were based entirely on analysis of conversational content in primary mathematics lessons.

The actual observation study took place during the Autumn term 1975 and Spring term 1976, with individual observation sessions lasting 20 minutes. Altogether 30 observers were involved, although the majority of the observations were made by 14 of these. Usually two observers worked together in a classroom, one recording the teacher's behaviour and the other observing one of the selected 'average' children. Although the teacher would naturally be more aware than the children of the nature of the exercise, neither the teacher nor any particular individual child was aware of exactly when, or even if at all, he or she was being specifically observed.

The original programme was for observations to take place in all 12 of the intensive study schools, with the teacher and each of the four selected average readers in every class being observed on 10 occasions. The supply of observers, however, was not adequate for this programme. In the event, observations were only undertaken in five of the schools, that is in 20 of the 33 classes in which the teachers had faithfully recorded their daily logs. Preference was given to lessons concerned with reading, writing and other language skills. 151 observation sessions were recorded for 20 teachers, the number per teacher varying from three to nine. 69 children were observed, this being between two and four per class. A total of 244 child observation sessions were recorded. The number of observations per child varied from two to eight.

As the various teachers and children were not necessarily observed in similar lesson situations, and as they were certainly not all observed in equal numbers of lessons, no extensive quantitative analysis of the results was attempted. However, a qualitative analysis proved fruitful in providing insights into the nature of different types of lessons involving reading and language work, and a limited quantitative analysis has served to furnish a general picture of the average proportions of time spent by teachers and by children in the various categories of activity into which their behaviour was catalogued.

## D. *Information Obtained from the Observation Schedules*

The observation record sheets show up fascinating patterns of what the teacher and child really do when reading and writing periods are in progress. What comes out very clearly is how hard the teachers work. Even so, the records indicate that the teacher does not always do what she thinks she is doing, nor is the child always doing what the teacher thinks he is doing.

### 1. Teachers' work patterns

(a) *Interruptions to teaching plans*
The first general point, already noted in Chapter 2, was that the actual total time devoted to reading and writing activities was considerably less than most teachers might imagine it to be. The main reasons for this were threefold and were similar to those noted in the NFER's reports *The Teacher's Day* (Hilsum and Cane 1971) and *The Teacher*

*at Work* (Hilsum 1972). They arose from alterations to normal school routines, interruptions by people coming into the classroom and interruptions by children within the class. Consequently, a period which the teacher might regard as thirty minutes or one hour devoted to reading and writing activities could be whittled away by perhaps a quarter or a third. As a result, the teachers' objectives for the term, which they had written out in advance, may not have been fully implemented because of these curtailments to anticipated time.

(b) *Breakdown of teaching time*
Data from the teachers' observation schedules made it possible to discover the proportion of teachers' time in reading/writing periods which was devoted to the various teaching activities and to other activities. This was done by averaging the breakdown figures over all lessons observed for individual teachers, and then averaging these over all teachers in each year-group. Ten teachers were observed in each year-group. The results were so similar in both year-groups that any slight differences found could be a function of the small sample sizes concerned, and for this reason the figures given are based on averages taken over all twenty teachers. It was found that, during periods set aside for reading/language activities, these teachers spent on an average 25% of their time in activities unrelated to the actual lesson. Some of this time was accounted for by the interruptions mentioned earlier: in the remainder of the non-teaching time, teachers were engaged in additional work not directly connected with current teaching-learning activities, for example, marking work unrelated to the current lesson or preparing equipment or materials for succeeding lessons, such as television, radio, art and craft. This result strongly supports the findings of Hilsum and Cane (1971), Garner and Bing (1973) and, particularly, of Boydell (1974).

The 75% of their time in which teachers were directly involved in teaching/learning activities was divided between the different categories on the observation schedules, in the proportions shown in Table 10-2.

Once more these results support the findings of Boydell (1974), especially in the low proportion (11%) of time spent in higher-level cognitive contributions (i.e. categories 3 and 8 in Boydell's definition). It is pertinent to note here that 'review and discussion' of books and other reading materials would be subsumed in these categories. Garner and Bing (1973) suggest that the very high incidence of teacher contact with individual children, (illustrated by the high rate of attention switches found in the present study and discussed later), may in fact serve to preclude any substantial work on a higher level than direct recall questions and factual statements.

Other points to note in Table 10-2 are that the highest proportion of the teacher's time (14%) was spent on listening to children's oral reading, while one of the lowest proportions (4%) was spent on direct teaching.

Table 10-2

*Proportions of teachers' observed time spent in categories of teaching activities (20 teachers)*

| Category | Activity | % of Time |
|:---:|:---|:---:|
| 1. | Gives direct reading instruction | 4 |
| 2. | Recounts or reads from a book | 5 |
| 3. | Explains or expands book content | 4 |
| 4. | Organises/supervises reading/writing activity | 13 |
| 5. | Hears oral reading | 14 |
| 6. | Supplies word/spelling | 6 |
| 7. | Directs copying or literal recall | 6 |
| 8. | Requires pupils' ideas on reading/writing | 7 |
| 9. | Comments on reading/writing | 11 |
| 10. | Engaged in other teaching activities | 5 |

(N.B. The remaining 25% of teachers' time, not accounted for in this table, was taken up with non-teaching activities.)

(c) *Attention switches*
One of the most striking features of the schedule data relating to teachers was the frequency with which teachers switched attention from one child or group to another during a 20-minute period. This was particularly noticeable in periods in which the teacher was listening to individual children reading orally to her, while the remainder of the class was engaged in other activities, and also during periods when a proportion or the whole of a class was writing and individual children approached the teacher for help with spellings. Indeed in some cases the teacher was engaged in both activities simultaneously, listening to one child reading aloud and, at the same time, writing a word in another child's spelling book after a short discussion with him.

The average number of attention switches for all teachers in a 20-minute period was 15, individual teachers averaging between 10 and 25. The maximum number of attention switches recorded for an individual teacher in such a session was 32. There were no marked differences between teachers of first- and second-year classes. Table 10-3 shows the average number of attention switches for individual teachers, together with the range of variation and number of reading and allied lessons on which the averages are based.

(d) *Time spent with individual children*
A further related, and most notable, finding resulting from the objective data, was the extremely short period of time spent by the teachers in listening to the oral reading of any one child. The average time spent by a teacher in total concentration on a child's oral reading was only

Table 10-3

*Numbers of attention switches by individual teachers*
*during 20-minute periods*

### 1st Year Classes

| Teacher | No. of Observations | Attention Switches | |
|---------|---------------------|--------------------|-----|
| | | Average | Range |
| A | 7 | 18 | 9–28 |
| B | 7 | 19 | 6–25 |
| C | 9 | 14 | 1–25 |
| D | 6 | 10 | 3–19 |
| E | 4 | 25 | 21–29 |
| F | 6 | 15 | 4–22 |
| G | 6 | 24 | 10–32 |
| H | 10 | 12 | 1–20 |
| I | 7 | 13 | 7–24 |
| J | 5 | 11 | 1–26 |

### 2nd Year Classes

| Teacher | No. of Observations | Attention Switches | |
|---------|---------------------|--------------------|-----|
| | | Average | Range |
| K | 6 | 15 | 7–20 |
| L | 8 | 12 | 7–23 |
| M | 6 | 16 | 1–24 |
| N | 6 | 14 | 4–29 |
| O | 3 | 12 | 7–19 |
| P | 6 | 19 | 10–28 |
| Q | 5 | 13 | 1–17 |
| R | 3 | 10 | 8–11 |
| S | 5 | 14 | 4–21 |
| T | 4 | 19 | 7–27 |

30 seconds. This objective result is one illustration of teachers not always doing what they think they are doing. The teachers' logs, for example, usually set this figure higher, but clearly no allowance had been made for the frequent interruptions which occur while the teacher is listening to one child's oral reading; for example, helping other children with spellings, commenting on other children's work, answering questions or issuing reprimands. Frequently this 30 seconds was the full time devoted to a single child. Furthermore only rarely was it observed that a teacher asked either a direct or open-ended question of a child on the content of his oral reading.

## 2. Children's work patterns

Bearing in mind that the children were a random sample from the band of children of average reading attainment in each class, teachers may be surprised at certain of the patterns of activities shown up by the records of children's observation schedules.

### (a) *Time spent on diversionary activities*

The first noteworthy feature arising from an examination of the children's observation schedules was the amount of time spent by many children in what are termed diversionary activities. These were activities which were not clearly directed towards the activity in hand. They include talking to other children, searching for pencils, wandering about the room or waiting to gain the teacher's attention. (The latter activity was differentiated from the other non-orientated activities on the record sheet.)

Of course, it would be unrealistic to expect children of seven and eight years-old always to concentrate totally on the task in hand. Analysis of the 244 children's schedules in this research indicated that the average proportion of time spent on diversionary activities was approximately one-third.

However, the proportion of approximately two-thirds of children's time being spent task-directed and one-third non-task-directed presents too optimistic a picture of what actually happens over a longer period. When observations covered a complete hour in one classroom, it was noted that the proportion of children's time spent on diversionary activities over the whole period was much greater. As every teacher knows, it often takes the first five or ten minutes of a period for all children to become task-involved. Then, after an initial period of reasonably high concentration for most children, as the hour progresses, task-involvement decreases while diversionary activities increase. Many of the 20 minutes' observation periods recorded, as they commenced five or ten minutes after the children had come into the room and actually started work, might be described as 'heavily saturated' with task-directed activities.

Both first-years and second-years spent on average 33% of their time on diversionary activities. These average figures form an interesting comparison with the results of a small experiment reported by Southgate and Lewis (1973). Children aged 5½ and 6½ years, when engaged in reading and writing activities, were found to spend on average 45% of their time on diversionary activities. The percentages of these two infant age-groups were identical and considerably larger than the figures given here for first- and second-year juniors. It would seem possible that, with an increase in age, there is a general improvement in children's ability to be task-orientated.

### (b) *Children differ in their work patterns*

A second, not unexpected, finding was that some children's general patterns of task-concentration were considerably higher than others. For example, average task-concentration over all observation periods could vary from 46% for one child, to 75% for another child.

(c) *Variability within an individual's general work pattern*
It was also noted that even when a child's general work pattern was recognized, his task-concentration in different periods still showed great fluctuations. One first-year girl, for example, whose average task-concentration over five periods was 67.5%, i.e. about average for her age-group, showed the following percentages of task-concentration in the different periods: 93%, 88%, 73%, 59% and 30%.

Quite often, the reasons for the variations shown could be traced to motivation. For example, one first-year boy (Basil) who was an avid reader showed an average task-concentration of 62.5% over seven periods. However, an examination of his concentration on the tasks he had been asked to do, showed how motivation and interest can dramatically alter the ratio of time spent in task-directed and diversionary activities. When asked to read his basic reading book or a self-selected book, his concentration was 90% and 80% respectively – which is extremely high. When writing about a book of his own choice, his task-concentration was 70%. However, when he was asked to write about a television programme which had clearly not captured his interest, his concentration dropped to 33%. This particular pattern of an increase in diversionary activities in free writing periods was one frequently noted in the observation records.

(d) *Task-concentration can be unproductive*
Details recorded on children's observation schedules also highlighted the fact that children can sometimes be task-directed without this proving fruitful. Table 10-4 presents a consecutive record of one observation session for a first-year girl (Sheila) of average reading ability, who was usually below average in task-concentration.

The totals at the bottom of the columns indicate that this girl spent 55% of her time concentrating on the task and 45% on diversionary activities, which was a much better performance than usual for her. What needs to be noted, however, is that this was a reading period. The task set by the teacher was for her to copy certain small pictures from her reading book, *Oxford Colour Reader* (Carver and Stowasser, 1963) and then write something under each one. However, although at a casual glance she was working fairly diligently on what her teacher had asked her to do, her reading and writing activities were minimal. Of the 22 recorded task-directed activities, 18 merely involved drawing. Only 4 of the recordings (i.e. 2 minutes) involved reading and writing activities and so were likely to contribute in any way to her reading progress.

(e) *Differences in work patterns between year groups*
Finally, one other interesting finding illustrated by the observation

Table 10-4

*Consecutive record of a child's activities over 20 minutes*

| Number of recordings at 30-second intervals | | | |
|---|---|---|---|
| Task-directed activities | | Diversionary activities | |
| | | 1 | |
| Draws | 2 | | |
| Reading Book | 1 | | |
| Draws | 3 | | |
| | | 1 | (speaks to another child) |
| Draws | 1 | | |
| | | 1 | |
| Draws | 5 | | |
| Writes | 2 | | |
| | | 1 | |
| Draws | 3 | | |
| | | 1 | (contacts another child) |
| Draws | 2 | | |
| | | 1 | |
| Draws | 1 | | |
| Writes | 1 | | |
| | | 7 | (waits for teacher) |
| Listens to teacher | 1 | | |
| | | 1 | |
| | | 4 | (waits for teacher) |
| | 22 | 18 | |

schedules was that, although the first- and second-year children spent, on average, equal proportions of time task-concentrated, there were quite noticeable variations between them in the time spent on particular types of activity. Table 10-5 shows the average proportions of observed time accounted for by the 12 categories recorded in the children's schedules. These figures were arrived at by averaging the data for each individual child and then finding the overall average of these values for each year-group.

It can be seen from this table that first-year juniors spent more time on category 1 activities, that is receiving instruction in reading, listening to the teacher reading or listening to the media, than second-year juniors. From the experience of the project researchers and from the schedule indications, this would seem to be explained by the fact that the first-year classes spent more time listening to school radio programmes or watching television than did the older children. This fact might also help to explain the contrasting types of written work engaged in by the two year-groups. The first-year children were often observed in television or radio 'follow-up' lessons, where they were

Table 10-5

*Changing patterns of activities between first-years and second-years*

| Category | Activity | Proportion of Time (%) | |
|---|---|---|---|
| | | 1st Year | 2nd Year |
| 1 | Listens to teacher/media/ instruction in reading | 17.3 | 11.0 |
| 2 | Listens to another child reading | 1.3 | 1.8 |
| 3 | Reads assigned book | 5.8 | 11.5 |
| 4 | Reads self-selected book | 2.2 | 4.0 |
| 5 | Writes referring to a book | 7.0 | 20.2 |
| 6 | Writes without books | 19.8 | 7.2 |
| 7 | Other activity work | 9.8 | 8.5 |
| 8 | Asks questions on reading/writing | 1.0 | 1.0 |
| 9 | Answers questions on reading/ writing | 0.5 | 0.5 |
| 10 | Volunteers an answer | 1.5 | 1.5 |
| 11 | Spontaneous contribution on reading/writing | – | – |
| 12 | Non-orientated activity | 33.3 | 32.8 |

asked to write about the subject of the programme previously seen or heard. The higher proportion of time spent by the second-year children in reading an assigned book related to the fact that they spent more time than did first-years on 'topic' work — which explains the greater proportion of time (20%) also spent by them in writing while referring to books rather than 'freely', without books, as the first-year children generally did. This figure of 20% also includes extra time they were engaged in English comprehension exercises. The change in activity emphasis in second-year classes has already been noted in the discussion of the information obtained from the teachers' daily logs.

One particularly important point which emerged from the children's observation schedules was the extremely small amount of time spent in both age-groups in questioning or answering on reading and writing activities (i.e. categories 8—11). In particular, children's spontaneous contributions on reading were observed on only nine occasions during the 177 recorded 20-minute sessions (i.e. 7,080 'random time points' on which Table 10-5 is based).

Finally, it should, perhaps, be mentioned that the 10% of time spent by both year-groups in 'other work' covers such activities as drawing (especially the practice of copying pictures from a reading book); 'thinking' (generally in free writing periods); examining the potential stimuli of free writing sessions (in one instance, for example, actual puppets were studied for some time); and also mathematics work in the occasional 'integrated' session.

## 3. Comparison of teachers' and children's output

(a) *Contrasting teacher/pupil output*
The optimum use of teachers' and children's time would seem to be desirable objectives. Accordingly, the intensity with which teachers work in most reading and writing sessions needs to be examined alongside the corresponding patterns of activities of their pupils. With regard to the girl, Sheila, previously mentioned, who spent only two minutes of a 20-minute period reading, it is worth examining what her teacher was doing during this reading period.

All the children were engaged in activities, such as reading, writing, answering questions or drawing, connected with their basic reading books. The teacher was sitting at her table and calling out individual children to read to her. Other children continued to ask the teacher's help with spelling or other queries. In other words, it was the kind of period which forms a regular feature of the majority of first-year junior classes.

Consecutive details of this teacher's activities are set out in Table 10-6.

From this table it can be seen that in this same 20-minute period, the teacher had contact with 18 children. In nine cases she was listening to a child reading, while nine other children came to show written work or ask for help. Most of the contacts with individual children were of 30 seconds or less. The longest contact was of two-and-a-half minutes − with one interruption. While the teacher was working at this terrific pace, at least one girl, and possibly other children, had not done anything likely to improve her reading.

The foregoing contact in teacher/pupil output was not uncommon as the three further, albeit extreme, examples set out in Table 10-7 illustrate.

Such patterns, although generally less pronounced than these examples, were observed quite frequently, particularly during free working periods.

(b) *Reasons for low pupil output*
The tremendous effort which teachers so obviously put into their teaching of reading and writing showed up very clearly in the data on their observation schedules. This being so, it must be disappointing for teachers to learn that the records on children's observation schedules showed equally clearly that, in certain cases, their pupils' own task-concentration was quite low. Fortunately, the data on the observation schedule provides certain clues to the reasons for some of the lack of concentration on the part of the children, and these are discussed here in the hope that teachers will find them helpful. At the same time, it should be borne in mind that no child can be expected to concentrate entirely on the task in hand − even self-disciplined adults would rarely expect such concentration from themselves.

Table 10-6

*Consecutive record of a teacher's activities over 20 minutes*

| Attention switch to another child | Teaching activity | * | Non-teaching activity |
|---|---|---|---|
| 1 | Listens to a child reading | 2 | |
| 1 | Comments on reading/writing | 1 | |
| | | | 1 |
| 1 | Listens to child reading | 1 | |
| | | | 1 |
| | Listens to same child | 4 | |
| | | | 2 |
| 1 | Comments | 1 | |
| 1 | Comments | 1 | |
| | | | 1 |
| 1 | Listens to reading | 2 | |
| 1 | Supervises reading activity | 1 | |
| 1 | Listens to reading | 1 | |
| | | | 1 |
| | Listens to same child | 1 | |
| | Comments on same child's reading | 1 | |
| 1 | Comments on another child's work | 1 | |
| 1 | Requests another child's ideas | 1 | |
| | Comments on same child's work | 2 | |
| 1 | Listens to child reading | 2 | 1 |
| 1 | Comments on child's work | 1 | |
| 1 | Comments on another child's work | 2 | |
| 1 | Listens to a child reading | 3 | |
| 1 | Comments on another child's work | 1 | |
| | | | 1 |
| 1 | Comments on child's work | 1 | |
| 1 | Comments on child's work | 1 | |
| 1 | Listens to a child's reading | 1 | |
| 18 | | 32 | 8 |

(* = number of recordings at 30-second intervals)

Table 10-7

*Contrasts in teacher pupil output*

| Teacher | Age Group | No. of Teacher's Attention Switches | Child's % of time task-directed |
|---|---|---|---|
| A | 1st year | 22 | 32 |
| B | 1st year | 27 | 25 |
| C | 2nd year | 27 | 15 |

Motivation is certainly an extremely important factor in children's concentration on a task. Yet it is clear that however hard a teacher tries, and whatever methods she uses, to inspire the children's interest in the task in hand, certain individual children will remain unmotivated, either occasionally or frequently. The details of the first-year boy, Basil, cited earlier, for example, show how his concentration dropped from 90% to only 32% when he was not interested in the prescribed task.

However, even when the children are highly motivated by the set task, discontinuity of work can occur owing to extraneous circumstances beyond their own control. For example, the observation data also indicated very clearly that many of the occasions on which a child completely ceased to work on the allotted task were related to the system in use for obtaining help from the teacher. There were also indications that different classrooms exhibited differing degrees of teacher-related non-directed activities on the part of the children.

An examination of all the observation data revealed a general decrease in the levels of task-orientation shown by children in two particular types of lesson, namely, the reading period and the free-writing period. The examples of a teacher's activities in Table 10-6 illustrates the common pattern of very many reading periods, in which different groups of children were engaged on various tasks relating to the basic reading schemes in use in the class. The teacher was listening to individual children reading aloud to her, while the queue of children coming to ask for various kinds of help grew longer, and finally obscured from her view many of the children supposedly working at their desks. Inevitably, the concentration of some of the children still working at their allotted tasks began to wander and they talked to or interfered with their neighbour's work. Meanwhile, the teacher herself was endeavouring to carry out an impossible threefold task: giving attention to one child's oral reading; interrupting that task to answer other children's queries; and ensuring that the remainder of the class were getting on with their tasks. This particular situation is not peculiar to the schools in which observations took place. It is certain that very many other teachers will recognize the description as a situation with which they are personally familiar.

The second example illustrates the kind of writing lesson with which every junior teacher is equally familiar. It was a one-hour period in which the children were to write their own stories, and it began with a class discussion for 10 minutes followed by 50 minutes in which the children were writing and occasionally seeking help with spellings. The teacher was observed over the first 20 minutes of this period. She switched attention from one child to another (and, during the class discussion, between individual pupils and the whole class) on 32 occasions. When the children were writing there were long queues of children at her desk, word-books in hand. The teacher's contact with individual pupils during this time was again about one every 30 seconds.

The collective observation records also showed that, as in this particular lesson, dictionaries were not always evident in classrooms during such writing periods, although many of the teachers had recorded dictionary practice in their daily logs. Of course, it is possible that children's dictionaries were present but were not noticed by the observers because of their infrequent use. It should also be remembered that dictionary practice as a class exercise, with the teacher directing the work, is a different matter from children, and especially first-year juniors, being adept at consulting dictionaries on their own, for the purpose of verifying spellings.

This particular lesson record was typical of many such, and is detailed here because one of the randomly selected average readers in the class was observed simultaneously and independently in this same lesson. The boy in question was generally less task-concentrated than the overall average proportion of two-thirds of lesson-time, but in this instance 65% of his time was spent in diversionary activities. Most of his time was taken up with talking to, or interfering with the work of, other children at his group table. These activities were interspersed with short bursts of writing activity, while towards the end of the observation session he waited four minutes in a queue at the teacher's desk before spending another three minutes talking to other children on the way back to his seat. This is a classical illustration of the way in which such free writing periods lend themselves to a work-defeating combination of diversionary activities.

This phenomenon could result from two possible major causes: first, the inappropriate demands made of a child of this age by the task concerned (see again Rosen and Rosen (1973) for an expansion of this point); and, secondly, the fact that while a teacher is so fully occupied with large numbers of individual children requiring differing degrees of help she cannot possibly fully supervise or direct the remainder of the class. Of course, the freedom of movement allowed in junior classrooms does render work-supervision much more difficult than otherwise might be the case, especially when this is associated with the usual group-seating arrangement. In fact, as noted on some of the observation records, complete groups of children can be inadvertently ignored for a whole period.

In only one classroom were different groups of children organized on a group-seating basis provided with different activities. On one occasion, one group was happily engaged in art work, another seemed absorbed in cutting out shapes in preparation for a future mathematics lesson, two more were quietly reading their library books or reading schemes, and the fifth group was involved in comprehension work. What this teacher did, which no other teacher was seen practising, was deliberately to select one or two children from each of the five main groups to come forward and cluster round the blackboard for extra tuition in an aspect of their mathematics work. In this way the teacher concerned was not only using the group approach to match activities to children appropriately but she was able, simultaneously, to 'keep an eye on' the rest of the class.

An interesting piece of research which indirectly strengthens the argument for continuous supervision of children at work was actually concerned with the problems of deviant behaviour in the classroom. A team of researchers (Kounin, *et al.* 1966) watched and recorded teachers at work in classrooms which contained a few emotionally disturbed children, but which were otherwise quite normal. The teachers who were found to be successful with the disturbed children were also more successful than others with normal pupils. These were teachers who managed to convey an impression of total awareness of all classroom activity, and they had more work involvement and less deviancy from their children than did the teachers who failed to demonstrate this facility.

# V  Summary

1. The information obtained in the 'intensive study year' about teachers' methods of teaching children to read, was based on work in 33 classrooms in 12 typical schools, staffed by teachers whose ages, training and experience, made it seem fair to regard them as a typical cross-section of primary school teachers. Accordingly, although the selection of schools was not based on a random sample, the members of the research team are certain that the majority of teachers will recognize many of their own practices in those described.

2. The two most important of the probing techniques used to discover teachers' methods of teaching reading were daily logs of all reading and related activities kept by the teachers themselves, and classroom observations made by trained observers based on the use of newly-devised observation schedules. The combination of these two techniques provided a very detailed picture of current practices relating to teachers' ways of extending the reading proficiency of children aged 7 to 9 years.

3. Teachers varied in the amount of time they spent on instruction in the basic reading skills, but it was generally much less than the time spent on listening to individual oral reading or in helping children with written work. The work on the basic reading skills included helping first-year children to increase their sight vocabulary and improve their phonic skills, although such teaching had decreased by the second year. Every teacher set aside some time for comprehension exercises; more of this activity taking place in the second year than the first year. Much of the comprehension work was based on text books, and was of an elementary kind, involving the answering of factual questions by the selection of words or phrases from the text.

4. Although teachers mentioned dictionary work in their daily logs, little use of dictionaries to check spellings was observed in writing periods, even among second-year children.

5. The predominating activity engaged in by teachers was listening to individual children reading aloud to them; most teachers regularly spending between 20 minutes and 40 minutes per day on it, and for the occasional teacher, 60 to 100 minutes. The books used for this purpose were almost invariably their basic reading books.

6. Children's written work also occupied a large proportion of both teachers' and children's time. Much of it was 'free' writing and 'topic work'; with the time devoted to the latter increasing during the second-year.

7. Even so, less time was spent on reading and writing activities than teachers might imagine. The reduction in the anticipated time can be attributed to:
(a) Alterations to the normal routine of class or school;
(b) Interruptions to lessons caused by other people entering the classroom.
(c) Interruptions caused by children in the class.

8. In most reading and writing periods the teacher worked extremely hard, continually switching attention from one child or group to another.

9. One result of this was that the time devoted to listening to any one child reading aloud was minimal, frequently being no more than 30 seconds per child.

10. Both first- and second-year children spent on average 33% of the time in which they were observed on diversionary activities. This average figure disguises wide variations in non-directed activities ranging from 0% (total concentration) to 88% (i.e. very little work being done).

11. Children demonstrated different overall patterns of work. Some showed up as usually task-orientated while others generally exhibited a low level of concentration.

12. Even so, the same child on different occasions exhibited quite wide variations in the proportion of time he spent task-orientated and non-orientated. Motivation seemed to be an important factor here, but interferences from other children and waiting to gain the teacher's attention were also contributory factors.

13. The high work output of teachers was not always mirrored by high task-orientation in their pupils. In fact, in certain lessons,

particularly when the teacher was engaged in listening to individual children's oral reading or helping them individually with spelling in a writing lesson, there were indications that with certain children an obverse effect took over; high teacher output was then related to low pupil output.

## VI  Implications for Teachers

These findings, obtained from teachers' daily logs and from the use of observation schedules, on the methods used by teachers in the intensive study year to increase the reading abilities of their pupils in first- and second-year junior classes should cause teachers to question many of their common practices. The following questions are among those which teachers will need to consider and discuss with each other.

1. Is sufficient time given to ensuring that all children have mastered the basic reading skills of immediate recognition of common sight words, and that they have a sound knowledge of phonic skills?

2. Should comprehension training not be much more broadly based than that found in many of the so-called comprehension exercises or comprehension tests?

3. One of the most time-consuming of teachers' activities is helping individual children to spell the words they want to use in their written work. Could this not be gradually reduced by more emphasis on teaching spelling, as well as more direct instruction and practice in using dictionaries?

4. Could not the stream of constant interruptions, caused by other adults and children coming into the classroom, be reduced? If so, how might this be effected?

5. There can be no doubting that teachers have high objectives in relation to the reading and writing progress of their pupils, and also that they work extremely conscientiously towards this end. But perhaps it would be helpful to think more about teachers' output of energy — which is great — in relation to children's learning. The question is mainly one of organization. As the actual time spent on reading and writing tuition (i.e. teaching/learning activities) is limited, teachers should be experimenting with procedures by which this precious commodity — their own time — will be most profitably spent, to ensure that as much learning as possible is taking place. If a teacher were not driving herself so hard, for example by trying to give individual attention to 32 children in 20 minutes, she could experiment with methods of organization which might result in a more profitable use of the children's time so that they learned more, practised more and used their developing skills more.

6. Consider the two types of lesson in which the teacher's output

of energy frequently shows an obverse relationship with certain of the pupils' patterns of concentration; the oral reading lesson and the free writing lesson. The pattern of the typical oral reading lesson would seem to indicate that teachers have been persuaded by educationists, and perhaps by reading experts, into thinking that individual help is *always* best. Teachers would do well to question whether individual tuition is always necessary or always the most profitable use of their time, particularly when the contacts are as short as 30 seconds. Are there never groups of children, or occasionally a whole class, ready for the same piece of teaching or learning experience at the same time? If so, would not 10 to 15 minutes spent with a group occasionally be a more valuable use of the teacher's time?

7. Regarding the typical free writing lesson, with queues of children wanting help with spellings, there is certainly scope here for experimenting with trying to reduce the queues. Children in first-year classes certainly do require a great deal of help with spellings. The teacher wants to encourage them to be courageous about using new and exciting words, and not just playing safe by using only the simple words they know how to spell. But it is not realistic to think that one adult can give individual help in this way to 35 or 40 young children at the same time, without there being a good deal of pupil-time wasted.

What might be done? First, could the number of children engaged in free writing at any one time be reduced by undertaking this activity less often? If so, only a proportion of the class could be writing, with the consequent demands on their teacher's attention, while the remainder were engaged in other fairly self-sufficient activities such as reading for pleasure or painting? Secondly, is it worth considering encouraging children to attempt to write all words on their own, with the help of dictionaries, word charts, card indexes, etc.? Then, when a piece of work is finished, the child might read it aloud to the teacher, who would help him with the spellings. Thirdly, perhaps one ought to ask if producing an imaginative piece of written work is not too difficult for certain of the children in first- and second-year junior classes? Some of them have difficulty in writing factual accounts, even when common spellings are written on the blackboard. Some children are lacking in imagination. Could their imagination be encouraged by asking them to tell or record a story, instead of trying to record imaginative ideas through a most difficult medium, not yet mastered by them?

# CHAPTER 11

# Encouraging and Training Children to Use Their Reading Skills

## I Introduction

As children's mastery of reading skills increases, so should their use of these skills for both recreational and functional purposes. Teachers of children aged 7 to 9 years are well aware of this, as has been shown by the discussion in Chapter 5 of their stated aims and objectives in teaching children to read. A number of the investigations in this research project throw light on how teachers set about teaching children to use their reading skills. The word 'teaching' in this context includes both encouragement and training.

The main factors involved in the process of ensuring that children make full use of their increasing mastery of the skills of reading may be described as follows:

(a) Motivation – the encouragement and promotion of children's interest in books;
(b) Provision of appropriate books and other reading resources;
(c) Deployment, classification and arrangement of the books;
(d) Guidance in locating and selecting books;
(e) Training in the use of books;
(f) Opportunities to read – i.e. the provision of places to read and time to read.

## II Fostering Children's Interest in Books

Visits to schools, the use of classroom observation schedules, and an examination of the daily logs of reading activities kept by teachers in the intensive study year, all indicated that it was common practice for teachers of first- and second-year juniors to read aloud to their classes. Discussions with teachers in the intensive study schools confirmed that they regarded the practice of reading to children as one of the main methods of motivating children to read. At the same time, teachers were eager to experiment with new ways of fostering children's interest in books, and they welcomed the opportunity to discuss their ideas with the interviewer. These discussions proved so fruitful that it was decided to enlarge this part of the enquiry. Accordingly, in July

1977, a questionnaire relating to ways of promoting children's interest in books was sent to teachers who had been members of the earlier research groups. 127 teachers responded and their replies, when amalgamated with those 27 teachers in the intensive study schools, provide many ideas for promoting children's interest in books.

## A. *Reading Aloud to Children*

The teachers' daily logs of all reading, writing and related activities in the intensive study schools give some indication of the amount and kind of reading aloud to their classes which was undertaken by the teachers. These records are more likely to be under-estimates than over-estimates of what actually took place, as the teachers had sometimes found it impossible to keep recording everything as it happened, throughout the day.

Information from the logs indicated that the story period usually lasted for 15—20 minutes, usually occurred once each week, and was generally found at the end of the day — often on Friday afternoon. Ten first-year and four second-year classes had weekly story sessions; four first-year and five second-year classes heard stories 2—3 times per week, one class in each year had daily story periods, while the remaining teachers either did not read stories to children or failed to record the fact. It proved the exception rather than the rule for these sessions to be devoted to complete short stories, the common practice being to read consecutive extracts from longer stories, and there was a great variety of books in use ranging from *Brer Rabbit* to *Tales from the Odyssey*.

The teachers' logs also showed that teachers sometimes read poetry to their classes and sometimes stories from scripture and history textbooks. Two teachers recorded reading pupils' own written work to their classes, as a follow-up to free writing sessions, and once a teacher recorded reading to her class a letter a child had received from his pen-friend. This happened a few weeks after the children had been helped to write their own letters to their pen-friends. Providing the opportunity for children to listen to stories being read on radio programmes was also regarded by teachers as a means of promoting children's interest in books.

The possibility that these teachers had frequently omitted to record in their daily logs the occasions on which they read aloud to the children, was confirmed by their interviews with one of the researchers and by the questionnaires which they completed. From these sources, it was discovered that many teachers read aloud to their classes four or five times a week in sessions of 15—30 minutes. The material shared with the class in this way included non-fiction as well as stories and poems; extracts from magazines, encyclopedia and information books on topics in which the class were currently interested. Some teachers read to their pupils snippets from books they themselves were currently reading. Books from which extracts or whole stories had been read were frequently placed in the class library so that children could read them for themselves.

The questionnaire completed by the 127 teachers from the reading research groups revealed similar patterns of story-telling practices. The results of the questionnaire analysis are shown in Tables 11-1 and 11-2.

Table 11-1

*No. of occasions teacher read to class*

| No. of Occasions | % of Teachers | |
| --- | --- | --- |
| | 1st year | 2nd year |
| 1 | 2 | 4 |
| 2 | 7 | 12 |
| 3 | 23 | 26 |
| 4 | 18 | 25 |
| 5 | 41 | 25 |
| 6 | 2 | 4 |
| 7 | – | 2 |
| 8 | – | 2 |
| 9 | – | – |
| 10 | 7 | – |

Table 11-2

*Time per week spent on reading to class*

| Time per week hr.  min. | | % of Teachers | |
| --- | --- | --- | --- |
| | | 1st year | 2nd year |
| – | 30 | 7 | 11 |
| – | 45 | 11 | 7 |
| 1 | 0 | 23 | 23 |
| 1 | 15 | 5 | 5 |
| 1 | 30 | 18 | 24 |
| 2 | 0 | 9 | 11 |
| 2 | 15 | 2 | – |
| 2 | 30 | 23 | 11 |
| 3 | 0 | – | 4 |
| 3 | 30 | – | 2 |
| 4 | 0 | 2 | 2 |

It can be noted from these tables that teachers of each age-group showed great variations in the amount of time they spent per week on reading to children; the range being from half-an-hour to four hours. The majority of the teachers, however, spent between one hour to two-and-a-half hours per week on this activity. The figures reflect the fact that sessions usually lasted between 10 and 30 minutes and generally occurred three to five times per week.

When asked what else besides stories they read to their classes, almost 75% of the teachers mentioned poetry, over 40% mentioned factual material (usually related to current topic work), approximately 20% (30% of first-year teachers and 15% of second-year teachers) listed children's free writing, almost 15% included news items from newspapers and magazines, and 6% mentioned Bible stories.

A number of teachers indicated that they occasionally read longer novels or 'sequence' books to foster their pupils' potential interest in books generally. One or two of the teachers listed ex-pupils' letters being read to the class, and also extracts from books brought into the class by the children — sometimes read aloud by an individual child.

## B. *Additional Activities*

In the questionnaire, teachers were asked to list activities, other than reading aloud to children, which they instigated with a view to promoting children's interest in books. The suggestions were many and varied. Most teachers gave two or three alternatives and an occasional teacher provided more. In contrast, a few teachers offered no alternatives. The most commonly mentioned methods of stimulating interest in books were the following:

(a) allowing free access to appropriately and adequately stocked class and school libraries – (38%);

(b) arranging book displays which could be centred around a particular author, related to current topic work, or simply an attractive random arrangement in the classroom book corner — ('book displays' were mentioned by 35% of teachers);

(c) encouraging the use of non-fiction books for reference in relation to topic work – (35%);

(d) the promotion of the local library, either by providing information about its use and contents, or by making visits in school time – (31%). Table 11-3 summarizes all the alternatives suggested.

It is clear from Table 11-3 that first-year teachers considered attractive book displays a useful aid in fostering interest in books, followed in order of popularity by promoting the local public library, allowing free access to adequately stocked class and school libraries, encouraging the use of reference books in topic work, and the existence of a book club where paperbacks may be viewed and bought.

Second-year teachers mentioned book displays less frequently (27%) than did the first-year teachers (40%), and gave more importance

Table 11-3

*Promoting children's interest in books — percentages of teachers (from a total of 127) using various methods*

| Categories of Activities Utilized by Teachers | % of Teachers | | |
|---|---|---|---|
| | 1st year | 2nd year | Totals* |
| 1. Free access to appropriately stocked class/school libraries | 32 | 44 | 38 |
| 2. Book displays — fiction or topic-related | 40 | 27 | 35 |
| 3. Topic work involving use of non-fiction reference books | 30 | 38 | 35 |
| 4. Promotion of local library — information/visits | 30 | 29 | 31 |
| 5. Discussion about books or a particular book | 17 | 33 | 23 |
| 6. Book clubs ('Chip', 'Bookworm', 'Puffin', etc.) | 27 | 16 | 23 |
| 7. Book records/reviews (including children's oral reviews) | 10 | 22 | 17 |
| 8. Encouraging introduction of books into classroom | 17 | 7 | 12 |
| 9. Allowing books to be taken home | 10 | 11 | 10 |
| 10. Children reading to class (often own work) | 3 | 13 | 7 |
| 11. Relating art/craft work to story or topic work | 7 | 9 | 7 |
| 12. Relating drama sessions to story content | 7 | 5 | 6 |
| 13. Reading chapter then using prediction or leaving book for children to read | 10 | 5 | 7 |
| 14. Encouraging hobby/interest reading | 3 | 7 | 5 |
| 15. Discussing authors (particularly of 'serial' books) | 3 | 5 | 4 |
| 16. Encouraging parental co-operation at home | 2 | 5 | 3 |
| 17. Miscellaneous | 12 | 7 | 12 |

*(N.B. 12 classes contained both first- and second-year juniors; while they are included in the total figures for all classes, they are not shown separately.)

to access to the school/class libraries (44%) and encouraging reference to reading matter in topic work (38%). Illustrative comments on topic work were the following: 'The children make their own booklets, using topic books and work cards. This enables them to follow up their own individual interests and learn how to find out information by reading' and, 'I give groups of children different topics, where research through reference books is essential.'

Book Clubs were listed less frequently by second-year teachers than by first-year teachers (16% and 27% respectively). On the other hand, the teachers considered discussion about authors, and books and their contents, to be more important for the older children (33% mentioned against 17% first-years). One teacher commented: 'We discussed various authors and why the children did or did not enjoy their books.' And another, 'When, occasionally, a book is reviewed by the children, I provide lists of books on similar subjects or books by the same author.' Promotion of the local public library was mentioned equally often by teachers of both years, and usually this took the form of class visits to the library, often with the librarian helping with book selection.

Television was mentioned by eight teachers as a promotional influence. The children either watched or listened to a programme concerning books or relating to a story, and were then encouraged to read related material. Some teachers drew their children's attention to the book underlying a television drama serial, and provided information about other work by the same author. An infrequently mentioned, although often used, method was that of displaying children's written work, possibly with related craft work, for other children to read. Displays were generally placed in the classroom reading corner, in a corridor or in the reception area.

Book records and reviews were considered valuable aids in fostering an interest in reading, particularly for the older children. Such reviews could be written or spoken. One other promising suggestion would seem to be a 'class review book' in which children record their views on recently read books for others to see.

A point often stressed was that books, and book corners, should be as attractive in appearance as possible; the introduction of new books into the classroom often being mentioned as an immediate stimulus to children's interest in reading. The following are examples of such comments.

> Occasionally have a book afternoon. Spread out all the library books on view, then browse around and talk about them.
> Children are encouraged to bring to school their book gifts, received as birthday or Christmas presents. These are shown to the class and usually greatly admired.

It is worth noting that only three teachers mentioned personal example as a motivating influence, although it may be that this is taken so much for granted that specific mention was not thought necessary. Instances of 'personal example' given were discussion by the teacher of interesting parts of the book she was currently reading, and the teacher being 'seen' to be engrossed in personal reading of a library book during the children's personal reading periods.

Also of interest is the fact that only three teachers mentioned involving parents in promoting children's interest in reading. This was done by encouraging parents to listen to their children reading in the evenings. On the other hand, some teachers may well follow this practice but perhaps did not think of including it in their lists.

Finally, it must be noted that a number of the suggestions for fostering children's interest in reading may be particularly relevant for both the backward and the reluctant reader. The most obvious of these was the encouragement of reading in the areas of their hobbies and interests. 'I talk to children about their interests and hobbies, then lend them books on these subjects and introduce them to fiction and non-fiction books in these areas'.

Every one of the suggestions mentioned by teachers – of which these quoted are only a small sample – would seem to be of great value and no doubt other teachers could add examples to the lists.

## III  Provision and Arrangement of Books

The value of promoting children's interest in books and reading is clearly lessened if the provision of books in the school is inadequate or inappropriate, if access to them is limited and if their classification and arrangement is not easy for the children to follow. The first three of these points were stated in positive form by teachers in the preceding examples, when 'free access to appropriately stocked class and school libraries' was given top priority among the various ways of fostering children's interest in reading.

In this project, information about the provision and arrangement of books other than teaching books, was gathered in a general way on visits to schools during the first two years and, in great detail, in the Reading Environment Exercise undertaken in eight schools during the intensive study of the third year, and is summarized in Chapter 7. Here it was noted that while most classrooms had book corners and books on display and all had contrived a central library – often in difficult circumstances – there was great variety between the different schools in practically every facet of their provision of 'books for using'.

Yet to 'surround children with books' is only the first stage of having them use the books to the best advantage. Children cannot be expected to locate the books they need or select those which interest them, and which they are able to read and understand, if they are merely surrounded by a haphazard assortment of books. Some classified system of arrangement of books on shelves is necessary. This is essential in a central library and helpful to children even in a class library. In nearly all the schools visited, fiction had been separated from non-fiction books in the central library. The non-fiction books were usually divided into categories of subject matter, sometimes based on a simplified Dewey system, and in certain libraries colour-coding was also used. Even so, the staffs of the schools were rarely fully satisfied with the systems they had devised. It was clearly evident that to devise a classification and borrowing system which is effective, yet sufficiently simple for younger children to understand, is not an easy task. No system is perfect; each having its own strengths and weaknesses, and compromises have often to be reached.

While a minority of the schools involved in the project employed colour-coding systems for grading the fiction books in the central library into fairly broad categories based on levels of difficulty, not one school visited in the whole four years had attempted to do this with non-fiction books. In this respect, junior schools as well as secondary schools would appear to be far from the ideal proposed by the Bullock Committee. The *Bullock Report* (Department of Education and Science 1975) indicated that 'retrieval systems' in 'resource areas' should '. . . incorporate information on the readability level of each printed text. A simple form of coding would enable the pupil to select material at an appropriate level and would save confusion and frustration'. To achieve such a result, even if it were considered essential, would be an extremely time-consuming task, if not impossible for primary school librarians who are almost invariably in full-time charge of a class. Nevertheless, if a combined effort on the part of the whole staff could succeed in separating the non-fiction books into even two broad categories of 'easier' and 'harder' books, it would prove a helpful guide for children.

It seems certain that the grading of books into broad categories of difficulty can prove helpful to younger and slower readers, by guiding them to shelves on which they will find books which they, and their teachers, know that they will be able to read. There can be a danger in such a system, however, if it is so rigidly adhered to that a child with a particular interest in certain books is prevented from attempting to read them because they are judged to be too difficult for him. A certain amount of flexibility would seem advisable. A guiding principle might well be that the use of a system of grading books according to levels of difficulty should be sufficiently flexible for a child to be guided towards books which the teacher knows he is able to read, yet not debarred from attempting more difficult books when highly motivated to do so.

## IV  Helping Children to Locate and Select Books

The training and supervision of children into the use of the central library was a matter of great concern to the teachers in the intensive study schools. Introducing children who had come straight from infant classes to the central library was a particular problem and, in certain schools, while the youngest juniors were allowed to borrow fiction books from the central library, initiating them into the classification system for non-fiction books was left until the second or third term in their first junior year. In a number of schools the restrictions imposed by the building itself, on the siting of the central library, seriously limited its use. Thus even fitting in one period per week when children could change their library books was difficult and opportunities for familiarizing children with the classification system were limited. In addition, in most schools, the various problems imposed by lack of adequate space for a central library area close to the classrooms of youngeɪ juniors, seriously reduced the guidance and training of children in locating and selecting books, which the teachers would have liked to provide. Even so, in a number of schools the school librarian spent one or more periods with first-year classes introducing them to the library and occasional periods with second-year classes. When class teachers had library periods in the library with their entire classes, a little time was occasionally spent on library skills, but the emphasis was more usually on promoting children's interest in books. In the majority of schools, little direct training was observed in the bibliographical skills, for example, the use of subject and author indexes and/or reference books. Where it did occur it was mainly in second-year classes.

## V  Training in the Use of Books

Discovery methods of learning in the primary school, which increased noticeably during the 1960s, and especially after the seal of approval was put on them by the *Plowden Report* (Department of Education and Science 1967), continued to develop during the 1970s. Two related effects of this emphasis on discovery methods of learning were an increase in the proportion of information books to fiction books found in primary schools, and a concomitant increase in the amount of 'topic work' in which children were engaged. By 1975, the Bullock Committee was able to report, from information gathered in 1972–4, that 94% of all nine year-olds were doing some topic work – which they described as 'reading and writing' based mainly on reference books. 42% of the nine year-olds spent over an hour of class time on it, and 68% also spent some of their optional time in this way.

This was the same kind of picture as the research team encountered in all their contacts with schools over the four year period of the project. First- and second-year juniors were frequently engaged in producing booklets on topics of common or individual interest. Some of these were of a very high standard, while in other cases the child had clearly been struggling in his effort to produce a few sentences.

In their report, the Bullock Committee stated: '. . . the experience of our visits was that much of the writing done in the name of topic work amounts to no more than copying.'

Lunzer and Gardner (1979) have also noted this same practice with twelve-year-old secondary pupils. In the current project, topic work of this kind was noted by members of the research team, most frequently in second-year rather than first-year classes. Often the procedure adopted was a class discussion on a topic, after which the children were directed to specific sections of certain reference books, which they then copied into their topic books. Other witnesses to such practices were Rosen and Rosen (1973), who provide an interesting discussion on the extent and, in their view, comparative value of this particular activity.

It should be said, however, that the child who can locate a relevant sentence or paragraph and copy it into his own topic book must at least possess a certain mastery of the earliest of study skills, namely literal comprehension. To progress beyond this, children must at some stage be trained to summarize in their own words. This is the crux of the problem about which class teachers involved in the research project were extremely concerned and which they often brought up in discussion with the research team.

Unfortunately, teachers in junior classes, through no fault of their own, are generally ill-equipped to teach the reading skills which extend beyond the beginning stage. This did not, until quite recently, form part of their initial teacher training. Neither are books on the subject of study skills, which might be of help to them, readily available as they are usually American publications. Even the *Bullock Report*, which stresses the necessity for teaching the more advanced stages of reading which follow the beginning stage, is lacking in concrete suggestions which could be of help to teachers of children aged 7 to 9 years. In fact, teachers of these two age-groups find themselves in a no man's land regarding study skills. Infants who produce simple topic books are applauded and their teachers commended. At the opposite end of the educational process, secondary school teachers frequently find that children of 11 and older have not been trained to use books as tools of learning. Yet teachers of junior classes, and particularly of younger juniors who are most concerned with bridging this gap, have not been helped to deal with this most important stage of reading development.

The only extensive work on the extraction of information from books, recorded in the teachers' logs in the intensive study year, occurred in just one class in each age group. The classes turned out to be the two which, at the end of the year, had made most progress in reading (as measured by Brimer's *Widespan Reading Test* (1972)). The first-year class was one whose teacher allowed lengthy personal reading sessions with regular oral and written review, and in the second term this teacher also gave instruction to the class on the general question of information retrieval using reference books.

The second-year class, which outstripped all others for reading progress over the year, again held class discussion and reviews on books. However, what most distinguished this class from all the others was the fact that, not only did the children engage more frequently on topic work in class time, but their teacher also set extensive topic work for homework in the Spring term. Work on a particular topic often extended over weeks, was usually inspired by a television programme, and was twice followed up with substantial tasks to be conducted outside school time and to be written-up and reviewed in class later. One of these projects to be undertaken at home, on a television programme 'Fun and Games', began with a class discussion and associated written work about leisure activities. The teacher then distributed as many different types of sport or hobby activity as there were children in the class, and each child was asked to spend the following weekend finding out as much as he could about the allocated activity; for example, how it began, when, where, how it spread from one country to another, and so on. In the following week, 30 minutes were spent in class discussing the information found by the children, and this was followed by a 40 minute period in which the children individually wrote up their findings.

The fruitful way in which this teacher built up such activity from the basis of the initial television stimulus is an excellent example of such practice as recommended by the *Bullock Report* (1975). The members of the Bullock Committee, whilst conceding that the most effective use of broadcasting material in the primary classroom involves the teacher in much careful preparation, stress the potential for learning of this level of integration into other classroom activities.

There were also other examples of teachers who, by means of work cards or oral suggestions, tried to direct children to appropriate books for topic work. For example, one teacher, during a project on dinosaurs, tried to get the children to use books as reference books, through the use of questions and directions on a work sheet. Nevertheless, effective training in the use of non-fiction books, even at a very simple level, was not widespread, even in second-year junior classes.

## VI Provision of Opportunities to Read

Fostering children's interest in books, surrounding them with books, and teaching them how to locate, select and use books are part of the long-term aim of making reading not merely an interesting pastime but an integral part of life; in other words, encouraging children to become habitual readers. Some children, no doubt, eventually become life-long readers because they belong to families in which all the members are readers. Certain other less fortunate children, are unlikely ever to become life-long readers unless the habit of reading, for lengthy periods, is established at school. As the *Bullock Report* (1975) states: 'The habit of reading should be established early and should receive unqualified encouragement from that point onwards.'

Two of the most obvious ways of helping to establish the habit of reading are, first, to allow time for children's personal reading and, second, to provide inviting places in which to read. All the junior classes visited had contrived 'book corners' in their rooms, often by arranging low book cases to demarcate the areas. These book corners varied in their size, equipment and attractiveness. Most contained a table and a few small chairs, some had carpet on the floor, and one or two possessed a few easy chairs. The number of books in the book corner, their appropriateness and attractiveness showed great variations from class to class. In some cases the books were exactly those likely to appeal to, and fulfil the needs of, the children in the class, and special displays and notices, designed to tempt children into the corner, were in evidence. In other cases, the shelves in the book corner appeared to be a repository for all the old, dull, out-of-date books which should have been discarded years before. Most of the book corners could only accommodate small numbers of children at a time, usually not more than about six, and they were seen to be used mainly by children who had completed set pieces of work in advance of their classmates. Observations suggested that the role of book corners in junior classes was that of tempting children to become interested in books, rather than that of training them to become habitual readers.

On the other hand, the provision of an area, centrally placed, equipped as a library and reading room, and sufficiently large to accommodate a whole class, could greatly help the establishment of permanent reading habits. The accommodation in so many of the junior schools had rarely been designed to meet this need and, consequently, even with the great efforts put forward by the staff, central libraries were compromises — as the teachers were the first to recognize. In contrast, in the one school in the intensive study which had a magnificent central library, constantly in use by whole classes and individual children throughout the day, this undoubtedly contributed to the forming of habitual readers.

Even so, the provision of places where children may read comes second in priority to the provision of time for personal reading. A child who enjoys reading can become absorbed in a book in whatever place or conditions he finds himself. Even more so than with adults who are avid readers, the child can become quite oblivious to hard seats and the noise made by his classmates. But to reach this stage, he needs to have had a continuing experience of extended periods of time, free from interruptions, which are devoted solely to reading for pleasure. The experiences need to be contrived, in school, for all children. It is not sufficient that children should be free to read when they have completed the task in hand or when the teacher is engaged with other pupils. In any event, the children who first complete most of their set work ahead of other children are usually the better readers. The struggling reader, who most needs to be manoeuvred into becoming a habitual reader, is thus the one least likely to be provided with free time in which to read for pleasure at his own level.

The results of the Bullock Committee's survey, referring to the amount of time spent by children on individual reading of stories indicated that 5% of nine year-olds spent no time at all on this activity and 27% of them devoted half-an-hour or less per week to it. Moreover, the balance of the time spent on the personal reading of stories was in children's optional time, as opposed to time set aside for the whole class for this purpose. In such circumstances, it would seem fair to assume that the children in whom the habit of personal reading was already established would be those most likely to devote optional time to reading stories. Incidentally, it was noted in the course of the project that children did not always choose 'stories' as personal reading: non-fiction books were also chosen by some children.

The researchers in this project noted on their visits to schools that, apart from the reading done by children who had completed other tasks, most of the personal reading done by first- and second-year juniors was in short periods of 10 or 15 minutes when the teacher was engaged, for instance, in registration. To see a whole class engaged in personal reading for longer periods, except on occasions when library books were being changed, was quite rare. This impression was confirmed by the daily logs kept by teachers in the intensive study schools.

Further evidence of the amount of time devoted to children's personal reading was obtained from the questionnaires completed by teachers in the intensive study schools and by 127 teachers from the Teachers' Reading Research Groups. One of the questions asked was, 'Do you set aside any time *regularly* each week for *all* the children in your class to do some personal reading for pleasure?' If the reply was in the affirmative, the teachers were asked to state approximately how long per week was set aside for this purpose. Other related comments were invited and, in many cases, the comments confirmed what observations had suggested.

93% of the teachers indicated that they did set time aside for the whole class to read for pleasure, and they indicated that such periods usually took the form of 10–15 minute sessions at morning registration, with odd additional periods of reading after set work was finished by individual children. Only rarely was it the case that longer periods of personal reading were time-tabled for the entire class.

The approximate times spent on such reading periods over a week by these classes are shown in Table 11-4.

It can be noted from Table 11-4 that 10% of teachers of first-year classes and 5% of teachers of second-year classes set no time aside for personal reading. In contrast, in 2% of the first-year classes and 4% of the second-year classes, the time spent in this way was 4 hours per week. The more usual pattern, however, was 1–1½ hours per week being set aside for personal reading: 42% of the classes falling into this range. This represents less than 20 minutes per day.

An interesting comparison can be made between Tables 11-2 and 11-4, in that the majority of teachers spent more time reading aloud to children than was set aside for children to engage in their own personal reading.

Table 11-4

*Children's personal reading time (no. of classes = 127)*

| Time per Week | | % of Classes | | |
|---|---|---|---|---|
| hr. | min. | 1st year | 2nd year | All* |
| | 0 | 10 | 5 | 7 |
| | 30 | 10 | 16 | 13 |
| | 45 | 10 | 4 | 6 |
| 1 | 0 | 23 | 20 | 22 |
| 1 | 15 | 17 | 9 | 3 |
| 1 | 30 | 12 | 18 | 17 |
| 2 | 0 | 8 | 9 | 9 |
| 2 | 15 | 3 | – | 3 |
| 2 | 30 | 5 | 15 | 9 |
| 4 | 0 | 2 | 4 | 2 |

(*This column includes 12 mixed classes not shown separately.)

## VII  The Role Played by Books

The fact that teachers involved in this research project appreciated the value of trying to promote children's interest in books and encouraging them to read books on their own, emphasizes the vital role which books should play in primary schools. The importance of this role has been reinforced by certain other research findings.

Chall (1977), for example, in her overview of reading in the decade 1967–1977, having noted the growing interest in the relationship between reading and language, goes on to say:

> Among the significant research in this area has been a study of the effects of exposure to books on language growth and reading achievement. This exposure includes the extent to which children are read to or read independently (Chomsky 1972). A substantial and significant correlation was found between reading exposure, language maturity, and reading achievement. In further analyses of what caused what, Carol Chomsky concluded that the key was the number of books read to or by the children, particularly those that were above the child's own level of linguistic maturity. Thus, it would appear that being read to and reading on one's own are major vehicles for learning the more complex literary language needed for progress in reading as well as in language.

## VIII  Summary

1. It has been suggested that the main factors involved in encouraging and training children to use their reading skills are: motivation; provision of appropriate books; effective deployment and classification

of the books; guidance for children in the selection of books; training in the use of the books; and ample opportunities for reading the books.

2. Teachers regarded the practice of reading aloud to children as one of the best ways of promoting their interest in books, with a view to motivating them to undertake personal reading.

3. Teachers did not only read fiction to their classes. Among the many other materials read aloud to classes were: poetry; Bible stories; excerpts from history books, children's own written work, magazines, newspapers, encyclopedia, and information books; and occasionally, passages from the books they themselves were currently reading for their own pleasure.

4. Quite wide variations were revealed in the amount of time which different teachers spent in reading aloud to their classes; these ranged from half-an-hour to 4 hours per week. The majority of teachers, however, spent between one hour and 2½ hours per week on this activity; the time being divided into sessions ranging from 10 to 30 minutes, occurring three to five times a week.

5. Apart from reading aloud to their pupils, teachers listed many other activities which they initiated in order to encourage the children's personal reading. The most frequently mentioned were: free access to appropriate books in school libraries; attractive book displays; encouraging the use of non-fiction books for topic work; and introducing children to the local library.

6. The provision of 'books for using' showed great variations between schools in their numbers, ratio of fiction to non-fiction books, apportionment of books between central libraries and class libraries, the suitability of the books, their arrangement and classification, as well as the degree of freedom of access to the books.

7. Although teachers were well aware of the necessity to initiate children into the organization and classification system of books in the central library, their attempts to do so were frequently curtailed by the lack of a specific room to be used exclusively as a library, and sufficiently large to accommodate a whole class. The result was that in a number of schools, little direct training appeared to be given in the bibliographical skills, such as, for example, the use of subject and author indexes. In fact, one of the important findings of this piece of research is that children in the first two years of the junior school require more specific training in the use of books, and particularly of non-fiction books.

8. While teachers were aware of the need to train children to use reference books for the 'topic' work in which they were so frequently engaged, they were rarely certain of how this might be achieved — and

this could generally be attributed to the fact that they themselves had received little or no training in the development of study skills.

9. Every classroom visited had contrived some sort of 'book corner'. These varied greatly, not only in their provision of furnishings, but also in the appropriateness of their books, their attractiveness and arrangement, and the quantity and quality of supporting displays and notices.

10. The children who did most personal reading, either in the book corner or in their own seats, were usually those who had first completed the tasks set by the teacher; in other words, the most able children and the better readers.

11. Replies to a questionnaire on specific periods set aside for a whole class to engage in personal reading showed that 10% of first-year teachers and 5% of second-year teachers never did this, while the remainder allowed total times varying from 30 minutes to 4 hours per week for this activity. Generally, the amount of time set aside for private reading was 1–1½ hours per week, spread over three to five occasions.

12. The time which teachers generally devoted to reading aloud to their pupils exceeded the time set aside for the children to read books of their own choice.

## IX Implications for Teachers

1. Any teacher who may be using only one or two of the methods of promoting children's interest in books, which were mentioned by teachers in this research project, should find it helpful to experiment with or adapt some of the ideas noted. While no individual teacher could be expected to engage in all these activities at any one time, staff discussions of possible ways of interesting children in reading as a leisure-time activity might lead to the development of fresh ideas particularly suited to the children in the school and the existing conditions.

2. The indications of the preponderance of non-finction over fiction books suggest the need for teachers to check on the ratio of the two classifications of books in their own schools and classes. This could well lead to a decision to ensure that the balance be redressed.

3. Similarly, the finding that the ratio of 'difficult' to 'easier' fiction books in junior classes was usually in favour of the more advanced readers, should encourage teachers of juniors to search out fiction books which will help average readers of 7+ to bridge the gap which exists between the completion of an infant reading scheme and the time when they are able to read the more 'adult' type of library books, at about a level of reading ages 9–10 years. Certainly, unless

generous provision of fiction books, as well as information books, is made for these progressive stages of reading development, many fluent infant readers are unlikely to have become habitual readers by the age of 11+.

4. Consideration needs to be given to the proportion of books allocated to central, as opposed to class libraries. This should be closely related to the ease of access which every class has to the central library.

5. Ways of making class library book corner displays sufficiently tempting to encourage *all* the children in the class to want to use them should be continually reconsidered.

6. Schools which have not previously attempted to grade 'books for using' into broad categories of levels of difficulty would be well advised to consider this possibility. A list of helpful publications, which include graded lists of books, has been provided.

7. Even though many primary schools are hampered by lack of appropriate spaces for library facilities, the staff of every junior school still needs to evolve a common policy of introducing children to the system of arrangement of books in force in the school, as well as beginning to train children in the bibliographical skills.

8. The training of children in methods of locating and extracting information from books relating to their topic work requires a detailed plan, worked out and agreed on by all members of staff — a plan which can be introduced in carefully graded stages throughout the four years of junior education.

9. As junior teachers frequently expressed themselves as doubtful about appropriate ways of training children in study skills, they would certainly appreciate an increase in courses of in-service education on methods of training junior pupils, and particularly the younger age-group, to use information and reference books effectively.

10. The efforts spent by teachers in fostering children's interest in books, providing and arranging the books, guiding children to find the right books and showing them how to use them, may all be partially or wholly wasted if the habit of reading is not established in the first two years of primary school. This means planning that *all* children will have the experience of *extended* periods for personal reading of books of their own choice in school time. Teachers need to ask themselves if the odd ten minutes or so at a time is sufficient, and also whether slower readers and duller children have equal opportunities for private reading as the more advanced pupils.

11. The fact that, on average, teachers spent more time on promoting children's interest in reading than in allowing them to satisfy the aroused interest — i.e. they spent more time on reading aloud to their pupils than on allowing them to read their personally selected books, should surely cause many teachers to reappraise their programmes, with a view to achieving an acceptable balance.

# CHAPTER 12

# Results of Teachers' Guidance on Children's Choice of Books

## I Limited Available Evidence on Younger Juniors' Personal Reading

Although the literature on both primary school children, and on reading, contains much about the value of children's voluntary reading, very little has been written, and practically no recent research undertaken, on the books which children aged 7 to 9 years actually do choose to read on their own. The gap in information and comments about this vital period can even be noted in the *Bullock Report* (1975) which concentrates more on the early stages of reading for infant pupils and the later stages of reading for secondary pupils than on younger juniors. For example, it states: '... one of the most important tasks facing the teacher of older juniors and younger secondary pupils is to increase the amount and range of their voluntary reading.'

Some of the findings of the project 'Extending Beginning Reading' would suggest that the statement should also be applied to children aged 7 to 9 years, as it could well be even more important to ensure that the reading habit becomes firmly established during the first two years of junior education.

The research of Whitehead and his associates (Whitehead, *et al.* 1975; 1977) into the reading interests and habits of children aged 10+, 12+ and 14+ is one of the few recent investigations relating to junior children. It was found that in one month, 13% of children in the 10 year-old sample had not read a single book on their own and that this percentage increased with age to 29% for 12 year-olds, and 36% for 14 year-olds; which must surely suggest the necessity for ensuring that children's personal reading becomes an established habit well before the age of 10 years.

Teachers of younger juniors are so conscious of the need to encourage children to read for pleasure — as was demonstrated in this project in their stated aims and objectives, as well as by the amount of time they spent on promoting children's interest in reading — they may not always be aware of the small amount of personal reading which many children actually do. At least part of the answer may lie in the following comments of the Bullock Committee:

The teachers were assiduous in their concern that the child should 'learn to read', but when he could decode to their satisfaction they came to see him as self-supporting. . . . We found, in fact, that some capable readers almost never read a book in school. They dipped into reference and information books, many of which did not give occasion for sustained reading, but they did not read novels. We also noticed that this was related to the teacher's discontinuance of any kind of record of the child's reading. . . . There were only comparatively rare instances of their knowing the pattern and balance of the child's reading, which is one of the essential features of a policy of expanding its range.

The knowledge that teachers are rarely fully aware of the pattern and extent of children's voluntary reading, led to the inclusion in the current project of a number of investigations in this area. The information obtained on the numbers, titles and levels of difficulty of such books selected and read by children aged 7 to 9 years, although not based on a country-wide sample, not only produced data of interest and value to the research team, but also provided teachers in the schools concerned with information on children's personal reading which was previously unavailable to them.

## II  Factors Affecting Children's Choice of Books

A child's choice of books for personal reading is affected by various factors, some personal, others concerning his home background, and a third set of factors relating to his teachers and the reading environment in the school.

Among the personal factors influencing a child's choice must be included his attitude to reading, motivation to read, personal interests and level of reading competence. Yet, before such personal factors can come into operation, the child's choice of books is partially predetermined by factors within his home background and school. In this research, the concern has been with school conditions and practices rather than with home conditions, although some aspects of the reading backgrounds in the children's homes emerged in the interviews with certain children, as mentioned in Chapter 13.

Among the school factors affecting a child's choice of 'books for using' are the extent to which his teachers have promoted his interest in books; the total supply of books from which he can choose and their arrangement; the opportunities available to him to examine these books; the training he has received in locating books of interest to him; the help he has been given in selecting books appropriate to his interests, needs and reading abilities; and the time set aside in which he can read his chosen books.

It would seem probable that for many children such factors relating to the total reading environment in school could have the greatest influence of all on the pattern of their personal reading. Accordingly, the majority of these components of the school reading environment have been considered in earlier chapters of this book (e.g. Chapters 6 and 7) and in particular Chapter 11, in which the focus was on the ways in which teachers encourage and train children to use their reading skills.

Now comes the crucial question of what children do choose to read on their own? One of the main themes of this research, and of the report, relates to a statement that has frequently been made by Southgate (e.g. 1975):

> In all reading tuition the first aim should be to produce children and adults who want to read and who do read; the second aim should be to help them to read effectively.

For this reason, in this project, various investigations were carried out into the books children actually did read on their own, as well as the books they said they liked. The latter enquiries into children's preferences and interests in reading are described in Chapter 14, while details of books being read by children aged 7 to 9 years are outlined in this chapter.

## III Books Read by Children on Their Own

Three separate enquiries on the books children read on their own were made in this research project. The first two concerned the levels of difficulty of the books, and were undertaken by teachers in the reading research groups. The third was based on the children's own records of the titles of books they had read in the intensive study year.

### A. Levels of Difficulty of Self-Selected Books

#### 1. Teachers' views on appropriate levels of difficulty

This particular assignment, undertaken by teachers in the first Teachers' Reading Research Group, was a preliminary enquiry designed to discover what teachers of children aged 7 to 9 years regarded as generally acceptable levels of difficulty for books which children read on their own. 'Difficulty' was to be assessed in the simplest terms, i.e. by error counting. Before carrying out this assignment the teachers had undertaken an exercise which provided them with a common experience on which to base their general assessment of acceptable levels of difficulty of books. They had listened to individual children of different reading ages reading aloud a passage from a specified book (e.g. *Wide Range Blue Book 3* (Schonell and Flowerdew 1953) or *Ladybird Book 12A* (Murray 1964)) and they had noted the number of errors each child made. Notes on error counting had been provided; and briefly, every error, including omissions, substitutions and repetitions with self-correction, was to be scored. Teachers were then asked, in the following terms, what they considered would be a generally acceptable level of difficulty.

Imagine you are trying to find a book of a suitable level of difficulty for a child (i.e. *any* child) to read *on his own*. Suppose that to check whether the book you had in mind was appropriate, you ask the child to read aloud to you a passage from it. What proportion of errors per number of running words would you consider to be acceptable? (Tick the appropriate category.)

20 categories were given, ranging from the easiest level — 0 errors in 500 words, to the hardest level — 19 errors in 100 words. It should be noted that, at this stage, none of the teachers was acquainted with any method of assessing the level of difficulty of a book by the number of errors made by a child when reading aloud passages from it.

Completed forms were returned by 73 teachers, of whom 59 were women and 14 were men. There was a large measure of agreement among teachers' acceptable levels of difficulty of books. 66% of the teachers considered three, four or five errors per 100 words to be an acceptable level of difficulty for a book which a child was to read on his own. At the two extreme ends of the judgements, however, there were two teachers who considered the easy level of one error in 500 words to be appropriate, while two others supported the difficulty level of 10 errors in 100 words.

If these teachers' responses are converted into McCracken's levels of difficulty (see Chapter 9), the results of this introductory enquiry are as set out in Table 12-1.

Table 12-1

*Teachers' judgements of appropriate levels of difficulty for books children could read on their own (n = 73)*

| No. of errors per 100 words | Level of Difficulty (McCracken) | % of Teachers |
|---|---|---|
| 1 or less | Independent Level | 10 |
| 2 or 3 | Instructional Level (definite) | 33 |
| 4 or 5 | Instructional Level (questionable) | 45 |
| 6 or more | Frustration Level | 12 |

(N.B. Rather than accept these levels uncritically, teachers are advised to try to regard actual errors as miscues — see Chapter 16.)

It can be noted from Table 12-1 that if only error counting were taken into account, just 10% of these teachers' pupils would be guided to select books at their own independent level of difficulty. Of the remainder, 33% of the teachers would find it acceptable for their pupils to read on their own, books at an instructional level which would require the teacher's help, while the remaining 57% of the teachers would consider it appropriate for children's personal reading to be at an even more difficult level. The judgements shown here indicate that the majority of these teachers had not generally appreciated that the books their pupils read on their own, i.e. 'books for using', should usually be easier than the books the teachers are using as 'teaching books'. The results also support the need expressed by teachers in their preferred outcomes of the project for more knowledge about the grading of books.

The findings of this small preliminary enquiry were confirmed in a second exercise undertaken by the teachers in the reading research group into the actual books that children in their own classes were reading.

## 2. Difficulty levels of books being read

Details of the way in which the second investigation made by teachers in the reading research group was carried out have already been given in Chapter 9. The books their pupils were currently reading were divided into two broad categories: 'teaching books', which the children were reading with the help of their teachers; and 'books for using' which the children were reading on their own for pleasure. 'Books for teaching' were discussed in Chapter 9, where it was noted that the general pattern disclosed was that half the children in first-year classes and nearly two-thirds of the children in second-year classes were reading, with the help of their teachers, books which they were perfectly well capable of reading on their own. In this chapter, the parallel information provided by the teachers in the first Teachers' Reading Research Group on the levels of difficulty of children's self-chosen story books and information books is considered.

The same 197 children of average reading attainment, drawn from 57 schools, already described in Chapter 9, were concerned in this enquiry. Directions to the teacher on testing children on self-selected books were also similar to those already outlined. Each child was to be asked to read aloud from a story book and an information book which he had previously chosen for himself and which he was currently keeping in his desk or locker to read, on his own, at convenient times. If the child did not have such a book in his possession, the teacher was to ask him for one he had recently chosen to read for himself.

If the concept of an 'independent level' of difficulty, represented by one or less error per 100 words, is accepted, one would expect that in his personal reading a child would only rarely encounter a word which he was unable to read on sight or guess from the context. One would expect that the book a child chooses – or is guided by his teacher to select – to read on his own, would usually be easier than the teaching book which he is reading to his teacher. (Of course, this generalization is not taking into account that high motivation to read

Table 12-2

*Percentage of errors in children's oral reading from story books of their own choice*

| % of Errors | Level of Difficulty of Book | % of Pupils | | | | | |
|---|---|---|---|---|---|---|---|
| | | 1st year (n = 121) | | | 2nd year (n = 76) | | |
| | | Boys | Girls | Total | Boys | Girls | Total |
| 0−1 | Independent Level | 30 | 45 | 38 | 59 | 50 | 54 |
| 2−3 | Instruction Level | 41 | 24 | 32 | 31 | 32 | 31 |
| 4−5 | Instruction Level (questionable) | 21 | 19 | 20 | 6 | 13 | 10 |
| 6 and over | Frustration Level | 7 | 11 | 9 | 3 | 5 | 4 |

a certain book can sometimes overcome difficulties in the text.) Yet the details provided by teachers about the errors made by children in reading passages from their personally selected story books and information books showed these books to be generally more difficult than their current teaching books. Table 12-2 shows the errors made by first- and second-year juniors in reading from story books of their own choice.

It can be noted from Table 12-2 that only 38% of first-year pupils were reading free-choice story books which were at their own independent level of difficulty, while the remaining 61% had chosen books which, according to McCracken (1969), were at their instruction level or frustration level. The hardest book of all was such that the child was failing to read 12 words in every 100. A second interesting feature of Table 12-2 is that 45% of the girls selected books at an 'independent' level of difficulty, in contrast to only 30% of the boys.

Turning to the second-years, it can be seen that they more often selected for their personal reading story books which were at an 'independent' level of difficulty than did first-year juniors. 54% of them chose books at this level of difficulty, leaving a corresponding drop to 45% of children with books at the instruction or frustration levels. It can also be noted that by the second year, boys seem to be a little better at choosing appropriate story books than girls − 59% as opposed to 50% selecting books at an independent level of difficulty.

A summary of the errors children made in reading from their chosen information books is presented in Table 12-3.

The trend shown was for children to be trying to read by themselves information books which were even more difficult than their selected story books. Among the first-years only 22% of the children were using information books at an independent level, leaving 79% with books at instruction or frustration level. Just as with fiction books

Table 12-3

*Percentage of errors in children's oral reading from information books of their own choice*

| % of Errors | Level of Difficulty of Book | % of Pupils | | | | | |
|---|---|---|---|---|---|---|---|
| | | 1st year (n = 121) | | | 2nd year (n = 76) | | |
| | | Boys | Girls | Total | Boys | Girls | Total |
| 0−1 | Independent Level | 18 | 25 | 22 | 40 | 43 | 42 |
| 2−3 | Instruction Level | 44 | 36 | 40 | 37 | 25 | 31 |
| 4−5 | Instruction Level (questionable) | 25 | 21 | 23 | 17 | 23 | 20 |
| 6 and over | Frustration Level | 13 | 18 | 16 | 6 | 8 | 7 |

there was an improvement with age, there being almost twice the pro-portion of older children (42%) as younger children (22%) using books at an independent level of difficulty. Unfortunately, it was not possible to judge whether more children chose difficult information books than fiction books because the collections of information books from which the children, in the 57 schools, made their selections, were harder than the corresponding collections of fiction books, or whether the children experienced more difficulty in judging the level of dif-ficulty of texts in information books. However, data gathered later in the intensive study year, in the reading environment exercise and in children's comments on books they had read, all suggested that information books available for children of these ages were usually too difficult for the majority of them. Whatever the reason, it is cause for concern that 79% of first-years and 58% of second-years may be attempting to gather information for their own projects or 'topics' from books which they are unable fully to understand.

First-year girls showed themselves superior to boys in choosing information books at what might be judged an appropriate level of difficulty, just as they had done with fiction books. By the second year, the boys had closed the gap but had not reversed the pattern as they had done in the choice of fiction books.

The results of this enquiry into the books children were supposedly reading on their own, even after making allowances for the fact that a mere error count, without some attempt at assessing comprehension, is a crude measurement of the difficulty of a particular book in respect of a particular child, must certainly cause teachers some concern. That the fiction books children are attempting to enjoy as part of their own personal reading are more difficult than the text books they are studying with their teachers' guidance, and that the non-fiction books from which they are supposed to be gleaning information for their 'topic' work are even more difficult, would surely represent a complete reversal of the expected practices.

## B. *Children's Own Records of Books Read*

In the records of the titles of books read throughout the year, made by children of all levels of reading ability in the intensive study schools, three categories of books were clearly separated: books the children had read with the help of their teacher, i.e. 'teaching books'; books they had read by themselves; and books they had consulted for project work. The first category of 'teaching books' was discussed in Chapter 9, where details were given of how the exercise was carried out. The remaining two kinds of books are regarded as 'books for using', and are considered here as the books which children chose to read.

As indicated in Chapter 9, children's records of the books they read by themselves were likely to be less accurate than those read with the help of their teachers, as the former recordings probably received less supervision than the latter. Some children's records of books read on their own would probably be under-estimates of the number of books actually read, as children may have forgotten to record certain titles of books they only glanced at.

To a large extent the accuracy of the children's records depended on the quality of the teachers' supervision. Teachers varied in how closely they considered it appropriate to supervise children's personal reading. In certain cases teachers guided children's choice, occasionally listened to them reading passages from the books, and would not allow them to record the titles until they were certain that every page had been read. In contrast, other teachers had a more relaxed attitude to children's private reading and relied on their pupils to select their own books, to reject unfortunate choices, and to read the books either in a desultory fashion, omitting pages and passages which they found dull, or to read and absorb every page.

The numbers of books referred to as having been consulted by the children in topic work also showed wide variations in different classes.

Table 12-4

*Range of books read in one school year by three first-year junior classes in three different schools*

| Books | Range in Numbers of Books Read | | |
|---|---|---|---|
| | School A | School B | School C |
| Read with teacher | 3–5 | 3–5 | 6–27 |
| Read by child himself | 3–8 | 0–44 | 0–47 |
| Consulted by child | 2–4 | 0–17 | 0–5 |

The range in the numbers of books read by children in three first-year classes in different schools is set out in Table 12-4.

In School A there was clearly careful supervision of all reading activities, for every category of book. Every child read three, four or five teaching books with the teacher during the year, read from three to eight books on his own and consulted two, three or four books for topic work. Although children in the first-year class in School B read the same number of books with their teacher, these children were obviously encouraged to do much more private reading (up to 44 books being read by one child on his own), and to use more books for topic work. In School C children read many more books with their teacher (from 6 to 27), many children read large numbers of books for pleasure (up to 47), but the range of books recorded as being consulted was small.

The numbers of books read by children on their own cannot, of course, be disassociated from the size of books. Some were substantial texts, while others were 16-page booklets with an illustration accompanied by only a few lines of print on every page. These differences in the sizes of books made it impossible to carry out computations on them and inappropriate to dwell too much on variations in numbers of books read. Nevertheless the lists of titles recorded did reveal to anyone who is at all familiar with the book titles, that some children did very much more personal reading than others, and the amount was not necessarily related to reading ability. For example, the numbers of books read on their own, in one school year, by children of average reading ability, in four classes in the same primary school, ranged from 2 to 77, as shown in Table 12-5.

Table 12-5

*Range in numbers of 'free-choice' books read by children of average reading ability in one school, in one year*

| Class | Age Group | Range in Numbers of Books |
|-------|-----------|---------------------------|
| 1A | 1st Yr. | 6−84 |
| 1B | 1st Yr. | 2−77 |
| | | |
| 2A | 2nd Yr. | 28−67 |
| 2B | 2nd Yr. | 13−44 |

The children's personal lists of books read were also useful to the teachers who were familiar with the titles recorded and, consequently, able to judge the amount and quality of reading done by the children, as well as the difficulty of the books selected. Few of the teachers had previously trained children to keep personal records in this way and, at the end of the year, many of them reported on the value of this practice, and indicated that they intended to continue it and, in some cases, expand it. For example, one teacher planned to have children keep records of poems read, while another intended to have page numbers included in references to books consulted.

The fact that the researchers were not as familiar with all the book titles as the teachers, when combined with some children's tendency to record incomplete titles of the books, made it impossible to differentiate accurately between fiction and non-fiction books which children read on their own. What was obvious from examining the children's records was that many children chose to read non-fiction books as well as fiction, and that the boys appeared to read non-fiction books more frequently than the girls.

Some of the other trends which showed up on an examination of children's records of the books they had read were as follows:

(a) The numbers of books read by children on their own was not necessarily related to their reading ability. One might have imagined that the better readers would read many more books for personal pleasure than the slower readers. In fact, although there was a slight tendency towards more proficient readers reading more books than less able readers, this trend was not marked.

(b) In certain schools, when children had finished the reading scheme, i.e. usually *Wide Range Book 6*, they spent all their reading periods engaged in personal reading. (This practice accounted for some of the better readers recording having read only one or two books, or even no books at all with their teacher.)

(c) In contrast, some of the slower readers who only struggled through one or two teaching books with their teacher did not record having read a single book on their own.

(d) Reading small numbers of books with their teacher was not necessarily compensated by children reading many books on their own.

(e) The titles of the books selected by children often provided very useful insights into their interests and, also, the fluctuating patterns in their choices. Some girls, for example, appeared to read all available books on horses or ballet, while others clung to fairy stories and traditional tales. Frequently, the children, having enjoyed one book in a series, continued to read others in the same series. Some above average readers occasionally dipped into series which were well below their reading ability. There were also examples of children recording titles of books well beyond the difficulty of the books they were reading with their teachers, and probably also beyond their understanding.

The children's records of books they had read proved a source of pride to them, as well as an incentive to further reading. These recorded titles were also of interest and value to their class teachers and to the researchers who had been in such close touch with many individual children for a whole school year. These records, however, do not lend themselves to generalizations: rather do they indicate the wide variations in children's patterns of reading. Examples of different children's records of books read by themselves are given in Appendix 12-A.

## IV Summary

1. It was suggested that the ages of 7 to 9 years represent a vital stage for ensuring that the habit of personal reading becomes established. Yet, although teachers are anxious that this should occur, they are not always fully aware of the small amount of personal reading done by certain children in their classes. At the same time there is little research evidence available about the personal reading of these age groups of children.

2. The factors affecting a child's choice of books for his own reading may be viewed in three groups: personal characteristics; factors relating to his home background; and factors relating to the reading environment of the school. In the context of this project, the latter are considered the most important. School factors include the supply, arrangement and availability of the books and the guidance the child is given in locating books of interest to him and in selecting those appropriate.

3. A small preliminary enquiry into the general level of difficulty, judged by error counting, which teachers considered appropriate for children to read on their own, showed that only 10% of the teachers would guide children to choose books at their own 'independent level' of reading difficulty. The remainder of the teachers considered that books at the 'instructional level' or 'frustration level' would be suitable for personal reading.

4. A second investigation, relating to the number of errors children made in reading aloud to their teachers passages from a story book and an information book which they were currently reading on their own, also indicated that such books were generally more difficult than the 'teaching books' they were reading under their teacher's guidance. The pattern was of story books being more difficult than basic reading books, and information books being even more difficult than story books.

5. A third method of investigating the actual books which children read on their own, took the form of children's individual records of the titles of the books they had read. While the reliability of such records cannot be regarded as entirely accurate, they did provide indications of different patterns of reading. It was shown that the number of books read on their own, in one school year, by different children, ranged from 0 to 84.

6. Children enjoyed recording the titles of the books they had read. Teachers also found these records to be helpful to them and many planned to continue this practice.

## V  Implications for Teachers

The reports of the fairly simple investigations mentioned in this chapter may well cause teachers to question whether their efforts to surround their pupils with attractive books, and so encourage them to read, are as successful as they had hoped. The following are examples of relevant questions to which teachers should give careful consideration.

1. If children are choosing to read on their own books which are more difficult than their basic reading books, are they gaining pleasure and/or information from this task? If not, is the experience of trying to read books at what might be their 'frustration level' likely to develop in children the habit of reading or to discourage them from such a pursuit? Alternatively, if the children are understanding and enjoying what they are reading privately, does this indicate that they are being 'understretched' by their teachers in being restricted to a 'teaching book' at an easier level?

2. If children are truly finding many of the books they have chosen for personal reading to be too difficult for them, how did this occur? Was it because the majority of the books from which they made their selection were at a more advanced level and so more suitable for older children? Was it because the arrangement of books from which they made these selections provided them with no guidance about the levels of difficulty of the books? Was it because their teachers had not been able to give them adequate help at the time when the choice was made?

3. When the non-fiction books from which children are supposed to be gathering information for their 'topic' work are very much more difficult than their basic reading books, is the amount of time devoted to this activity in junior classes likely to be time which is fruitfully spent?

4. If a teacher does not have records of the books each of her pupils reads or attempts to read on his own, how can she know whether or not her efforts to foster his interest in books and to ensure that the habit of reading is being established, are successful?

5. If the staff of a school does not have some information about the proportion of available 'books for using', which fall into various bands of difficulty, as well as into different subject categories, how can they be aware of the gaps which need filling when new books are ordered?

# PART SIX

## Children As Readers

# CHAPTER 13

# What Children Think About Reading

## I Interviews

As a child's attitude to reading represents a significant factor influencing not only his motivation to read but also the manner in which he learns, the progress he makes and also his eventual use of his ability to read, it was considered important in this research project to try to gauge the attitudes to reading of certain children of average reading ability within the 7 to 9 year-old age groups. The most fruitful line of enquiry seemed likely to be personal interviews, undertaken by members of the research team with whom the children concerned were familiar.

Individual interviews were conducted with 50 children, randomly selected from children of average reading ability who were already under review in the intensive study schools. Usually one girl and one boy from each first- and second-year class were selected in this way. The interviews followed, to some extent, the pattern of those described by Reid (1958). They were carried out in an informal and friendly manner, so that although based on a number of set questions, they took the form of informal discussions, in which questions could be rephrased, if necessary, and interesting replies could be followed up. As these particular children had already undertaken various tests for the interviewer, the fact was stressed that on this occasion they were not being tested, but that the interviewer was very interested in their views. The interviews were tape-recorded so that the interviewer could concentrate on the discussion with the child, without the need to make notes.

The interviews were based on the following 15 questions which began with general questions about the children's own reading and the reading done by their families, before probing their views on reading difficulties and their ideas of the purpose of reading.

1. Do you like reading or not? (Why?)
2. Do you think you are a good reader? (What makes you think that?)
3. Do you prefer to read quietly to yourself or to read aloud to someone else? (Why is that?)
4. Do you read a lot at home?

5. What kind of books do you like best?
6. Where do you get the books from?
7. Do the people at home read much?
8. What sort of things do they read?
9. What made you choose this book?[1]
10. Is this a difficult (hard) book?
    Is it more difficult or less difficult than the book you are reading with your teacher?
11. Why (or how) is this book difficult? What is difficult about it?
12. Show me a difficult word. What makes it hard?
13. When you are reading by yourself, if you come to a word you don't know, what do you do about it?
14. Do you think children should learn to read? Why?
15. Why do you think grown-ups need to be able to read?

The children's replies to Questions 5 and 9, which refer to their views about books and their reasons for choosing particular books, are discussed in Chapter 14. The information gathered from replies to the remaining 13 questions, relating to the children's attitudes to reading and their ideas about reading are presented in this chapter.

## II Information Obtained From Interviews

### A. *Children's General Attitudes to Reading*

**Question 1 – Do you like reading or not? (Why?)**
In considering children's replies to this first question, it should be remembered that they had known the interviewer for many months and were well aware that she was particularly interested in reading. Consequently, it is possible that certain children said they liked reading in order to please the interviewer.

Most of the children interviewed seemed to regard the act of reading without anxiety. Over two-thirds of the 50 children professed to like reading, with numbers evenly divided between years and sexes. Reasons for liking it fell into three broad categories: it was regarded as either easy, interesting or useful. More reasons fell into the second category than into either of the other two: 'I like nice stories'. An example of the third category was, 'It helps me to learn new words.' The few children who said they did not like reading gave as reasons either that they found it hard, or that they preferred to do other things, for example, mathematics, writing or making things. Only two of the first-year boys were unable to give their reasons for not liking eading.

---

[1] Each child had been asked to bring with him, to the interview, the book he was currently reading with his teacher, and one which he was reading on his own. Questions 9-13 referred to the latter book.

Some of the first-year girls who like reading linked it with their mastery of the techniques. For example, one girl said, 'I know the words'; while another said, 'Because I keep getting the right words. I learnt in the top class at the infants'—and, as an afterthought, 'It's interesting.' One girl liked it because, 'It learns you how to get clever'; and another, 'Because you get more practice. You start getting on to a different reading book every time.'

In general, it appeared from the replies of these 'average' readers that most of them were just emerging from the stage in which they were preoccupied with the mechanics of reading.

It seems as if the positive attitude of these first-year girls may derive mainly from their pleasure in having recently mastered the techniques, since they showed no firm preferences for particular books or stories, merely expressing a mild interest in the kind of stories which they had encountered most frequently during the early stages of listening to adults and learning themselves; that is, fairy stories. Robinson and Weintraub (1973) discuss this point interestingly.

First-year boys gave more varied responses. Some used the word 'interesting' and one boy went further in saying, 'It's nice to read and I enjoy reading.' There were signs here that some boys had begun to recognize the usefulness of the activity; for example, 'You can find things out.' There were also indications of developing discrimination in the comment, 'I like it a very lot when I find a good book.' Some boys, like the girls, said they enjoyed reading more than other subjects because it was easier. One first-year boy, however, who only liked reading 'a bit', said that he found some of the words too hard.

All the second-year girls, except one, showed equally positive attitudes towards reading. This girl thought 'It has too many hard words and small print', and so she would rather watch television. Some children were able to elaborate with reasons. Some girls mentioned the excitement or interest of certain stories, for example, the fact that stories were about people and 'children doing exciting things.' One girl showed that she was prepared to persevere even if a story did not hold her at first – 'Some that you haven't heard of get interesting in the middle'. It seems that these girls were beginning to enjoy stories because they could identify with the characters, and were also willing to tackle substantial texts. Only two girls, like the first-years, liked reading because it was easy. Some responses implied that reading was a time-filler for inactive moments: 'I like reading because it's something to do'; while others got more positive pleasure from it, for example 'I like reading just for the fun of it.' It seems a pity that so few children were willing to admit to reading being 'fun', without tacking on such reasons as 'It learns you', or 'You're reading lots of words and you're finding new words.' On the other hand one may have to accept that this is a transition stage in motivation, and the less that children read for pleasure at home – or at school for that matter – the longer they are likely to regard reading as a task to be mastered, made up of such discrete components as learning new words or being able to 'sound out' unknown words.

Only two second-year boys were dubious about liking reading and in both cases they gave the difficulty of words and the presentation as reasons. The others who liked it gave reasons such as: 'It's kind of exciting when you get to the good part in books.' These boys were showing, like the girls, that the suspense of narrative was beginning to grip them. Some boys still connected liking with facility. One boy, for instance, said: 'I like it because I don't like anything else — not much anyway, at school. I like reading because all the other things are hard.' Another boy replied: 'I like books with quite small writing and words that aren't too difficult for my standard of reading.'

Size of print was mentioned by several children. It appeared to have a prestige value, and so the ideal book for many at this age, as for the above-mentioned boy, might well be a book which *looks* difficult, that is, with small print and few illustrations, but which contains familiar vocabulary. Many of the published reading schemes, incidentally, do not cater for this combination of tastes, since they tend to progress simultaneously to small print and hard vocabulary.

Although most of the measures carried out in the intensive study year showed substantial development between first- and second-year reading achievement, the information gleaned from the interviews demonstrated that reasons for liking reading showed little change across the two years, except in detail.

## B. *Children's Concepts of Themselves as Readers*

### Question 2 — Do you think you are a good reader? What makes you think that?

In reply to the question, 'Do you think you are a good reader?', half the children interviewed saw themselves as good readers, one-third were doubtful, and the remaining seven children were sure that they were not good at reading. There was little difference in the pattern of responses between the two years.

The answers to the follow-up question, 'Why do you think so?' or 'What makes you think that?', made it clear that most children derived their opinions of themselves as readers from the extent to which they found the task easy or difficult: this was particularly the case with second-year readers. Examples of such answers are: 'There aren't many words I don't know', (first-year boy); and 'Not so many difficult words now,' (second-year girl). Those doubtful about their ability usually cited difficulty with techniques: 'Well, I'm a bit good — I sometimes get stuck on words, but I don't get stuck on all of them'; 'I can't pronounce words properly', (second-year girl); 'I keep stopping if I don't know a word', (second-year girl). Question — 'Are there a lot of words you don't know?' Reply — 'Quite a few. Words I've never heard of.'

In every case of doubt it was the difficulty in decoding individual words that was raised, not the intricacies of following a story-line or general lack of confidence in, for instance, phonic rules. The children's mastery of strategies, like using phonic cues or guessing from context, seemed therefore to operate at an intuitive level; the children were not aware of applying rules, although they must have been doing so. They were only aware that they were unable to tackle individual words, and so doubts arose when a passage of text contained a high proportion of words which they did not recognize.

These children were very much aware, however, of their achievements in relation to others, and many of them built their self-concepts from comparison with other children. One first-year girl thought that she read as well as her eleven-year-old brother. Clyde (first-year), who thought his reading was 'O.K.', said 'Some people are on higher and some on lower books.' Stephen, a first-year who did not think himself a good reader, explained this by saying, 'Not the best in our class, because there are people on higher reading books.' A similar comparison was made by a second-year girl — 'I'm not all that good. Half good.' Question — 'Are some people better?' Answer — 'Yes, because some are on library books and they're all past me. They're not on *Wide Range*.' Robert, a second-year, judged his position by stating: 'I'm not the worst reader. I'm in the top group. I think I've only got two more *Wide Range* books to go before I go on to library.' James, a second-year boy who was actually a good reader but in a high-achieving school, said: 'I'm not really good. I don't find the words hard, but I'm almost bottom. Mrs. H. has got a chart and you see your name, whether you're first, second, third, fourth, fifth, sixth, seventh. It depends how you read when she comes round to the group.' A second-year boy from the same school considered himself a good reader because 'People ask me about words.'

Some children were influenced by adults' opinions of their reading skill; that of both teachers and parents. A first-year girl said 'My mum thinks I am [good]. I read two pages to her every night.' Pamela (first-year) said 'My mum says so. Because I read one book a day.' A first-year boy mentioned that both teacher and mother approved his achievement. A second-year girl said, 'I read every night to my mother and she says I'm quite good.' And Amanda said — 'My uncle says I can read like an eleven-year-old'. It is interesting that more mention was made of the opinions of adults at home than of teachers.

Other reasons given by children with a high self-concept of their reading were connected with the amount read and the time spent on the activity, but these reasons were only given by second-years. Examples of such replies were: 'I read quite a lot of pages every day'; 'I have thick books and can read them'; and 'I read every night in bed.'

Amanda (second-year) was confused about her own ability, though it was considerable, because there was an apparent clash between her instructional and self-chosen material. She stated: 'I don't know really — yes or no. I was off the reading scheme, but I went back on. I've read all the books in the main library and there weren't any left.'

It seems therefore that the children's concept of their reading achievement was based partly on subjective feelings about their skill in overcoming difficulties, and partly on comparisons with peers and the opinions of their elders. In no case did a child connect being good at reading with understanding or appreciation of any particular story. Therefore, it seems fair to deduce that to these children, being 'good at reading' meant the mastery of word-recognition skills and the ability to proceed speedily through a graded reading scheme, using comparison with others' oral reading achievement as a yard-stick.

An examination of the relationship between self-concept and liking for reading showed that 20 of the total sample of children interviewed both liked reading and thought that they were good at it (slightly more in the first-than the second-year); while sixteen liked reading but were doubtful about their ability (more second-than first-years). Five children were doubtful on both counts, although nobody admitted to both disliking reading and being a bad reader. It appears therefore that second-years may be slightly more realistic, or even at times, pessimistic, about their reading skill, though the majority had a positive attitude towards reading and their belief in their own ability.

## C. *Children's Preferred Mode of Reading*

When children learn to read they are usually engaged in a public, and often competitive, activity, arising from the emphasis placed on reading aloud to teachers which is found in most of today's primary schools. Some time during the first two years of junior school most average readers progress to more or less efficient silent reading, in the sense that sub-vocalizing is not obvious, and fingers are not used to point to words. The nature of the act thus seems to change from the public, often competitive activity of working through the reading scheme with frequent checks by the teacher, to reading for personal goals such as finding out or for enjoyment and reflection — purposes similar to those of adults when reading. Many teachers give as one of their reasons for listening to children's oral reading that it is a social contact and that pupils like it and would feel deprived without it.

In order to find out children's preferences between oral and silent reading, the next question they were asked in the interviews was:

**Question 3 — Do you prefer to read quietly to yourself or to read aloud to someone? (Why is that?)**
It was hoped to discover, from this particular question, whether the children's views supported the teachers' theory. The results were, that of the 48 children who answered this question, 36 preferred to read to

themselves, and this total was evenly spread across both years and sexes. Only seven children in all preferred to read aloud, and four of these were second-year girls. Five children liked both oral and silent reading equally. It is almost impossible to classify the children's reasons, but the answers overall, and the certainty with which the initial question was answered, showed that these children, unlike those in Reid's (1958) sample, knew what 'reading to yourself' meant.

Although there was little difference in totals between age and sex in this preference for silent reading, the actual reasons given varied somewhat across the age-range. Most first-years liked reading to themselves because it did not disturb others, or because they were shy of reading aloud. Reasons given by first-year girls were: 'Cos it disturbs my mum watching the telly'; 'I'm a bit shy of reading out loud'; 'I don't like shouting.' Clyde (first-year) was more concerned with the peer group: 'Because people tell me to shut up and that.' Second-year girls did not offer this reason, unlike second-year boys, one of whom said 'I don't like people listening.'

Most first-years, though, were unable to say why they preferred silent reading, apart from two who felt it helped them to concentrate. Six children in the second year (two boys and four girls) thought it was quicker than reading aloud and several thought it was easier to miss out words which caused difficulty. Some of the replies are quoted in full to convey the complexity of the thinking:

*Alana* (*first-year*) 'To myself. If you're reading quietly in your head and you don't know some words you can just think.'

*Sean* (*first-year*) 'To myself. Because I can read in my mind.'

*Linda* (*second-year*) 'To myself. Because when you read to other people, it makes you go slower and you always stop on words you might not know when you do it in your mind.'

*Karen* (*second-year*) 'To myself. 'Cos I can read faster and I can read the whole story to myself, but when I read to Mr. T. you have to stop halfway through the story.'

*Robert* (*second-year*) 'Reading to a grown-up because sometimes I cheat to myself somehow. I miss out words and pages when I'm reading to myself. It took me half-an-hour to read a book with 150 pages once.' Question — 'Did you get anything out of it?' Reply — 'No. I read it again and it took me five weeks. And then I enjoyed it.'

*Ewobt* (*second-year*) 'To myself. If you say words wrong it's easier to yourself. You don't have to stop to get breath. I lose myself in it. I get away from the rest of the class in my head. I work myself into the book.'

From these responses it can be seen that there are wide differences in the development of skill in silent reading at this age, and it is therefore understandable that many teachers do not feel that they can assess reading progress other than orally. However, it would appear preferable to aim towards helping children to 'work themselves into books' as Ewobt did, rather than to imply that missing out words or phrases as Robert did is 'cheating'. If the purposes of silent reading are clearly defined for the children by the teacher, then even at this early stage it would appear that many of them could begin to develop study skills at a simple level, and come to realize that skimming and scanning are legitimate strategies if they help them in such activities.

## D. Children's Reading Habits

### Question 4 – Do you read a lot at home? Do you read more at home or at school?

While it was realized that the answers to these two connected questions could not be interpreted as objective answers, it was interesting to discover the children's impressions of where they believed most of their reading to be done. The results were somewhat surprising, as it might have been anticipated that children in these age groups would associate the reading of books more with school than with home. In fact, two-thirds of the children (with equal numbers in each year) said they read more at home than at school. Just under a third of the children thought they read more at school and three children thought they read about the same amount at home and at school.

The following comments, giving examples of when and how reading occurred at home, substantiate the importance these children placed on reading at home – often done in bed in spite of parental disapproval.

*First-Years*
'Sometimes before tea and sometimes when "Policewoman" is on'.

'Saturdays and Sundays I spend the whole day. Yes, when I go to bed, my mummy doesn't know, but I turn the light on and read. Cartoons and comics – whole books of cartoons. *Dandy* or *Bunty*.'

'A bit in bed until my mum says I have to have the light out, then I put my book away on the chair next to my bed.'

'Sometimes I read in bed and sometimes as soon as I get home.'

'I read a book last night. *The Faraway Tree* I think it was. The whole book. I bought it about a week ago. I asked my mum to buy me another in the same set – *The Enchanted Wood*.'

*Second-Years*
'I read every night. Any time.'

'More at home than school, but not every day. Sometimes I read a comic at tea. If I've got nothing to do. And in bed.'

'More at school. At home when I come in at night if there's nothing good on, or in bed.'

'Yes, I usually read at the weekends when I don't have a lot to do – my friends are out.'

'Yes, quite a lot,' [at home] 'Every night when my sister's gone to bed and I read *Oliver Cromwell.*' (Ladybird History Book)

'I sit on the settee and read for about half-an-hour.'

While it is impossible to draw general conclusions from the remarks of so few children, there does seem to be a difference between the child's concept of himself as a reader in school, where he is aware of his lack of skill, particularly in relation to others, and his happy acceptance of reading as pleasurable relaxation at home. As this gap between school book knowledge and home reading widens, it may be that older pupils will lose their pleasure in the activity and look on it only as a chore. Such an attitude is seen in the example of Mark, who, still a first-year pupil and a very good and confident reader, was not interested in reading for its own sake, but only wanted to master it 'so that he could stop it.'

It is vital that children at this crucial stage should begin to form their own concepts of the purpose of reading, and there were signs in some of the interviews that this was not happening. Britton (1977) suggests that the usual practices of teaching children to read in primary schools, with the help of reading schemes, kits and apparatus, may prevent children from discovering what reading is and what it is for. He goes on to suggest that the infant who pretends he is reading a story from a book may, in one vital respect, be further on the road to success than these children.

**Question 6 – Where do you get the books from?** (i.e. the books the children read at home)

Most of the children interviewed were able to state quite clearly where they obtained the books they read at home; and usually they mentioned more than  one source. Table 13-1 summarizes the sources from which the children said they obtained the books they read at home.

Table 13-1

*Sources of supply for books children read at home*

| Sources of Supply | No. of Mentions | | |
|---|---|---|---|
| | 1st year | 2nd year | Total |
| Public Libraries | 9 | 13 | 22 |
| Gifts | 8 | 12 | 20 |
| Personal Purchase | 6 | 10 | 16 |
| School | 10 | 4 | 14 |

(NB  As many children mentioned more than one source of supply, the totals across the different categories is greater than the number of children interviewed.)

Perhaps the most interesting fact to be noted in Table 13-1 is that the lowest number of mentions relates to borrowing library books from school as one of their sources of supply. This is at variance with information gathered in the reading environment exercise, in which nearly all the teachers indicated that they encouraged children to take books home, and seemed to be of the opinion that the majority of children borrowed library books regularly once a week. It is, however, impossible to know whether some children forgot to mention school library books as a source of supply for the books they read at home, whether they did take books home from school but did not read them because they were unattractive or inappropriate, or whether teachers were not fully aware that many children did not actually borrow library books from school on a regular basis. Several children did, however, volunteer the fact that they never took books home from school. Susan (a first-year) said : 'Mrs. D. never gives us books to read at home. We can take our *Wide Range* home.' A second-year boy stated:'School books are kept at school', while another said 'I don't get books from the school library. I've got my own – lots at home.'

As can be seen from Table 13-1, borrowing from public libraries was the highest source of home-read books and this did not vary much from school to school. This borrowing habit could well be the result of the practice mentioned by nearly every teacher in the intensive study schools of introducing their pupils to the local libraries – often taking whole classes at a time. Country children used the village library or the circulating library van. One second-year boy was clearly very proud of belonging to the local library: 'I have my own tickets', he reported. A few children belonged to more than one library. Of course, there is no knowing from the interviews how often books were borrowed, or how thoroughly they were read – but the same doubt could be applied to adult borrowers.

Presents, expectedly, were often spoken of as sources of supply and the varied collection of titles mentioned by the children demonstrated the doubtful merits of indiscriminate purchase of gift books for children. The gifts were received for Christmas and birthdays, or bought in the presence of the children on weekend shopping expeditions or the like. Mark, a competent although unenthusiastic first-year, obviously expected his books to be bought for him – 'People buy them for Christmas and birthday. I spend my money on ice-creams', he said. One first-year boy showed a more co-operative approach: 'My mum chooses and I help her. Sometimes she buys me one when I'm at school.' Leanne, a second-year, had been given a dictionary for her birthday, while Susan had a book as a gift from a friend: 'I have a big shelf-ful at home. Quite a lot that Mum and Dad have bought and one that Elspeth gave me for my birthday as a surprise.' Another second-year said: 'I got three for Christmas: *James and the Giant Peach, The Little Wooden Horse* and *Mrs. Pepperpot's Outing.* I like all of them.' Robert, a second-year who never borrowed books from school, said: 'I had two last Christmas — *Alexander The Great* and *Captain Scott*. I haven't read *Captain Scott* yet.'

One of the most encouraging findings was the number of times the children mentioned, voluntarily, that they bought their own books, and this occurred in all types of catchment area. Harry, a first-year, said, 'I've got about 200 books at home. I buy them from jumble sales.' Paul, a second-year, 'I buy them any place — Smiths. I buy them with my own money.' Other children also indicated that they purchased books from Smiths the bookshop. The replies of two second-year girls were, 'I bought one myself. *James and the Giant Peach*. Mrs. S. was reading it to us last year and so I bought it. I'm half-way through it.' 'When I had my birthday I buyed some books from Smiths. I save up my spending money and buy it with my own money.' Stephen, a first-year boasted: 'I've got a great big bookcase of my own. Most are presents, but I buy a lot as well.' Deborah had costed her purchases: 'I buy some Ladybird books 15p or 18p. My own money, but mummy gives it to me.' Julie had other commitments, as she explained: 'I get them as presents. I don't buy them 'cos I'm going on holiday.'

Some differences were apparent between the age-groups in the sources of reading material, as can be seen from Table 13-1. More second-years, especially girls, bought their own books and borrowed from public libraries, whereas more first-years took books home from school.

The comments on the sources from which they obtained books were generally heartening. They showed that most children at this age have books available from different sources, and many of them make use of more than one source. The fact that school borrowing did not feature more strongly in children's comments, however, may be a cause for some concern as it might indicate that already some children may be sensing a dichotomy between 'learning to read' at school and experiencing the pleasures of books at home.

## E. *Family Reading Habits*

It has already been noted that many children, in their attitudes and approaches to reading, were influenced by the reaction of adults in the family. In this, perhaps more than any other skill, the atmosphere of the home has an early and deep-seated influence (for example, see Clark 1976). This, of course, underlies much of the work on 'linguistic deprivation', as even when children have adequate spoken language, their ability to deal satisfactorily with the language of written texts is affected by early home background. In this particular project, although it was not possible to make case-studies involving home visits, in an attempt to assess the numbers of books in active use in the children's homes, two questions relating to the reading habits of adults in the home were included in these interviews. They were 'Do the people at home read much?' (specific mention of fathers or mothers was avoided because of one-parent families) and 'What sort of things do they read?'

## Question 7 – Do the people at home read much?

In answer to this question, father and mother were mentioned most frequently, with mother quoted as reading more often than father. Other members of the family were referred to, but usually in the context of siblings still learning to read.

It was decided to compare 'positive' with 'negative' responses about family reading habits; the 'negative' responses being when children said definitely 'No', or were unable to quote examples of adult reading other than, for instance, 'My dad sometimes reads the newspaper.' 24 children gave positive answers and 23 negative. This does not necessarily mean, of course, that half the children's parents read widely and half did not; it does convey what the children's impressions were, which were bound to be influenced by what seemed important to them. So it could be said that half the children interviewed did not think that reading played a very important role in their families. (In this context, the fact that parents may read after these children aged 7 to 9 years have gone to bed in the evening, should not be overlooked.)

Some children elaborated on parents who did not read. The following are examples of such comments:

'My mum is too busy washing and ironing. Dad has to wash the car.'

'They don't read as much as me. My dad used to but he doesn't now. My mum reads on holiday.'

'Dad reads the paper, otherwise they don't read.'

'Daddy doesn't read because he's often at work, doing work or watching TV.'

## Question 8 – What sort of things do they read?

Those children who gave positive answers to the question 'Do the people at home read much?' were asked the follow-up question, 'What sort of things do they read?' Replies to this question indicated that second-year girls seemed to notice what was being read by their parents more than others, but many children offered some information about the nature of the reading done at home.

Newspapers and magazines were mentioned 27 times, and evidently formed the bulk of family reading. Some parents read newspapers intermittently: for example, 'Dad reads the newspaper – bits of it'; and 'Dad reads the paper on a Sunday'; whereas others read them avidly: 'My dad reads the newspaper – he can't go without it.' Other informational material was cited, such as: 'My mum does crosswords with a bit of reading'; 'Dad reads how to fix the car'; 'Mum reads cookery books'; 'Dad reads something about motor-racing always'; 'My mummy and daddy read Yoga books.' In all, nine references were made to this type of functional reading matter.

Eighteen children said that their parents read books, and in some cases they were able to detail contents and frequency of such reading. It should be remembered, however, that the term 'books' is used synonymously with 'magazines' in some homes. Examples of comments on books read by parents were as follows:

'Mum reads love stories. Dad reads battles and wars.'

'My mum reads two books a night. She likes love stories.'

'My dad buys great big books.'

'Mum reads rude books. She's got *Confessions of a Private Soldier* from my uncle. My dad reads it too.'

'My dad reads every night. Books about sex and all that.'

One might have expected the responses to these two questions to reflect the socio-economic status of the parents but there was no apparent difference in the replies of children from schools in different socio-economic areas, either in the type or amount of reading done by parents (as seen by the children). The general conclusion is that some children were much more aware than others of the presence and use of reading matter in their homes with girls apparently noticing more than boys.

Since there seemed to be such variety in the amount of reading being done in different homes, and the class teacher cannot always be aware of the varying amounts done in different children's homes, it is clearly important that all children should be encouraged to undertake out-of-school reading. Information obtained in the Reading Environment Exercise indicated that teachers were conscious of this need and tried to fulfil it by means of book fairs, book clubs, taking children to the public libraries and interesting them in the books available in the school for borrowing to take home.

## F. *Children's Views of Reading Difficulties*

The questions put to the children in this part of the interview were concerned mainly with finding out how they tackled the difficulties which they met in their own reading. Each child had been asked to bring with him, to the interview, a book of his own choice which he was currently reading. The questions and replies were related to these particular books. Not all the children interviewed were able to provide answers to every question in this part of the interview. (Replies to Question 9 – 'What made you choose this book?' are discussed in Chapter 14.)

**Question 10 – Is this book more difficult or less difficult than the book you are reading with your teacher?**

Of the 27 children who answered this question, 16 thought that their self-chosen book was harder than their reading book, and 11 thought it easier. A slight divergence occurred between boys in the two age groups, as 6 first-years thought their self-chosen book was harder than the book they were reading with their teachers, while two thought it easier; compared with 5 second-years who thought their self-chosen book easier while two considered it to be harder. But these differences may only be a result of the small sample.

The next three questions asked were designed to probe the nature of the difficulties which children experienced and their strategies for dealing with them. Reid (1966) found in her interviews with 5 to 6 year-olds that most of them did not admit to difficulty in reading. When they did so, reference was usually made to hard words, though some could not find examples in the texts they brought with them. Similar questions were asked of the children aged 7 to 9+ interviewed in this project, with regard to the book(s) they brought to the interview.

### Question 11 – Why (or how) is this book difficult?
### What is difficult about it?

When the children were asked this question about what made a book difficult, the responses were closely in line with Reid's (1966) findings. 27 comments emphasized *hard words,* by far the greatest cause of difficulty in both years. Many children referred to *long words.* There was some evidence, though, of awareness of other elements developing in the second-year responses. Four references were made to the difficulty caused by *small print,* and three to the problems of 'bigger stories'. Such difficulties, however, did not necessarily daunt the readers. One boy, for example, said: 'The writing is smaller and there are harder words. It doesn't put me off – I try to look closely, but I am slower.'

As Reid (1966) says, it is difficult to know how far the children are selecting what seems the most obvious cause of difficulty, and also what exactly they mean by 'hard words'. It is sometimes a hitherto unencountered word that is referred to, or an 'easy' word in an unfamiliar context. However, it seems clear that most of these children aged 7 to 9 were still concerned with words in isolation, rather than difficulties caused by density of text or concepts. The picture of these average readers' view of reading becomes clearer as their answers to the various questions are amalgamated. It can then be seen that most of them still regarded reading as a skill to be mastered at the decoding level. Their progress into mature reading is likely to be affected by such attitudes; those who consistently choose books for their phonic simplicity are unlikely to incorporate active contextual prediction unless they are given direct guidance by the teacher. The possibility of children being put off reading by books which are too difficult for their independent reading seems, from evidence obtained, to be less likely to occur.  These children's self-pacing appeared to be generally modest, even at times laggardly. The few second-years who did choose books which they saw as difficult seemed to take pride in this choice and to make a conscious effort to master the difficulties.

## Question 12 — Show me a difficult word. What makes it hard?

When each child was asked to indicate a word in his book which he found difficult, the majority of them could not find an example. When the interviewer then went on to point out possible words which they might find difficult, in most cases the children either knew them, or were able to decode them successfully. This was so with such words as: 'hippopotamus', 'slithered', 'mechanical', and 'vegetables'.

The words the children did point out as being difficult, fell into certain categories. Some were multi-syllabled words which were hard to guess from context because of their abstract qualities; for example 'enthusiasm', 'organization', 'authorities', and 'protection'. Others were shorter but beyond the direct experience of the readers, for example, 'blizzard', 'oasis', 'prairie'. The children were often puzzled by foreign names like 'Ivanovitch', 'Mitshutzka', and 'Cassioepia'. One child said that he found abbreviations difficult: 'All these R.A.F. things and P.C. things', as he said. It is clear, therefore, that the few words the children found difficult were those which could also cause adults some hesitation. In many cases, the children were able to guess the meaning of difficult words by linking them with their own experience: for example, 'precious' — 'If they break it they'll get smacked'; and 'desperate' — 'If some-one wanted the toilet and they had to go.'

Unfamiliar names really cause less trouble than they appear to, since if a mature reader encounters them, for example in a Russian novel, he will quite happily use his own version of the name, whether it is correct or not, keeping it a constancy throughout. It is when children are still struggling with decoding that an analysis of miscues reveals different attempts at such a name each time it is encountered, showing the reader's insecurity in phonic skill. Help may be needed for the child who finds difficulty with polysyllabic words, to provide him with word-building techniques.

Reid (1966) found that the children in her research chose 'look-and-say' words as the most difficult. As she wrote: 'One was left in no doubt about the feeling of helplessness and frustration . . . of words which the rules they had been given did not suffice to illuminate.' From the preceding examples, it seems that these older average readers did not often experience such frustration, and that most of them had satisfactory strategies for decoding all but the most abstruse words.

The final question asked in this part of the interview was intended to probe how children tackled words which caused them problems.

## Question 13 — If you come to a word you don't know, when you are reading it by yourself, what do you do about it?

Most children were able to describe what they did when they met unknown words, and many of them mentioned more than one tactic. Table 13.2 shows the varying emphasis placed on self-help or seeking help from others.

Table 13-2

*Children's methods of dealing with difficult words*

|  |  | Numbers of Responses | | |
|  | Strategies Employed | 1st Years | 2nd Years | Total |
|---|---|---|---|---|
| Asks others for help | Asks Adult | 15 | 20 | 35 |
|  | Asks Friend | 7 | 5 | 12 |
| Uses decoding skills | 'Sounds out' | 14 | 15 | 29 |
|  | Uses groups of letters | 7 | 10 | 17 |
| Miscellaneous | Uses dictionary | – | 2 | 2 |
|  | Guesses | 10 | 13 | 23 |
|  | Misses word out | 5 | 13 | 18 |

(NB   As most children suggested more than one strategy, the totals shown in the various categories are greater than the number of children interviewed.)

It can be seen from Table 13-2 that asking an adult – usually the teacher – was the response most frequently given; it was mentioned as often by second-years as first-years, with girls in both years proving slightly more reliant on the teacher than the boys. Of course, it cannot be taken for granted that this is actually what happens; indeed, it seems unlikely that the teacher would be approached every time a difficult word was encountered. The important conclusion is that in making these statements children obviously believed that this was a reasonable and acceptable action to take, and moreover, many children, especially the younger ones, mentioned it first in their replies, showing that they *expect* to rely on the teacher. The categories in the table show how much these readers depended on help from others and on decoding skills, at the word level. Although some admitted to 'guessing' and 'missing out' words – and they usually only did this when pressed – certain children said quite firmly that they *never* missed a word out. Although these replies may have represented their beliefs rather than the facts, they do indicate that the children considered it wrong to miss out or even to guess words when they were reading.

Second-year girls were more prepared than any other group to admit that they missed words out. Only two children (second-year boys) mentioned looking up a word in a dictionary, showing that they were prepared to take independent action. Dictionaries do not help to decode a word, but give its meaning, so it appears that these boys accepted 'a word you don't *know*' as 'a word you don't understand' thereby showing a more mature attitude to the reading act.

Table 13-2 does not convey one important element of these answers, which was the order in which strategies were offered. The first tactic suggested can be presumed to be either what the child does most frequently when he encounters difficulty or what he believes he is *expected* to do. It can only be surmised from further knowledge of the children concerned which was most likely.

Examples of complete answers to Question 13, given by some of those interviewed, will illuminate the variety of approaches.

*First-Year Girls*
*Alana*
1. 'Look at the first letter then sound it out.'
2. 'Cover one bit then the other.'
3. 'Ask Miss P.'
4. 'Never miss it out.'
5. Sometimes guesses.

This child, who had apparently learnt all the right strategies, was one who made the lowest scores on the assessments administered.

*Paula*
1. 'Put three or four letters together.'
2. 'Ask the teacher.'
3. 'If he was busy I'd work on it.'
4. Wouldn't guess it or ask other children.
5. Wouldn't miss it out because 'it might be one of the words at the back of the reader and I'd have to say it then to the teacher.'

*Michaela*
'I try and read it. I try and make it right. If I don't get it right then I leave it.'

*First-Year Boys*
*Harvey*
1. 'I just spell it "magazine" (covers up 'azine') — "mag".
2. 'If I can't get it I go on to the next word.'
3. 'I might guess it by going on and then I go back to it.'
4. Never asks the teacher — asks one of his friends.

*Clyde*
'I used to try and guess in the infants but not any more.'
*Second-Year Girls*
*Julie*
1. "gradually". I'd put my finger over that and say "grad" and then I'd say "ually".

2. 'I make sounds out of it. And then I add it on to the other if I know the first word.'

*Rebecca*
1. 'I go to the teacher.' (*Q* – What if she's busy?)
2. 'Yes, she is often – listening to other people reading. In that case I don't know.'
3. 'Sometimes I guess.'
4. Never misses out.

*Amanda*
1. 'Try to spell it out – "des-per-ate" and then I just say "desperate".'
2. 'Might go and ask teacher' or
3. 'Just try.'
4. Never misses it out – 'I'd go on struggling. If it took me from quarter-to-one to five-to-one.'
5. Sometime guesses.

*Second-Year Boys*
*Ewobt*
1. 'Try to work it out.'
2. 'Look in the dictionary.'
3. 'Ask teacher.'
4. 'I would think there are other words I can remember that look like it.'

It appears that what children *say* they do may be actually very different from what they *do* when encountering difficulties. Even at this early stage, they responded by suiting what they said to what they believed the teacher expected of them. They know that they are supposed to 'sound out' words and often attempt to do so, letter by letter; they think they should never guess or miss out a word, although in reality they often, sensibly, do so. Some of their faulty strategies probably emanate from their teachers' concentration on listening to oral reading.

## G. *The Purpose of Reading*

Reid (1958), in her investigation of thirteen 5 to 6 year-old boys and their reading, found that all her sample thought that the purpose of reading was 'So that they could read when they were big or grown-up; to read newspapers or books in connection with work.' No child said anything about reading being necessary in school, or having an immediate usefulness. The results of the interviews in this project showed a similar trend, but with certain differences, particularly in the upper age range. Children were asked two questions about their views on the purpose of reading.

**Question 14 – Do you think children should learn to read? Why?**
Not all the children interviewed were able to formulate a reply to
this question. Table 13-3 shows the number of occasions on which
different purposes were mentioned.

Table 13-3

*Reasons provided by children on why children should
learn to read*

| Categories of Reasons | No. of Mentions |
| --- | --- |
| An aid to further learning | 12 |
| To help with spelling, writing, etc. | 11 |
| For information | 8 |
| For pleasure | 3 |
| Some use (no reason given) | 4 |
| No use | 3 |

The 12 children who regarded reading as an aid to further learning
were equally divided between the two age-groups. These examples of
children who could see a direct purpose in reading for school work
contrasted with Reid's younger sample, none of whom gave such
reasons In the group of 7 to 9 year-olds in the current project, even
some first-years were aware of the need to read to prepare for future
schooling. The following are examples of such comments:

'When you're a teenager you get lots of books and you have to study
Chapter 2 or Chapter 4 sometimes. If you can't read it's a bit too bad
for you.' (Second-year girl)

'When they go to secondary they'd get into trouble (without reading) –
like my sister.'

'When they go to secondary school they'll be doing harder work and
harder sums.'

The second most common reason given by six first-years and five
second-years was to help with spelling and writing – that is, a kind of
circular activity. The following are examples of such comments from
first-years. 'When they've learnt to read they get the hang of it –
learn difficult words'; 'You can spell as well.' One child mentioned
the need for 'practice at doing it' in order to get on to *Wide Range*
and *Through The Rainbow* reading schemes. Another boy, one of the
best readers in the sample, thought it useful for children to know how
to read 'and then they can stop.' Second-year boys began to realize
the social drawbacks of not being able to read: 'If they didn't read
they'd have to go to a special class'; and 'You sometimes get teased if
you can't read.'

The third reason provided, namely reading to gain information, was given by six second-years, but only two first-years. One of the first-year girls thought reading useful to '. . . find out things about animals, in case I go somewhere where there are dangerous animals.' But, in general, there was no recognition among first-years of any existing or imminent practical use in reading. It was the second-year boys who realized its value most. Typical answers were: 'If you get an invitation.' 'Train and bus signs, like "Stockport".'

Only three suggestions from the total implied enjoyment as an aim, and all three came from boys. For example, Peter, a first-year, said: 'It's a lot more exciting than just writing. You get things that are going to be exciting in a minute.'

The final question referred to children's ideas of the necessity for adults to be able to read.

**Question 14 – Why do you think adults need to be able to read?**
Children's replies to this question are categorized in Table 13-4.

Table 13-4

*Reasons provided by children on why adults need to be able to read*

| Categories of Reasons | No. of Mentions |
|---|---|
| For information | 28 |
| For work | 10 |
| To help their children | 7 |
| For pleasure | 5 |
| An aid to further learning | 5 |
| Some use (no reason given) | 5 |
| No use | 3 |

(N.B. As many children suggested more than one reason, the total across the various categories is greater than the number of children interviewed.)

The children's theories about adult reading emphasized its functional purposes. Many children realized that grown-ups did not read in order to better their spelling and writing, although some of the younger children found it difficult to project themselves into the adult mind: one first-year boy thought that adults who did not read 'would be sad and they'd start crying' and another thought that 'they might forget the words.' Seven girls mentioned that adults need reading to help their own children, for example:

'If their children don't know a word they'll have to go and ask them (i.e. the parents) and if they (the parents) don't know, they'd (i.e. the children) just have to miss it out.'

'If you've got children who aren't at school you can teach them to read if they're at home a bit.'

'They can tell stories to children.'

The great majority of children, however, plumped for the usefulness of being able to read newspapers, letters and such like. The following are examples of such responses from second-year boys:

'In case a man from the garage sends a note they need to read it – and the licence.'

'They couldn't read newspapers and newspapers tell you more about what happens than the news.'

Several boys referred to reading about cars, for example, 'books about cars breaking down.' One obtains an intriguing picture of family reading from the acute observations of many of the children, and it is encouraging that they are so aware of reading as essential for the minor encounters of ordinary life. What seems strange is that they did not link this consciousness of adult reading needs more closely with their own newly-mastered skill, the direct usefulness of which was so rarely mentioned.

It was interesting to note that ten children referred to the value of reading in adult work. In two of these cases their parents were teachers. One second-year boy said: 'Like my father, he's a teacher. He'd have to read boys' or girls' work.' Two other second-year boys said that it would be useful to adults to 'read important matters in work' and 'when they get a job, signing letters.'

There were only five suggestions which implied that adults might get enjoyment from reading. A first-year girl said 'To read in bed at night' but emphasized the penalties of such self-indulgence by adding 'But if you leave the light on every night it's expensive.' A first-year boy said simply 'They enjoy it'; and a second-year boy more doubtfully, 'They might read for pleasure.' As against these, three children thought reading would be no use at all for adults, one first-year boy stating firmly that adults would *not* read for fun.

The overall picture that emerged from these particular questions relating to the reasons for learning to read, showed a developing awareness in children of the varied purposes of reading. The result which should perhaps cause teachers most concern is children's lack of emphasis on reading for enjoyment and the fact that few children saw it as a directly useful activity for themselves.

## III Summary

1. Of the 50 children aged 7 to 9 years, of average reading ability, who were asked whether or not they liked reading, over two-thirds replied in the affirmative, although it is possible that some children may have given the reply which they thought would be approved of. The main reason given by the children for liking reading was that they

found it interesting or enjoyable; the two subsidiary reasons were that it was easy and that it was useful.

2. Those children who professed not to like reading, gave as their reasons either that they found it too hard or that they preferred to do other things.

3. There were indications that certain children still regarded reading as mastery of techniques, while others had reached the stage of being absorbed by a story or taking pleasure in the information to be gained from books.

4. Half the children considered themselves to be good readers, one-third were doubtful, and the remaining seven children were sure they were not good at reading. Their concept of their reading achievement was based partly on subjective feelings about their skill in mastering the mechanical difficulties of reading, partly on comparisons with their peers, and partly on the opinions of their teachers and parents – particularly the latter.

5. Of the 36 children who said they liked reading, 20 thought they were good at it, while 16 were doubtful about their ability. Five children were doubtful on both counts. Nobody admitted to both disliking reading and being a poor reader.

6. Approximately three-quarters of the children said that they preferred to read quietly to themselves rather than read aloud to someone. This contrasts with the beliefs of most teachers that children like to read aloud to them.

7. Two-thirds of the children thought they did more reading at home than at school. Many made a practice of reading in bed at night. Many children appeared to regard reading at home as a pleasurable activity, in contrast to some children who regarded reading in school merely as the mastery of skills.

8. Children said that the books which they read at home were obtained from the following sources: public libraries, gifts, personal purchases and school libraries – in that order. Most children obtained books from more than one of these sources.

9. Regarding reading habits at home, although half the children gave the impression that not much reading was done by their parents, the fact should not be overlooked that some parents may do most of their reading after their children have gone to bed in the evening. The remaining half of the children considered that one or both of their parents did a considerable amount of reading. In the latter case, examples of the kinds of reading materials were frequently quoted, with newspapers and magazines featuring more often than books.

10. When children were asked about the difficulty of the books they had selected to read on their own, the larger proportion of them

considered these books to be harder than the books they were currently reading with their teachers.

11. In speaking of difficulties encountered in reading books, the majority of the children emphasized 'hard words', while others referred to 'long words'. A few children mentioned either 'small print' or 'bigger stories'. Their replies indicated that most of the children still regarded reading as a skill to be mastered at the decoding level.

12. When each child was asked to indicate a word in his book which he regarded as difficult, the majority could not find an example. When the interviewer pointed out words they might find difficult, children were generally able to 'guess' them from the context. Words which caused real difficulty were either polysyllabic words, foreign names or words with abstract meanings.

13. On being asked what they did when they came across a 'difficult' word, most children were able to describe how they tackled it, and many mentioned more than one tactic. Asking help from an adult, usually a teacher, was the most frequently named strategy. Next in the order of responses was 'sounding it out', followed by 'guessing'. Frequently, however, 'sounding it out' was the first method mentioned by the children. The older children spoke of 'missing out' difficult words more often than did the younger age-group.

14. When asked why they thought children should learn to read, not every child was able to formulate a reply. Of the reasons given by other children, the three which headed the list were: an aid to further learning; to help with writing and spelling; and to obtain information. Only three suggestions mentioned enjoyment as an aim.

15. When asked why they thought adults needed to be able to read, children again emphasized the functional purposes of reading, for example the usefulness of being able to read letters and newspapers. Some saw the need for reading in their fathers' occupations, while others mentioned reading as an aid to hobbies and interests. There were only five suggestions which implied that adults might gain enjoyment from being able to read.

## IV Implications for Teachers

1. The fact that three-quarters of the children stated that they preferred to read silently to themselves rather than aloud to their teachers or parents, contrasts with the views held by most of their teachers, who spend most of their reading periods listening to children's oral reading. It could be that the practice of reading aloud to the teacher, and being prompted on individual words which they find difficult, or alternatively, encouraged to 'sound out' these words, is the cause of certain children, even at this stage, still regarding reading as the mastery of techniques. More emphasis on silent reading for pleasure, with an

encouragement to 'guess' the meaning of unknown words from the context, would be likely to produce more fluent readers who regarded reading as an enjoyable pursuit.

2. The pleasure which so many children expressed about the reading they did at home, contrasted with the views of those children who clearly regarded reading at school in terms of word recognition and the application of phonic skills to unknown words. This finding reinforces the preceding suggestion that it would be profitable for teachers to emphasize silent reading, in order either to gain interesting information or to enjoy narrative prose. At the same time, it would help if teachers provided more time in school for these purposes, while decreasing the amount of time devoted to individual oral reading.

3. That large proportions of children borrowed books from public libraries and bought books for themselves must certainly be attributed, in no small measure, to teachers' encouragement of these practices by introducing children to the public libraries, to book clubs and to book fairs. These practices are clearly well worth following, and even increasing. On the other hand, the fact that borrowing books from school libraries was the source of supply least frequently mentioned by the children could imply that either the school libraries are not always stocked with sufficient appropriate books, or that there is insufficient time and opportunity for teachers and their classes to have access to the schools' central collections of books so that teachers may help children in their choices and be aware of how much borrowing of books actually occurs.

4. The majority of the children considered that the book they had chosen to read on their own was more difficult than those they were currently reading with their teachers. This confirms earlier findings in this research report (e.g. see Chapters 7, 9 and 12). There are two opposing implications which teachers need to consider in relation to these findings. If the books which children are supposed to be reading with the help of their teachers are sufficiently easy for them to read on their own, why do teachers devote so much time to individual oral reading from these books which inevitably results in very slow progress through 'teaching books'? Also, if children are gaining meaning and enjoyment, on their own, from more difficult self-selected books, should the easy 'teaching books' not be discarded? Alternatively, are children selecting for their personal reading books which are too difficult for them? If so, is this because the majority of the books from which they made their choice are too difficult for them, or is it because teachers lack the opportunities and time to guide their choices? (See Chapter 7).

5. The fact that children emphasized 'hard words' and 'long words' as the main cause of their reading difficulties no doubt reflected their teachers' frequent concentration on decoding. Yet, most children were

unable to pick out a difficult word from their self-chosen books. Furthermore, the majority of children could read or 'guess' from the context possible difficult words which were pointed out to them. The implications of this for teachers would seem to be that average readers of 7 to 9 have usually reached a stage when an insistence on decoding should be replaced by an encouragement to concentrate on global meaning so that minor errors and the omission of unimportant words are disregarded. The question teachers should be asking themselves is whether or not the child is making sense of what he is reading, rather than concentrating on whether or not he can pronounce every word correctly.

6. Answers to questions relating to the purpose of learning to read again showed that few children placed enjoyment at the head of their lists of reasons why children should learn to read and why adults needed to be able to read. Certainly teachers should be concerned about children's lack of emphasis on reading for enjoyment and the fact that so few of them saw it as directly useful for themselves. If the time spent on listening to oral reading was seriously reduced, more time could then be devoted to inculcating an appreciation of the usefulness of reading and the pleasure it can bring.

7. As these individual 'interviews' with children, conducted by members of the research team, produced such interesting and valuable insights into children's ideas about reading, as well as the difficulties they experienced and their ways of tackling these problems, teachers might like to consider the value of trying to arrange 'mini-interviews', on somewhat similar lines, with their own pupils. For example, instead of spending practically every reading period in trying to listen to large numbers of children reading orally to them for an average of 30-60 seconds each, certain periods could be set aside in which the teacher would devote her entire attention to a small number of individual children, for say 10 minutes each, while the remainder of the class was engaged in personal reading or other quiet work which did not involve interrupting the teacher. The aim would be to listen to the child's ideas on reading, his interests, attitudes and difficulties. These discussions would also, of course, provide diagnostic pointers which would be of value to the teacher. Such personal conversations with individual children could be based on a few of the questions used in the interviews just described and/or they might develop along more diagnostic lines in what many American writers describe as individual 'conferences' with their pupils. (See, for example, Duker (1971), Spache and Spache (1969) and Strang (1969)). Even one reading period per week set aside solely for four or five individual interviews or conferences would mean that each child in the class would have the teacher's undivided, and uninterrupted, attention at least once per term, while those most in need of such help could have more frequent conferences.

# CHAPTER 14

# Children's Views On Books

## I Introduction

The books children had chosen in schools for their own personal reading were discussed in Chapter 12. The emphasis in that chapter was on those factors in the school environment which had influenced the children's choice; for example, the supply of available books in the school, their deployment and arrangement, and the guidance and training provided by their teachers in locating and selecting appropriate books. It was also noted that children's choice of books was greatly influenced by their attitudes to reading and by their personal interests. Children's attitudes to reading were discussed in Chapter 13, while in this chapter information gathered in the project about children's views on books are reported.

Two enquiries were made into the kinds of books children said they preferred to read. First, two questions relating to children's choice of books were included in the interviews (described in Chapter 13) with 50 selected children of average reading ability in the intensive study schools. The second method of exploring children's interests in books was by asking whole classes of children, i.e. children of all levels of reading ability, in the intensive study schools to supply written answers to a questionnaire.

When the information from these two probes is added to the account of the investigations of the books children actually did read, (as described in Chapter 12), they provide a fairly detailed, and generally mutually supportive picture of children's personal reading in the first two years of the junior school.

## II Questionnaire

Supervision of the task of completing the questionnaire at the end of the school year was undertaken by the class teachers concerned. As it related to children's own records of books they had read during the year, each child had beside him his record of 'Books I have Read', open at the pages headed 'Books I Have Read By Myself'. The questions asked of the children were as follows:

1. Which book did you like best?
2. What did you like about it?
3. What kind of books do you like best?
4. Which book did you *not* like very much?
5. What did you *not* like about it?

The teachers were asked to begin by reading the questions aloud to the children, while they followed them on their own questionnaire papers, and to ensure that everyone understood the task. The teachers were then requested not to help children in any way with their written answers.

The written responses on 597 questionnaires were analysed – these being all the questionnaires returned by 10 first-year and 10 second-year junior classes. The detailed breakdown of sample size is set out in Table 14-1.

Table 14-1

*Children in categories of reading ability*

|  | 1st Years | | | | 2nd Years | | | |
|  | AA | A | BA | Total | AA | A | BA | Total |
|---|---|---|---|---|---|---|---|---|
| Boys | 52 | 59 | 30 | 141 | 64 | 51 | 33 | 148 |
| Girls | 72 | 53 | 16 | 141 | 82 | 57 | 28 | 167 |
| Totals: | 124 | 112 | 46 | 282 | 146 | 108 | 61 | 315 |

AA, A and BA represent 'above average', 'average' and 'below average' respectively, in terms of reading ability as categorized by the results of *Southgate Group Reading Test 2* (Southgate 1962), administered at the beginning of the school year.

## A. *Children's Reasons for Liking Particular Books*

In children's responses to the first question – 'Which book did you like best?', the titles of particular books liked and disliked were too varied and numerous to detail; in any class as many books might be mentioned as there were questionnaires completed.

Children naturally showed great differences in the quantity and quality of their answers to the second question – 'What did you like about it?' Some merely commented 'It is funny', or 'It was boring', while others went on to give lengthy accounts of the story line or provided quite mature expansions on their original general comments. However, the main reasons for a child liking the particular book he had mentioned in reply to the first question were that the books were amusing, interesting, exciting, educational, fairy tales, about animals, or about some character or situation with which the children obviously identified. Comparisons of the percentages of children, divided into categories by sex and reading ability, who gave the various reasons for liking particular books, are illustrated diagrammatically in Table 14-2.

The categorization, 'character identification', subsumes identification with any activity or situation of particular interest to the individual child, as well as with the usual identification with the male/female character of the story. The following are examples of comments in this category. (It should be noted that more of the examples are drawn from the answers of children of above average (AA) and average (A) reading ability than from children of below average (BA) reading ability, as the latter tended to express themselves less fluently in written replies.)

*1st Year Girl (AA)* – on *Coppelia*
'. . . because it was about ballet. I love ballet. I like ballet so much I wanted to read about it like Copplia . . . and I have been to Northen Dance Thearter.'

*1st Year Girl (A)* – on *The Little Cat That Could Not Sleep*
'I like this book because it is about a cat, because I had a cat called Scamp . . .'

*1st Year Boy (AA)* – on *Football*
'. . . and I like the game of football. But I don't like it when I get fouled.'

*2nd Year Boy (AA)* – on *Moonflight*
'It was about rockets and planets and was very exciting. . . . P.S. I keep watching for rockets in the sky.'

*2nd Year Girl (AA)* – on *The Magic Finger*
'It was good to hear a story about Cheshire, somewhere very near to where you live. It had the places I had been to (which somehow come up in my dreams) . . . it made commen remarks in the story that people really would say.'

*2nd Year Boy (BA)* – on *Some Different Farms*
'I like books about farming because my Dad brought a farm and My Dad and me go down the field to get the cows. . . .'

The categorization 'interesting' applies only to fictional story material. Whenever the general comment 'It was interesting' referred to a non-fiction title, the reason for liking the book was categorized as 'educational'. Comments of the 'educational' type included the following:

*2nd Year Boy (AA)* – on *Camping and Outdoor Fun*
'I liked it because when I go camping I know everything. How to set my tent and how to make a fire. . . .'

*2nd Year Boy (AA)* – on *Chemistry by Experiment*
'It told scientific words and told you some chemicals you can buy and find in the house.'

*2nd Year Boy (BA)* – on *The Monsters*

'. . . in the book it shows you how to make a monster you can make a monster out of paper.'

Table 14-2

*Children's reasons for liking particular books*

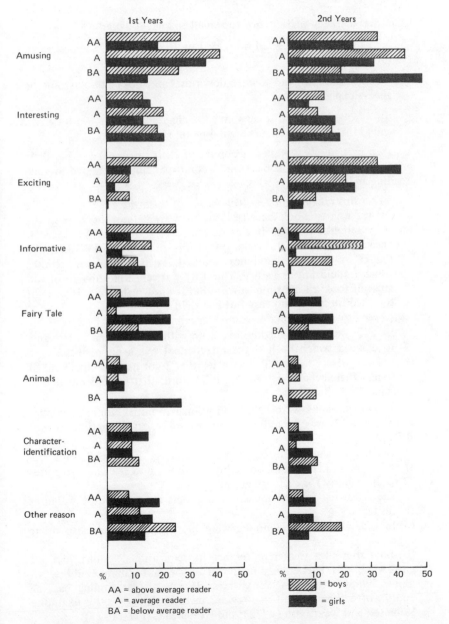

AA = above average reader
A = average reader
BA = below average reader

= boys

= girls

Only very occasionally in this section on reasons for liking a particular book did children comment on pictures, story length or word difficulty — these were frequently given as reasons for disliking books. The following are examples of such comments which did arise in this section:

'. . . it had easy writing, not too small and not too big.'

'. . . I also found it good because I understood it and there were no difficult words.'

'. . . if the author put a word down that may not be understood, he always explained it.'

'It was exciting. It was easy and the chapters weren't too long . . . and at the front they made a good picture.'

Two particularly detailed accounts of their reasons for liking their most favoured books came from second-year boys of above average reading ability.

### 2nd Year Boy (AA) — on *The Weirdstone of Brisingamen*
'It was a good book because you knew what the characters in the story felt like because it was described very well. . . . I enjoyed it because I was able to make out in my mind what it looked like thanks to the very good describing. I learnt lots of new phrases which I could put in a story. The story was very well thought of and must of took a long time to write but it was worth it. . . . It was not too hard for me or too easy but just right.'

### 2nd Year Boy (AA) — on *Professor Branestawm*
'. . . He was always getting mixed up with words. When I first came to a word which he had got mixed up I was a bit confused and had to go out to Mr. T. But after that I got used to that kind of thing. There were very few big hard words that I could not understand.'

As such expansions were always additional to initial emphatic comments such as, 'It was funny' or 'It was exciting', categorization was not difficult.

Table 14-3 shows the distribution of categories of children's reasons for liking particular books, broken down into sex and categories of reading ability for each age-group.

The following are the most striking facts illustrated by the figures in this table:

(a) In general, humorous books were more often preferred to other types.

(b) Boys showed a greater preference for 'educational' books than did girls, while girls, particularly in the first year, far outnumbered boys in liking 'happy' stories or fairy tales. This particular finding has, of course, often been noted in previous investigations (see, for example, Robinson and Weintraub (1973), and Whitehead, *et al.* (1977)).

Table 14-3

*Children's reasons for liking particular books (percentages of children giving the various reasons)*

| REASONS | 1st Years | | | | | 2nd Years | | | | | 1st Years | 2nd Years |
|---|---|---|---|---|---|---|---|---|---|---|---|---|
| | Above Average Readers | Average Readers | Below Average Readers | Boys | Girls | Above Average Readers | Average Readers | Below Average Readers | Boys | Girls | | |
| Amusing | 20 | 37 | 20 | 30 | 23 | 26 | 34 | 31 | 31 | 29 | 27 | 30 |
| Interesting | 13 | 15 | 17 | 16 | 14 | 9 | 13 | 16 | 12 | 11 | 15 | 12 |
| Exciting | 11 | 4 | 4 | 11 | 4 | 36 | 21 | 7 | 22 | 28 | 7 | 25 |
| Educational | 14 | 9 | 11 | 16 | 6 | 7 | 13 | 8 | 18 | 2 | 11 | 9 |
| Fairy Tale | 14 | 11 | 13 | 4 | 21 | 7 | 7 | 10 | 2 | 13 | 12 | 8 |
| Animals | 5 | 4 | 9 | 3 | 8 | 3 | 2 | 7 | 5 | 2 | 5 | 4 |
| Character Identification | 10 | 7 | 6 | 8 | 9 | 6 | 5 | 8 | 4 | 7 | 9 | 6 |
| Other (Poems etc) | 13 | 13 | 20 | 12 | 16 | 7 | 5 | 13 | 6 | 8 | 14 | 7 |

(c) The above average readers outnumbered the average and below average readers in their preference for excitement books.

(d) The percentage of second-year children appreciating excitement (adventure/mystery) showed a great increase over that for first-years; most other categories having reduced percentages.

## B. *Children's General Preference for Books*

The third question moved from the specific to the general by asking the children 'What kind of books do you like best?' Responses to this question fell into the same categories as replies to the preceding specific question, except that the 'character identification' and 'interesting' categories were not in evidence. The 'exciting' category shown in Table 14-3 is represented by 'adventure' which subsumes adventure, mystery, Enid Blyton (particularly the *Famous Five* series which was often mentioned) and war/crime/science fiction.

The factual category includes specific preferences such as 'motorcycles', 'football', 'the army', as well as the general 'non-fiction', 'scholastic' and 'the true story'. Again a graphical representation of the findings may be helpful, and is given in Table 14-4.

The 'other' category covers those comments not easily assigned to specific headings such as:

'I liked the poetry books best, because it covers your spare time up . . .' (2nd Year Boy – AA)

'. . . ones with a lot of ritting.' (1st Year Boy – A)

'I like harder ones because I am too old for easy ones.' (1st Year Girl – AA)

The percentage distribution of children's preferred types of books, in response to the third question, is set out in categories in Table 14-5.

Children's comments on the kinds of books they liked in general showed, as one would expect, a number of similarities with the reasons given for liking their favourite book. The main points to note in Table 14-5 are the following:

(a) While the preference for adventure/mystery books heads the list of both first- and second-year juniors, it shows a dramatic increase among the older age-group.

(b) As before, girls consistently outnumber boys in appreciating fairy stories and boys outnumber girls in their liking for factual material.

(c) The preference for amusing books, although it does not head the list as it did in Table 14-3, in general remains stable over the two age-groups.

(d) One interesting fact to emerge, which was not so evident from the figures for particular likes, is the increase with age in the preferences of below average readers, and decrease in preferences of above average

Table 14-4

*Children's general preferences for types of books*

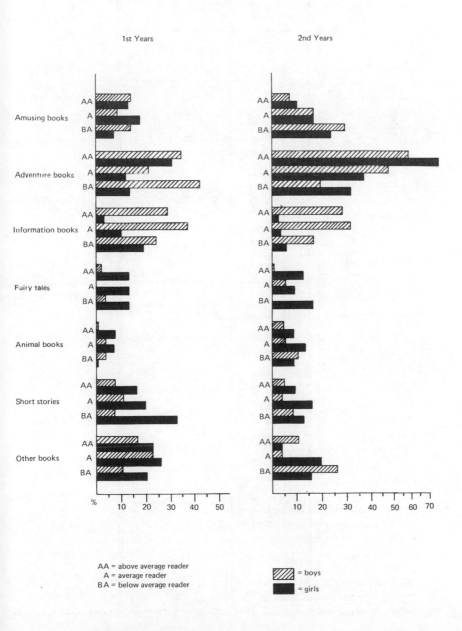

1st Years                    2nd Years

Amusing books

Adventure books

Information books

Fairy tales

Animal books

Short stories

Other books

%   10  20  30  40  50        10  20  30  40  50  60  70

AA = above average reader          = boys
 A = average reader                = girls
BA = below average reader

Table 14-5

Children's general preferences for books (percentages of children giving the various preferences)

| Preference | 1st Years | | | | | 2nd Years | | | | | 1st Years | 2nd Years |
|---|---|---|---|---|---|---|---|---|---|---|---|---|
| | Above Average Readers | Average Readers | Below Average Readers | Boys | Girls | Above Average Readers | Average Readers | Below Average Readers | Boys | Girls | | |
| Amusing | 13 | 13 | 11 | 11 | 13 | 7 | 14 | 24 | 13 | 12 | 12 | 13 |
| Adventure | 31 | 16 | 30 | 29 | 21 | 60 | 40 | 23 | 43 | 48 | 25 | 46 |
| Factual | 14 | 23 | 22 | 31 | 7 | 13 | 15 | 10 | 25 | 2 | 19 | 13 |
| Fairy Tales | 8 | 7 | 7 | 2 | 13 | 5 | 6 | 7 | 1 | 10 | 7 | 6 |
| Animals | 4 | 5 | 2 | 2 | 6 | 5 | 7 | 8 | 5 | 8 | 4 | 6 |
| Short Stories | 12 | 14 | 15 | 9 | 18 | 5 | 8 | 8 | 3 | 10 | 14 | 6 |
| Other | 18 | 22 | 13 | 16 | 22 | 5 | 10 | 20 | 10 | 10 | 19 | 10 |

readers, for amusing books. The reason for this is not evident but one might speculate that humorous stories may be easier to understand than the plot or theme of books of adventure.

## C. Children's Reasons for Disliking Particular Books

The fourth question asked was, 'Which book did you *not* like very much?' The most common reason children gave for disapproving of one of the books they had read but did not like was that it was boring: this was often expressed as 'not interesting', 'not exciting', 'boring — not funny'. However, quite often a child would expand on this general statement when it would seem that 'boring' really meant 'difficult to understand', 'hard words', 'babyish', 'unreal' or 'silly'. Whenever a further definition was given this was the categorization noted. A graphical illustration of the general findings is given in Table 14-6.

Table 14-6

*Children's reasons for disliking particular books*

AA = Above average reader
A = Average reader
BA = Below average reader

= boys

= girls

An interesting variation on the 'boring' theme was the complaint that the book was repetitive in some sense, either because words or because situations were continually repeated. Examples of such comments are the following:

*1st Year Boy (BA)* – on *I Can See*
   'Every page – I can see. I can see.'
*2nd Year Boy (BA)* – on *I Went Shopping*
   '. . . it keeped sayind the same thing over and over agen.'
*2nd Year Boy (AA)* – on *The Old Gang*
   '. . . they kept going to football matches . . . You would have thought
   I would have liked it very much because I am a boy but they went to
   about twenty football matches before the book ended.'

The 'easy/babyish' category includes comments such as 'big writing',
'too many pictures', 'too short', or 'silly'. The following are some
typical comments in this category:

*2nd Year Boy (A)* – on *White Elephants*
   '. . . it is a baby book it has fifteen pages with four lines in it so I
   don't like it now.'
*2nd Year Boy (BA)* – on *The Circus*
   '. . . there were no adventures in it and it had nearly a picture on
   every page . . . and it had big words* in it and it was not very long.'
   *(the child here clearly means 'big print').
*2nd Year Girl (AA)* – on *The Big Pancake*
   '. . . it had big writing in it and big spaces in between the writing
   and the pictures were baby pictures. There was about six lines of
   writing on each page and they were easy words. It was much too
   easy for me.'

The foregoing examples, which represent only a sample of many
similar comments, must be related to the fact that the children were
referring to books which they had read by themselves and had, pre-
sumably, selected for themselves. Yet clearly, these books were written
for younger children, with lower reading ability. One wonders if these
children had read them because the stock of books from which they
were free to choose were all at this level or whether the children needed
more guidance in selecting books for their personal reading.

Many interesting comments in this same category related to the
unrealistic nature of occurrences in the story. Apparently fairy stories
which are naturally unreal are at least plausible, and are therefore
acceptable. Unbelievable situations, which the children considered to
be silly, were strongly objected to by some children, as the following
comments demonstrate.

*2nd Year Girl (BA)* – on *Baba The Elephant*
   '. . . it is daft becos elephants live in a zoo not in a big house . . .'
*2nd Year Boy (BA)* – on *Too Many Dogs*
   'How they get a lot of dogs all in one day it is impossibull to get that
   manny dogs in one day.'
*1st Year Girl (A)* – on *Mr Mead and His Garden*
   '. . . because the things in it are not true I think this book is stupid
   there cod not be a hill of slugs and they would not go round a
   house . . .'

*1st Year Boy (AA)* – on *Jungle Book*
'I did not like it because of the wolves because I never knew that wolves could speak.'

*1st Year Boy (AA)* – on *The Clumsy Cowboy*
'. . . it is nothing like cowboys. I think that children should start learning from the day they are born and this is a bad impression on young children who are ready and willing to learn. How could a cowboy ride a cow. I do not like silly books.'

In contrast to the many complaints which fell into the easy/babyish/silly category, criticism of a different nature related to the difficulty of books. Such critical comments included reference to hard words, small writing (i.e. print), long stories, much writing, dull pictures and difficulty of understanding. The latter comment was often added as an afterthought, as in the following two quotations:

*2nd Year Girl (AA)* – on *The Tree That Sat Down*
'. . . it was boring and it was a boys book and I could not understand it.'

*2nd Year Girl (AA)* – on *Weighing and Balancing*
'I did not like it because it had lots of questions in it. And it got me muddled up.'

Inability to understand the book was also given frequently as a major reason for disliking it:

*1st Year Boy (A)* – on *Heroes and Saints*
'When I was reading it I could not understand what was going on.'

*2nd Year Boy (AA)* – on *Sir and Abu Kir*
'. . . it did not make much sense to me . . . I could not work this book out. I do not know what the aurthor of that book was trying to tell the owner of it. I thought he has not concentrated enough to make a good story.'

Besides complaining that a book was too long, contained 'hard words', had small writing, or was generally 'boring', many children also referred to dullness of the pictures which were variously described as 'dull', 'grey', 'black and white' or 'purple'. In general it seems that a moderate number of attractive coloured pictures are appreciated by children of this age.

The final 'miscellaneous' category of dislikes contains comments which show that some children dislike books that predominantly feature the opposite sex. Such comments may be regarded as the equivalence of the character identification category of reasons for book preference. The following are two pertinent examples of reasons for disliking a book:

*1st Year Boy (A)* – on *The Beast of Outdoor*
'. . . it has too many girls in it.'

Table 14-7

Children's reasons for disliking particular books (percentages of children giving the various reasons)

| Reasons | 1st Years | | | | | 2nd Years | | | | | 1st Years | 2nd Years |
|---|---|---|---|---|---|---|---|---|---|---|---|---|
| | Above Average Readers | Average Readers | Below Average Readers | Boys | Girls | Above Average Readers | Average Readers | Below Average Readers | Boys | Girls | | |
| Boring/Repetitive | 26 | 18 | 22 | 26 | 18 | 32 | 34 | 31 | 33 | 32 | 22 | 33 |
| Easy/Babyish | 31 | 35 | 16 | 33 | 27 | 24 | 17 | 18 | 25 | 16 | 30 | 20 |
| Hard/Long | 26 | 22 | 40 | 25 | 29 | 16 | 19 | 13 | 16 | 16 | 27 | 16 |
| Other | 17 | 25 | 22 | 16 | 26 | 14 | 20 | 33 | 15 | 25 | 21 | 20 |
| No Dislikes | – | – | – | – | – | 14 | 10 | 5 | 11 | 11 | – | 11 |

*1st Year Girl (A)* – on *Tommy's New Engine*
'. . . I don't like this book because it is a boy's book and I am a girl.'

Besides this 'opposite sex' theme, diverse additional reasons for dislike of particular books are included under the heading of 'other'. The following are some of the examples of unique and individual complaints:

*1st Year Girl (AA)* – on *Jack and the Beanstalk*
'. . . because the page was old and tatty.'
*2nd Year Girl (AA)* – on *Grandad and the Magic Barrel*
'. . . a counened read it properly cause it didn't have many speech marks or any full stops and commers . . .'
*2nd Year Girl (AA)* – on *Black Beauty*
'. . . because black beauty keeps getting hit.'
*2nd Year Boy (AA)* – on *The Human Body*
'. . . because it shows you parts of the body that are not very nice like your brain.'

The percentage distribution figures of children's reasons for disliking a particular book are shown in Table 14-7.

These general findings show that not only did these children aged 7 to 9 provide numerous reasons for disliking particular books they had read, but they also demonstrated that they possessed keen critical faculties already fairly well developed. Some of the main points to be noted from the figures presented in Table 14-7 are as follows:

(a) Similar numbers of first-year children disliked particular books because they were either too difficult for them (27%) or because they were too easy and/or babyish (30%). These proportions reduced to 16% and 20% respectively for second-years.

(b) The complaint that particular books were boring or repetitive was the most frequently noted comment for second-year children (33%), but took third place in first-year children's responses (22%).

(c) In total, about half of the children in each age-group gave as their reasons for disliking particular books that they were either boring or else were too easy, babyish or silly.

(d) The 10% of older children who registered no dislikes in the books they had read by themselves – meaning they had liked them all – pose an interesting question. All of these children come from two classes in one particular school, and a number of them stated, 'I did not choose any titles I did not fancy.' It would be interesting to know whether this liking for all books read is a sign of a generally healthy attitude to reading (and, if so, how this was achieved), the result of careful guidance by teachers on children's book choices, or perhaps a reflection of entirely appropriately stocked class and/or school library.

## III General Patterns of Children's Views on Books

The clearest pattern emerging from the general expressed preferences for books was that in the first year adventure books were greatly favoured by all children, with amusing books, factual material (for boys) and fairy tales (for girls) following closely in popularity. By the second year, information books tended to lose their appeal slightly for the middle and lower reading ability groups, adventure books became even more popular for the highest and average ability readers, while 'funny books' retained their attraction for average readers, lost it substantially for good readers and gained it even more strongly than before for poorer readers.

On looking for these precise patterns in the figures relating to specifically considered books, interesting differences were found. For instance, it appeared that the book chosen as the most enjoyable by the children was more often an amusing book and less often an adventure book than might be expected from their stated general preferences. This was true for all levels of reading ability, but more particularly for the average and above average readers. For example, twice as many girls who were average readers in each year-group enjoyed a book for its amusing characteristics than might have been expected from their general statements of preferences, while for boys who were average readers the picture was even more dramatic with five times as many first-years and three times as many second-years showing this discrepancy.

In fact, while the expressed preference figures are interesting in revealing information on the developmental patterns of perceived opinions about reading matter, the criteria on which the children actually based concrete judgements about books really provided more relevant knowledge for the teacher about children's reading interests.

These general findings were reflected in the interviews with the 50 children of average reading ability referred to in the previous chapter, but it is their responses to the question 'What made you choose *this* book?' which are particularly interesting in this context. Few of the first-years were able to give coherent reasons for their choice. Many offered no response to this question, and those who did could only think of one reason. Of the 12 who answered, three implied that they were concerned with progress in techniques: for example; 'If it's got easy *and* hard words.' (Question: 'Why do you like hard words?' Reply: 'Because you can learn better.') Here can be seen further evidence of children's concept of reading which was described in Chapter 13, namely, a desire to master the techniques of reading; and also evidence of one child who was sufficiently aware to self-monitor her own reading development. Another child, however, chose a book because 'the words looked easy'; and this would appear to be a more universal reason for children's choices in the first year.

Three first-years said that they chose a book by the pictures, though one of them realized that this was not necessarily fool-proof, since she discovered that the book was too hard for her when she started reading it. Three chose because they had previous experiences of the book, through seeing it on television or because it contained a familiar story: for example, 'The Wombles — because I watch it every time on the telly.' Only one first-year, a boy, said that he looked in the front 'and it tells you about the story'.

Most first-years, therefore, had no real policy or strategy for choice of books and were, consequently, likely to encounter many disappointments. While freedom of choice must inevitably include freedom to make a bad choice, and this is desirable up to a point so that children's tastes can develop gradually, it also carries dangers for some children who might well be put off reading altogether by making unsuitable choices. This finding supports what has been said in Chapter 12 about the importance of teachers guiding children to make appropriate choices. It is also reinforced by the fact that none of the children in either year mentioned choosing according to a colour banding system or other form of classification, although some of the schools had initiated such aids.

Second-year readers differed from the first-years in that several mentioned more than one reason for their choices. Two girls said that they had not chosen the book they brought to the interview — the teacher had done so. Five children chose on readability criteria; for example, 'I look to see if it's too difficult. I read a page to see if there are hard words', and 'I look to see if it's too easy for me.' Another said 'If it's too easy I don't pick it — (after reading the first page); while one child looked to see 'what the words are like.'

Four children mentioned the influence of pictures, but usually combined this reason with another. Some referred to 'interest' factors, which the first-years did not mention; for example, 'It looked interesting and exciting — and had small writing'. or 'Because it was adventure.'

Some children gave more detailed replies, for example, 'I chose a book that I haven't read before. The name gave me some idea of what it was about.' James 'read the summary in front' and another boy said 'I looked at the tops of chapters'. One child said that she had chosen it 'because my friend had it.'

It seems reasonable to suppose that, given a large variety of reading materials easily accessible to the children, and a positive motivational force encouraging them to read widely, then by trial and error the children will form their own opinions about the types of reading matter they prefer. The teacher can to some extent guide the children towards 'good' books once their reading interests are established, but the most important task for the teacher, in this area, at this stage in reading development, would seem to be to promote in the children motivation to read. This seems particularly important in the case of average readers who may not feel as attracted by the activity as do more able children, and it is here that knowledge of children's criteria for judging books becomes especially relevant.

It is undoubtedly important to have a class library as appropriately stocked as resources will allow, and it seems from the evidence that even first- and second-year classes need rather different emphases. From their comments on dislikes made by the younger children in particular, and also by the older children to some extent, it appears that they are greatly impressed by the appearance of books. If a book looks verbose and, therefore, possibly too hard, or if it appears babyish by virtue of large print and many pictures, or if it simply appears moth-eaten and old, then many children will not choose it, or, if they do, they will not enjoy reading it. It is only if the general appearance of a story book appeals to the children that they will later judge the book on interest value or vocabulary difficulty. The teacher must, therefore, try to ensure that a sufficiently diverse collection of reading materials is available in the classroom to suit all tastes, and also attempt to match the book presentation to the age-group so that the appearance of individual books and of the library area in the classroom is such as to stimulate children's reading interests.

The knowledge about children's preferences on the content of books may be most useful in cases where children have difficulty reading, or for some other reason are not immediately attracted to the idea of reading books for recreation or information. Apart from general patterns such as the younger girls' penchant for fairy stories (and, though to a lesser extent, the boys' enjoyment of myths and legends), and the attraction to animal stories experienced by girls, especially in the lower ability band, the number of children who enjoyed a book because it was a fictional story or an information book about a subject or theme in which they already held an interest is revealing. It is a restatement of a fact often noted by junior teachers that reluctant readers can often be won over by being introduced to books at an appropriate level concerned with their individual hobbies, pets or other interests.

Children's records of books read, their written reviews of their self-chosen books, and class discussions of books are some of the possible ways of reminding children of the variety of books available and of the sorts of books they had previously found enjoyable. Many other ways of promoting children's interest in books are mentioned in Chapter 11.

## IV Summary

1.   In general a preference for humorous books headed the list of children's reasons for liking particular self-chosen books.

2.   Girls, in both age-groups, far outnumbered boys in expressing enjoyment of 'happy' stories and fairy tales.

3. Boys showed a greater preference for information books than girls in both age-groups.

4. Second-year children appreciated excitement/adventure/mystery in books very much more than first-years; and more above average readers preferred such books than did the rest of the children.

5. The item in the questionnaire which provided the greatest insight into children's views on books, was one in which they were asked to look at the list of books they had read during the year, select a book they had not enjoyed and write down their reasons for disliking it. Their replies indicated that keen critical faculties were already fairly well developed in many children of 7 to 9 years.

6. There were three main types of complaint about particular books, and these were that the books concerned were 'boring', difficult in some sense, or else were too easy, babyish or silly.

7. 30% of first-years and 20% of second-years expressed dislike of books they had read on their own because they had found them to be too easy, repetitive, babyish or silly (meaning unrealistic).

8. 27% of first-years and 16% of second-years disapproved of books they had chosen for their personal reading and had found too difficult for them to read or understand. For first-year boys of below average reading ability this figure rose to 45% (a figure to be treated with some caution as it is based on a sample of only 13 children).

9. The results obtained from the various enquiries about the children's personal reading, highlight the need for a much better match between the reading abilities of the children and the difficulty of the books many of them are supposed to be reading on their own. Even when allowance is made for the fact that high motivation can, to some extent, override difficulties in the text, large numbers of children were clearly struggling with books which were too difficult for them to understand.

## V Implications for Teachers

Teachers will have noted that, while certain of the findings outlined in this chapter relating to children's views on the books they read confirm some of the points made in Chapter 12, others extend one's knowledge of, and insight into, the personal reading of children aged 7 to 9 years. Particular points to consider are as follows:

1. Teachers would gain valuable information on their pupils' ideas about books if a written questionnaire such as the one described were to be undertaken by the whole class, perhaps once a year.

2. As so many children in both age-groups demonstrated keen critical faculties in judging the merits and demerits of books, are such abilities being fully utilized? Are children encouraged to record their comments on books, for others to read? In addition, do teachers arrange class

discussions and perhaps group discussions, which will draw on children's general views on books and personal judgements of particular books, while helping them to crystallize their own ideas and express them more fluently, orally?

3. As so many children expressed enjoyment of 'amusing' or 'funny' books, is there a good supply of such books in both class and school libraries?

4. Is not the fact that about half of the 30 first-year boys of below average ability found the books they were trying to read on their own to be too difficult for them to understand, likely to convince them that they are poor readers and that reading is never likely to be a pleasure to them? If this is so, then could such a situation be avoided if teachers were to ensure that these children's free choice of books operated within a framework of books which the teacher knows are within the children's capabilities?

5. A situation in which children themselves level a variety of criticisms at the personal books they have actually read, merits a good deal of thought and discussion. This is a valid and most important point whether the criticisms are directed towards the subject matter, the content or the levels of difficulty of the books. The following are some of the questions which need to be asked and answered in this context.

(a) Do children's criticisms reflect an inadequate supply of books within the school which cater for their expanding interests and widely dispersed reading abilities, inappropriate deployment and arrangement of the books, insufficient access to the books, or lack of adequate guidance in choosing books for personal reading?

(b) Alternatively, or in addition, has a practice been established whereby a child, having once selected a book, is expected to read it right through, however ill-advised his choice might turn out to have been?

(c) Would a simple system of grading books according to their levels of readability, eliminate some of children's criticisms about the books they have read being 'too hard' or 'too babyish'?

(d) What would be the most satisfactory methods of grouping books so that those children who preferred 'adventure' or 'fairy' stories could locate them?

(e) How might children be encouraged to find interest in additional categories of books to those they currently prefer?

(f) Could children's views on the sort of books they like and dislike, with particular reference to existing gaps in the provision of available books, be elicited and acted on at the time when new books are about to be purchased or borrowed from a library service? In other words, could children of these ages be given a greater measure of responsibility for choosing appropriate replenishments for the collection of books from which they make their personal selections?

CHAPTER 15

# Reading and Related Assessments

## I Selection of Tests

### A. *Testing for Different Purposes*

The various forms of individual assessments and standardized group tests used in this project were selected or devised for two main purposes. The first in importance was the need to attempt an assessment of the relative performances of individual children in those elements usually deemed to be related to reading competence.

The second purpose, and this applied particularly to the standardized group tests selected, was to confirm or establish that the schools used in the intensive study in the third year of the project showed such a spread of ability and reading attainments that they could, quite fairly, be regarded as typical primary schools.

### B. *The Selected Assessments*

An outline of the various forms of assessments and standardized tests employed in the course of the project, and particularly in the intensive study year, has already been provided in Chapter 2. In this chapter, further details of the tests themselves are considered and the results presented, under two headings; first, assessments of particular elements contributing to reading proficiency and, second, standardized tests of reading and general intelligence. The particular elements assessed consisted of:

A sight vocabulary of basic words – *Key Words to Literacy* McNally and Murray (1962);

The ability to define the meanings of words – the *Crichton Vocabulary Scale* (Raven 1951);
Phonic skills – a new diagnostic test.

The standardized tests comprised:

*Southgate Group Reading Test 2* (Southgate 1962);
*Wide-Span Reading Test* (Brimer 1972);
*Coloured Progressive Matrices* (Raven 1949).

At this point, attention should be drawn to the fourth element in reading mentioned in Chapter 3, namely comprehension, which is undoubtedly the most important aspect of all. In this project, the research team have not been so much concerned with reading comprehension as a skill but rather with mastery of the whole reading process, which it was believed involved an element of information processing in the sense that children inevitably bring their own experiences to bear on their interpretations of the text. For this reason the major probes used into children's efforts to understand what they are reading were centred on the use of Miscue Analysis and Cloze Procedure. The investigations undertaken in these two areas are described and discussed in detail in Chapters 16 and 17.

## C. *The Testers*

The initial screening test administered at the beginning of the intensive study year (*Southgate Group Reading Test 2* (Southgate 1962)) was undertaken by ten experienced teachers who were following an advanced Diploma course at Manchester University, and by one retired headteacher. *Wide-Span Reading Test* (Brimer 1972) (both pre-tests and post-tests) were administered by the three members of the research team, as was the *Coloured Progressive Matrices* (Raven 1949).

The testing of children's knowledge of *Key Words to Literacy* was carried out by teachers in the first Reading Research Group. Teachers in both Reading Research Groups also undertook preliminary investigations into children's phonic skills. The new phonic test devised for use in the third year was administered by the three researchers, as was the Crichton Vocabulary Scale (Raven 1951).

# II Details of Particular Assessments

## A. *Key Words to Literacy*

One of the prerequisites for reading competence is that the reader should be able to recognize, immediately, on sight, a large proportion of the words he encounters in passages of prose. (As noted in Chapter 9, reading experts are not in total agreement about the desirable proportion of such words but the suggested figure tends to be in the region of 95% of the running total of words in any particular passage.)

In this context, *Key Words to Literacy* (McNally and Murray 1962) can be of inestimable value to teachers. The authors produced a list of 200 words to which they gave the term of 'key words', describing them as:

> ... words very commonly used in reading and the ready recognition of which is essential for the development of basic reading skill. These are key words in reading. They account for a half to three-

quarters of the running words occurring in everyday reading matter.

Twelve of these words, namely 'a', 'and', 'he', 'I', 'in', 'it', 'is', 'of', 'that', 'the', 'to', 'was', comprise 25% of everyday reading matter. A further 20 are so common that they contribute at least a further 10%. A list of these 200 words is provided in Appendix 15-A.

It can be noted that only a small proportion of these words are nouns — which are frequently the words which children first learn to recognize, and also that many, such as 'was' and 'one', are not phonically regular. These features of the 'key words' make it particularly important that teachers should help children to recognize them on sight. The authors say of the 200 words:

> The words we list are not of passing importance. As and when they arise they should be given priority of treatment for learning purposes. They are key words in verbal communication for child or adult. Their immediate recognition is essential for fluent reading. No matter the age at which the average child enters on a formal reading programme the aim should be to have him read these words with little or no hesitation some time towards the end of his second year of reading.

Teachers in the first Reading Research Group tested the knowledge of these 200 words possessed by certain of their pupils of average reading ability. The first-year children had chronological and reading ages of 8 years ± 2 months, and the second-years had chronological and reading ages of 9 years ± 2 months (reading age based on Schonell's *Graded Word Reading Test* — using original norms). The children were tested individually by being asked to read aloud the 200 'key words', while the teacher recorded the number of errors made. 57 schools returned the results of this assessment for 197 children, of whom 121 were 8 years old and 76 were 9 years old. The results are set out in Table 15-1.

Table 15-1

*Percentages of average readers making errors in reading 200 'key words'*

| Number of Errors | Percentage of children | |
|---|---|---|
| | 8 year-olds | 9 year-olds |
| 0 | 20 | 31 |
| 1–3 | 29 | 49 |
| 4–6 | 19 | 11 |
| 7–9 | 15 | 5 |
| ≥ 10 | 17 | 4 |

The main points to be noted from Table 15-1 are as follows.

1. Approximately 20% of average readers of 8 years recognized all

200 of the 'key words' on sight, while the proportion of 9 year-olds was approximately 31%. While these percentages show, as one would expect, an improvement with age, they are still very far from what McNally and Murray saw as the ideal.

2.   If the category of an acceptable number of errors were to be extended to three, it would include half of the average readers of 8 years and 80% of the 9 year-olds.

3.   17% of average readers of 8 years and about 4% of average readers of 9 years were unable to read 10 or more of the words. (The highest number of errors recorded for an 8 year-old was, in fact, 35.) This range of errors from 0—35 illustrates that children of equivalent chronological ages and reading ages, as measured by a graded word reading test, can show quite wide individual differences in particular reading skills — in this case, immediate recognition of 200 of the most commonly used words in the language.

A knowledge of the importance of these 200 words, and information on the particular words each child does not recognize, is clearly of diagnostic value to every teacher of these two age-groups. As these 200 words make up half to three-quarters of the running words in everyday reading materials, one may wonder what happens to the children who fail to recognize 10—35 of the words. How many times must such children hesitate or stumble in attempting to read passages of prose and how does this halting progress detract from their understanding of what they are reading? Furthermore, children of below average reading ability will be likely to fail to recognize many more of these 200 key words than do children of average reading ability. Teachers who diagnose the particular errors and take steps to ensure their pupils' mastery of the words not recognized would certainly note improvements in the reading fluency of these pupils.

One further point should be emphasised about these 'key words'. The majority of them are what might be termed 'carrier words', which, when they are unsupported by nouns, verbs and adjectives, have little meaning on their own. They are, therefore, more difficult for children to recognize on sight than those words which carry greater intrinsic meaning. In helping children to achieve instant recognition of 'key words', teachers should make use of the most interesting games in their repertoire for mastery of sight words, rather than relying solely on flash card drill. McNally and Murray (1962) suggest a number of such games and no doubt every teacher will have her own favourite means for extending children's instant recognition of sight words. A sensible practice would be to reserve the most enjoyable or exciting games for use with the dullest words, i.e. most of the 'key words'.

## B.  *Word Meanings*

### 1. Selection of a test

In considering 'key words' in isolation, the emphasis on immediate recognition inevitably centred on the child's ability to pronounce individual words, as it is only the flow of speech or text which eventually clothes these words with real meaning. However, many of the other words which are included in the vocabulary of the average reader of 7+ consist of such words as nouns, verbs and adjectives which he can not only recognize and understand when he hears them spoken, but he can also pronounce and understand when he sees them in print. They hold meaning for him even in isolation. Thus, as mentioned in Chapter 3, a second element contributing to effective reading is an ever-increasing knowledge of word meanings.

Of course, the young child when he first learns to speak attaches only one meaning to a word. It is only as he grows older and his facility with language increases that he begins to appreciate that the same word sometimes has different meanings depending on the context. In normal, everyday life a child or an adult usually encounters unknown words in the context of oral or written language. Frequently the situation enables him to make a fairly accurate guess at the meaning of the word from its context, whereas defining the meaning of a word in isolation is a more difficult task. Children's ways of relating the meaning of words to the context in which they find them are explored in Chapters 16 and 17. As various researchers, for example Davis (1970) and Spache and Spache (1969), have noted high correlations between children's knowledge of word meanings and their reading ability, here the emphasis is on the children's knowledge of the meanings of individual words, unrelated to context. As Raven's *Coloured Progressive Matrices* (1949) had been used to assess the intellectual ability – uncontaminated by verbal ability – of the children in the intensive study schools, the complementary test, the *Crichton Vocabulary Scale* (Raven 1951), was selected as being the most appropriate vocabulary test for use with these same children.

The test is basically one of oral definitions and consists of two lists of isolated words, arranged in order of difficulty. It is individually administered. The tester simply asks the child 'to explain in his own words the meaning of each word in turn', by saying 'what is a cap?', 'Tell me what a cap is?', 'What is a cap like?', without helping him regarding the meaning. The child progresses through each list in this way, until he is able to go no further. His final score is the total number of words correctly defined in the two lists. As an individual test of this nature is fairly time-consuming to administer, it was used only with the four randomly selected children of average reading ability in each class in the intensive study schools. The number of children tested was 134 and the testing took place half way through the school year.

## 2. Scores on the Crichton Vocabulary Scale
The Test Manual norms are given as percentile scores at half-yearly intervals from the ages of 4½ to 11 years. The age norms relevant to the sample of children of average reading ages in this study extended

from 7½ to 9½ years. While the average score for the child at the centre point of each age group is determined by the 50th percentile, the children who may be described as 'verbally average' are defined in the test manual as those whose scores fall between the 25th and 75th percentiles. In Table 15-2 the scores provided in the test manual are compared with those achieved by the sample of average readers in the intensive study schools.

Table 15-2

*Results of administering Crichton Vocabulary Scale to children of average reading ability*

| Chronological Age | Project Sample | | | Test Manual Figures | |
|---|---|---|---|---|---|
| | $n$ | Average Score | Range | Average Score | Range |
| $7^6$ | 19 | 40 | 28–54 | 28 | 23–30 |
| $8^0$ | 36 | 40 | 16–62 | 30 | 24–34 |
| $8^6$ | 29 | 43 | 25–59 | 33 | 28–39 |
| $9^0$ | 35 | 47 | 35–59 | 38 | 32–44 |
| $9^6$ | 15 | 45 | 33–59 | 41 | 36–48 |

The first point to notice in Table 15-2 is that the children in the sample gained much higher scores than the children on whom the test had been standardized in 1951. Two reasons for this may be suggested. First, it could be due to the age of the test and the possibility that in the intervening years there has been a genuine increase in children's knowledge of vocabulary. This would seem a feasible explanation in view of the linguistic stimulation (e.g. see Vernon 1969) children receive in current primary schools, not only in the amount of discussion which takes place but also in the time now spent by primary school teachers in reading aloud to their pupils. It could also be related to the quantity of books currently available to the children. Children's exposure to television, both in the home and the school, has also no doubt helped to enlarge their vocabulary, and this could be noted in the children's performance on one or two particular words in the test. Two such examples are the words 'tornado' and 'elevate', both these words occur late in the lists of test questions, which indicates that the children on whom the test was standardized in 1951 found them difficult to define. Yet in the current testing, having failed on many of the preceding words, children were frequently able to define these two words correctly. Children's unexpected familiarity with the first of these comparatively difficult words might well be connected with the well-known television advertisement for 'White Tornado', while the second could relate to the children's television programme entitled 'Trumpton', which has been running for many years, and in which the command 'elevate' is regularly given.

The second possible reason for the increase in test scores may be related to the scoring procedure for this vocabulary test, which rests partly on judgements made by the tester, which are to some extent subjective. While the three researchers concerned aimed to be absolutely objective in this test situation, the possibility cannot be ruled out that as they had had many contacts with these children in the preceding six months and so had grown very friendly with them, this may have slightly affected their judgements regarding the acceptability of certain definitions in favour of the children. Even experienced testers may occasionally err on the side of leniency in such circumstances. However, even a slight leniency in scoring could hardly have accounted for the large differences in average scores and, consequently, the first possibility mentioned seems the most likely.

The second point of interest in Table 15-2 is the very wide range of scores achieved by these children of average reading ability. Among the 8 year-olds, for example, the range of scores was 16 to 62. (The differences in the quality of the verbal responses of these pupils can be seen in the examples which follow.) Nevertheless, despite these extreme examples, as one would expect, in general the children's performances on the *Crichton Vocabulary Scale* showed a fairly high positive correlation with their scores on both the non-verbal intelligence test and the reading comprehension test. (Correlations of 0.45 were shown with Raven's *Progressive Matrices,* and of 0.55 with Brimer's *Wide-Span Reading Test,* both based on a truncated ability sample.)

### 3. Examples of children's definitions of words

The wide range of scores made by children of similar chronological ages and reading ages, already noted in Table 15-2, was further emphasized by the differences shown in the quality of many of the children's responses, which provide fascinating insights into the contrasting patterns of verbal facilities of children of similar ages and levels of reading ability.

Some of the children whose scores on the verbal test were very low were frequently unable to go beyond the stage of reiterating the given word. Such children rarely either offered synonyms or gave explanations, as did the children with higher scores, even when the permitted follow-up questions were asked. The following two examples of answers given by a first-year boy who only scored 20, are typical of the low scorers.

Q. What does the word *warm* mean?
A. When you're warm.
Q. Yes, so what does warm mean?
A. Warm.

Q. Do you know what *vanish* means?
A. When something vanishes.
Q. Yes. So what does vanish mean?
A. You can't see it.

This child's first response was generally a repetition of the test word. Frequently even a follow-up question elicited the same response — as in the first example. On other occasions the follow-up question revealed that he did actually know the meaning of the word, as in the second example given.

In marked contrast are the following responses of the first-year boy who scored 62 on the test.

Q. Do you know the meaning of the word *prosper*?
A. I know the word 'prosperous' but I don't know prosper.
Q. What does 'prosperous' mean then?
A. Well, when you get on.

Some of this boy's other definitions show the same kind of knowledge and verbal precision as can be seen in the following examples.

*rage* — When you are very, very angry.
*perfume* — It's some liquid which ladies put on to make them smell nice.
*warm* — It's the opposite of cool. When you're just hot, but not too hot — you've just been warm.
*effort* — When you do something, you have a good try at it.
*shrivel* — It's like a leaf in winter, when it curls up.
*precise* — When something is exactly right.

Some of the definitions given by the second-year boy who made the highest scores on the vocabulary test (i.e. 56) were as follows:

*lock* — Another name for a lake, in Scotland.
*sob* — Just getting over crying.
*triumph* — You win something with great glory.
*tornado* — A kind of whirlwind — knocks everything down.
*echo* — Well, I was walking once and there were some hills in the background, and I shouted and I heard an echo because my voice rebounded off the hills.
*entrance* — Opposite to exit. The place you wouldn't go out, you would go in.
*cargo* — Yes. It's mmm . . . luggage that a ship carries. It could be ten tons of bricks or something.
*release* — Oh! If a man had been in prison for about fifteen years, and the time had come for him to be released, they'd just let him go — he is a free man again.

The following interesting replies were provided by other second-year children. (The total score each child made on the test is given in brackets.)

## 2nd Year Girl (Score 45)

Q. What is a *patch*?
A. When you've got 'an 'ole' in something and your Mum sews it up.
Q. So what is a patch, then?
A. The material that you put over the hole.

Q. What does *connect* mean?
A. (child touching the lead from the tape-recorder which was on the table)
Like connecting your tape to that plug.

Q. What does *effort* mean?
A. When you are trying to do something and you keep on getting it wrong.
Q. Yes, so what does effort mean?
A. Trying hard to do it.

*echo*     — when you shout out loud somewhere, like in a cave or tunnel, and you shout 'Hello' and you get another voice coming back saying 'Hello'.

## 2nd Year Girl (Score 38)

*near*     — Say there was a lamp-post over the road. Well, if you go close to it, you're really near.

*view*     — Yes, like the flats. You go up to the top, on the balcony, and you look down and you see a view of houses or something like that.

## C. *Phonic Strengths and Weaknesses*

When attempting to read a passage of prose, the child who recognizes on sight and understands the meaning of 90–95% of the words in the text, is in a fairly strong position to begin to make sense of the whole passage. His elucidation of the remaining unfamiliar words will also be eased if he has some background knowledge relating to the subject matter of the text. In his efforts to gain meaning from the passage, he will then utilize the various clues provided by the text: namely, phonic cues; semantic cues — related to his awareness of the meaning of phrases, sentences and the whole passage; and syntactic cues — related to his latent knowledge of the grammatical structure of sentences in spoken and written English. The latter two types of cues are discussed in Chapters 16 and 17. Here the investigations into children's phonic skills are reported.

## 1. Preliminary investigations

The 700 teachers in the two Teachers' Reading Research Groups engaged in quite extensive investigations into the phonic strengths and weaknesses of the average readers in their own classes. These exercises were in the nature of pilot studies on which the final investigation of phonic skills in the intensive study year could be based. The areas investigated were: their pupils' mastery of the sounds of the letters of the alphabet and of various letter combinations and phonic rules; and the feasibility of utilizing 'nonsense words' as a diagnostic phonic testing device. The findings highlighted those areas of phonic weakness in children aged 7 to 9 years which merited further investigation. They also confirmed the use of 'nonsense words' as a useful diagnostic assessment technique and focussed attention on certain problems which needed to be avoided or overcome.

Although a number of available phonic tests employ the device of 'nonsense words', when closely examined none was found to be exactly what was required for children in these two age-groups. Accordingly, a new diagnostic phonic test was devised. Three succeeding drafts of possible test items were devised before the final version was arrived at. A notional order of the difficulty of the words was then established and a small pilot study undertaken with 30 children of the appropriate ages. The results of the pilot study led to minor amendments in the items themselves and in their order.

## 2. The new phonic test

The final test consisted of 55 nonsense words. The range of items was such that the poorest reader of $7^0$ years would be able to 'read' some of the items, whilst only the most proficient readers of $9^{11}$ years would be likely to score all items correctly. The nonsense words were devised so that they had the format, construction and rhythm of English words, which means that when pronounced they would create an impression of feasibility as possible English words. In other words, English speaking children would find it possible to 'get their tongues round them'.

The test was diagnostic in character. While it could not hope to provide a complete picture of a child's total knowledge of phonics, it could indicate areas in which he was confident and, even more important, highlight those areas in which his knowledge was either doubtful or non-existent. These latter areas could then form part of the basis of a teacher's forward teaching plans for the child in question.

Children's mastery of the following phonic skills could be assessed by administering the test:

(a)   The common sounds of the letters of the alphabet in the different positions in words which they usually occupy;
(b)   Blending sounds together in simple three-letter words;
(c)   Combining together, in a word pattern, two and three syllables;
(d)   Phonic rules to which there are few exceptions, for example the

pronounciation of 'ee', 'ing', or 'ph'. (Clymer (1963), Pratt (1939) and Wijk (1966) were consulted on this score);
(e) Rules which, although they have certain exceptions, are nevertheless in fairly common use; for example, the rule that a silent 'e' at the end of a monosyllabic word such as 'cake' often causes the preceding vowel to have its long sound.

The seven categories of phonic skills being tested in the nonsense words fell into the groups shown in Table 15-3.

Table 15-3

*Categories of phonic skills tested in new diagnostic test*

| No. of items | Categories of Skills | Example |
|---|---|---|
| 5 | Consonant blends | sp |
| 5 | Consonant digraphs | sh |
| 10 | Vowel digraphs | ee |
| 5 | Murmur vowels | er |
| 5 | Rule of silent 'e' | as in ma*ke* |
| 3 | Silent letters | 'k' as in '*k*nife' |
| 7 | Common word endings | ing |

In addition there were five examples each of words of one, two and three syllables. As certain vowel digraphs have alternative, common pronunciations in different words in English, for example *ea* – as in t*ea* or h*ea*d, *ow* – as in c*ow* or bel*ow*, either pronunciation in the nonsense word was counted as correct. The test was intended for individual administration. Each child was to be given introductory instructions about the items being 'silly' words, as they didn't make any sense at all. If, during the testing, a child appeared to be trying to make an item into a known word, the tester would say:

'Don't try to make it into a word you know. You won't know any of these words. They are not real words.'

The words were presented singly in the order of difficulty which had been established in the pilot trial. The following are examples of nonsense words included in the test:

| | |
|---|---|
| hix | shaff |
| plon | towk |
| roxer | exchinfer |
| kide | umbasade |

The method of scoring was such that the child received credit for a correct response to the crucial part of the word, for example a vowel digraph, even though he made an error elsewhere in the word.

## 3. Children tested

The testing took place in 10 of the 12 schools in the intensive study. The test was administered not only to the four randomly selected children of average reading ability in the relevant classes, but also to four randomly selected children of below average reading ability and to four of above average ability — based on performance on *Southgate Group Reading Test 2* (Southgate 1962) administered in September 1975. The original testing took place early in February 1976, and in order that some measurement of progress might be made, the test was repeated with the same children in July 1976. The total number of children involved in the initial testing was 434 (of whom 226 were first-years and 208 were second-years). By the time the second testing occurred, a few of the original children had left the schools, while others were absent through illness or on holiday, thereby reducing the number to 367. It should, however, be noted that the reduction in sample size was evenly distributed across all three reading ability bands. The distribution of children according to reading ability, in the pre-test and post-test samples, is set out in Table 15-4.

Table 15-4

*Distribution of sample of children tested on new diagnostic phonic test*

| Date of Testing 1976 | No. of Children | | | | | | Totals |
|---|---|---|---|---|---|---|---|
| | 1st Years | | | 2nd Years | | | |
| | AA | A | BA | AA | A | BA | |
| Feb | 77 | 93 | 56 | 72 | 68 | 68 | 434 |
| July | 63 | 82 | 44 | 61 | 61 | 56 | 367 |

AA = Above Average Reading Ability
A = Average Reading Ability
BA = Below Average Reading Ability

## 4. Results of administering the diagnostic phonic test

(a) *Raw score distirbution*

Although with a diagnostic test a total score is less important than the details of a child's success or failure on particular items, in this instance some interesting patterns can be noted in the distribution of total scores between children of different ages and general reading proficiency. Although the number of test items was 55, the maximum possible score on the test was 110. This was the result of awarding scores for each correct response to the rule being tested in a particular word, as well as to correct total pronunciations for each nonsense word.

Table 15-5(a) shows the raw score distributions with their average scores and standard deviations.

Table 15-5(a)

*Distribution of children's average scores on diagnostic phonic test*

(Maximum possible score = 110)

| | 1st Years | | | 2nd Years | | | Combined Age Groups | | | |
| | AA | A | BA | AA | A | BA | AA | A | BA | TOTAL |
|---|---|---|---|---|---|---|---|---|---|---|
| Feb | | | | | | | | | | |
| mean | 86.0 | 56.0 | 40.0 | 96.1 | 76.5 | 54.0 | 90.9 | 64.7 | 47.7 | 68.9 |
| s.d. | 16.3 | 24.0 | 21.7 | 10.6 | 16.6 | 25.7 | 14.7 | 23.4 | 24.9 | 27.5 |
| July | | | | | | | | | | |
| mean | 91.1 | 67.1 | 51.0 | 98.9 | 86.2 | 61.6 | 94.8 | 75.3 | 57.0 | 76.9 |
| s.d. | 14.4 | 24.8 | 24.8 | 9.2 | 14.2 | 24.1 | 12.8 | 23.0 | 24.8 | 25.4 |

AA = Above Average Reading Ability
A = Average Reading Ability
BA = Below Average Reading Ability

This raw score distribution for the separate bands of reading ability clearly illustrates a relationship between phonic strength and general reading ability, and the fact that there is a correlation of 0.74 between the pre-test phonic scores and the pre-test results on *Southgate Group Reading Test 2* gives strong support to this.

It can be seen from the figures in Table 15-5(a) that the average scores for any reading ability classification are always higher than those for an inferior reading ability group irrespective of year-group, and that the July score for any first-year reading ability group almost, but not quite, reaches the February score for the same reading ability group in the second-year — implying a systematic improvement in phonic strength with time. For example, note the following scores.

Table 15-5(b)

*Mean score abstracted from Table 15-5(a)*

| | | AA | A | BA |
|---|---|---|---|---|
| 1st Years | Feb | 86.0 | 56.0 | 40.0 |
| | July | 91.1 | 67.1 | 51.0 |
| 2nd Years | Feb | 96.1 | 76.5 | 54.0 |
| | July | 98.9 | 86.2 | 61.6 |

This time trend is further clearly illustrated by the graph in Appendix 15-B showing mean raw scores and median scores against chronological age in months. Although both first- and second-year groups of average and below average reading ability improved their mean scores by approximately 10 points between testing sessions, the graph of mean raw scores against age in fact shows steady improvement in phonic strength over the first year with a levelling-off after about 8 years 2 months.

(b) *Sex differences*
Performance on the test for the two sexes are everywhere exactly similar, the average raw scores produced by girls and boys being 68.7 and 68.8 respectively, with sample sizes of 211 girls and 223 boys and standard deviations of 27.1 and 28.1

(c) *Mastery of phonic skills and related weaknesses*
As seven of the specific sound categories were scored separately from the total phonic score which children achieved on the test, it was possible to formulate a hierarchy of these categories according to how well they were known by children in the sample. Table 15-6 indicates this hierarchy when all scores are totalled for those children of both age-groups and all levels of reading ability who could, at the first testing, pronounce correctly four out of five of the sounds selected as representing each category.

Table 15-6

*Percentages of children achieving 80% success in pronouncing specific phonic sound categories*

| Categories Tested | % of Children | |
|---|---|---|
| | 1st Year | 2nd Year |
| Consonant Blends | 89 | 93 |
| Consonant Digraphs | 78 | 89 |
| Silent Letters | 59 | 71 |
| Common Endings | 53 | 73 |
| Murmur Vowels | 43 | 70 |
| Long Vowels | 43 | 59 |
| Vowel Digraphs | 26 | 51 |

In reading Table 15-6 it should be remembered that had the criterion of success in each category been to read every example correctly, the percentages of children succeeding would, in every category, have been considerably less. Within each age-group, and within each category, children with different levels of reading ability were correspondingly more or less successful as one would expect. For example, in the least well-known category of vowel digraphs 85% of above average readers in the second-year were successful eight times out of ten, as opposed to only 21% of below average second-years and only 5% of below average first-years.

Table 15-6 therefore shows clearly that mastery of quite frequently occurring phonic skills is not complete even for the best readers in the second year. Even above average readers of 9 years still require some help and a little practice with the best known category of consonant blends, while all children aged 7 to 9 years require a good deal of help with the least well-known categories, particularly vowel digraphs and long vowels (i.e. the rule that the silent 'e' at the end of a mono-syllabic word generally causes the preceding short vowel to become long).

With regard to lack of success with consonant blends, for example 'sp', 'tr', or 'qu', this is not surprising in the light of one of the findings from the first Teachers' Reading Research Group. When 197 children of average reading ability were tested on their knowledge of the *sounds* of the letters of the alphabet, the results were as shown in Table 15-7.

Table 15-7

*Percentages of children making errors in giving the sounds of the 26 letters of the alphabet*

| No. of Errors | 1st Years | | 2nd Years | |
|---|---|---|---|---|
| | Boys | Girls | Boys | Girls |
| 0 | 39 | 32 | 49 | 39 |
| 1–4 | 44 | 58 | 37 | 56 |
| 5 or more | 17 | 10 | 14 | 5 |
| Range | (0–12) | (0–22) | (0–21) | (0–5) |

The main points to be noted in this table are as follows:

(i) Approximately 35% of first-years and 45% of second-years knew the sounds of all 26 letters of the alphabet, leaving 65% and 55% of the respective age groups who could not provide correct sounds for all the letters. It is thus understandable that certain children, when faced with the diagnostic phonic test, were unable to blend together the sounds of two consonants.

(ii) The number of errors made by individual children extended to 21 and 22; and, incidentally, the highest number of errors forecast by their teachers for any child was four.

(iii) There was little noticeable improvement in the performance of second-years over first-years.

These latter two points suggest that the teachers in question were not fully aware that so many of their average readers were not familiar with the sounds of all the letters of the alphabet. It also seems fair to assume that many of the below average readers in these classes were even less proficient at this preliminary stage of phonic competency. This same finding was also demonstrated when the new phonic test was used in the intensive study; for example, certain children still showed confusion between such letters as 'm' and 'n' or 'b' and 'd'. Once again the need for individual diagnosis is quite obvious.

The main value of a diagnostic test, however, does not lie in its ability to measure children's success in various areas; the purpose of the test is rather to discover the weaknesses or failures of individual children so that the teacher's attention may be directed to those areas which require tuition and practice. Accordingly, a more fruitful method of considering the results of this diagnostic test is to highlight what was not known. In Table 15-8, therefore, the figures have been reversed, in order to demonstrate the percentages of children, separated according to age and reading ability, who were *not* sufficiently familiar with certain frequently occurring sound combinations and phonic rules as to be able to deal correctly with four-fifths of the selected examples provided in the test.

From Table 15-8 it can be noted that in only two categories, consonant digraphs and consonant blends, did a whole group of children succeed with four-fifths of the sample of nonsense words. In both cases they were second-year children of above average reading ability. At the opposite end of the order of difficulty, i.e. vowel digraphs, 95% of below average readers and 85% of average readers in the first-year succeeded on fewer than 80% of the examples provided in the test. In fact, it would seem fair to suggest that both vowel digraphs and long vowels had either not been taught, or had been touched on so fleetingly that they had not been learned by the majority of first-years and a large proportion of second-years.

The figures provided in Table 15-8 are illustrated diagrammatically in Table 15-9 in order to highlight two important points; the wide discrepancies in phonic proficiency between children with different levels of general reading ability and the amount of teaching and/or learning which takes place in one school year.

The histograms in Table 15-9 provide a diagrammatic illustration of the results obtained from the diagnostic test, which very clearly show up the following points:
(i)  Very large proportions of children in both year-groups failed to recognize many of the common phonic rules in the English language.
(ii)  The portions of the columns indicated by diagonal lines denote the differences between the failure rates of first- and second-year children, which means that these areas represent the amount of successful teaching and/or learning which has occurred in a period of six months. In some cases, and particularly for the below average readers, these gains represent less than half of the original areas of failure. Yet a rule half-known can, with a little direct teaching, very easily be

Table 15-8

*Percentages of children succeeding on fewer than 80% of the examples of specific sound categories or rules*

| Categories | Reading Ability | % of Children | |
|---|---|---|---|
| | | 1st Years | 2nd Years |
| Vowel digraphs | BA | 95 | 79 |
| | A | 85 | 57 |
| | AA | 42 | 15 |
| Long vowels | BA | 91 | 69 |
| | A | 68 | 41 |
| | AA | 17 | 12 |
| Murmur vowels | BA | 79 | 62 |
| | A | 68 | 29 |
| | AA | 22 | 3 |
| Common endings | BA | 86 | 65 |
| | A | 50 | 9 |
| | AA | 10 | 1 |
| Silent letters | BA | 64 | 56 |
| | A | 44 | 22 |
| | AA | 16 | 11 |
| Consonant digraphs | BA | 37 | 28 |
| | A | 26 | 6 |
| | AA | 5 | 0 |
| Consonant blends | BA | 20 | 9 |
| | A | 13 | 3 |
| | AA | 1 | 0 |

converted into complete mastery. Therefore, it would seem that many teachers may be unaware of the specific examples of sounds embodied in a phonic rule which are not mastered by individual children; and thus have failed to ensure that they are learned.

In the foregoing context, teachers might find it useful to know that within each category of sounds or rules, the following examples in the test showed the highest failure rates:

| | *Example* |
|---|---|
| Vowel digraphs | *ou* (as in sh*ou*t) |
| Long vowels | *u* (as in t*u*ne) |
| Murmur vowels | *ir* (as in s*ir*) |
| Common endings | *tion* (as in ac*tion*) |
| Silent letters | *b* (as in lam*b*) |
| Consonant digraphs | *ph* (as in *Ph*ilip) |
| Consonant blends | *qu* (as in *qu*een) |

Table 15-9

*Percentages of children succeeding on fewer than 80% of the examples of specific sound categories or rules*

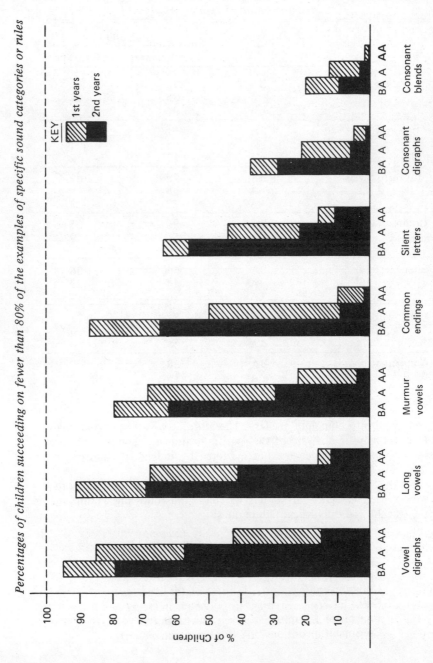

It has already been stated that all the figures so far given for success with phonic items in the diagnostic test have been based on children's knowledge of 80% of the individual items in that category. It follows from this that if the criterion for mastery had been 100% success with the items in any category, the failure rate would have been considerably higher. At the other end of the scale, none of the tables provided so far shows any evidence of children who failed to get even one example correct in a sound category. Table 15-10, therefore, sets out to show the percentages of children who were so unfamiliar with certain common phonic rules that they were not successful with even a single example.

Table 15-10

*Percentages of children who failed to get even one example correct within each sound category*

| Categories | Date | 1st Years | | | 2nd Years | | |
|---|---|---|---|---|---|---|---|
| | | BA | A | AA | BA | A | AA |
| Vowel digraphs | Feb | 5 | 1 | – | 3 | – | – |
| | July | 4 | 1 | – | 3 | – | – |
| Long vowels | Feb | 34 | 13 | 1 | – | – | – |
| | July | 14 | 2 | – | – | – | – |
| Murmur vowels | Feb | 25 | 10 | – | 12 | – | – |
| | July | 13 | 2 | – | 5 | – | – |
| Common endings | Feb | 7 | – | – | – | – | – |
| | July | 4 | – | – | – | – | – |
| Silent letters | Feb | 25 | 19 | 5 | 17 | 4 | 1 |
| | July | 25 | 7 | 3 | 9 | – | – |
| Consonant digraphs | Feb | 2 | – | – | – | – | – |
| | July | 2 | – | – | 2 | – | – |
| Consonant blends | Feb | – | – | – | – | – | – |
| | July | – | – | – | – | – | – |

Table 15-10 illustrates once again the close relationship between knowledge of phonics and general reading ability, in that by far the greatest majority of children who failed all the items in any one category were children of below average reading ability, whereas only a very small proportion of above average readers appear in the table – apart from the category of silent letters. This latter category is evidently one of which many children have no knowledge, even by their second year in the junior school. This is rather surprising in that two of the silent letters tested are in fairly common use in the reading material used by children of these ages, and are also used frequently by the children in their own writing. For example:

silent *k* as in knock, knit, knob, know, knight, etc.

silent *w* as in write, wrong, and wrap.

A second rather disturbing result is the large proportion of children in the first year who did not even know one of the five murmur vowels — not even the easiest one 'er', which is in such common use. Fortunately, by the second year all the average and above average readers recognized at least one of the murmur vowels — even though, as illustrated in, other tables, many children had not mastered them all. The other point to be noted in Table 15-10 is that in certain categories very little, if any, improvement was shown between the two testing dates.

## 5. Conclusions about phonics

Teachers might wonder whether the findings of the project have led the team to advocate a return to phonic methods of teaching beginning readers, or for that matter, ineffective older readers. Nothing could be further from the truth. The total findings of the project have strengthened our belief that the major portion of the reading programme for 7 to 9 year-olds should be exactly that — uninterrupted reading of books the children understand and enjoy. It is fluent reading which aids comprehension, rather than stumbling, halting progress. If comprehension is the ultimate goal of extending beginning reading, the practice of continuous fluent reading, rather than hesitant oral reading with frequent halts for coaching, will be most likely to achieve this goal. Therefore, we have concluded that periods of phonic teaching, when required, should be brief. Probably no more than 5-10 minutes once or twice a week should be all that is necessary — and just for those particular children in whom specific phonic weaknesses had been discovered.

At the particular stage of reading competency reached by the majority of children of 7 to 9 years, it would seem that the semantic cues in the text relating to meaning, and the syntactic cues relating to grammatical structure, are more important than the phonic cues — although the latter certainly play a part in the global understanding of what is read. We would agree with Smith, *et al.* (1976) who state:

> Most of the simple panaceas in reading instruction are not methods but sets of tactics that emphasize the learner's use of one set of cues or a group of related cues. Phonics, for example, is a set of tactics for handling letter cues. These tactics, if they are based on a sound understanding of letter—sound relationships, can be fitted into a method of reading instruction. . . . Any strategy of reading instruction based on a single principle or tactic is incomplete, no matter how valid the principle.

# III  Details of the Standardized Tests

## A. *The Selected Tests*

### 1. Reading tests

As mentioned in Chapter 2, the first requirement at the beginning of the intensive study year was a screening test of general reading ability, in order to identify those children of average reading ability in each of the two year-groups. An easily administered group test of general reading ability was needed, and *Southgate Group Reading Test 2* (Southgate 1962) was selected as suitable for the purpose. This standardized test requires a child to complete each of 36 sentences – having always the last word omitted – by choosing one of five words listed and underlined at the end of the sentence. It is administratively simple to use with large groups of children, as two parallel forms are available and a whole class can be tested in 20 minutes. Also the scoring procedure is very straightforward.

As the intended age range for this test is 7 to 9 years, it was expected that the ceiling was likely to be reached by a proportion of the children concerned before the end of the second year. An additional test of general reading ability was, therefore, required. It needed to have a much higher ceiling, and also to be a group test with at least two alternative test forms. *Wide-Span Reading Test* (Brimer 1972) was chosen as the most suitable for the purpose of monitoring reading progress during the school year, despite the fact that at first sight the procedure to be followed seemed exceedingly complicated for such young children to follow, and consequently it appeared that there might be the risk of a loss of pre-test information for some of the younger children. In the event, few problems arose in administering the test.

### 2. A test of general intelligence

As mentioned earlier, it was not only necessary to determine that children in the classes in the intensive study should have reading attainments extending over the full range, but also that the same was true of their general intellectual abilities. Once more it was necessary to select a group test and also, as the project itself was focused on reading, one in which the results would not be contaminated by reading ability. The *Coloured Progressive Matrices* (Raven 1949) was selected as fulfilling both conditions. It is, in fact, a pattern perception test and, according to the author, is intended to indicate 'a person's present capacity for intellectual activity, irrespective of his acquired knowledge'. It is a standardized test and the results are expressed as percentiles, accompanied by a classification into five grades of intellectual ability.

## B. *Test Results*

### 1. Southgate Group Reading Test 2

The scores achieved on the screening test, *Southgate Group Reading Test 2,* by the 1,395 children tested in the intensive study schools were found to be somewhat higher (particularly for the younger children) than might have been expected from the published norms. A comparison between the average scores detailed in the test manual for three broad age-bands and those achieved by similarly aged children in the sample is given in Table 15-11.

Table 15-11

*Comparison between Test Manual\* data and project results for Southgate Group Reading Test 2*

| Chronological Age | Test 2A | | | | Test 2B | | | |
|---|---|---|---|---|---|---|---|---|
| | Boys | | Girls | | Boys | | Girls | |
| | No. | Mean | No. | Mean | No. | Mean | No. | Mean |
| $8^6 - 9^2$ | 107 | 30.0 | 110 | 31.4 | 116 | 31.1 | 99 | 30.4 |
| | *173* | *26.7* | *160* | *30.4* | *193* | *27.3* | *148* | *30.4* |
| $7^9 - 8^5$ | 137 | 23.3 | 130 | 29.0 | 123 | 23.2 | 118 | 27.1 |
| | *179* | *23.5* | *170* | *24.2* | *192* | *20.8* | *159* | *23.5* |
| $7^0 - 7^8$ | 105 | 16.8 | 111 | 19.1 | 118 | 14.5 | 113 | 18.4 |
| | *146* | *14.5* | *184* | *15.2* | *169* | *11.8* | *177* | *14.6* |

(\*Test Manual figures italicized.)

It is, of course, possible that the differences apparent in Table 15-11 simply result from the regional nature of both the project sample (four LEAs in the north-west of England) and the original standardization (using complete populations of children in the relevant age-groups in the city of Worcester). It is also possible, though, that achievement levels have genuinely changed in the 20 years since this test was constructed and the norms established.

The other point worth noting was the generally higher level of achievement for girls compared with that for boys. The overall mean scores achieved by the girls and boys were 26 and 23 respectively, and this difference is statistically significant at the 1% level. The sex difference is most marked at the younger end of the age range, virtually disappearing by the middle of the second year.

## 2. Wide-Span Reading Test

*Wide-Span Reading Test* (Brimer 1972) has been standardized much more recently, and the project results for this test correspond in general with those expected according to the test manual. As mentioned previously, there was a risk of losing pre-test information on this test for some of the younger children. It was the case, in fact, that 14% of all first-year children failed to score on the test: this varied within classes from zero to about 30%; the latter percentage referring to one of the youngest classes in the sample, in which the average age at the start of the year was 7 years 4 months. There were a few children who handed in blank answer sheets at the end of the session, and it may be that a proportion of these were due to lack of understanding of the procedure to be adopted. It could be noted that the less able children often chose any arbitrary word from the right hand sentence to copy onto an answer sheet, and sometimes they substituted semantically associated words or even word associations neither syntactically nor semantically appropriate in the context of the target sentence. Commonly, a less able pupil would simply copy the responses of his immediate neighbour, despite having been told previously that adjacent children were using different test papers. The pre-test results for each class within each school are shown in Table 15-12.

The overall mean scores for all first-years and for all second-years were 7.3 and 17.2 respectively. These are rather lower than those given for these age-groups in the test manual (p. 13); the figures being about 12 and 19 respectively. However, the overall means for the project test session held at the end of the school year (July) were 13.2 and 24.2. The discrepancies, then, between these sets of figures and those given in the test manual are probably accounted for by the period within the school year during which the Brimer test was administered for standardization.

It is clear from Table 15.12 that, at the beginning of the school year, there were great variations in the achievement levels of the various classes in each year group, and indeed marked differences between complete schools, as well as between the four LEAs involved. Such differences strongly reflect the different socio-economic catchment areas of the schools concerned, and partly the average chronological age differences between the classes. For example, the first-year class 12, with its low average score of 2.1, was the class in which the average chronological age was only 7 years 4 months at the beginning of the school year compared with the more usual 7 years 6 months.

An important point to note in Table 15.12 is that, at the start of the school year, classes of the same age within the same school tended to have very similar levels of reading competence.

## 3. Raven's Progressive Matrices

For the purpose of this project, the raw scores resulting from the administration of Raven's *Progressive Matrices* were of primary interest

Table 15-12

*Pre-test results on Brimer's Wide-Span Reading Test (raw scores)*

| School | 1st Year Classes | | | | | 2nd Year Classes | | | |
|---|---|---|---|---|---|---|---|---|---|
| | Class | n | mean | s.d. | | Class | n | mean | s.d. |
| 1/Z | 1 | 28 | 5.4 | 4.5 | | 1 | 36 | 12.3 | 6.5 |
| 2/Z | 2 | 34 | 7.7 | 7.6 | | 2 | 33 | 17.6 | 6.2 |
| | 3 | 31 | 6.0 | 6.5 | | | | | |
| 3/Z | 4 | 28 | 11.1 | 8.2 | | 3 | 32 | 18.8 | 10.3 |
| 4/Z | 5 | 35 | 6.0 | 6.6 | | 4 | 30 | 14.8 | 10.8 |
| 7/Y | 6 | 27 | 12.7 | 8.2 | | 5 | 29 | 19.6 | 9.9 |
| | 7 | 27 | 13.1 | 6.5 | | 6 | 35 | 19.6 | 7.5 |
| 8/Y | 8 | 17 | 5.7 | 5.7 | | 7 | 20 | 24.1 | 7.6 |
| 5/Y | 9 | 28 | 8.6 | 7.6 | | 8 | 33 | 20.9 | 11.8 |
| | 10 | 24 | 8.2 | 7.1 | | 9 | 29 | 18.6 | 10.5 |
| 6/Y | 11 | 25 | 6.8 | 5.2 | | 10 | 22 | 12.6 | 8.3 |
| | 12 | 26 | 7.6 | 6.2 | | | | | |
| 9/X | 13 | 27 | 5.4 | 6.0 | | | | | |
| 12/W | 14 | 28 | 2.1 | 3.8 | | | | | |
| 11/W | 15 | 18 | 5.9 | 6.4 | | 11 | 31 | 13.6 | 9.7 |
| | 16 | 22 | 4.9 | 5.0 | | 12 | 27 | 13.9 | 7.6 |
| 10/W | 17 | 21 | 6.9 | 6.2 | | 13 | 33 | 19.3 | 10.9 |
| | 18 | 19 | 4.8 | 3.9 | | 14 | 28 | 16.4 | 10.6 |
| | | | | | | 15 | 36 | 17.2 | 10.7 |

in establishing whether or not the children observed and assessed in the intensive study year covered a normal range of intellectual ability, and it was anticipated that this was all that would be reported about the results obtained. However, it happened that, according to the test norms, the scores achieved on the test by all the children concerned were so much higher than those expected, that some comment on them would seem appropriate here.

In order to illustrate clearly the anomaly, every child in the intensive study was graded into one of the five grades as defined by the Test Manual. These grades range from Grade I ('Intellectually Superior — score lies at or above the 95th percentile for people in the same age-group') to Grade V ('Intellectually defective —score lies at or below the 5th percentile for the same age-group'). Table 15-13 shows the percentages of pupils falling into each of the five grades for each of the intensive study schools.

Table 15-13

*Classification of pupils according to Raven's Progressive Matrices Test Manual (percentage of pupils in each of 5 grades)*

KEY

| Grade | Expected % |
|---|---|
| I = intellectually superior | 5 |
| II = definitely above average in intellectual capacity | 20 |
| III = intellectually average | 50 |
| IV = definitely below average in intellectual capacity | 20 |
| V = intellectually defective | 5 |

| | 1st Years | | | | | 2nd Years | | | | |
|---|---|---|---|---|---|---|---|---|---|---|
| School | I | II | III | IV | V | I | II | III | IV | V |
| 1/Z | 20 | 26 | 28 | 17 | 9 | 8 | 33 | 36 | 14 | 8 |
| 2/Z | 36 | 25 | 23 | 9 | 1 | 19 | 41 | 32 | 5 | 3 |
| 3/Z | 24 | 41 | 26 | 9 | — | 21 | 35 | 29 | 9 | 6 |
| 4/Z | 24 | 37 | 29 | 8 | 3 | 29 | 29 | 36 | 7 | — |
| 7/Y | 67 | 25 | 8 | — | — | 50 | 37 | 12 | 1 | — |
| 8/Y | 46 | 36 | 9 | — | 9 | 65 | 22 | 9 | 4 | — |
| 5/Y | 39 | 35 | 18 | 7 | 2 | 56 | 23 | 15 | 6 | — |
| 6/Y | 31 | 38 | 20 | 6 | 5 | 36 | 16 | 32 | 12 | 4 |
| 9/X | 22 | 22 | 34 | 9 | 13 | 38 | 31 | 12 | 6 | 12 |
| 12/W | 35 | 35 | 19 | 9 | 2 | 20 | 13 | 47 | 7 | 13 |
| 11/W | 33 | 29 | 27 | 10 | 2 | 10 | 43 | 33 | 8 | 6 |
| 10/W | 42 | 38 | 13 | 4 | 2 | 41 | 27 | 25 | 3 | 3 |

Although the distributions shown in Table 15-13 reflect fairly accurately the different socio-economic catchment areas of the schools concerned, they do not correspond in absolute terms with those expected by the team in the light of their project requirements and on the basis of their knowledge of these particular schools.

In order to investigate further these levels of achievement, figures were derived from the project data which would correspond with the age norms quoted in the Test Manual. Sufficiently large sample sizes were available for the calculation of new 'norms' at each of five age points — 7½, 8, 8½, 9 and 9½ years. Each age represents the mid-point of a six-month span. The project and associated Manual norms are given in Table 15-14. It can be noted that the project-calculated norms are everywhere higher than those quoted in the Test Manual, and this is particularly clear for younger children.

This test was originally standardized on approximately 100 children per age-group, whereas the sample size on the which the project figures are based was four to five times larger than this. Furthermore, the schools in the intensive study were chosen as 'typical' primary schools by the advisers concerned, and the project team's judgements of these schools on the basis of long experience of visiting such schools supported the advisers' opinions. Although there still remains the possibility that the discrepancies noted result from the regional nature of the project sample, it seems more likely that the levels of achievement on this kind of test have increased since the test was first standardized[1]. Similar increases were noted also for the associated *Crichton Vocabulary Scale* as mentioned earlier.

Test sophistication cannot realistically be held responsible for the improved scores on Raven's *Progressive Matrices* as these children had met the test for the first time during the project's investigation. It would seem more plausible that the increased interest in recent years in 'modern mathematics', with its emphasis on spatial relationships and tessellation exercises, has caused all children to be more attuned to the similarities and differences to be observed in the type of patterns of which this test consists.

Accordingly, for the purpose of the project, and in the belief that the sample of schools used in the intensive study year covered a full range of intelligence, approximate IQs were calculated from the raw scores achieved by the children on Raven's *Matrices,* on the basis of the usual mean of 100 and standard deviation of 15. Those for first-year classes are shown in Table 15-15 alongside the average chronological ages and average reading ages (*Southgate Group Reading Test 2*) for each school at the beginning of the school year.

Table 15-14

*Raven's Coloured Progressive Matrices 'Project Norms' and Test Manual Norms (italicized)*

| Percentile Points | Age | | | | |
|---|---|---|---|---|---|
| | 7½ | 8 | 8½ | 9 | 9½ |
| 95 | 33 *25* | 34 *26* | 34 *28* | 35 *30* | 35 *32* |
| 90 | 31 *23* | 32 *24* | 33 *26* | 34 *28* | 33 *31* |
| 75 | 28 *30* | 29 *21* | 30 *23* | 31 *26* | 30 *28* |
| 50 | 23 *17* | 24 *18* | 26 *20* | 27 *22* | 27 *24* |
| 25 | 19 *15* | 20 *16* | 22 *17* | 23 *19* | 23 *21* |
| 10 | 16 *14* | 17 *14* | 18 *15* | 19 *16* | 18 *18* |
| 5 | 15 *12* | 15 *13* | 15 *14* | 17 *15* | 15 *16* |
| Project Sample size | 133 | 281 | 263 | 249 | 157 |
| Mean raw score | 23.3 | 24.1 | 25.4 | 26.9 | 26.2 |
| s.d. | 5.9 | 5.6 | 5.8 | 5.8 | 5.9 |

[1] This test is now being restandardized.

Table 15-15

*Comparison of mean chronological age, reading age and mean IQ of 1st year children in 12 schools*

| School | Mean Chron. Age | Mean Reading Age | Mean IQ |
|---|---|---|---|
| 1/Z | $7^{10}$ | $7^{10}$ | 95 |
| 2/Z | $7^8$ | $7^8$ | 100 |
| 3/Z | $7^8$ | $7^{11}$ | 100 |
| 4/Z | $7^6$ | $7^6$ | 98 |
| 7/Y | $7^6$ | $8^1$ | 112 |
| 8/Y | $7^4$ | $7^{10}$ | 104 |
| 5/Y | $7^6$ | $7^7$ | 105 |
| 6/Y | $7^7$ | $7^6$ | 100 |
| 9/X | $7^6$ | $7^6$ | 91 |
| 12/W | $7^3$ | $7^2$ | 96 |
| 11/W | $7^7$ | $7^4$ | 100 |
| 10/W | $7^7$ | $7^6$ | 106 |

It can be seen from Table 15-15 that the average IQs in the 12 schools could be divided into three categories of above average, average and below average, with four schools falling into each group. It can also be noted that, in general, the three results are in concordance: when the IQ is above average the mean reading age tends to be slightly higher than the chronological age; similarly below average levels of intelligence usually result in reading ages lagging behind average chronological ages.

## 4. Comparison of reading and other assessments

The relationships between the two reading tests and each of the other reading-related assessments and the non-verbal intelligence are of interest. The correlations between these assessments are set out in Table 15-16.

Table 15-16

*Correlation matrix for reading and other assessments*

| | Brimer Test | Raven's Matrices | Phonic Test | Crichton Scale* |
|---|---|---|---|---|
| Southgate Test | 0.81 | 0.47 | 0.73 | 0.41 |
| Brimer Test | | 0.55 | 0.63 | 0.44 |
| Raven's Matrices | | | 0.33 | 0.45 |
| Phonic Test | | | | 0.16 |

(*Truncated sample of approximately 134 children of average reading ability.)

Table 15-16 illustrates the strong relationship between general reading ability as measured by the two reading tests and the three other related measures. The two general reading ability assessments are themselves highly correlated, but it is interesting to note the differences in the correlations between each of these and the non-verbal intelligence and phonic assessments. The very low correlation between phonic proficiency and knowledge of word meaning is also interesting although it must be remembered that this was based on a truncated sample of *average* readers.

## C. *Reading Progress*

### 1. Comparison of pre-test and post-test results
As *Wide-Span Reading Test* (Brimer 1972) had been administered to whole classes of children in the intensive study schools in early October, and again in July, at the end of the school year, it was possible to assess the children's reading progress over the year. As was to be expected, not only were there found to be marked differences in the progress made by individual children in the same class, but also in the general progress made by different classes.

The first important finding was that, although different classes within the same age-group in the same school may have begun the school year with very similar average raw scores on the *Wide-Span Reading Test*, these classes sometimes ended the year with vastly different levels of achievement. Table 15-17 illustrates this point clearly.

Such differences in average class progress within the same schools strongly suggest some kind of link between the different levels of progress and as yet unknown class-based factors. Naturally, chronological age, preliminary reading ability and socio-economic background (reflected to some extent in the assessments of non-verbal intelligence) must all contribute towards varying amounts of reading progress, as also must a number of school-based factors. Here, though, there appears to be strong evidence of classroom-based factors which have influenced progress over and above these other contributors.

Before investigating this point further, the classes within each year-group were ranked in order of degrees of average reading progress. This was done on the basis of post-test scores; these being statistically adjusted for the effects of differences in initial reading achievement, chronological age and non-verbal intelligence between the classes concerned. This statistical reordering resulted in only minor changes in the order which would have been produced solely on the basis of magnitude of difference between pre- and post-test mean raw scores. The adjusted ordering is shown in Table 15-18.

### 2. Tentative conclusions about reading progress
Although the programme for the intensive study year was not designed

Table 15-17

Pre-test and post-test performances on Brimer's Wide-Span Reading Test for different classes within the same schools
(raw scores)

| School | 1st Years | | | | | | 2nd Years | | | | | |
|---|---|---|---|---|---|---|---|---|---|---|---|---|
| | Class | pre-test | | post-test | | Change | Class | pre-test | | post-test | | Change |
| | | mean s.d. | | mean s.d. | | | | mean s.d. | | mean s.d. | | |
| 2/Z | 2 | 7.7 7.6 | | 15.7 9.7 | | 8.0 | | | | | | |
| | 3 | 6.0 6.5 | | 15.7 8.6 | | 9.7 | | | | | | |
| 7/Y | 6 | 12.7 8.2 | | 19.6 8.2 | | 6.9 | 5 | 19.6 9.9 | | 33.3 10.1 | | 13.7 |
| | 7 | 13.1 6.5 | | 15.4 6.7 | | 2.3 | 6 | 19.6 7.5 | | 27.7 8.6 | | 8.1 |
| 5/Y | 9 | 8.6 7.6 | | 15.3 8.0 | | 6.7 | 8 | 20.9 11.8 | | 29.4 9.4 | | 8.5 |
| | 10 | 8.2 7.1 | | 14.8 10.7 | | 6.6 | 9 | 18.6 10.5 | | 22.4 11.2 | | 3.8 |
| 6/Y | 11 | 6.8 5.2 | | 12.2 9.5 | | 5.4 | | | | | | |
| | 12 | 7.6 6.2 | | 9.8 4.9 | | 2.2 | | | | | | |
| 11/W | 15 | 5.9 6.4 | | 9.9 8.4 | | 4.0 | 11 | 13.6 9.7 | | 21.4 12.2 | | 7.8 |
| | 16 | 4.9 5.0 | | 8.0 5.1 | | 3.1 | 12 | 13.9 7.6 | | 18.3 7.8 | | 4.4 |
| 10/W | 17 | 6.9 6.2 | | 15.0 9.3 | | 8.1 | 13 | 19.3 10.9 | | 28.5 13.4 | | 9.2 |
| | 18 | 4.8 3.9 | | 10.0 5.5 | | 5.2 | 14 | 16.4 10.6 | | 22.4 13.6 | | 6.0 |
| | | | | | | | 15 | 17.2 10.7 | | 23.7 11.0 | | 6.5 |

with the aim of discovering and/or comparing the amounts of reading progress made by different classes, the figures for the average gains in reading progress shown in Table 15-18 — which have been adjusted for differences in chronological age, non-verbal intelligence and pre-test reading level — certainly posed the question of how these different levels of progress had occurred. This suggested that it might be worth re-examining the various available records of classroom practices, in order to discover if they contained clues to the answer.

It will be remembered that the teachers in the intensive study schools had kept daily logs of all reading and allied activities in their classes for four and six week periods during the autumn and spring terms respectively. An analysis of this data was made on the basis of a detailed examination of the collections of every teacher's daily logs, from which a broad description of the emphasis on such activities within each specific classroom was arrived at.

One important finding was that, with rare exceptions, the activity pattern remained stable within a classroom over the two periods during which the logs were kept. A second finding was that, although teachers in general engaged in very similar activities (for example, listening to children reading, relating a story, teaching phonics and initiating free writing), the relative emphasis placed on these activities was often quite different even for classes within the same school.

Unfortunately, some areas of practice (for example, spelling, grammar and comprehension) could not be directly related to the progress lists because the relative amounts of time devoted to these activities in the various classrooms was often impossible to calculate. While all teachers engaged their pupils in free writing and in listening to stories being read aloud to them, the times spent on these activities varied apparently randomly across the progress lists. Relationships between reading progress and other activities are equally unclear; for example, those classes in which phonics were taught or not taught were also scattered throughout the progress list.

However, further examination of the data on classroom activities, viewed in the light of the order of reading progress made in the classes during the year, revealed two clear pointers. First, there was the suggestion of a relationship between the time teachers spent on listening to oral reading, and the average reading progress of the class. Furthermore, the relationship may come as a surprise to many teachers, in that classes higher up the progress list tended to be those whose teachers placed the least emphasis on listening to children's oral reading. The second clear difference between classes at the top of the reading progress list and the less successful classes, was the greater time devoted to uninterrupted private reading and to discussion about books read in those classes where most reading progress was made. The pupils in the second-year class which was far ahead of all others by the end of the year, also engaged in fairly advanced topic work, with extensive homework in the spring term.

Table 15-18

*Order of classes in terms of reading progress in one school year
(Adjusted for differences in chronological age, non-verbal intelligence
and initial reading achievement levels)*

| 1st Year Classes | | | 2nd Year Classes | | |
|---|---|---|---|---|---|
| School | Class | Progress* | School | Class | Progress* |
| 2/Z | 3 | 9.7 | 7/Y | 5 | 13.7 |
| 8/Y | 8 | 8.5 | 10/W | 13 | 9.2 |
| 2/Z | 2 | 8.0 | 5/Y | 8 | 8.5 |
| 10/W | 17 | 8.1 | 11/W | 11 | 7.8 |
| 1/Z | 1 | 7.4 | 1/Z | 1 | 7.7 |
| 4/Z | 5 | 7.0 | 7/Y | 6 | 8.1 |
| 7/Y | 6 | 6.9 | 8/Y | 7 | 7.8 |
| 3/Z | 4 | 6.5 | 10/W | 15 | 6.5 |
| 5/Y | 9 | 6.7 | 10/W | 14 | 6.0 |
| 5/Y | 10 | 6.6 | 4/Z | 4 | 6.2 |
| 6/Y | 11 | 5.4 | 3/Z | 3 | 5.1 |
| 12/W | 14 | 5.3 | 2/Z | 2 | 4.9 |
| 10/W | 18 | 5.2 | 11/W | 12 | 4.4 |
| 11/W | 15 | 4.0 | 6/Y | 10 | 4.1 |
| 11/W | 16 | 3.1 | 5/Y | 9 | 3.8 |
| 7/Y | 7 | 2.3 | | | |
| 9/X | 13 | 2.2 | | | |
| 6/Y | 12 | 2.2 | | | |

(*i.e. the mean gain in raw score for the class. Reference to the Manual suggests that a 'typical' class would progress by about 6–7 raw score points in a 9 month period.)

The following Tables 15-19(a) and (b) provide brief summaries of the oral reading practices in the different classes; the classes being listed in the order in which they were presented in the reading progress lists in Table 15-18, that is, the classes with the greatest reading progress appearing first.

A careful examination of these two tables will reveal a gradual increase in emphasis on oral reading practice as one moves down each of these progress orders. The pattern is particularly noticeable for the first-year classes and, in fact, a correlation of −0.46 was found between average raw score improvement on the *Wide-Span Reading Test* (Brimer 1972) and average time spent per week in each first-year class on this activity. The negative sign simply reflects the fact that as time spent on oral reading decreases, the average Brimer score improvement increases, and this correlation is significant at the 5% level. The equivalent correlation for the second-year classes is −0.35, and it can be seen from Table 15-19(b) that in fact there is rather more uniformity in the

Table 15.19(a)

*Oral reading practice in 1st year classes*

| School | Class | Time* | |
|--------|-------|-------|---|
| 2/Z | 3 | 66 | *Below average readers only.* Group and individual. 5 min each *2 days only.* |
| 8/Y | 8 | 25 | *Groups only* (10 per group). 10 min per group. Once weekly. |
| 2/Z | 2 | 156 | *Groups for better readers* (3–4 per group). 10 min per group or individual. Once weekly. |
| 10/W | 17 | 93 | Individual. 2–4 min each. Once weekly. |
| 1/Z | 1 | 196 | Not clear, but 2–3 min per child if individual. Weekly. |
| 4/Z | 5 | 228 | Individual. 5 min for AA, 10 min for A and BA. Once weekly. |
| 7/Y | 6 | 69 | Individual. 3 min each *A and BA only.* Weekly A, twice BA. |
| 3/Z | 4 | 113 | Individual. 4 min each. Once weekly. |
| 5/Y | 9 | 157 | Individual. 3–5 min each. Once weekly. |
| 5/Y | 10 | 124 | Individual. 3 min each. Once weekly. |
| 6/Y | 11 | 271 | Individual. 10 min each. *AA and A once/twice BA three times* weekly. |
| 12/W | 14 | 338 | Individual. 2–3 min each. *Daily.* |
| 10/W | 18 | 118 | Group and individual. 10 min per group, 5 min per individual. *Daily.* |
| 11/W | 15 | 259 | Individual. 2–5 min each. *AA 4 times/ week. BA once/twice weekly.* |
| 11/W | 16 | 81 | Group and individual. *40 min per group* (8). *3 min per individual. A and BA up to 3 times/week.* |
| 7/Y | 7 | 207 | Individual. 3 min each. *Often half the class each day.* Average once/twice per child each week. |
| 9/X | 13 | | Individual. 2–3 min each. Once weekly. |
| 6/Y | 12 | 215 | Individual. 5–10 min each. *AA and BA once to three times* per week respectively. |

(*Average time (minutes) spent per week by the teacher listening to individual children reading aloud.)

average time spent in these classes on the oral reading practice – this general time being lower than for first-year classes. A lower emphasis is often reflected in a lesser amount of time, in general, being spent on the activity, and this is achieved either by engaging fewer children in the activity or by spending less time per child, perhaps by using a more effective organizational approach such as grouping readers at similar levels.

It would seem reasonable to suppose that the less time a teacher spends hearing children reading (and simultaneously helping queues

Table 15-19(b)

*Oral reading practice in 2nd year classes*

| School | Class | Time* | |
|--------|-------|-------|---|
| 7/Y | 5 | 111 | Individual. 2–3 min each. Weekly. *AA fortnightly*. Remedial group. |
| 10/W | 13 | 33 | Individual. 5 min each. *Poor readers only (6)*. Remedial group. |
| 5/Y | 8 | 153 | Individual. 3–4 min each. Once weekly. |
| 11/Y | 11 | 129 | Individual. 3–15 min each. (Spring 1–2 min.) One to three times per week. |
| 1/Z | 1 | 99 | Individual. 2–3 min each weekly. |
| 7/Y | 6 | 141 | Individual. 2–3 min each weekly. Remedial group. |
| 8/Y | 7 | | Individual. 2–5 min each weekly. |
| 10/W | 15 | 56 | Group and individual. 10  15 min per group (3–5). 3–4 min per individual. Weekly. |
| 10/W | 14 | 163 | Group and individual. 10–15 min per group (6). Weekly. |
| 4/Z | 4 | 191 | Individual. 3–10 min each. *Not AA*. Once/twice weekly. Occasionally 15–20 min each. |
| 3/Z | 3 | 200 | Individual. 5 min each. Weekly. |
| 2/Z | 2 | 246 | Individual. 5–10 min each. Weekly. |
| 11/W | 12 | 113 | Individual. 1–2 min each. *Often half the class each day*. |
| 6/Y | 10 | 116 | Individual. 5–10 min each. Once/twice weekly. |
| 5/Y | 9 | 139 | No detailed information given. |

(*Average time (minutes) spent per week by the teacher listening to individual children reading aloud.)

of children with their spellings), the more opportunity that teacher would have to be aware of what other children in the class were doing, to help or encourage them as necessary, and to discuss their reading experiences with them. Some of the time thus released could also be spent on individual diagnosis and/or direct teaching of groups of children known to have particular weaknesses.

## IV Summary

1. During the first two years of the project, certain assessments of the reading proficiencies of average readers in their classes were carried out by teachers in the two large Teachers' Reading Research Groups. These assessments were followed in the intensive study year by a battery of individual assessments and standardized tests of intellectual

ability, and reading and related skills, administered by the researchers and their helpers to whole classes, selected groups of children, and individual children in the 12 schools.

2.   When children's sight vocabulary was tested on the first 200 words of *Key Words to Literacy*, it was found that 20% of average readers of 8 years recognised all the words, while the proportion for 9 year-olds was 32%. The remaining 80% and 68% of pupils respectively, made errors ranging from 1–35. Of these, 17% of average readers of 8 years and nearly 4% of average readers of 9 years failed to read 10 or more of the words.

3.   When knowledge of the meanings of discrete words possessed by average readers of 7 to 9 years was assessed on *Crichton's Vocabulary Scale*, it was found that the children gained much higher scores than the children on whom the test was standardized in 1951. It is suggested that this could probably be attributed to the greater verbal stimulation of current primary schools and to the increase in television viewing. It was also noted that children with about the same levels of reading ability displayed wide variations in their success in defining words out of context; the words correctly defined by average first-year readers ranging from 16–62 and for second-years 25–59.

4.   Pilot investigations carried out in the Teachers' Reading Research Groups into children's phonic skills showed that even average readers in first- and second-year junior classes were not always familiar with common phonic rules, while some children were unable to give the sounds of all the letters of the alphabet.

5.   A new diagnostic phonic test, in the form of 'nonsense words', was devised for use in the intensive study schools. It was used with children of above average, average and below average reading ability and was found to be effective at diagnosing phonic weaknesses at every level. It should prove equally valuable for use by class teachers.

The results of the test showed that while many children, especially those of above average reading ability in each age group, demonstrated a working knowledge of the common phonic rules represented in the test, there were still many children, and particularly those of below average reading ability, whose knowledge was either sketchy or non-existent. In general, the categories of phonic skills least well known were vowel digraphs, the rule of the silent 'e', and murmur vowels, in that order; followed by common endings of words and silent letters. The test also indicated that a number of children still confused letters such as 'b' and 'd'.

The fact that only part of the deficiencies shown by first-years had been overcome by second-years suggests that either teachers were unaware of the particular areas of weakness displayed by individual pupils or that the teaching provided may not have been effective because it was not aimed at the precise problems experienced by individual children. (As it happened, the phonic teaching observed in the intensive study schools usually took the form of class lessons, whereas the results of the diagnostic test indicate that a much more diffuse and varied programme is required for different groups of children, and for individual children.) The importance of teachers diagnosing phonic weaknesses in individual children and taking measures to rectify them is further emphasized by the fact that performance on the phonic test showed high correlations with the results of the two reading tests. (0.73 with *Southgate Group Reading Test 2*, and 0.63 with *Wide-Span Reading Test.*)

6. A battery of three standardized tests, two of reading ability and one of intellectual capacity, was administered to all the children in the classes used in the intensive study schools. *Southgate Group Reading Test 2* (Southgate 1962) was used for the first screening test and proved suitable for this purpose, as whole classes could be tested in less than half-an-hour and the scripts were easy and quick to mark. It was followed by *Wide-Span Reading Test* (Brimer 1972) which had a much higher ceiling and so could be used to assess reading progress over the year. *Coloured Progressive Matrices* (Raven 1949) was selected to test children's intellectual ability on the grounds that it was uncontaminated by verbal ability. All three tests fulfilled the purposes for which they had been selected, although with both Raven's *Matrices* and, to a lesser extent, *Southgate Group Reading Test 2,* the children tended to score more highly than the children on whom the tests were standardized, (Raven's *Matrices* in 1947 and *Southgate 2* in 1962).

7. When scores from these three standardized tests were compared with each other and with the scores achieved on *Crichton's Vocabulary Scale* and on the new diagnostic phonic test, it was found that the two reading tests agreed very closely with each other (r=0.81). Scores from the phonic test also correlated highly with the two reading tests as already mentioned under point 5. The tests of intellectual capacity and verbal ability, as one would expect, also showed fairly close relationships with the reading tests, correlations ranging from 0.73 to 0.41 (based on a truncated sample of average readers).

8. A comparison of the pre-test and post-test scores on Brimer's *Wide-Span Reading Test* revealed that even when classes commenced the year with similar average reading standards, there were great variations in the progress they made by the end of the year, (even for classes within the same school). This still held good after adjustments had been made for chronological age, intellectual capacity and initial reading achievement, which strongly suggests the influence of class-based factors.

9. The tentative conclusions drawn about possible reasons for the wide differences in reading progress between the classes were based mainly on the teachers' logs, i.e. their own written records of the daily activities related to reading and related skills in their own classes. Two

pointers emerged from a further examination of this data. There was a tendency for classes which made most reading progress to be those in which the teachers spent the least time in listening to children's oral reading. Furthermore, in the most successful classes, a greater proportion of time was devoted to children's uninterrupted private reading and to discussions about books read.

# V Implications for Teachers

1. As the first 200 of *Key Words to Literacy* account for half to three-quarters of the running words occurring in everyday reading matter, it is essential that teachers of 7, 8 and 9 year-olds should ensure that all their pupils have instant recognition of all these words. Teachers would find it helpful, particularly near the beginning of the first junior year, to check which of these words each child does and does not recognize. The actual errors made by each child should be noted and arrangements made for practice and constant review until children have not the slightest hesitation in recognizing every word. This same procedure would be equally applicable to average and above average infants and to slower older readers. When those children who were making errors have reached a stage of instant recognition of all 200 *Key Words*, there should be a noticeable improvement in their fluency in reading.

2. As children's knowledge of word meanings was shown to be closely related to their reading progress, teachers would be wise to continue, and even increase, those activities in which they are already engaged, and which are designed to extend children's vocabulary. Children with poor verbal fluency could benefit particularly in this way. Teachers who take every opportunity to stimulate, in all their pupils, a permanent interest in enlarging their vocabularies by collecting and using new and exciting words will be likely to see improvements not only in the children's reading progress but also in their spoken and written language.

3. As it has been shown that some children show a complete lack of knowledge of the simplest and/or most common phonic rules in the English language, while even average and above average readers in second-year classes have not achieved complete mastery of these rules, and, furthermore, that knowledge of these rules bears a close relationship to reading progress in general, the implications for teachers of children aged 7 to 9 years are absolutely clear. Diagnosis of individual children's phonic strengths and weaknesses is the first essential step — and the new phonic test is an effective instrument for this purpose. The aim need not be to test every child in the class at the beginning of the school year, but a start should certainly be made, as rapidly as possible, with those children who appear to be the least proficient readers. Accurate records of individual weaknesses need to be kept for every child and these records should be updated as skills are mastered.

Steps then need to be taken to teach children those skills which are found to be weak. Class teaching will only be the appropriate means for doing so if the entire class is ignorant of the rule in question. In most other cases group teaching of only those particular children who have shown lack of mastery of certain sounds or rules would be most effective. The members of such groups would vary on different occasions, depending on which children did or did not know the skill to be taught and practised. In certain cases, individual tuition would be called for. The fact that the smallest number of phonic deficiencies are usually displayed by children of above average reading ability means that once a teacher has diagnosed and rectified the few phonic weaknesses among the most fluent readers in her class, further attention can be devoted to providing phonic tuition for average and below average readers, in the required proportions and in the deficient areas disclosed by diagnosis. (A list of publications and aids to the teaching of phonics, which should prove helpful to teachers, is provided in Appendix 15-C.)

4.  The implications, drawn in this chapter, about reasons for some classes making so much greater reading progress than other classes, in one school year, will probably come as a surprise to many teachers who devote so much of their time to listening to children's individual oral reading. Yet the inferences are clear. A lesson in which a teacher listens to large numbers of individual children reading aloud to her, for only a brief period each, while other children are supposed to be reading or writing – and constantly interrupting her to ask for help with spellings – does not provide a peaceful atmosphere in which children can become absorbed in their reading or in which teachers can undertake diagnosis or engage in interesting discussions about books with the children. A reading programme, based on these findings, would include: lengthy periods in which every child was reading silently, and uninterrupted, for his own information and pleasure; some time when the teacher was discussing their books and reading interests with the whole class or a group of children; and periods in which the teacher would devote fairly substantial amounts of time to diagnosing individual children's strengths and weaknesses, as well as their interests in reading, and arranging with them programmes designed to fit their individual needs.

# CHAPTER 16

# The Strategies Children Use in Reading: Miscue Analysis

## I The Act of Reading

In Chapter 3, entitled 'Learning to Read – and Reading', it is made clear that the process of reading is closely bound up with total language experience. Although teachers may plan to help children's reading by teaching progressively more difficult reading skills, they become aware that some children seem to succeed although by-passing certain steps in this programme, while others still find difficulty however carefully they have followed the teacher's instructions. It appears, then, that a plan for teaching 'sequential skills' may not be the most helpful teaching programme.

When a young child looks at books he learns to recognize whole words which fulfil a function for him. His name, for instance, will probably be the first word which assumes a real identity for him. Usually, however, it is only when he comes to writing for himself that he begins to realize the need to distinguish single letters and realizes the need to build up words. As he enters school he meets written symbols in the form of single letters: A, B, C, etc. The letter is a shape on the page which he may be taught corresponds with a single sound. For example 'G' 'stands for' the *sound* 'g' which 'stands for' his name – Gilbert. He will learn to recognize the letter via some perceptual distinctions of his own invention (perhaps helped by the tactile sense while writing it), but he will initially only recognize it as corresponding to one sound – the one which served the role of starting the word 'Gilbert'.

Now the child has to accommodate the letter written in different forms – that is, not 'G' but 'g' or 'g'. He has to learn that what he thinks is the same letter upside down – 'b', is a completely different entity. He begins to select the *distinctive features* of letters and words. It is not necessary to make a complete inventory list to find out what these are; it is done by rapid *unconscious* comparing and discarding prompted by recognition of similarities and differences between the two like objects.

He then finds that 'g' is not always found at the beginning of a word. He may discover it at the end of 'bag'. He accepts this, because although it is in a different place it is stall making more or less the same sound as it did in 'Gilbert'.

When he finds 'g' again in 'laugh' or 'huge', however, the child's conceptual framework has to expand considerably. He reaches one of the crucial points in reading acquisition — a link has to be developed conceptually between the identity of letters and their varying functions, and the whole-word recognition which has usually been proceeding in parallel. He has to realize that 'laugh', which he may have recognized as a whole word in his reading book, has elements *within it* which can be recognized separately. And he is also faced with the fact that one element, the letter 'g', is not doing the same thing at all that it did in 'Gilbert' or 'bag'. The child gradually acknowledges the fact that the recognition of a letter on its own does not mean very much. His attention shifts from preoccupation with the distinctive features of the letter to the incorporation of it as one of the possible distinctive features of a word — and from there to recognition of certain words as distinctive features of a sentence. At that stage he will now *only* register the letter if it is a helpful way of recognizing a word.

As the experience of reading builds up, we do not discard our awareness of any particular level of recognition completely; it is just that one way of perceiving the text comes to the fore on certain occasions. For example, in the sentence: 'He laughed in agony when the huge weight ground him into the ground', there are a number of instances of the letter 'g' appearing. In normal adult reading none of them would have been isolated. They exist in the sentence, carrying some sort of invariate quality of 'g'-ness with them, although playing very different roles. It is also unlikely that the separate words would be consciously distinguished at first, until the reader comes up against something which is unexpected in the sentence. If the words are found to be playing unexpected roles he will go back to re-read them. Two phrases in the above sentence are likely to be picked out in this way, for different reasons — first, 'he laughed in agony'. This is correct grammatically, but surely the verb must be wrong? The reader looks again at 'laughed'. Is it a mis-spelling or has he read the word wrongly? Similarly he looks at 'ground' when it appears for the second time in the phrase 'ground him into the ground'. It is an unusual literary convention to repeat a word in such a short phrase, especially as the juxtaposition emphasizes the two different uses of the word. As he considers these questions the reader is working from the meaning, from his expectations; from the whole to the part. This is not at all the same operation as the young child's 'whole word' recognition of 'laugh' in his early reader. The adult has a wealth of experience behind him which complicates the mental processes. If he had been reading one word at a time (as children often do in learning to read), no incongruities would have struck him. He is expecting certain conventions, both syntactic and semantic, to be followed, and his selection of distinctive features is governed by the extent to which these expectations are brought into doubt.

The child, who may not yet be motivated to grasp meaning from the text, has to be shown that he must learn to operate as a skilled reader as quickly as possible. Working sequentially through a programme of letter recognition, word recognition and syllabification to contextual guessing is not necessarily the best way to achieve this. The number of items which can be held in short term memory are relevant here, too. If it can only hold up to seven items at a time, these items are better as meaningful units than, for example, phonemes.

Much interest has been shown recently in the nature of mental planning and the structuring of behaviour. Learning most skills involves the ritualizing of certain patterns which results in making some thinking 'automatic'. This will occur through the repeated practice of sequences of events, and is right and necessary. But we must be able to discriminate, when teaching, between the elements which need to be automatized and what may merely be 'superstitious' learning on the child's part; there is often a great deal of this, particularly in the assimilation of phonics. For instance, the child believes he ought to sound out a word letter-by-letter, and does so regardless of the fact that the sounds he mumbles could never make up the word — which, however, he often gets successfully in the end! He believes that he should never leave out a word; should never guess. Automatization is not *empty* ritualization, but an economical way of packaging knowledge which has initially been *understood*. Teachers need, therefore, to give children a chance to exploit their expectations of a text, already present through their experience of life and language.

There are two main ways in which expectations can be fulfilled in reading text; the first is the human proclivity to find *patterns* which are repeated regularly, although the repetition is not always distinguishable at first. Once the elements of a pattern are recognized, however, we look for them again and are thereby able to incorporate apparently meaningless features into a coherent whole. Spelling exceptions, for example, are often elements in a pattern if viewed from the aspect of word derivation.

At the stage of reading under investigation children are already finding patterns which may be visual or syntactic, but which will in time become automatized as the same patterns emerge over and over again in print. We travel on railway lines rather than in a car when we read. We have a regular base to work from.

The second way in which expectations will be aroused and fulfilled develops from the belief that reading should make sense, should mean something. The determination to break the code comes from the confidence that there is a reward of meaning to be gained. The thinking that the reader uses to fulfil this type of expectation is different, though, from the automatized responses developed from pattern finding. He begins to make associations with what he finds on the page and what already exists in his conceptual framework. This operation is rarely

automatized – we are in the train looking out of the window and noticing what we see and explaining it to ourselves. Some phrases which
originally involved conscious awareness of meaning do get assimilated
automatically and become 'pre-processed phrases'. They are sights
which we observe so often on the journey that we hardly notice them
although they are still part of the scenery. For very young children
'once upon a time', 'long ago and far away', 'they lived happily ever
after' become ritual phrases (if, of course, they are still fed on a diet
of fairy tales). The most vivid understanding will occur, however,
when the reading matter changes existing concepts radically – in other
words, when it surprises the reader, although he can only be surprised
if his expectations are refuted, so he must have a backcloth of relevant
experience for this to occur. Alternatively, when his expectations are
reinforced totally by reading he will be deeply satisfied.

Many other factors, including cognitive style and attitudes to reading
affect the extent to which it can become a necessary adjunct to existence. As soon as possible it should serve real needs, should be just another
way of receiving language which is almost as natural in a literate society
as listening to speech. Teachers should be aware of the whole process,
both in children and in themselves. It is a mixture of conscious and
unconscious processes with subtle interactions.

In this project, an attempt was made to disentangle some of these
processes in the children observed; the children of average reading
ability who had reached the point of becoming skilled practitioners.
Measures were devised to see how far the ability to see patterns had
become automatized, and if the children realized that they could
extract meaning from the written word. The following devices were
employed in an attempt to isolate the strategies in use, rather than to
grade the readers on a ladder of sequential skill mastery.

## II Detection of Strategies

Standardized reading tests provide a measure of the reader's achievement in relation to the expected development for his age. A teacher
needs, however, additional information to allow her to give aid to
individual children. It has already been emphasized how crucial the
7 to 9 year-old stage is, since the utilization of phonic cues reaches its
peak at about this stage in average readers. After this, strategies, if not
different in kind, need to be different in emphasis, in order to encourage
the shift from 'word-by-word' reading to 'mature' reading. The practice
of hearing children read aloud has traditionally constituted the main
method of instruction in the classroom, but is often associated merely
with the mastery of word-recognition skills. In trying to investigate the
overall strategies in use, it was necessary to devise a way of using oral
reading more searchingly, in an attempt to diagnose how far these
children were utilizing their existing language experience, their awareness of collocation and syntax, and their phonic skills.

The use of strategies can only be surmised, particularly with children of this age, many of whom would be unable to verbalize their mental activities. It was therefore necessary to insert obstacles in the way, and to observe the methods by which children overcame these obstacles. Two diagnostic procedures were used:

1. A fairly difficult passage was selected for oral reading, to tax the child's decoding skills, although not to the point of complete frustration; the errors made were then categorized;
2. A passage from which words had been deleted was presented, and the children were asked to fill in the missing words during silent reading.

Both methods have been used extensively in research and classroom practice; the first is known as 'Miscue Analysis' and the second as 'Cloze Procedure'. During the first two years of the project, a great deal of preliminary work was undertaken with these two methods of diagnosis, both in pilot tests and in the Teachers' Reading Research Groups, in preparation for the intensive study in the third year. The investigations based on Miscue Analysis are reported in this chapter, while those utilizing Cloze Procedure are reported in Chapter 17.

## III Miscue Analysis

### A. *Previous Research in Miscue Analysis*

It is debatable whether the same strategies are used in oral as in silent reading. Golinkoff (1975), surveying the literature dealing with the links between decoding and comprehension of text, found that some information on comprehension may be gained from factors in oral reading *(viz.* the rate of reading, the recognition of phrase boundaries and the nature of errors incurred). The comparison of results of comprehension tests following silent and oral reading imply that it is valid to use the study of errors in oral reading as a partial reflection of silent reading processes.

Although it is possible for oral reading to appear fluent with little real understanding occurring, some idea of the suitability of strategies can be achieved by analysing errors made during reading aloud. The theory was introduced by Goodman (1965, 1968), who preferred to replace the term 'error' by 'miscue', since he believed that some errors are positive indicators of good strategy. An analogy may be drawn with early language acquisition; the child learning to speak devises his own grammar, showing that he realizes the presence of structure in language although he may mis-apply the rules: for example, 'Me want', 'I goed'. Although Goodman's methods of analysing miscues are complicated and time-consuming, an attempt will be made to suggest simplified methods for teachers to adopt the same principles in the normal classroom routine.

The bulk of research into oral reading has occurred since 1960, although some studies go as far back as 1940. It is difficult, though, to detect a clear pattern of procedure, largely because there is still no really satisfactory model of the reading process. It is only since a psycholinguistic model was set up (see Chapter 3: 'Learning to Read and Reading'), that the importance of observing reading *in context*, rather than single word-recognition skills, was recognized.

Originally, the errors made in an orally read passage had been viewed only as evidence of a lack of skill on the part of the reader. The classroom application of this theory was exemplified, in the USA, by the development of Informal Reading Inventories of which the first was by Betts (1946). These have been discussed in Chapter 9. In using Informal Reading Inventories, errors are not classified, but are merely counted as indicators of failure to achieve a target of 100% accuracy of word recognition and correct pronunciation.

Certain researchers, however, soon began to realize that the strategies in use by the reader could be diagnosed by examining the nature of the errors made, rather than by counting them all as signs of failure. MacKinnon (1959) and Merritt (1969) typified this approach. Intensive analyses in case-study form were carried out by Goodman (1967), Clay (1968) and Weber (1968). The *Neale Analysis of Reading Skills* (1958) was one of the few diagnostic reading tests which classified types of error, though it still did so with a view to eradicating the *faults* thus identified. In 1965 Goodman published the first of a series of papers describing attempts to look more positively at errors, and it was at that time that he coined the term 'miscues'.

Clay (1968) and Weber (1970) looked at the miscues of readers made during normal class routine, analysing reading over a period of time, which meant that they had little control over the variable of text. Most studies, however, arising from Goodman's approach have been qualitative and descriptive, examining the miscues of individual children in great detail (for example, Burke and Goodman 1970).

Biemiller's research (1970) is one of the few to trace developmental trends on a small sample of 42 children in the first-grade (i.e. 6 to 7 year-olds). He concluded that this method of examining oral reading can be a powerful diagnostic tool, both for regular and remedial reading. He noticed that in the higher grades it was retarded readers who over-used or misused graphic information.

Hood (1975) criticized the lack of standard procedure in oral reading analysis, and showed how difficult it is to achieve standardization because of the nature of the exercise. Because the observation is confined to errors, there can be no prior information on the number or nature of those errors and subjective categorization is likely to affect results. There is thus very little real consensus, and in choosing one way of analysing errors one may omit many valuable clues as to the use of strategies. Clay and Imlach's (1971) attempts to categorize juncture, pitch and stress in oral reading might well yield equally valuable information or the extensive corpus of work on eye—voice span (Gibson and Levin 1975). The investigations described in this project, therefore, used Goodman's methods of analysis but it is emphasized that it is the *attitude* towards oral reading which is important, rather than any one particular approach.

## B. *Miscue Analysis in the Intensive Study Schools*

### 1. Procedure

The immediate aim was to see how children were utilizing, in a test, the different cues available to them in an active, problem-solving, and systematic way. The miscues of four 'average' readers in each first- and second-year class in the schools in the intensive study year were analysed, in order to see how they were utilizing language cues. A total of 127 children from 10 schools were included: 32 boys and 31 girls were first-year juniors, and 30 boys and 34 girls were second-years.

The following passage taken from *More About Paddington* (Bond 1959) was used. (Reading level of 9+ on Spache Readability Formula (1953).)

> Mrs Bird's contribution had been some bright new curtains for the windows, which Paddington liked very much. In fact, the first night he spent in his new room he couldn't make up his mind whether to have them drawn together so that he could admire them or left apart so that he could see the view. He got out of bed several times and eventually decided to have one drawn and the other left back so that he could have the best of both worlds.
>
> Then something strange caught his eye. Paddington made a point of keeping a torch by the side of his bed in case there was an emergency during the night, and it was while he was flashing it on and off to admire the drawn curtain that he noticed it. Each time he flashed the torch there was an answering flicker of light from somewhere outside. He sat up in bed, rubbing his eyes, and stared in the direction of the window.
>
> He decided to try a more complicated signal. Two short flashes followed by several long ones. When he did so he nearly fell out of bed with surprise, for each time he sent a signal, it was repeated in exactly the same way through the glass.
>
> Paddington jumped out of bed and rushed to the window. He stayed there for a long while peering out at the garden, but he couldn't see anything at all. Having made sure the window was tightly shut, he drew both curtains and hurried back to bed, pulling the clothes over his head a little farther than usual. It was all very mysterious and Paddington didn't believe in taking any chances.
>
> It was Mr Brown at breakfast next morning who gave him his first clue.

As a 'Paddington' series was currently being televised, it was expected that the extract would be within the children's experience. Before reading the passage each child was asked to read to the tester ten of the most difficult words in the passage, presented singly on flash cards. He was then told something of the context of the passage and the names of the characters, before reading the passage aloud to the tester. He had been warned that he would not be helped with words unless it was absolutely necessary (i.e. after a lengthy pause). No corrections were made. The reading was tape-recorded.

A note was made of whether the passage was read word by word or with normal intonation. This was bound to be a somewhat subjective judgement but, in pilot tests, timing the rate of reading a passage had not proved useful, as children's natural rates of reading vary greatly. At a later stage the tape-recorded reading was coded for miscues onto a transcript. (In the normal school routine children could easily be trained to tape-record themselves without the teacher's presence.)

## 2. Classification of miscues

All deviations from the original text were marked on the transcript, coded in the categories shown in Table 16-1. An example of a marked transcript is given on p. 270.

Table 16-1

*Classification of miscues – in passage from 'Paddington' test*

| Original Text | Miscue | Coding Symbol | Explanation |
|---|---|---|---|
| Mrs Bird's contribution | Non-response | contribution | Prompting required |
| made a point of keeping | Hesitation | made a point of/keeping | Hesitation, but word finally supplied |
| whether to have them | Repetition | whether to have them | Underline word or phrase repeated (1 repetition) |
| It was Mr Brown | Self-correction | It was Mrs Mr Brown | Substitutes or makes other error, but then supplies right word |
| a more complicated signal | Substitution | a more complicated complashant signal | Substitutes one word for another |
| fell out of bed | Insertion | fell out of/the bed | Inserts word or phrase |
| peering out at the garden | Omission | peering out (at) the garden | Omits word or phrase |
| to have one drawn | Reversal | one ⌐ drawn | Reverses word or phrase |

## Example of Coded Transcript

*Words Correct In/Out of Context* (Out of context -7, In context -7, Difference -0)

view ✓✓    farther ✓✓    caught ✓✓    exactly ˣˣ    direction ✓✓
emergency ✓✓    answering ✓✓    contributioñs ˣˣ    eventually ✓✓    mysterious ×✕

Mrs Bird's /contribution had been some bright new curtains for the win-

dows, which Paddington liked very much. In fact, the first night he

spent in his new room he couldn't make up his mind whether to have

them ~~drawn~~ *dawn* together so that he could /~~admire~~ *admoor* them or left apart so that

he could see the view. He got out of bed several  times and/eventually

~~decided~~ *excited* to have one drawn and the other left back so (that) he could

have the best of both worlds.

Then something strange caught his  eye. Paddington made a point of

keeping a torch by the side of his bed in case there was an emergency

during the night, and it was <u>while</u> he was flashing it on and off ~~to~~ *he* /

~~admire~~ *admeer* the drawn curtain that (he) noticed it. Each time he flashed

the torch there was an answering /flicker of light from somewhere out-

side. He sat up in bed rubbing /his eyes, and ~~stared~~ *stared* in the direction of

the window.

He decided to try a more ~~complicated~~ *competition* signal.  Two short flashes foll-

owed by several ~~longer~~ *long* ones.  When he did so he nearly fell out of ˄the bed

with surprise, for each time he sent a signal it was repeated in ~~exactly~~ *extraly*

the same way through  the glass.

Paddington jumped out of bed and rushed (to) the window. /He stayed

there for a long while / peering out at the garden, but he couldn't see anything at all. Having made sure the window was tightly shut, he drew

both curtains and hurried back to bed, pulling the clothes over his head

a little/farther than usual. It was all very /mysterious̶ *mystrious* and Paddington

didn't believe in taking a̶n̶y̶ *the* chances.

It was Mr Brown, at breakfast next morning, who gave him h̶i̶s̶ *the* first clue.

| Miscue Totals | | | | Word by Word Reading | | |
|---|---|---|---|---|---|---|
| Non-responses | 1 | Substitutions | 11 | Yes/No | | |
| Hesitations | 10 | Insertions | 1 | GRA | SYN | SEM |
| Repetitions | 1 | Omissions | 3 | % | | |
| Self-corrections | 4 | Reversals | – | | | |

Total errors (omitting self-corrections) = 27

| Graphic Similarity | | | | Grammatical Strength | | | | | Comprehension Strength | | | |
|---|---|---|---|---|---|---|---|---|---|---|---|---|
| Column | Y | P | N | Column | Y | P | N | o/c | Column | Y | P | N |
| Total | 7 | 1 | 3 | Total | 7 | 3 | 5 | | Total | 11 | 0 | 5 |
| % | 69 | 9 | 27 | % | 47 | 20 | 33 | | % | 69 | | 31 |
| Miscue Total | 11 | | | Pattern Total | 15 | | | | Miscue Total | 16 | | |

Y = Yes, P = Partial, N = No

### 3. Analysis of miscues

The main purpose of the analysis was to see how far the strategies used indicated a varying emphasis on different levels of language. As described earlier in this chapter, the mature reader samples on the most convenient level for his needs. If he is familiar with the subject-matter and is confirming expectations he will be using mainly the *semantic* level. His knowledge of the way language fits together, for example, word-order and grammatical features, will enable him to use the *syntactic* level as a cuing system. The syntactic and semantic levels together imply the use of *context*. Unfamiliarity with a text, or immaturity in reading, will force a greater concentration on the *grapho-phonemic* level, in which the perception of the visual display is matched to phonic knowledge. Here *word-recognition* skills are likely to be utilized without the use of context.

The analysis, based on Goodman's procedures, is described in detail in Appendix 16-A. The assumption behind this is that comprehension can be assessed to some extent from oral reading, since if a reader hypothesizes from the context he must be understanding it. If many of his miscues show a similarity on the grapho-phonemic level, but do not make sense, it is possible that understanding is not occurring.

## 4. Results of miscue analysis

Certain questions, arising from expectations of children's reading development at this stage were asked; the answers were obtained from the data provided by the analysis.

*Question 1: Did the relationships between the use of the three language levels indicate differences in strategy?*

It was hypothesized that younger or less able readers would make greater use of grapho-phonemic cues, whereas more mature readers would employ all three levels of language, showing that they were also aware of contextual constraints. The analysis produced three final percentages for each child, worked out according to a modification of Goodman's analysis. One showed *graphic strength* (the extent to which miscues approximated to the visual/auditory constraints), the second showed *grammatical strength* (the extent to which miscues are syntactically suitable), and the third *comprehension strength* (indicating the extent to which semantic constraints were recognized).

The correlations between the levels of language in use, judged by miscues, were very high. The miscues made by both years were in many cases suitable on all three levels.

So, in attempting to solve problems which arose in the passage, these readers showed that they were aware that the word they supplied should look and sound like the original, and should make good sense.

*Question 2: Did difference in age indicate different strategies in use?*

The children's miscues were analysed in an attempt to reveal any age or sex differences which might exist in their use of strategies. Table 16-2 shows the mean scores achieved by the children in terms of the grammatical, graphic and semantic appropriateness of their miscues.

Table 16-2

*Mean scores for graphic, grammatical and comprehension utilization for sex and sex-by-age classification*

|  |  | graphic | grammatical | comprehension |
|---|---|---|---|---|
| 7–8 year-olds | boys | 29.2 | 44.4 | 48.5 |
|  | girls | 27.6 | 43.4 | 50.0 |
| 8–9 year-olds | boys | 18.2 | 24.9 | 23.6 |
|  | girls | 22.4 | 31.5 | 28.3 |
| combined age groups | boys | 23.7 | 34.6 | 36.1 |
|  | girls | 25.0 | 37.4 | 39.2 |

(*Low* scores imply *high* utilization.)

Even allowing for the small sample sizes, it is clear that *chronological age* proved a crucial factor in the ability to use all three levels of language suitably. The mean score for graphic, grammatical and comprehension strengths showed that the older children:

(a) were generally superior in using all available cues;
(b) used semantic and syntactic cues relatively more often and more efficiently than younger children.

This means that the second-years used the visual display less and placed more emphasis on surmising from the context. The first-years tended to substitute words which bore a sight/sound relationship to the original but did not make good sense. Syntax seems to be the pivot on which sampling develops; within normal development, the reader will move from reliance on within-word graphic cues to the incorporation of syntactical awareness, using the pattern of language with which he has become familiar through usage. He also realizes that reading has meaning, and unless he encounters material which is outside his conceptual framework, the cues derived from context will become his chief source of information.

*Question 3: Did differences of sex indicate the use of different strategies?*
Although, from the data available, there did not appear to be any significant sex difference in strategies, there was a tendency for the *older boys* to be slightly more efficient than girls at using all the available cues (see Table 16-2). However, it is impossible to know whether this tendency was an artefact of the small sample or a true indication of sex difference.

*Question 4: What effect did methods of teaching reading have on use of strategies?*
Unfortunately, the small numbers of children which it proved possible to involve in this exercise from each class precluded any investigation of this possible link.

*Question 5: Did readers succeed more on recognizing words in or out of context?*
No significant differences were found here between the sexes or between the two age groups. 20% of all children read more words correctly from flash cards than the same words presented in the text. 31% of all children read words on flash cards equally well as the same words in context. 49% of all children read more words correctly in context than the same words presented on flash cards. Goodman (1965) found a more positive result in favour of reading words in context successfully. Half the readers in the present test were making good use of context, although it is surprising that second-years were no more successful in this than first-years.

*Question 6: What was the relationship between word-by-word reading and use of normal intonation?*

Exact figures are not given since judgement was subjective to some extent. There is no doubt, however, about the general trend; only a fifth of the first-year readers used a normal intonation, whereas half the second-years were reading aloud fluently. Somewhere between the first and second year, therefore, most average readers leave a word-by-word attack.

*Question 7: How did individual types of miscue indicate differing strategies?*

Some indication of development of strategies can be gained by analysing particular types of miscue, as follows.

*Substitutions:* This type of miscue can yield more diagnostic information than any other, because of the inferences to be made about the levels of language in use. Findings have already been described and a simplified method of analysis for classroom use can be found in Table 16-7.

*Non-responses:* As might be expected, the older children refused on fewer words. 24 first-year children attempted every word in the passage, and this rose to 44 children in the second-year. In the first-year 5 boys and 2 girls refused on 10 words or more; in the second-year no child refused on more than 3 words. The overall figure of 50% who attempted every word shows the confidence with which many children approached the text (which was at a readability level of 9+).

*Self-Corrections:* According to Biemiller (1970) the use of self-correction is an interim phase which disappears as reading becomes more skilful. If this is so, children in both age-groups in the present research were at this interim stage, as there was no significant difference between years on the number of self-corrections with an average of 4 in both years.

*Hesitations and refusals:* The results showed a fairly high correlation (r=0.6) between hesitations and refusals, miscues which indicate a reader lacking in word-recognition skills. There was also a fairly high correlation (r=0.6) between *hesitations and substitutions* with more of both in the first year. The correlation between self-corrections and substitutions was lower (r=0.5), with self-corrections occurring more in the second-year; the awareness of language constraints is therefore more evident with the older children. It looks as if *hesitations and repetitions* are employed as delaying devices by readers at different stages of development, since there was a negative correlation between these types of miscue. On the whole, those who repeat do so to keep the flow of reading going, while the hesitators are operating on a word-by-word basis. Those who omitted words tended not to hesitate or refuse. Omissions are often made by skilled readers, who preserve the sense while unconsciously omitting unimportant words.

Although the small numbers of children participating in the research make it impossible to generalize, further experimentation along these lines by teachers themselves may reveal emerging patterns in the type of miscue made by particular readers, dependent on a stage of development, attitude to reading, or cognitive style.

## 5. Examples of two readers

A great deal of information on strategies can be gained by qualitative evidence gained from individual children. To illustrate this, the responses of two children, in their oral reading of the Paddington passage, were examined in greater detail, with a view to practical diagnosis. One child was chosen from each year group and both fell into the band of children of average reading ability within their respective age-groups. The children were selected because analysis revealed that they used very different strategies.

The miscue analysis for each child was made solely from one reading. It may seem presumptuous to attempt diagnosis from a single transcript, and of course deductions must be tentative. Even so, these two children's strategies show up as being quite different and, consequently, it is hoped that these contrasting profiles will enable teachers to see the practical possibilities of miscue analysis. It is also interesting to note that, although according to an Informal Reading Inventory (Christenson 1969) both children would be reading this passage at frustration level, the analyses show that this was far from the truth. It seems, therefore, that making judgements on the basis of the total number of errors in oral reading is not helpful in diagnosing strategies.

### (a) *Diane (1st Year)*

The available information about Diane, other than that obtained from the Miscue Analysis, came from two sources — test results from the intensive study year and the comments her teacher was asked to provide. The teacher's comments were as follows:

> Diane reads well and with expression. She enjoys reading stories but often chooses below her age level. Her written work is imaginative and well written, but of a fairy tale quality. Diane is a quiet, dreamy little girl who comes from a very good home. There is a gap of about ten years between her and the older children.

Diane's test results during the intensive study year were as follows:

Table 16-3
*Diane's (a 1st year) Test Results*

|  |  | Pre-Test | Post-Test |
|---|---|---|---|
| Southgate Group Reading Test 2 | (Reading Age) | $7^6$ | $8^5$ |
| Brimer's Wide Span Reading Test | (Raw Score) | 5 | 14 |
| Crichton Vocabulary Test |  | absent | |
| Diagnostic Phonic Test | (Raw Score) | 78/110 | 91/110 |
| Cloze Test | (Raw Score) | 5/45 | |
| Raven's Matrices | (Raw Score) | *16/36 | |

(*This score fell into category IV — defined as 'definitely below average in intellectual capacity'.)

The marked transcript of Diane's oral reading of the Paddington passage follows.

*Diane (1st Year) Oral Reading Miscues (Paddington)*

*Words in/out of Context* Out of context - 6, In context - 6, Difference - 0

view ✓✓    farther ✓✓    caught ✓✓    exactly ✗✗    direction✓✓
emergency✓✓    answering✓✗    contribution✗✗    eventually✗✗    mysterious✗✓

Mrs Bird's contri~~bu~~tion [*continued*] had been some bright new curtains for the win~~dow~~s [*window*], which Paddington liked very much. In fact, the first night

he spent in his new room he couldn't make up his mind whether to

have them drawn together so that he could ad~~mi~~re them [*admeer*] or left apart

so that he could see the view. He got   out of bed/se~~v~~eral [*serval*] times and/

eventually decided to have one drawn and the other left/back so that

he could have the best of both worlds.

Then so~~meth~~ing [*Sometimes*] strange caught his eye. Paddington made a point of

keeping a torch by the side of his bed in case there was/an emergency

during the night, and it was while he was flashing it on and/off to

ad~~mi~~re [*admeer*] the drawn curtain that he noticed it. Each time he flashed

the torch   there was an answ~~er~~ing [*answer*] flicker of light from somewhere

outside. He sat up in bed, rubbing his eyes, and st~~ar~~ed [*started*] in the dir-

ection of the window.

He decided to try a more/comp~~li~~cated [*compated*] signal. Two short flashes

followed  by several lo~~ng~~er [*long*] ones. When he did so he nearly fell out

of ᴧbed [*the*] with surprise, for each time he sent a signal  it was/repeated

in/exactly the same way through the glass.

Paddington jumped out ofᴧbed [*the*] and rushed to the window.  He

stayed there for a long while peering out at the garden, but he couldn't see anything at all. Having made sure the window was tightly shut he drew both curtains and hurried back to the bed, pulling the clothes over his head a little f~~ar~~ther *further* than usual. It was all very mysterious and Paddington didn't believe in taking any chances.

It was Mr Brown, at /breakfast next morning, who gave him his first clue.

The various analyses of the miscues shown in Diane's reading of the passage are set out in Tables 16-4(a) and (b).

Table 16-4(a)
*Diane (1st Year) – analysis of miscues*

| Table 16-4(a) Miscue Totals | | | | | |
|---|---|---|---|---|---|
| Non-responses | 2 | Substitutions | 11 | *Word-By-Word Reading* | |
| Hesitations | 10 | Insertions | 2 | ~~Yes~~/No | |
| Repetitions | 4 | Omissions | 1 | | |
| Self-corrections | 3 | Reversals | 0 | | |

Total errors (omitting self-corrections) = 30

Table 16-4(b)
*Diane's strengths*

| Strength | Yes | Partial | No | Over Correction | % Yes + Partial |
|---|---|---|---|---|---|
| Grapho/Phonemic | ·10 | 0 | 0 | – | 100 |
| Grammatical | 5 | 3 | 3 | 2 | 61 |
| Comprehension | 7 | 1 | 7 | – | 53 |

Diane had seen the Paddington programme on television, and also had a Paddington book at home, though she had not read this particular story. She made a score of 6/10 on reading words from the list and the same on words in context, although there were discrepancies within the score ('answering' and 'mysterious').

Diane read the passage with apparent ease. She managed to avoid a 'word-by-word' delivery by employing a very slow overall pace, within which she maintained a natural intonation and a well-modulated tone. She made a total of only 29 miscues overall, which compared well with many of even the second-year readers. Her scores on graphic/ grammatical/comprehension strengths, though, show an imbalance which warrants further investigation. She reflects the tendency of first-year readers to use graphic clues extensively, so that all the substitutions she makes bear a strong grapho-phonemic resemblance to the original. Grammatical and semantic suitability are less in evidence.

Diane made two *refusals* — 'eventually' and 'exactly', but since she managed to succeed on 'emergency' and 'tightly' it is difficult to detect a pattern in her refusals.

Her *repetitions* usually occurred a few words before a stumbling-block, suggesting that her eye-span was carrying her some words ahead (further than many other first-year children). Having repeated a word to gain time, her next ploy was to pause immediately before the word in doubt. It is difficult to see a connecting link in the words which did cause trouble. 'Contribution' (line 1) and 'admire' (lines 4 and 9) were frequently miscued by both first- and second-years, but it is surprising that Diane, who was successful on 'mysterious' and 'emergency' found trouble with 'several' (line 5) and 'stared' (line 11). There is, perhaps, a clue here, however, to the particular strategies of this child; although she relied on graphic cues so much, her phonic skill was not really very good, and she seemed to get many of her words correct by means of whole-word recognition. She made no overt attempts to sound out such words as 'mysterious' and had no trouble in guessing it. Occasionally she made an unpremeditated incorrect substitution, for example, supplying 'continued' for 'contribution' in line 1, possibly indicating the same 'look-and-say' strategy, here unsuccessfully applied.

The examination of different responses to the same word can be a helpful guide towards strategies. It is often possible to see a child discarding attempts which do not fit and working his way through to the right response which 'fits' at all levels. This gives some support to the hypothesis that, rather than the sampling of all language levels more or less simultaneously which skilled readers employ, children at this stage look at one level at a time, especially when they encounter difficulties. The child who makes an incorrect response and sticks to it when the same word re-occurs is demonstrating a lack of flexibility in approach. 'Admire' remained 'admeer' for Diane on both occasions. Of course, it is impossible without further questioning to know whether she understood the word in its context, but it can be said that in persistently thinking of it as 'admeer' she could not have connected it with the words 'admire' or 'admiring' which she may well have encountered in speech. Her lack of flexibility in use of strategies seems to be a more important finding than the fact that she has not yet learnt the rule of the silent 'e' successfully.

In all her substitutions Diane began with the right *syllable*, not just the right letter. With more advanced readers this could imply a considered use of syllabification (e.g. 'continued' for 'contribution' (line 1) and 'answer' for 'answering' (line 10)). As long as the word seemed satisfactory and recognizable *as a word,* it did not matter if it fitted syntactically or semantically.

Diane made four self-corrections. Usually this is a sign of awareness of context in the reader, but sometimes corrections are made which are not really necessary, which Goodman terms 'over-correction'. Two of Diane's self-corrections, which were comparatively high compared with the other children, showed this tendency. Supplying 'further' for 'farther' (line 20) was a miscue made by the majority of the children, most of whom did not self-correct, since 'further' and 'farther' are synonymous here; 'further' is probably easier to say and more likely to be in their spoken vocabulary. Diane, however, did correct herself on this, and with similar lack of economy corrected the response 'fell out of bed' (line 14). Other substitution errors, more detrimental to the meaning, were not corrected or even debated, showing that here she was not *aware* of discrepancies in meaning.

Diane appears to be a reader who has got beyond the word-by-word stage, whose style of reading implied that she was accustomed to listening to stories, but who still seems to be relying on a memorized repertoire of words to some extent. Her apparent 'fluency' masks the fact that she does not apply phonic knowledge systematically and does not yet utilize contextual guessing sufficiently. Because of an apparently excellent visual memory she does not often encounter difficulties but when she does she has insufficiently good strategies to overcome them.

It would probably be unwise in Diane's case to return to an intensive programme of phonic teaching. It might be better to build on her potential ability to see and read syllables, and to encourage a heightened awareness of meaning and the cues offered by the text, so that she would begin to employ context cues more successfully.

Diane's results on the various tests given during the year bear out the general conclusions of this analysis. Although she scored highly on the phonic test, she performed poorly on measures involving contextual guessing. She may now be reaching a plateau because she will not be able to progress further while relying on the particular strategies she is now using. Her low score on *Raven's Matrices* indicates that it may be low general ability which is hampering her rather than lack of motivation.

This example shows that a high score in grapho-phonemic approximation does not necessarily subsume good phonic knowledge, and that apparently fluent oral reading does not ensure that what is read is also being understood.

(b) *Deborah (2nd Year)*
Deborah's test results from the intensive study year, other than those obtained from the Miscue Analysis, are set out in Table 16-5.

Table 16-5

*Deborah's (a 2nd year) Test Results*

|  |  | Pre-Test | Post-Test |
|---|---|---|---|
| Southgate Group Reading Test 2 | (Reading Age) | $8^3$ | $>9^7$ |
| | | | |
| Brimer's Wide Span Reading Test | (Raw Score) | 14 | 21 |
| Crichton Vocabulary Scale | (Raw Score) | 51 | |
| Diagnostic Phonic Test | (Raw Score) | 77/110 | 82/110 |
| Cloze Procedure | (Raw Score) | 37/45 | |
| Raven's Matrices | (Raw Score) | *25/36 | |

(*This score fell into Category II — defined as 'definitely above average in intellectual capacity'.)

Unfortunately, her teacher's comments were not available, as in the case of Diane. The marked transcript of Deborah's oral reading of the Paddington passage follows.

*Deborah (2nd Year) — Oral Reading Miscues (Paddington)*

*Words in/out of context*　Out of context -8, In context -9, Difference +1

view ✓✓　　farther ✓✓　caught ✓✓　exactly ✓✓　direction ✓✓
emergency ✓✓ answering ✓✗ contribution ✓✓ eventually ✗✓ mysterious ✓✓

Mrs Bird's/contribution had been some bright new curtains for the

window, which Paddington liked very much. In fact, the first night

he spent (in) his new room he couldn't make up his mind whether to

have  them drawn together so that  he could admire them  or  left

/apart so that he could see the view. He got out of bed several times

(and)/ eventually decided to have one drawn and the other left back

so that he could have the best of both worlds.

Then something strange caught his eye. Paddington made a point of/

keeping a torch by the side of his bed in case there was an emergency

during  the night, and/it was while  he was flashing (it) on and (off)(to)

admire the drawn curtain that he noticed it. Each time  he flashed
_(admiring)_ _(curtains and)_ _(that)_

the torch there was an answering  flicker of light from somewhere
_(answer)_ _(the)_

outside.  He sat  up in  bed, rubbing his eyes, and stared in the
_(else)_ _(rubbed)_ _(at)_

direction of  the window.

He decided to try a more  complicated signal.  Two short flashes
_(Some)_ _(complashant sign)_ _(Some)_

followed by  several longer ones. When he did so he nearly fell out
_(long)_ _(was)_

out of  bed with surprise, for each time  he sent a signal it was

repeated in exactly  the same way  through the glass.
_(repeating)_

Paddington jumped out of  bed and rushed to  the window.  He

stayed   there for a long while  peering out at the garden, but he
_(time peeping)_

couldn't see anything at all.  Having made sure the window was

tightly shut he drew both curtains and hurried back  to bed, pulling

the  clothes over  his head/a little farther than usual. It  was all very
_(further)_

mysterious and Paddington didn't believe in  taking any  chances.

It  <u>was</u> Mr Brown, at breakfast next morning  who gave  him his

first clue.

The various analyses of the miscues shown in Deborah's reading
of the passage are set out in Tables 16-6(a) and (b).

Table 16-6(a)

_Deborah (2nd Year) — Analysis of Miscues_

| Table 16-6(a) — Miscue Totals | | | | |
|---|---|---|---|---|
| Non-responses | 0 | Substitutions | 21 | _Word-By-Word Reading_ |
| Hesitations | 5 | Insertions | 2 | Yes/No |
| Repetitions | 3 | Omissions | 13 | |
| Self-Corrections | 0 | Reversals | 0 | |

Total errors (omitting self-corrections) = 44

Table 16-6(b)

*Deborah's strengths*

| Strength | Yes | Partial | No | Over Correction | % Yes + Partial |
|---|---|---|---|---|---|
| Grapho/Phonemic | 11 | 1 | 12 | – | 35 |
| Grammatical | 20 | 7 | 11 | 0 | 70 |
| Comprehension | 32 | 2 | 3 | – | 92 |

Deborah had seen the Paddington series on television, and had read some Paddington stories. She read eight words correctly out of context and also managed to get 'eventually' right in the text, although she could not read it as an isolated word. She read the passage quickly, rather breathlessly, with a slightly exaggerated intonation, as if she were conscious of an audience; she had probably assimilated the intonation which adults used in reading to her. She often ignored sentence junctures, however, and tended to omit or replace conjunctions.

Her many omissions were never words she did not know, but always short items showing that she was possibly processing the content load too speedily for accurate oral reading. It is interesting that she made few miscues in the first paragraph; it was only when she 'got into the story' that her mistakes occurred. Most of her miscues, in fact, support the likelihood that she was re-encoding the text in her own language, often quite successfully. When she came to a word she was unsure of, instead of 'wasting' time sounding it out, she substituted a roughly equivalent nonsense word, as though to keep the flow of the reading going, e.g. 'complashant' for 'complicated' (line 13). Her substitutions were often reasonable, though, on all three language levels, apart from discarding graphic similarity – 'time' for 'while' (line 18) and 'some' for 'two' (line 13). She made no self-corrections because she was confident in her reading and felt that it made sense. This was reasonable because few of her miscues broke the sense or the syntax. The mistakes she made at the syntactical level could occur through rapid processing and re-encoding of the internalized text.

Deborah's oral reading seems to show that reading aloud by a confident skilled practitioner may be indicative of the process of skilled reading itself. It is likely that the visual message is absorbed without subvocalizing, and that the oral reading is a re-encoding of the already internalized message. This is supported in Deborah's case by her low graphic similarity score.

This reading, therefore, indicates that Deborah is well beyond the early stages of decoding. She is at home with narrative, and is probably now actually hampered by having to read orally, unless it is intended for an explicitly communicative purpose. She still needs wider experience of the formal conventions of written language and she sometimes alters meaning by imposing her natural speech junctures on the text. Her ability to predict means that her comprehension strength is high and should be supported by an equally competent grammatical awareness.

The results of the other assessments undertaken during the year reflect this analysis very closely. The fairly low rise in phonic score is off-set by high scoring in Cloze and the reading test post-scores. Deborah  is using contextual guessing extensively and the number of overall errors bears no relationship  to her well-developed reading skill.

### (c) *Conclusions about the two readers*

These two examples of miscue analysis were selected because the children were near the 'average' of the average readers with Deborah making more miscues than Diane. Therefore, Deborah might have been accepted by a teacher listening to her reading aloud as less well advanced in her reading achievement. Yet it can be seen that each had her own characteristic strategies, and that Deborah was actually a much more mature reader than Diane.

## IV  Summary

Mature reading  involves the sampling of the text on three levels of language: grapho-phonemic; syntactic; and semantic.  The reader will use his expectations of the text to achieve understanding as economically as possible. It is advisable to encourage even beginning readers to approach the text in an active problem-solving way, training them to use economical sampling methods.

In this project, the analysis of errors made in oral reading was adopted to assess the strategies in use by children from 7 to 9 years old. The errors were termed 'miscues' to indicate that they often show a positive approach towards reading. They were analysed on the basis of Goodman's 'Miscue Inventory'.

It was found that the strategies adopted by children develop with age, younger children using visual/auditory matching methods rather than exploiting contextual cues, whereas older children achieve a more balanced use of language levels. There was no apparent difference between the sexes in their use of strategies.

A high degree of fluency in oral reading was demonstrated by the older children, most of whom had progressed beyond the stage of a word-by-word attack.

Profiles of two readers showed that great differences in strategy may occur in readers who make a similar number of errors in oral reading of a passage.

# V Implications for Teachers

## A. *Listening to Reading*

The research shows that at the age of 7 most of the children were reading aloud adequately, although they were often operating at the level of word-recognition. It is clear that at this stage many children need the guidance towards the mature reader's strategies described at the beginning of the chapter. The children were no longer much hampered by difficulties at the phonic level. Many, however, had not learned to use context well or to look across the text for clues.

It seems that children may vary in their approach towards reading; those who have not had a wide reading background before school entry may encounter it primarily in the light of phonic decoding skills to be mastered through sequential instruction. Such children tend to read haltingly and to give up easily if they come across a phonically irregular word. Others may approach reading with an awareness of its function, indeed coming to school with the expectation of rapid mastery and a readiness to use context, including visual illustration, without the systematic backing of phonic teaching. It follows that not all children will need the same type of instruction, or even the same reading materials, and it should perhaps be accepted that good reading is not always achieved through a uniform programme, based on a graded reading scheme.

The team's observations in classrooms showed that teachers invariably placed great emphasis on hearing children read as frequently as possible. However, the time allocation for any one child proved minimal. The exercise was rarely used instructionally: the main purpose seemed to be to check regularly that a page was read. When a child failed to recognize a word, he was usually prompted immediately, and there was rarely any discussion of word-recognition difficulties, or of context. It might be more profitable if oral reading to the teacher was carried out less frequently, but with more positive aims in view.

Such a decision would involve two approaches. The first would utilize miscue analysis see pp. 285−7). The resulting diagnosis would lead to 'instructional' reading sessions, often with groups of children who were exhibiting similar strategies, including the possibility of using contextual cues. Many children interviewed in the research did not admit that they 'guessed' words, evidently thinking that this was the wrong tactic. It is thus an *attitude* rather than a skill which is to be developed; a willingness to look ahead, to use all the resources of language. Above all, children must be helped to use sound independent strategies, so that they do not rely on tactics likely to prove ineffective, such as 'sounding out' a word letter by letter because they think it is expected of them. Some children seem to be held back from independent reading because they have not learnt to rely on their own judgement as problem-solvers. Phonic skills are important, but only as part of the whole reading task.

The second approach would involve a greater emphasis on the content of the book. Instead of actually reading a passage aloud to the teacher, the individual contact would take the form of a 'reading interview'. Goodman used direct recall of a story as part of his assessment; this could be adopted in a modified form as a request, 'Tell me what you can remember about the story you have just read' or 'Find me the part in the story that you liked best and read it to me.' Questions on context would follow, emphasizing affective as well as cognitive aspects. Some of the questions used in the interviews with children (see Chapters 13 and 14) would help to find out what attitudes towards reading were developing. The sessions would become a relaxed and enthusiastic dialogue between teacher and pupil.

Inevitably, this type of interview would lead to the development of intermediate and higher order skills. The child could be sent away with questions on content, short-term goals set *in advance* of his reading. These would often encourage quick scanning of a whole paragraph rather than word-by-word reading. The individual contact between teacher and pupils would not disappear, but its emphasis would change, and there would be a growing awareness of the *function* of reading rather than of techniques.

## B. *Diagnosis from Oral Reading*

There is no one method of analysing miscues; teachers will adapt the procedure to the stage of development of their pupils. The system described below is suggested as a simplified version of that used in the research, and it has been tried out successfully by teachers in the normal classroom situation.

### 1. Choice of text

For children with reading ages below about 6 years, diagnosis can be made from whatever reading materials the children have in hand. For children with reading ages above 6 years, a passage should be chosen which has a readability level about six months to one year higher than their reading age. The *Spache Readability Formula* (Spache 1953) is suitable for assessing books for younger readers. (See Appendices 16-A and 16-B).

It is useful to duplicate key passages for presentation at appropriate times. The preparation of about three passages for one term would enable the teacher to collect valuable data on a class. From this the teacher would find out how little real information is conveyed by a reading age, and how strategies can vary within it. The coded transcripts could be collected in individual folders, along with personal cassettes, to form a comprehensive reading record.

## 2. Procedure

(a) Set up a tape-recorder (one cassette per child if possible), and ask the child to read the passage in the following terms:

'I would like you to read this story for me. I am not going to help you on the hard words, unless you get really stuck. The story is about . . . (brief contextual information). We are going to tape-record your reading, so please say your name onto the tape.'

On other occasions, the child may record his own reading without the teacher's presence.

(b) Next, code the miscues on to a transcript of the passage according to the following key (see Table 16-1 for suggested symbols).

*Non-response:*    teacher has to supply word finally.

*Hesitation:*    pause before word, which is eventually supplied by reader.

*Repetition:*    repetition of word or phrase (phrase counts as one repetition).

*Substitution:*    substitution of one word by another.

*Reversal:*    reversal of word or phrase. Count reversal of whole line as one reversal.

*Omission:*    word (or phrase) of original omitted in reading.

*Insertion:*    word (or phrase) inserted, not present in original.

*Self-correction:*    any of the above miscues may be subsequently corrected by reader. If so, tick above original error coding. This will count both as *miscue* and *self-correction.*

(c) Total the individual miscues and fill in on grid as follows:

| Non-responses | Hesitations | Repetitions | Substitutions | Self-Corrections | Omissions | Insertions | Reversals | Total Words in Passage | Total* Miscues |
|---|---|---|---|---|---|---|---|---|---|
|  |  |  |  |  |  |  |  |  |  |

*Omit self-corrections

(d) The substitutions should be coded separately, as they indicate most clearly the levels of language in use (see Table 16-7). Normal progression will be from Box 4 to Box 1. The boxed results should show the balance in the use of language levels. The eventual aim will be to have all the miscues in Box 1. A majority of ticks in Box 4 will indicate imbalance in strategy.

Table 16-7

*The Coding of Substitutions*

|  | Graphically correct* | Graphically incorrect |
|---|---|---|
| Contextually correct | √ in this box if the first phoneme of response is same as original<br><br>*and*<br><br>if response fits context of sentence | √ in this box if the first phoneme of response is *not* the same as original<br><br>*and*<br><br>if response fits context of sentence |
| Contextually incorrect | √ in this box if first phoneme of response is same as original<br><br>*and*<br><br>if response does *not* fit context of sentence | √ in this box if first phoneme of response is *not* the same as original<br><br>*and*<br><br>if response docs *not* fit context of sentence |

(*A word is counted as graphically correct if the first phoneme is the same as in the original word. This may seem a crude criterion, but Weber (1970) has shown that first-letter correspondence associates highly with letter-matching in the rest of the word.)

(e) In using the results, there is no intention of calculating norms or standardized scores. The main aim is to weigh up 'positive' and 'negative' uses of strategies and to suggest helpful corrective procedures from the resulting profile. (See Readers' Profiles earlier in this chapter.) Examples of diagnosis from types of miscue are given below.

| Positive strategies | Negative strategies |
|---|---|
| *Self-corrections*<br>Reader must be considering meaning and be aware of original error | *Non-response*<br>Over-dependence on teacher — no independent strategies |
| *Omissions and insertions*<br>Usually made on short structural items, showing that reader is internalising text and re-encoding it in his own language | *Over-correction*<br>If reader self-corrects unnecessarily, he is probably placing too much reliance on graphophonemic level |
| *Repetitions and hesitations*<br>Negative in so far as they hold up flow of reading, but may be used positively as time-gainers ||

## C. *Individual Analyses*

It would be impossible for a teacher to analyse oral reading in the depth envisaged more than two or three times a term for any individual. The teacher would decide on ways of making this feasible, which would probably involve a change of pattern in the practice of hearing children read. She may decide to carry out the analysis with a few children only, and to let others tape-record their own reading. The diagnoses should provide a good record of reading development within a class, which would provide the basis for grouping children for instruction, always bearing in mind the need for flexible movement between groups.

It is emphasized that there is room for great variety of approaches in miscue analysis. Several personal communications from teachers indicate its possibilities, particularly for remedial readers. One teacher adds a cautionary note:

> I doubt very much whether I would be able to gain as much information from this kind of approach had I not initially done several very detailed miscue analyses based on the Goodman inventories. The insights gained during that type of in-service activity ensures that the act of hearing children read becomes an active one of *listening* to children read where one is all the time questioning rather than simply correcting errors.

## D. *Oral Reading as Communication*

The analysis of oral reading as a guide to the development of strategies is very different from oral reading as a shared communicative activity. Though most children interviewed in the research stated that they preferred to read to themselves, there is still a place, particularly at this transitional stage, for an individual to read with a teacher, or for groups to share reading of a book. There are two main purposes behind this: learning to read aloud with the express aim of bringing the text to life for others; and for the pleasure which comes from shared experience of content. Both these purposes presuppose a fairly high level of skill mastery. It was noticeable in the research that the second-year children usually moved into oral reading with natural intonation and some tonal 'colour', whereas many first-years were still reading 'word-by-word'. The exhortation to read 'with expression' is probably meaningless for a child. Expressive oral reading only comes from a full understanding of the text, and an ability to look ahead across fairly large chunks of material. This may be best achieved by providing suitable outcomes which necessitate communicative reading aloud, for instance, one child reading out simple instructions to another, reading his own writing to a group, reading stories or poems on tape to make a programme, or reading plays together. (Penguin *Take Part* books, or Black's *Read Together* books would prove useful here. The Penguin *Take Part* books have reading parts which are graded for readability so that children can contribute at their own level.)

## E. *Shared Reading*

A teacher can begin to develop appreciation and evaluation of text by reading aloud with a child, the teacher often taking the larger share of the reading. This should be accompanied by discussion of content, and questioning which even with young readers can progress beyond the literal level. The discussion should include prediction on the possible developments of the story as well as recall of events. Once children have realized what can be gleaned from a story or informational text, there is no reason why small groups of children should not be able to work together in discussion, beginning on a superficial level, but developing towards the type of analysis which they will need in secondary school.

To carry out the purposes suggested earlier would require a variety of reading matter of intrinsic interest for children. It follows that the still widespread practice of continuing with reading schemes and supplementary readers with the 7 to 9 year age-range may be misplaced. The advantages which they offer — careful grading of readability, systematic introduction of phonic rules, etc. — are frequently outweighed by their irrelevance to the real interests of the children and by their lack of stylistic merit. Instruction in reading skills will, of course, still be necessary for many children of this age, but it may be better to give such instruction specifically when needs have been demonstrated.

## F. *Silent Reading*

As a corollary to a diminished emphasis on oral reading, it follows that silent reading should be encouraged at an earlier stage than at present. There has been little research on silent reading since the 1930s, reflecting perhaps the lack of interest in it in the schools. Useful discussions of the development of silent reading can be found in Pugh (1975 and 1978). Clearly many children experience difficulty in the change of mode, although many teachers seem to accept that once children have reached a fairly competent standard in oral reading, there will be an automatic transfer to the very different skill of silent reading. It is not, of course, so easy to assess achievement in silent reading. It can only be done by organizing specific purposes to produce observable outcomes of such reading. The Open University Reading Development course gives valuable help in this field.

The Americans, always more aware of the need to instruct directly in the different stages of reading acquisition, have shown more sustained interest in silent reading. As far back as 1913, Huey stated:

Reading as a school exercise has almost always been thought of as reading aloud, in spite of the obvious fact that reading in actual life is to be mainly silent reading. The consequent attention to reading as an exercise in speaking . . . has been heavily at the expense of reading as the act of thought getting.

This concept of 'thought-getting' was re-emphasized by Bamman (1963):

After pupils have mastered a fair-sized vocabulary, children should do much silent reading and considerable selective oral reading where only a part of the story is read aloud.

and

In every instance, a sentence is read 'with the eyes' before a pupil reads it aloud. The teacher prefaces the reading with a question so that reading is a thought-getting process.

There are two important aspects here which were rarely observed in the schools where the research was carried out. The first sees oral and silent reading as skills which should be developed concurrently, and the second implies that children should be 'focused' on an outcome in their reading, so that they are geared towards prediction and awareness of meaning even in the early stages. As Pugh (1975) says, '. . . the major factor which effected change in reading speed was motivated practice in reading quickly.' Silent reading requires a different technique from oral reading and it needs to be taught.

One practising teacher outlined two major ways of fostering silent reading which she had found successful in classroom work. First, where the writer's purpose is paramount, for example in a mathematics text book, the procedure might be as follows:

(a) Read quickly through the passage to find out the nature of the task (calculation, diagram, etc.);
(b) Note keywords, including any new words;
(c) Carefully examine any examples, and imagine explaining them to someone else;
(d) Read through again, considering every keyword carefully.

Secondly, where the reader's purpose is paramount, for example in topic work, it is advisable for the pupil to have a list of questions worked out in collaboration with the teacher, or alone. For younger children or difficult texts, a possible formula is 'Read, Talk, Understand, Remember'. For more experienced readers, it is 'Read, *Think,* Understand, Remember'.

Examples of 'motivated goals' which would help focus on outcomes of silent reading might be carrying out written instructions such as:

Jobs in the classroom
Looking after pets
Following a treasure trail from written clues
Following recipes
Playing games from written instructions
Constructing models from diagrams and instructions
Carrying out scientific experiments from written instructions
Adapting narrative for drama.

It is not always extended reading which will develop skill, but accuracy in interpreting even one sentence. Such examples may of course vary in detail and sophistication according to the ability of the children concerned, but all of them provide self-evident outcomes. The proof of the pudding is in the eating!

The much more widely used outcome of requiring written answers on a text is less satisfactory as a teaching aid for the development of silent reading, since it is often possible to transfer factual information at a literal level from the original text without comprehending the vocabulary or the concepts involved. At this stage particularly, where children are still at the concrete operational stage, it seems advisable to concoct goals where the outcomes involve either *doing* something or giving an oral response (not oral reading), as far as possible. This should also support a gradual transition to the realization that skimming and scanning are as legitimate for certain purposes as reading every word in a text.

These suggestions point towards a programme balanced carefully between oral and silent reading, with the aim of encouraging all children towards independence in reading, able to use text for learning and enjoyment.

## G. *Classroom Organization*

The practice of teaching reading in the majority of classes observed in this project was centred round the often ritualized activity of 'hearing children read'. This meant, almost invariably, the teacher listening to individual children reading. This practice caused great difficulties in organization because of the constant interruptions from other children seeking help from the teacher. It seems that this organization is perhaps in need of drastic reappraisal. We do not advocate a return to class-teaching, or to reading groups of children chanting together from a scheme. It does, however, appear that there should be more group teaching, based on versatile and flexible group activities. It seems uneconomical to teach every new element incidentally to individual children. If the balance were to be shifted more towards silent reading, as previously suggested, the organization of reading teaching should be eased considerably.

# CHAPTER 17

# The Strategies Children Use in Reading: Cloze Procedure

## I Introduction

In this project two complementary investigations were undertaken in an attempt to discover the strategies used by average readers of 7 to 9 when, in their reading, they encounter unfamiliar words. One method, described in Chapter 16, was the application of miscue analysis to the errors the children made in oral reading. The second method, which is described in this chapter, was the use of what is termed Cloze procedure. A simple introduction to this technique was provided by Moyle (1972), who wrote:

> ... it is a technique based on the human tendency to complete an incomplete pattern or sequence. Thus if a word is omitted from a sentence the reader attempts to supply the word to complete the meaning.

An example of such a passage is given below.

### Example 1(a) – Cloze Passage

#### PADDINGTON TURNS DETECTIVE

Paddington jumped out of bed and rushed to the window. He stayed there for a long while peering out at the garden, but he couldn't see anything at all. Having made sure the window was tightly shut, he drew both curtains and hurried back to bed, pulling the clothes over his head a little farther than usual. It was all very mysterious and Paddington didn't believe in taking any chances.

It was Mr Brown, at breakfast next ——, who gave him his first clue. 'Someone's stolen my —— marrow!' he announced crossly. 'They must —— got in during the night.'

For some weeks —— Mr Brown had been carefully nursing a huge —— which he intended to enter for a vegetable show. He —— it morning and evening and measured it every —— before going to bed.

Mrs Brown exchanged a glance —— Mrs Bird. 'Never mind, Henry dear,' she said, 'You've —— several others almost as good.'

'I've a good —— to offer a small reward' said Mr Brown. Paddington —— up his ears at the mention of a ——. As soon as he had finished his —— and marmalade he asked —— be excused and disappeared upstairs —— even having a third cup of tea.

On reading through this Example 1(a) one can quickly realize that in order to insert the words which have been deleted, it is necessary to search the surrounding context for clues. Thus the words which the child inserts in the blanks can provide the teacher with clues to the uses which the child is making of the context.

Cloze procedure was first introduced by Taylor (1953), in the USA, with a view to measuring the readability of texts. He believed that reading depends on the ability to make choices 'within meaningful overall combinations'. Obviously, a passage will never carry the same readability for all readers, since they will bring different experiences to the task. However, making good guesses to fill the deletions is possible, according to Taylor, largely because of two elements. The first he calls 'transitional probabilities'; it is possible to guess which word is likely to follow another because of constraints of syntax or meaning. The second he terms 'dispositional language habits', which he explains as 'bundles of skill sequences' — chunks of language which have become so automatic that they 'run themselves off in pertinent situations'. These 'chunks' may also be termed 'habitual associations'.

## Example 1(b) — Cloze Passage with Deletions Inserted

It was Mr Brown at breakfast next (1) *morning*, who gave him his first clue. 'Someone's stolen my (2) *prize* marrow!' he announced crossly. 'They must (3) *have* got in during the night.'

For some weeks (4) *past* Mr Brown had been carefully nursing a huge (5) *marrow* which he intended to enter for a vegetable show. He (6) *watered* it morning and evening and measured it every (7) *night* before going to bed.

Mrs Brown exchanged a glance (8) *with* Mrs Bird. 'Never mind, Henry dear,' she said, 'You've (9) *got* several others almost as good.'

'I've a good (10) *mind* to offer a small reward' said Mr Brown. Paddington (11) *pricked* up his ears at the mention of a (12) *reward.* As soon as he had finished his (13) *toast* and marmalade he asked (14) *to* be excused and disappeared upstairs (15) *without* even having a third cup of tea.

A skilled reader tackling a Cloze passage is likely therefore to be carrying out two interlocking operations. He will, on one hand, be consciously searching for clues, scanning the passage both before and after a deletion, to find clues which will help him to guess correctly on the content level. In the completed Cloze passage, for example with Deletion 12, 'Paddington pricked up his ears at the mention of a ——', 'reward' can easily be guessed because it has already been used in the previous sentence. Deletion 7 — 'measured it every —— before going to bed' requires the reader to look ahead to the following phrase before he can identify the redundancy and supply the word 'night'.

Before he can complete Deletion 2 'someone's stolen my —— marrow', with the correct word 'prize', he must look ahead across two sentences to discover that Mr Brown is going to enter his marrow for a show. Such guesses would equate with Taylor's 'transitional probabilities'.

At the same time, the skilled reader would unconsciously be using his 'dispositional language habits' to complete deletions; these would include knowing, for example, that 'a glance' is 'exchanged' 'with' 'someone' (Deletion 8), and that 'I've a good —— to offer a small reward' (Deletion 10), necessarily demands 'mind' for its completion. Sometimes, both strategies will be needed to solve one deletion; where, for instance, a verb participle is deleted, the reader will perhaps need to guess tense at the semantic level, but will be helped by internalized syntactical restraints. In all skilled reading, levels of language are sampled whenever necessary. It is the mixture of conscious strategies and the application of internalized rules which makes the skills employed difficult to disentangle. The developing young reader, however, is unlikely to have achieved this synchronization of skills. At the stage with which we are concerned, he is often reliant on recognizing words largely through sound—symbol association (the grapho-phonemic level) and is only just beginning to use the constraints of context extensively.

The skills involved in Cloze are apparently those of prediction and model-making, that is, the conscious use of all available cues linked with analogies made through knowledge of language patterns, both very necessary components in the more advanced skills of reading. The age range of children aged 7 to 9+ examined in the project is crucial, since the children are probably at one of the transition stages discussed by Powell (1973). A child is moving from a stage where he has utilized the grapho-phonemic associations almost exclusively and where his spoken language system is in advance of his written system, to one in which automatization of visual/auditory processing will enable him to increase prediction on syntactic and semantic levels.

## II Cloze Experiment in the Intensive Study

Levitt (1970) has suggested that:

> the primary focus for a first-grade reader is mastery of a code, whereas that for more advanced readers is efficient application of that code: thus it is probable that context is used differently at different stages of reading.

The prediction in the project's work was that the foregoing statement would be reflected in the results of Cloze procedure measures. It was expected that younger readers would make fewer correct or functionally correct guesses, and that more of their guesses would be inappropriate; and that there would also be differences between age-groups in the pattern of response to individual words. It was hoped to find reasons for success or failure.

## A. *Procedure*

The Cloze experiment was devised in order to find out how far children were successful when forced into using syntactical and semantic
clues. Obviously it is impossible with children of 7 to 9 years to
ascertain the exact nature of the mental operations. Accordingly, the
same test was administered to 80 teachers, unconnected with the
project, and 20 of these were asked to verbalize the reasons for making
their choices. The children participating in the exercise were the 127
who had already been used for the Miscue Analysis exercise, that is
four children, two boys and two girls, randomly selected from the
band of average readers in the first- and second-year classes of eight
of the schools in the intensive study year.

The selected passage of 300 words (see Example 1(a)) was taken
from Bond's (1959) *More About Paddington.* The same passage was
used with all the children, to identify developing strategies more
easily. The chosen passage followed on immediately from the passage
used for oral reading for the Miscue Analysis, three weeks earlier.
There had, therefore, been an adequate run-in, the first sentence
of the Cloze passage having in fact been presented as the last sentence
of the Oral Reading passage.

Deletions in Cloze procedure are usually made on a regular basis
of every 5th, 7th or 10th word. Since, however, in keeping with the
short concentration span of children of these ages, the number of
deletions was limited to 15, the arbitrary rate of deletion was modified
to include as many different constraints as possible. The deletions
occurred at intervals of from 5 to 10 words, with an average of 8.7
words between deletions.

The exercise was carried out with groups of from four to eight
children, by members of the research team. Each child was given a
duplicated copy of the passage (Example 1(a)), lines of equal length
inserted where a word was omitted. The following instructions were
given to each group.

Do you remember reading to me from the story about Paddington?
I have typed out the next part of the story. This tells you what
made the noise that disturbed Paddington. I want you to read it to
yourself, and every time you come to a space with a line in it, try
to guess what the word might be which has been left out, and write
it on the line. There is only one word to be filled in for every space.

Don't worry too much about spellings, just fill in the word as
well as you can. Don't get stuck too long on one space. Perhaps
you will be able to go back and fill it in later. If you can't guess a
word at all, leat it. Now remember, only *one* word for each space.

No specific time limit was set, although if a child was obviously de-
feated he was relieved of his paper.

## B. *Method of Scoring*

The testees were not expected to identify so completely with the passage that the criterion for scoring would be an identical response with the original. Although many researchers adopt this criterion, they are assessing readability rather than the strategies of young readers. In this instance, the aim was to identify the extent to which children made reasonable sense of the passage by means of active structuring in relation to their own, at this stage, limited experience. The following system was devised.

| Score | Response |
|---|---|
| 3 | Identical word to the original |
| 2 | Functionally correct word, suitable both syntactically and semantically, i.e. a word which makes good sense, even though it is not a synonym. |
| 1 | Word which is suitable either semantically or syntactically, but not both |
| 0 | Incorrect guess, both syntactically and semantically inappropriate |
| 0 | No Response |

*Maximum Possible Score* = 45
As long as words were recognizable, incorrect spelling was not penalized.

## C. *The Results*

### 1. Total scores

Out of a possible maximum correct score of 45, the average score for first-year children was 15 and for second-year children 26, showing that, as expected, second-years performed considerably better than first-years. Table 17-1(a) shows the relative success rates by age-group on individual words. For this table, and for the graph (Table 17-1(b)), the children were credited with success if they supplied the correct word or one which fitted the context, both syntactically and semantically (i.e. *functionally correct*).

In most cases the pattern of gussing indivudial words suitably is similar across the two gears, although the first-year achievement is lower; that means, on the whole, that the same words caused difficulty. The reasons for the different scoring on certain words is discussed later in the chapter.

### 2. Refusal and unsuccessful guesses

The foregoing details, however, do not provide information as to the strategies which the older children were using to gain their successes; whereas an examination of the refusals and unsuccessful guesses made by the children is helpful in this respect. Again a clear difference was found between the age-groups. Out of the total of 15 words, first-years averaged 8 unsuccessful guesses or refusals, while for second-years the

Table 17-1(a)

*Percentage of pupils making identical or functionally correct responses on individual words*

|         | % of pupils |          |         | % of pupils |          |
|---------|-------------|----------|---------|-------------|----------|
|         | 1st year    | 2nd year |         | 1st year    | 2nd year |
| morning | 88          | 92       | watered | 28          | 60       |
| night   | 66          | 90       | mind    | 25          | 60       |
| have    | 40          | 75       | to      | 17          | 55       |
| toast   | 40          | 75       | with    | 33          | 50       |
| got     | 42          | 73       | reward  | 12          | 50       |
| pricked | 35          | 73       | without | 10          | 25       |
| prize   | 45          | 65       | past    | 6           | 25       |
| marrow  | 20          | 65       |         |             |          |

figure was only 4. There was also a marked difference in the proportion of guesses to refusals. Children in both age-groups made consistently more guesses than refusals. The ratio was approximately;

1st Years:    9 guesses to 7 refusals
2nd Years:    3 guesses to 1 refusal

In general, first-years, as was expected, made more unsuccessful guesses, and refused more frequently than second-years. There were no sex differences in the number of guesses/refusals.

The results show that children of average reading ability in both first- and second-years were able to tackle the Cloze task with some confidence, though the first-years were less successful in their responses.

A shift of emphasis is necessary in order to find out what was happening when the children actually made guesses, by examining whether they were more successful on some deletions than others. This can be done quantitatively to only a limited extent, as the deleted words provide a very small sample of linguistic classes and constraints. The 15 words deleted were first categorised into *content* and *function* words. There is some variability of definition in the literature, but the categories devised by Fries (1952) were used for classification, based on the function of words within the context of the sentence, *viz*:

Certain parts of speech carry the *content* of the message. These include nouns, main verbs, adjectives and adverbs. In the Paddington passage they were:

reward   (noun)              pricked (verb)
morning (noun)              watered (verb)
prize     (adjective)         night    (noun)
past      (adjective)         got      (verb)
marrow (noun)                 mind    (noun)

Nouns and verbs allow for a wide variety of possibilities in any particular slot, so that high scores are likely within the 'functionally

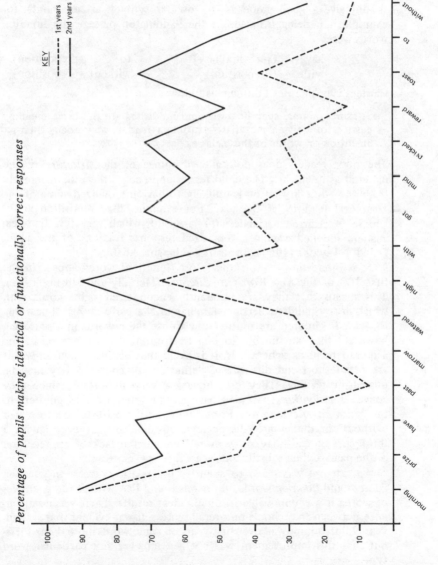

Table 17-1(b)

Percentage of pupils making identical or functionally correct responses

KEY
------- 1st years
——— 2nd years

correct' category.

Other words may be described as *function* words; structural words which act as the mortar between the bricks of the vocabulary items. If the reader is aware of the correct syntactical pattern, choice will be more limited for this type of word, and the reader is likely to guess either correctly (i.e. response identical with original), or incorrectly, since there are fewer viable alternatives. Success with these words should give a good guide as to how far syntactical constraints, for example, are being utilized. In the Paddington passage the function words were:

| have | (verb auxiliary) | to | (preposition) |
| with | (preposition) | without | (preposition) |

Harner (1966) quotes Loutham as follows:

> ... since nouns, specific verbs and modifiers are the basic meaning carriers of written material – problem readers may focus their . . attention on words of these classes.

The poor reader 'does not take advantage of the *structure* of the material as he might'. The child reader approaches the task differently from the adult in that he is unlikely to have internalized some of the structural features of the text. For example, the preposition in the phrase 'exchanged a glance *with* Mrs Bird' which very few first-year readers supplied was an automatized response for 90% of the adults tested – Taylor's (1953) 'dispositional language habits'.

It is interesting to note that most 'function' words appear in the first 100 of the *Key Words to Literacy* (McNally and Murray 1962). This means that they are frequently encountered sight words with which many children become familiar in the early stages of learning to read. If children are unsure how to use these words in a sentence, however, they are unable to benefit from the advantage of having acquired them as sight words. It is likely that because function words are often short and difficult to define out of context, they may be missed in reading. They are, however, very important, since they convey *relationships* within a passage and often serve as pointers to the tenor of the message. For example, to substitute 'because' for 'without' in the phrase 'disappeared upstairs without even having a third cup of tea', may show more fundamental lack of appreciation of the passage than substituting 'vegetable' for 'marrow'.

An attempt was made to quantify the relative success in guessing *content* and *function* words, but it was found that with so few examples of words it was impossible to obtain clear results. There was no difference between the schools on overall scores. It was evident that second-year children improved over first-years on some words more than others, but that this improvement was not general over any particular word type.

There was indication of an interesting interaction between schools and word type, a negative relationship seeming to exist between content and function strength. That is, content strength was present at the expense of function strength; which could suggest that children might have been taught with emphasis on one aspect at the expense of the other. The available data indicated that second-years were more successful in supplying the correct function word, but there was so much variation in success on different individual function words that this tended to mask any developing overall patterns which might exist.

### 3. The use of syntactic and semantic cues

The mature reader utilizes the clues given in the language on both the syntactic and semantic levels. It was thought likely that young readers would make more use of the syntactic level, using the language patterns which they had internalized from an early age. Information on this score was obtained from analysing unsuccessful guesses, wrong either syntactically or semantically. It was found that all children made more successful use of the syntactic level, with insignificant variation between age and sex. The mean ratio between the two levels was 5 syntactically correct guesses to 1 semantically correct guess. This is an indication of the strength of syntactical constraints on these readers, and shows that they were using internalized knowledge to make guesses, rather than approaching the task as an active search after meaning.

### 4. The use of the surrounding text

Nine of the 15 words deleted could be guessed by using only the *preceding* text, while 5 necessitated looking ahead to gain information. Table 17-2 gives the percentage of correct responses in relation to these

Table 17-2

*Number of pupils using preceding or succeeding text successfully*

| Age Group | No. of Pupils | % of Pupils Deriving Cues From | |
|---|---|---|---|
| | | Preceding Text | Succeeding Text |
| 7−8 | 56 | 26% | 12% |
| 8−9 | 54 | 46% | 30% |

two types of cues. The development pattern is clear; the second-year readers improve considerably on the first-years in successful use of context, although looking ahead for clues is still less in evidence than using only the preceding text. These results have a very clear implication for classroom practice: readers need to be shown the necessity for reading ahead to make maximum use of all available clues.

### 5. Habitual associations

Habitual associations may be equated with Taylor's (1953)

'dispositional language habits'. They are phrases which have been 'pre-processed'by the individual through frequent use. This means that when any one part of the phrase is presented, the reader is likely to respond automatically with the rest of the phrase. These phrases can only be assimilated in this way through frequent encounters, and are part of the linguistic and cultural tradition of a speech community. (Their acquisition proves a great source of difficulty for learners of a foreign language.) The build-up of such phrases seems to be an important element in spoken and written language maturity. Their acquisition should be of great help in reading, both from the point of view of the amount of 'chunking' that they allow in short-term memory, and because they require minimal visual cuing for recognition, as we do not actually read such phrases word by word.

Categorization of habitual associations is bound to be subjective to some extent. The phrases selected from the Paddington passage to exemplify this feature were:                                          .

'exchanged a glance *with*'
'I've a good *mind*'
'*toast* and marmalade'

Once more, the older age-group were markedly better in this respect than the younger group. Out of 3 possible correct responses, first-years averaged 0.5 and second-years 1.5 correct responses. Even so, the second-years were still far from achieving an adult facility with habitual associations. There were no sex differences.

It is interesting to surmise how this particular development occurs, since it is unlikely to be the result of direct teaching. One suspects that it might be that children coming from homes which provide a rich and varied language background may gain familiarity with such phrases, although such experience *may* have the opposite effect of developing lateral thinkers, who would insert unexpected, though functionally correct, words in such instances.

## 6. Discussion of responses to certain deletions

Because a variety of clues are present at every choice point (the higher the redundancy of the passage, the more clues), it is of course difficult to know why any specific decision is made. It is likely that any word which involves using less well-tried strategies is less often guessed correctly by children. To illuminate this, certain individual deletions were examined in the light of the constraints they carried.

(a) *Deletion 2: 'Prize'*

'Someone's stolen my *prize* marrow.'

This is a *content* word involving the preceding clue 'my' and the need to look ahead for further information about the vegetable show. It is an adjective that would only be supplied by the children with relevant background experience.

There were *no* correct responses from first-years, and only 5 of the 54 second-years guessed the correct word. However, 25 of the 56 first-years and 32 of the 54 second-years supplied words which fitted the sense and the syntax, showing that they recognized linguistic constraints although they did not recognize the circumstances. The idea of quality was preserved by frequent offers of 'best', 'big', 'nice', etc. The backward acting nature of the clue did not impede guessing, as it was so near the deletion.

### (b) *Deletion 3: 'Have'*

'They must *have* got in during the night'

This proved an interesting deletion since 22 first-year readers and 11 second-years inserted 'of' showing that they were associating with the spoken pronunciation 'must've'. This demonstrates the close but sometimes unsteady connections between speech and written language, and the fact that adults very rarely diagnose what children *think* they are hearing in listening to talk. Apart from this, however, this word was one of the highest-scoring in the passage, with 27 first-years and 36 second-years guessing the correct word — a *function* word, needing the use of *preceding* context only.

### (c) *Deletion 4: 'Past'*

'For some weeks past Mr Brown had . . .'

This adjective involves the use of the immediately *preceding* context. Nobody guessed it correctly, either in the first- or second-years. The word is superfluous, to a certain extent, and children might easily have glossed over the gap. This is supported by the fact that 22 first-years and 12 second-years did not supply any word. Varied suggestions made by children in both age-groups showed that they recognized the time element: 'now' 'already', and 'before' were all perfectly reasonable alternatives, but others like 'time', 'when', 'later', 'ago' did not fit *syntactically*.

### (d) *Deletion 5: 'Marrow'*

'Mr Brown had been carefully nursing a huge *marrow*.'

This should have been an easy clue. It had already been used in the preceding text, the surrounding words exerted high constraints, and it is a *content* word. Confusion was likely to be caused by an ignorance of 'nursing' used metaphorically. This accounts for many of the alternatives. Only 10 of the first-years got the correct word, and 11 made no guess at all. Of those who did attempt it, 15 supplied quite unsuitable words (e.g. that, round, to, by, in, for), while the syntactically correct guesses included garden, nose, house, bath, elephant, bear, baby and man! Only one first-year managed a reasonable alternative 'vegetable'. In the second-year, 27 correct guesses were made, with only 2 refusals. There were in addition 10 reasonable alternatives (e.g. plant, vegetable) with fewer completely unsuitable suggestions. Such responses demonstrated that the second-years were using their experience of the whole content of the passage, and the preceding text, much more successfully than the first-years and were more aware of the specialized connotation of 'nursing'.

(e) *Deletion 7: 'Night'*

'Measured it every *night* before going to bed'

This was one of the most successful completions – 23 first-years and 31 second-years got it correct. As with 'morning' in the first sentence, it is a *content* word, involving clues in the preceding text, and a clue immediately following the deletion.

(f) *Deletion 8: 'With'*

'. . . exchanged a glance *with* Mrs Bird'

This is a habitual association in a formal mode and a *function* word. Only 2 first-year children supplied the correct solution, and only 3 in the second-year. 8 first-years made no attempt to guess compared with 5 in the second-year. The first-years offered many unsuitable guesses (e.g. the, for, Paddington, said, about), but in the second-year 30 children offered the feasible alternatives 'at' or 'to', showing that they had got the sense but not the idiom. This then was one of the least successful deletions for both first- and second-years.

(g) *Deletion 10: 'Mind'*

'I've a good *mind* to . . .'

Here is another habitual association, perhaps more likely to have been heard in speech. There was a much wider gap in correct scores between the answers of the two years. 13 first-years and 27 second-years guessed correctly. Nearly all the alternatives offered fitted syntactically and some were reasonable, e.g. 'idea', 'chance', 'offer'.

(h) *Deletion 13: 'Toast'*

'. . . *toast* and marmalade'

This deletion involved looking ahead, though only to the immediately succeeding text. For adults with a particular cultural background it would be a habitual association, and since it is a *content* word with high syntactical constraints, it should have proved an easy gap to fill with a reasonable alternative. Only 8 of the first-year children guessed 'toast' correctly and 12 gave the reasonable alternatives of 'bread' or 'tea'. 7 of the children did not complete this blank. The interesting fact about alternatives supplied is that they showed a lack of awareness of class hierarchies. For example, 9 children suggested 'breakfast' without realizing that it must subsume 'marmalade'. There was a big improvement in the second-year, with 24 succeeding, and a further 16 supplying 'tea' or 'bread'; with only 2 refusals overall. Some children still suggested 'breakfast', 'honey', 'sandwiches', 'jam', etc. again showing awareness of context but not of adult classificatory concepts.

(i) *Deletion 15: 'Without'*

'. . . disappeared upstairs *without* even having a third cup of tea'

The last sentence is complex and involves perception of relationships, and this particular clue was difficult in that it involved looking ahead for a solution. Conscious guessing was necessary on both syntactic and semantic levels, and the negative element was quite difficult to disentangle. 'Without', moreover, is a pivot word which links the sense across the whole sentence. Only 3 of the first-years and 8 of the second years guessed it correctly. 16 of the first-years left a blank, compared with 8 of the second-years. Of the alternatives offered, most first-years supplied 'and', showing some awareness of the syntactic constraints, but no recognition of the negative element. A number of alternative prepositions and adverbs were offered by both years, but with a much greater variety among the second-years (e.g. 'now', 'after', 'then', 'though'), including the functionally correct 'before', 'never' and 'not'.

## 7. Overall patterns of children's responses

From the examples quoted it can be seen that there was no obvious pattern of success or failure on particular parts of speech. Among both first- and second-years, however, individual children did seem on the whole to be guessing either well or badly on the same words; which would seem to imply that the approach to the exercise did not differ between the two years. The significant gains of the second-year were made across the board.

Children guessed most successfully on deletions where only the immediate context was involved. There were implications that children were still reading on a word-by-word basis. They failed on clues which were infrequently met in speech or which were part of habitual associations which they had not internalized. Such failures imply a lack of relevant experience rather than a deficiency in reading skill or cognitive reasoning.

Table 17-3

*Percentages of readers making responses identical to original deletions*

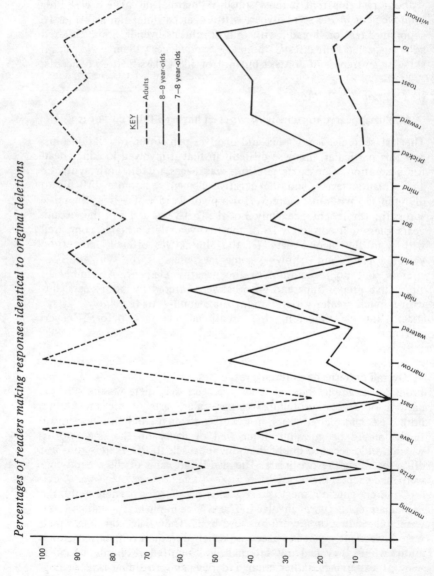

# III Cloze Procedure with Adult Readers

## A. *The Results*

80 teachers were given the same Cloze test as the children. Since the teachers were, expectedly, much more accurate in most of their guesses, comparisons were only made on a 'correct' response basis. The graph in Table 17-3 shows correct scores made on individual words by adults, first- and second-year children. What is informative here is the difference in pattern between the three groups. Although second-year children improved considerably on first-years in the number of their correct responses, they still tended to fail on the same words as the younger children while the adults, not surprisingly making much higher scores than both groups of children, also varied in relative success on certain words.

Another factor is that (apart from Deletion 4 'past') the adults showed success at a consistently high level while there is a fall-off towards the end of the test with the children, especially the first-years. This might have been due to a combination of fatigue, on the children's part, added to the fact that the last two deletions were function words contained in a complex sentence.

## B. *Adults' Reasons for Responses*

20 of the adults who had completed the Cloze passage, were asked to give reasons for their solutions. Although it would have been inappropriate to demand this from the children, one may surmise that the closer their completions agreed with those of the 'adult', skilled solutions, the nearer their strategies might be to those verbalized by adults.

Although the terms used by the adults varied in sophistication, there was a strong consensus about, first, the factors involved in guessing and secondly, the distributions of these factors among the deletions. Table 17-4 lists the strategies used, in order of the frequency with which they were mentioned.

It was clear that 'automatized' processing was by far the most frequently used strategy, followed by the use of information derived directly from the text. The use of 'habitual associations' was mentioned more frequently than any other strategy.

It seems that although many children tackled the Cloze exercise with reasonable success, they did not use as wide a range of strategies as adults. When children were using automatized responses, they were more successful in their use of syntax than in their awareness of habitual associations, and when they were consciously using context they used the preceding text far more than the succeeding text. Their utilization of 'previous experience' or 'knowledge of style' was still severely limited. So children were *not* operating in the same manner as adult readers.

## IV Summary

Two important questions should be considered. First, how far is the outcome of reading to convey new information and how far does it confirm existing experience? On this question will depend the amount of active contribution that a reader can be expected to make. Secondly, what do teachers expect of reading from their pupils? The answers to such questions may differ according to the ethos of the school and the extent to which the reading programme is structured. The continued use of a basic reading scheme, by its nature high in repetition may affect the development of the learner's skill in absorbing new information.

One of the most important elements that seems to be isolated by use of Cloze procedure is the way in which a reader uses the redun-

Table 17-4

*Strategies mentioned by 20 adults – in order of priority*

| 1. | *Automatized Response* |
| | (a) Habitual Associations |
| | (b) Use of Syntax |
| 2. | *Meaning Within Text* |
| | (a) Reading *back* for Information |
| | (b) Reading *on* for Information |
| | (c) 'Makes Sense' |
| 3. | *Search Within Text and Previous Experience* |
| | (a) Previous Experience |
| | (b) Knowledge of Style |

dancies of the passage and the associations from his existing conceptual framework. The element of redundancy is important: it follows that suitable material for any stage of development should be *either* highly redundant *or* should contain familiar syntactical patterns. For example, story books with easy predictability of plot could include a fairly high proportion of new words, whereas informational material should be syntactically simple, since the vocabulary is likely to be unfamiliar. In all reading material, however, there needs to be a strong connecting link through a paragraph. Children completing the Cloze passage in this experiment managed to 'hold a thread' across the passage; it was fiction and they were already used to a 'story line'. Children probably develop efficient reading habits most easily when this clear narrative sequence is present, but they could also be helped to look for it by teachers.

Cloze procedure, then, forces children to use contextual clues. How far they do this in the normal reading situation is more difficult to judge. But if scores rise with age, as they do, this surely indicates that older children are improving in their use of context. It seems that, for average readers between 7 and 9 years, this stage of development sees a great step forward in the use of a variety of strategies in attacking reading material. Teachers need to be aware of this period as one of transition, and will find it helpful to devise and experiment with direct and structured means of helping children to look on reading as an active, problem-solving process.

## V  Implications for Teachers

Cloze procedure is a flexible instrument, and examples of its usefulness for the classroom are available to teachers (for example, Walker (1974) and Lunzer and Gardner (1979)). It has not been used very often for diagnosing strategies, however. With experience, teachers could build up profiles of their pupils from the analysing of responses they make (remembering, in this case, that 'functionally correct' answers can yield as much, if not more, information than completely correct responses). It is also important to sub-divide 'refusals' and 'unfounded guesses'. The use of preceding and succeeding context, and the relative success in guessing content and function words are also revealing. It is clear that teachers of children in these age-groups need to encourage their pupils to *look ahead* in the text as a means of providing clues to words with which they are experiencing difficulties.

In general, deletions in passages to be used for Cloze procedure exercises should be made as far as possible at regular intervals, probably every tenth word for younger children, progressing to seventh-word deletions, and there should always be a good run-in. A minimum of 15 deletions is advisable. It is, however, also possible to delete particular types of words to encourage awareness of both content and function words. For example, it was found in our research that relationships within a sentence were often poorly grasped. Deletions of function words only should help to show the importance of the 'little' words which so often affect the meaning.

Cloze exercises can be carried out in a variety of types of class organization. Asking individuals to complete a Cloze task verbally would complement the written Cloze exercise. For this it would be useful to tape a passage with a clear signal to mark each deletion. The tape should be played right through once while the children listen, and then repeated as many times as necessary, so that they can make suggestions for filling in the gaps.

According to some researchers, Cloze not only *tests* comprehension, but can also *help* it. Here it is probably best used on a group-organized basis, where discussion among children can precede the completions. They may thus become aware of different ways of reasoning to reach a common goal, and vocabulary may be extended through shared experience. The teacher could also encourage increased reflection, the core of understanding, by discussing with an individual or group why certain words were suggested. Children may be helped towards an awareness of the variety of languages used in different types of writing, by realizing that in some texts the identical response to the original is essential, for example in scientific texts, whereas in imaginative writing, more open-ended responses may be reasonable.

There are many exercises in English work-books and course-books which use sentence-deletion techniques. It should be emphasized that Cloze procedure is not the same as leaving a gap in a sentence in order to check that a particular item of vocabulary has been learnt, although word deletions in sentences are often used in this way to test previously learnt facts.

Both Miscue Analysis and Cloze procedure stem from the same theory of reading — the belief that children should be using all levels of language even in the early stages of learning to read, and that they can be given structured help in so doing.

# PART SEVEN

## Conclusions

CHAPTER 18

# Conclusions and Recommendations

## I Introduction

The main aim of this four-year research project has been to help practising teachers to extend the reading proficiency of average readers of 7, 8 and 9 years, in ways which could be expected to lead them eventually to become effective and habitual readers. At the same time it was expected that the findings would have practical implications for younger, more advanced readers and older, slower readers. To this end, a variety of probes has been made into existing practices in many first and second year junior classes; the attitudes, ideas and habits of both teachers and pupils have been explored; and the reading environments in certain schools have been investigated. Throughout the project the teachers concerned co-operated fully with members of the research team, disclosed and discussed their beliefs, ideas and problems and, most difficult of all, opened their classroom doors and exposed to the closest scrutiny all their daily activities. The information gathered and reported in this book owes as much to the openness and willingness of all these teachers as to the work of the researchers and their helpers. It is hoped that nothing reported in this book will be taken as a denigration of the very great efforts which teachers put into helping their pupils to read.

The practical implications of the findings have been spelt out at the end of every relevant chapter, in the hope that teachers might be led to discuss and closely question their current practices and that this might, in turn, lead to experiments with innovatory practices which could prove to be even more effective than existing methods of extending beginning reading.

One further point — a gulf is frequently said to exist between teachers and researchers. This research project has demonstrated not only that teachers are eager to be involved in educational research, especially in practical areas relating to their own teaching practices and their pupils' learning patterns, but also that they have an important role to play. If researchers will take teachers into their confidence, state clearly their aims and the practical results which may be expected from the work, and, most important, supply them with as many of the results of their work as soon as possible, an extremely valuable partnership can exist. It has also been demonstrated by the large Teachers' Reading Research Groups set up (440 and 258 teachers) that it is not always necessary to enlist only small groups of teachers.

## II  Main Findings

### A.  *General Statement*

Teachers of 7, 8 and 9 year-olds give high priority to the improvement of their pupils' reading abilities. They are aware of the need to achieve a balance between recreational and functional reading. They devote a great deal of time to helping their pupils to improve their reading and to fostering their interest in books. In these circumstances, providing that adequate facilities such as appropriate books are available, it might be expected that the desired results would be achieved with the majority of normal children. Accordingly, the findings relating to children are reported first in order that certain important questions may be considered: for example, are the results of teachers' strenuous efforts reflected in a continuing improvement in children's reading competencies, their attitudes and ideas about reading and about books, their ability to use books for gaining information and the establishment of the habit of reading for interest and pleasure? If the teachers' aims and objectives are appropriate but the end products are not always what they might hope for, these disappointments will need to be viewed in the light of existing teaching techniques and practices, as well as the available book provision and facilities in the school.

### B.  *Children As Readers*

1. When 50 children in first- and second-year junior classes were questioned in individual interviews, two-thirds of them said they liked to read; the main reasons being that they found it easy and/or interesting. (Their replies, however, may have been tempered by their awareness of the interviewer's interest in reading.)

2. In contrast, when these children were asked why children and adults should learn to read, their replies showed that the majority perceived merely the functional usefulness of being able to read. Only a few children suggested that reading might be a source of enjoyment for themselves and for adults.

3. Children who said they did not like reading frequently indicated that they found it too difficult. Those who were doubtful about their own reading competence or who were certain they were poor readers, based their judgements partly on subjective feelings about their lack of skill in mastering mechanical difficulties in reading, partly on comparisons with their peers, and partly on the judgements of their teachers and parents, especially the latter.

4. Approximately three-quarters of the children said they preferred

to read quietly to themselves rather than read aloud to someone. Two-thirds of them thought they did more reading at home than at school and these children appeared to regard reading as pleasurable, in contrast to those children who regarded reading in school as merely the mastery of skills.

5. When nearly 600 children of all levels of reading ability in first- and second-year junior classes completed questionnaires on their reasons for liking and disliking books they had read, they showed themselves to be keen judges of the kind of books they liked or did not like to read.

6. The most common reason given by children for disliking a book was that it was 'boring' or 'not interesting'. Such books included two extremes: books the children found difficult, to long or incomprehensible and those they found 'too easy', 'silly', or 'babyish'.

7. Many children took three or four months to get through a teacher-selected reading book, while a few spent a whole school year on one such book — even though these 'teaching books' were frequently sufficiently easy for them to be perfectly capable of reading on their own.

8. When children in both first- and second-year junior classes were set tasks of reading and/or writing activities — usually concerned with basic reading books — while their teacher was engaged in listening to individual children reading to her, on average they spent one-third of their time on diversionary activities. In extreme cases this figure rose to 88% — that is only 12% of the child's time being devoted to the designated reading/writing task.

9. The books children chose to read on their own were often found to be more difficult than those 'teaching books' they were currently reading under their teachers' guidance. The non-fiction books from which they were trying to gather information for different topics were usually even more difficult than their self-chosen story books.

10. The various enquiries into children's personal reading highlighted the need for a much better match between the reading competencies of the children and the books they were supposedly reading on their own. Even when allowances were made for the fact that high motivation can, to some extent, override difficulties in the text, large numbers of children were struggling to read on their own books which were too difficult for them to understand.

11. In contrast to the lengthy periods of time when children were supposed to be reading or doing work connected with their basic reading books, there were few occasions when every child in a class was engaged in silent, uninterrupted personal reading — a practice which would be likely to encourage the establishment of permanent reading habits.

12. In general, apart from the more able children who quickly completed other set tasks, most children spent only scattered, brief periods

in uninterrupted silent reading of books of their own choice.

13. Children of below average reading ability had fewer opportunities for personal reading than children of average or above average reading ability.

14. Although there was a slight tendency for more proficient readers to read more books than less able readers, this trend was not marked. The number of books which children read on their own was closely related to the classes they were in. In classes in which teachers laid great emphasis on personal reading, larger numbers of books were read by all the pupils than in those classes where this activity was given a lower order of priority. Even so, in most schools and classes there were certain children who, in the entire school year, read few books on their own.

15. Many second-year children as well as the majority of first-year children had little idea of how to locate, select or use information books.

16. Only one-fifth of average readers of 8 years were able to read all of the 200 most commonly used words in the English language (*Key Words to Literacy*, McNally and Murray 1962), while for 9 year-olds the proportion was about one-third. 17% of average readers of 8 years and nearly 4% of average readers of 9 years failed to recognise 10 or more of these frequently used words.

17. While certain children in both age-groups, and especially those of above average reading ability, demonstrated a working knowledge of some of the common phonic rules in the English language, there were still many children, particularly those of below average reading ability, whose knowledge was either sketchy or non-existent. Moreover, many of the rules which children had failed to master in the first-year classes still showed deficiencies in second-year classes, which suggests that these weaknesses may not have been diagnosed.

18. Most of the average readers in first-year junior classes had mastered the mechanics of reading aloud, although many of them lacked natural intonation, and were reading word by word, which indicated that they were operating only at the level of word recognition. When they encountered unknown words their main tactic was to try to apply phonic rules, rather than use the context for clues. By the second year more children were demonstrating their growing awareness of the meanings of words and of the grammatical structure of the language by utilizing the semantic and syntactic cues of the passage to read.

## C. *Teachers of Reading*

1. The time set aside by teachers for language work of all kinds was mainly devoted to the following activities (in the order given):

(a) listening to individual children reading to them short passages from teacher-selected reading books;

(b) helping individual children with their written work — either 'free writing' or 'topic work' — by providing them with the correct spellings of words requested;

(c) work on the basic skills.

2. The predominating activity engaged in by teachers was listening to individual children reading to them, while the remainder of the class were engaged in set activities, frequently related to their teacher-selected reading books. The majority of teachers spent 20—40 minutes per day on this activity, while a minority spent 60—100 minutes per day.

3. Almost as much time was spent by teachers in helping children with spellings for their written work. Indeed, often these two activities ran concurrently; the class being engaged in reading and/or writing activities, the teacher sitting at her table and listening to one child reading on one side, while on her other side a queue of children formed to request help with spelling.

4. In such reading and writing periods the teachers worked extremely hard, continually switching their attention from one child to another, as well as interspersing this with comments to the remainder of the class and dealing with disciplinary problems and various interruptions. It was not unusual to note that in the 20 minute period when they were being observed, teachers made 20—30 attention switches, i.e. moved their attention from one child to another or from child to class or group. One result of this was that the actual time devoted to listening to any one child reading aloud was minimal, frequently being no more than 30 seconds for each child.

5. This high work output of teachers was not always mirrored by concentrated task-orientation in their pupils, the actual time devoted by a proportion of the children to the set reading and writing being extremely small. In fact, there were strong indications that in these types of lesson, with certain children, an obverse effect took over; high teacher output being related to low pupil output.

6. Moreover, the brief amount of time a teacher was able to devote to any one child in such a lesson was inadequate for:

(a) diagnosing individual weaknesses in order that they might be rectified;

(b) assessing anything other than the child's literal comprehension of the passage read;

(c) probing the reading strategies he was using;

(d) or discussing his views, interests or reading problems.

7. The non-stop pace of teacher's activities in these kinds of reading lessons also meant that teachers of first- and second-year juniors rarely had the time or opportunity to keep records of children's weaknesses, their progress in various areas or the books they had read — apart from teacher-selected reading books.

8. All teachers were interested in promoting children's interest in books.

They generally regarded the practice of reading aloud to their classes as one of the best ways of motivating their pupils to undertake personal reading. The materials read by the teachers included fiction, poetry, Bible stories, excerpts from magazines, newspapers and encyclopedias, as well as children's own written work. The majority of teachers spent between one hour and two-and-a-half hours per week on this activity. (It was also interesting to note that children spent more time in school listening to their teachers reading to them than the time they were allowed for their personal reading which the teachers were trying to promote!) Other means employed of fostering children's interest in books included book displays, book clubs, book fairs and introductions to local libraries.

## D. *Reading Resources*

1. The number of fiction books in the schools was generally smaller than for non-fiction books and, of the total fiction books, the numbers of those suitable for third- and fourth-year juniors usually exceeded those at readability levels appropriate for first- and second-year juniors.
2. Of the total of non-fiction books in the schools, the proportion sufficiently easy for younger juniors to use on their own was usually much smaller than that of books suitable for older juniors.
3. The result was that though teachers' aims were to encourage their pupils to read many fiction books and learn to consult non-fiction, the supply of sufficiently simple books was rarely adequate for children of 7, 8 and 9 years with average reading ability, much less for children of below average reading ability.
4. Only a small proportion of the schools had devised simple systems of grading fiction books according to levels of difficulty — to help children to choose books from a selection which they would be able to read.
5. No school visited had developed a grading system for non-fiction books.
6. The lack in most primary schools of a central library room of sufficient size to accommodate a whole class, and with free access at other times, made the task of initiating children into the system of classification and arrangement of books a formidable one, although school librarians and class teachers did their best in this respect. Consequently, the beginnings of bibliographical skills were rarely taught, even to 9 year-olds.
7. Training in the use of dictionaries was not often noticed in first- and second-year classes and, when the children were writing, they were rarely seen to refer to dictionaries to check the spelling of words.
8. Few teachers in charge of younger juniors had been trained to teach bibliographical skills or study skills and, consequently, most of them were unsure of their ability to do so and were eager for guidance or advice in this area of reading which they regarded as important.

## E. *A Brief Summary of the Findings*

First, it should be stated that undoubtedly many children aged 7 to 9 years were learning to read effectively and enjoyed using their reading skills for both recreational and functional purposes. On the other hand, certain children of average reading ability at the beginning of the school year had by the end of the year made considerably less progress than might have been anticipated, and certainly less than their teachers must have hoped for. There were some children who professed not to like reading; some who said they found it difficult; others who struggled through only a very few 'teaching' books with their teacher's help, in one year; and those who read very few books on their own. There were other children who were considered good readers but who did not appear to be sufficiently stretched. Yet teachers undoubtedly worked diligently and consistently in their efforts to improve their pupils' reading; in ways which are common practice in the majority of primary schools in the country.

Generally, even when their pupils make relatively good progress in reading, teachers are never entirely satisfied with what has been achieved — and the teachers involved in this project were no exception. Primary school teachers are continually hoping for guidelines which will help them to ensure greater success with children's reading. This report will be read by them with a view to gleaning suggestions of practices or techniques which may be expected to make their teaching more effective. The key question is whether or not it was possible in this research project to identify particular practices which could be shown to be more successful than others.

The twelve schools most closely observed in the project, and so most likely to provide possible answers to this question, were those which participated in the intensive study year. Part of the programme for that year involved testing children's reading ability at the beginning of the school year and again at the end of the school year (using *Wide-Span Reading Test* (Brimer 1972)). A measure of progress for individual children and for whole classes was thus available and could be related to observations of the teachers' practices and their personal records of the reading and related activities in which they had been engaged. When these different amounts of class progress were examined in the light of variations in teachers' practices, two clear pointers emerged. The classes which made most reading progress were those in which the teachers placed the *least* emphasis on listening to children's oral reading. Furthermore, in these same most successful classes, a greater proportion of time was devoted to children's uninterrupted personal reading and to discussions about the books the children had read. Accordingly, our suggestions for planning a more effective reading programme for children aged 7, 8 and 9 years are hinged on these two findings.

## III  Recommendations for a More Effective Reading Programme

The suggestions which follow are not intended to be taken as a blue-print for all reading programmes for children aged 7, 8 and 9 years. We should never contemplate advocating one system of organizing reading tuition which would be likely to prove equally effective if used by all teachers with all pupils. These suggestions spring from the findings of this research project and the many discussions which took place between team members and practising teachers about possible ways of planning more effective use of teachers' and children's time, as means of forwarding reading progress. Every teacher contemplating changes might first consider the suggestions in the light of her own beliefs, the needs of her pupils and their individual differences, and the school situation. Staff discussions in schools might then follow and it is hoped that they would result in decisions to try out some of these proposals.

The backbone of the proposals rests firmly on the following four major modifications of existing practices.

1. A drastic curtailment is needed of teachers' almost universal practice of spending the major portion of their time in reading periods in attempting to listen to large numbers of individual children reading to them for extremely brief periods each, from teacher-selected reading books.

2. An increase in the length of time which teachers spend with individual children is recommended, but with such contacts occurring at less frequent intervals.

3. The provision of periods in which every child in the class is silently reading, without interruptions, books of his own choice, should be extended. The length of such periods should be progressively increased as children grow accustomed to them.

4. Experimental plans for radically reducing the lengthy amounts of time in which teachers are acting solely as consultants for individual children on the correct spellings of words, should be made and put into practice as a matter of urgency.

### 1.  The ineffectiveness of short sessions with individual children

Although most teachers of 7, 8 and 9 year-olds are firmly wedded to the practice of listening to individual children reading aloud to them, the findings of the research show that the average time solely devoted to any one child at one session was 30 seconds. No effective teaching or help can be given in such a short time, particularly when the teacher is constantly being interrupted by other children asking for help or advice, or is dealing with other kinds of interruption. Nor is merely prompting the child when he fails to read a word an effective teaching technique. Teachers say that children enjoy the personal contact with which this activity provides them but the majority of the 50 children questioned said that they preferred to read by themselves rather than read aloud to other people. Effective individual reading teaching requires longer, uninterrupted periods. It is suggested that longer time for such periods could be gained from two sources: time formerly devoted to daily periods of listening to large numbers of children's oral reading; and the lengthy periods usually devoted to supplying individually requested spellings.

## 2. Longer individual contacts with children

Teachers in this project were aiming to listen to all children reading to them individually at least once a week, and poorer readers two or three times per week. If a new system were set up whereby the time teachers formerly spent on this activity (i.e. 2½ to 3 hours per week— and sometimes more) were used in longer sessions with each child, for example 15 or 20 minutes, it should be possible to have these extended sessions with 8 or 9 children per week. This would work out, depending on the number of children in the class, in a teacher having these much more fruitful contacts with each child every three or four weeks.

These longer periods of contact with each pupil, in which the teacher's time could be devoted to those particular activities suggested throughout this report which merit greater attention, would take the form of individual consultations leading eventually to case-studies. The following are some examples of what might be undertaken on occasions in such sessions:

(a) The child reading aloud a few pages from a self-chosen book;

(b) Discussion of the content of the book, reasons why it was chosen, the child's particular interests and hobbies related to books, and how he sets about finding books which interest him;

(c) His comprehension of what he is reading — not just literal comprehension;

(d) Checking whether or not he recognises the first 200 *Key Words to Literacy* (McNally and Murray 1962);

(e) Administering a diagnostic test of his phonic competencies;

(f) Vocabulary extension, in the context of his reading;

(g) Carrying out a miscue analysis of the errors he makes in oral reading, with a view to discovering the strategies he is using;

(h) Encouraging him to use his knowledge of the meaning of words, the sense of phrases and sentences and the normal grammatical structure of the English prose to provide cues to words or phrases he does not recognize;

(i) Keeping notes, records, tape-recordings, etc. of these sessions and thereby gradually building up a comprehensive file of his reading and its progress;

(j) Examining and discussing with the child his record of books he has read in the preceding few weeks and comments, reviews, etc. he may have written;

(k) Planning, with the child's help, the course of his reading activities for the succeeding few weeks.

### 3. Supplying individually requested spellings

Teachers of first- and second-year juniors were quite frequently involved for a whole hour in helping individual children to spell correctly the words they had requested for use in some written work in which they were engaged. An attempt to reduce this drain on teachers' time could help to release some of it for the sort of diagnosis, teaching and guidance which has been proposed. The following suggestions are some of the ways in which children might be helped to be more self-reliant and/or more confident about attempting to spell words for themselves without always consulting their teachers:

(a) Encouragement for children to try to be independent about spelling by first seeing if they can check the correct spelling on blackboard, chart, card index or dictionary and, when this is not possible, trying to spell it for themselves;

(b) Charts of commonly used, irregularly spelt words on display so that children may consult them;

(c) When children are all writing on a similar topic, *key* words for that topic on the blackboard (not a whole blackboard full of words);

(d) Simple card index boxes of words — with pictures where possible — always available, together with picture dictionaries;

(e) The teacher making children aware that good endeavours at spelling, even if incorrect, will be praised;

(f) Diagnosis of spelling weaknesses, followed by regular teaching of spelling to a group of children found to have a particular weakness;

(g) Regular graded training in dictionary skills;

(h) Arranging for fewer children to be engaged in written work at any one time would reduce or even obviate the need for heavy demands on the teacher's time.

### 4. More personal reading for children

The habit of reading is much more likely to become established if definite measures are taken early in the junior school not only to promote an interest in reading, but to set aside regular and increasingly lengthy periods when every child in the class reads in a quiet atmosphere without interruptions. It is not sufficient that children should be allowed to read for ten or fifteen minutes in the morning when the teacher is engaged in registration or the collection of dinner money, nor that those pupils who complete set tasks early should be free to read. At such times there may well be various interruptions which create opportunities for certain children to distract others. The following suggestions may help to establish a habit which eventually becomes a pleasurable activity for all pupils.

(a) Set aside a particular period every day for personal reading – perhaps the end of the morning or the afternoon.

(b) See that every child has a personally selected book at a level which he is likely to be able to understand, and, if he has nearly completed reading it, a second one to hand.

(c) Tell the children that they will be allowed, say, ten minutes to enjoy their chosen books without anyone interrupting them.

(d) The teacher should sit at her own table, preferably also quietly reading and trying to avoid speaking, for example by merely catching the eye of any child who is not reading and perhaps raising an eyebrow.

(e) Every effort should be made to establish the pattern that children neither talk nor leave their seats during this period.

(f) A notice on the door might read: 'Class reading – please do not disturb.'

(g) As children become accustomed to this procedure, gradually increase the period devoted to this personal, uninterrupted reading.

## 5. Study skills

Children in primary schools spend a great deal of time on what is termed 'topic work' and this usually involves them in locating relevant information in non-fiction books and other reading materials. Teachers of 7, 8 and 9 year-olds in this project were concerned about how they might initiate their pupils into the skills required for the successful undertaking of this quite difficult task. One answer would seem to lie in not expecting too much from children whose reading ability is less than that of an average 7 year-old, as abstracting information from non-fiction texts is a complex task and the skills of paraphrasing and summarizing are notoriously difficult. The following are a few suggestions which may help.

(a) First ensure that first-year juniors understand the classification system for non-fiction books in the school library and their own classroom, so that they may find their way to the section of books in which they are interested.

(b) Be certain that there are some very simple books in each section.

(c) Teach the use of an index.

(d) Arrange class or group discussions on paragraphs or small articles relating to topics of current interest, with a view to devising one or two simple sentences to represent the whole. (Children cannot be expected to summarize, *in writing*, what they have read if they have not first been encouraged and trained to do it mentally and then express it in spoken words.)

(e) Prepare cards or other guide-lines for children searching for information. These might include, among other pointers, the name of a relevant book, with the page number and paragraph of interest and a suggestion that the information in the paragraph might be condensed into one or two simple sentences.

## 6. Appropriate books

All that has been suggested in this section implies that there will need to be available an adequate supply of appropriate books, arranged in such a manner as to help children to locate and select those to suit their needs, and which they know will be within their capacity to read. The following are some of the deficiencies which teachers involved in the project pointed out about their own schools' book resources.

(a) The most common deficiency was that there were insufficient fiction books at the level which average and below average readers in first- and second-year junior classes could read with ease, while non-fiction books at an appropriate level for such pupils were even more sparse.

(b) In such cases, it is important that future book requisitions and borrowings from Schools Library Services should be used to rectify these deficiencies.

(c) The optimum use of the book resources in many primary schools would be more likely to be achieved if simple systems of grading both fiction and non-fiction books were undertaken and some system of colour coding or other identification system adopted.

(d) Teachers should seriously question the value of attempting to extend the reading proficiency of children of 7 and older, who can read at the level of an average 7 year-old and/or beyond this level, by making them work their way through basic reading schemes. It has been shown that this is not an effective way of extending reading proficiency. The *teaching* of reading should spring from diagnosis of weaknesses, with appropriate measures being taken to overcome the weaknesses, with individual children, groups of children or whole classes, as the need is exposed. The practice or use of reading skills would be better undertaken by children using books they had personally selected. Books forming parts of reading schemes could, of course, be included on appropriate shelves of graded books, so that children might choose them if they wished.

## 7. Individual, group and class teaching

Many teachers of 7 to 9 year-olds seem to have grown to accept the view that individual tuition for reading and writing is always the primary aim. The findings of this project are that it is frequently unnecessary, rarely of sufficient duration to be effective, and wasteful of the teacher's time. Furthermore, the attempt to pursue it by current practices more often than not leads to many of the remaining members of the class becoming engaged, for varying proportions of their time, in diversionary activities rather than the designated reading and writing activities.

Throughout this report, suggestions based on the findings have been made of occasions when class and group teaching would seem appropriate, and also of when individual teaching is called for and how such time might be most profitably employed. The diagnosis of individual strengths and weaknesses usually calls for individual attention. If deficiencies in any particular area of reading are found in all children, e.g. dictionary skills or study skills, then class teaching would be the appropriate remedy. If only certain children are unfamiliar with a phonic rule, those particular children should be gathered into a temporary group and taught it. On other occasions, a consultation period between a teacher and a child may reveal an individual problem which requires individual guidance. We would support wholeheartedly the following statement in the *Bullock Report:*

> We therefore consider the best method of organizing reading to be one where the teacher varies the experience between individual, group and class situations according to the purpose in hand.

## IV  Concluding Word

Teachers who read this report, as well as the researchers who have written it, owe a great debt to the many practising teachers who cooperated by so willingly exposing their current practices, ideas and problems. We are convinced that if other teachers of 7, 8 and 9 year-olds, as well as teachers of other age-groups, are equally willing to learn from the picture presented, and experiment with at least some of the suggestions made, more effective reading programmes will emerge. Teachers will then experience the pleasure of watching their pupils make better progress in extending their beginning reading skills in the direction of pleasurable and effective adult reading.

# Appendices

## Appendix 1-A

### *List of Schools in Which the Headteachers and Staff Worked Closely with the Project Team*

Ainsworth C. of E. Primary School, Bolton.
Alexandra Park Junior School, Oldham.
All Saints R.C. School, Eccles, Salford.
Altrincham Cloverlea County Primary School, Timperley,
    Altrincham, Cheshire.
Ascension C. of E. Junior School, Salford.

Baguley Hall Junior School, Manchester.
Bamford County Primary School, Rochdale.
Beech Street County Primary School, Eccles, Salford.
The Beeches Primary School, Sale, Cheshire.
Bexton County Junior School, Knutsford, Cheshire.
Birchwood County Primary School, Swinton, Salford.
Bishop Bilsborrow R.C. School, Manchester.
Bradshaw Hall County Primary School, Cheadle Hulme,
    Stockport.
Brandwood Street County Junior School, Bolton.
Breightmet County Primary School, Bolton.
Brentnall Primary School, Salford.
Briscoe Lane, Junior School, Manchester.
Broad Walk Junior School, Salford.

Cavendish Primary School, Manchester.
Cheadle Lum County Junior School, Gatley, Stockport.
Cheetwood Primary School, Manchester.
Chelford C. of E. Primary School, Macclesfield, Cheshire.
Chesham County Primary School, Bury.
Christ Church C. of E. School, Denton.
Church Road County Primary School, Bolton.
Claremont Road Junior School, Manchester.
Clifton Green County Primary School, Swinton, Salford.
Corporation Road School, Audenshaw, Manchester.
Corpus Christi R.C. Junior School, Denton.
Crawshawbooth County Primary School, Rossendale,
    Lancashire.

Denton Corrie County Junior School, Denton.
Derby Street School, Oldham.
Dial Park County Primary School, Stockport.
Disley County Primary School, Disley, Cheshire.
District C. of E. Junior School, Newton-le-Willows,
    Warrington.

Elmridge County Primary School, Altrincham, Trafford.
Elton County Junior School, Bury.

Fitton Hall Junior School, Oldham.
Freehold County Junior School, Oldham.

Gorton Mount Junior School, Manchester.
Green End Junior School, Levenshulme, Manchester.

Halton Bank Primary School, Salford.
Hargher Clough Junior School, Burnley, Lancs.
Harpur Mount Junior School, Manchester.
Haslingdon C. of E. School, Rossendale, Lancashire.
Haslingdon County Primary School, Rossendale, Lancashire.
Heald Place Junior School, Manchester.
Highfield Primary School, Urmston, Trafford.
Hillside County Primary School, Bury.
Hilton Lane County Primary School, Worsley, Salford.
Hollingworth County Primary School, Hyde.
Hollins County Primary School, Bury.
Holy Family R.C. Primary School, Rochdale.
Holy Trinity C. of E. Primary School, Blackley, Manchester.
Hough Fold County Junior School, Bolton.
Hulton C. of E. School, Bolton.
Hurdsfield County Junior School, Macclesfield, Cheshire.

Irlam Endowed School, Irlam, Manchester.

Kearsley Mount School, Kearsley, Bolton.
King David Junior School, Manchester.

Ladybarn County Junior School, Manchester.
Ladybridge County Primary School, Bolton.
Ladybridge County Primary School, Cheadle, Stockport.
Langley County Junior School, Langley, Middleton,
    Lancashire.
Leigh Central County Primary School, Leigh, Manchester.
Leyland Seven Stars County Junior School, Leyland,
    Lancashire.
Light Oaks Junior School, Salford.
Littleborough Dearnley C. of E. School, Littleborough,
    Manchester.
Lowton St. Mary's School, Warrington.
Lum Head County Junior School, Gatley, Stockport.

Marlborough Road Junior School, Salford.
Marton and District C. of E. Aided Primary School,
    Macclesfield, Cheshire.
Millbank Junior School, Urmston, Trafford.
Milnrow C. of E. Junior School, Rochdale.
Morris Green Junior School, Bolton.

Moss Hey County Junior School, Bramhall, Stockport.
Moss Park County Junior School, Stretford.
Moston Lane Junior School, Manchester.
Mytham County Primary School, Little Lever, Bolton.

Nelson Street Junior School, Manchester.
New Moston Junior School, Manchester.
Norbury Booth County Junior School, Knutsford, Cheshire.

Ordsall Junior School, Salford.
Our Lady and  the Lancashire Martyrs School, Worsley,
    Salford.

Park Road Primary School, Timperley, Cheshire.
Peel Hall County Junior School, Worsley, Salford.
Peel Hall Junior School, Manchester.
Pemberton County Primary School, Wigan.
Poundswick Junior School, Manchester.
Poynton Worth County Primary School, Poynton, Cheshire.
Presfolee County Primary School, Radcliffe, Manchester.
Princess Junior School, Manchester.
Puss Bank Junior School, Macclesfield, Cheshire.

Queen's Road Primary School, Cheadle Hulme, Stockport.
Queensway School, Higher Folds, Leigh, Lancashire.

St. Aidan's R.C. Primary School, Wigan, Lancashire.
St. Andrew's C. of E. School, Ramsbottom, Bury.
St. Andrew's C.of E. Primary School, Blackburn.
St. Anne's C. of E. Primary School, Royton, Oldham.
St. Anne's County Primary School, Denton, Tameside.
St. Antony's R.C. Junior School, Blackburn, Lancashire.
St. Benedict's R.C. Primary School, Handforth, Cheshire.
St. Brigid's Junior School, Manchester.
St. Catherine of Siena School, Lowton, Wigan.
St. Clement's C.of E. Primary School, Higher Openshaw,
    Manchester.
St. Clement's Primary School, Lower Broughton, Salford.
St. Edward's R.C. Primary School, Manchester.
St. Elizabeth's Primary School, Hale, Trafford.
St. Hilda's C. of E. Primary School, Oldham.
St. Hugh's R.C. Primary School, Timperley, Trafford.
St. James C. of E. Primary School, Farnworth.
St. James R.C. Primary School, Hyde, Tameside.
St. James C. of E. Primary School, Darwen, Lancashire.
St. James School, Royton, Manchester.
St. John's C. of E. Primary School, Bury.
St. John's C. of E. Primary School, Kearsley, Bolton.
St. John's C. of E. Primary School, Dukinfield, Tameside.
St. Joseph's Junior School, Bury.
St. Kentigern's R.C. Primary School, Manchester.

St. Malachy's R.C. Junior School, Manchester.
St. Margaret's C. of E. Primary School, Hollinwood, Oldham.
St. Mark's R. C. Primary School, Swinton.
St. Mary's Junior School, Blackburn.
St. Mary's R.C. Primary School, Bacup.
St. Michael's School, Bolton.
St. Osmund's R.C. Primary School, Bolton.
St. Paul's Primary School, Marley Road, Poynton, Cheshire.
St. Peter's C. of E. Primary School, Farnworth.
St. Peter's C. of E. School, Rochdale.
St. Peter's C. of E. School, Ashton-under-Lyne.
St. Simon's R.C. Primary School, Hazel Grove, Stockport.
S.S. Simon and Jude's School, Bolton.
St. Stephen's C. of E. Junior School, Blackburn.
St. Teresa's R.C. Junior School, Altrincham, Cheshire.
St. Wilfred's C. of E. Primary School, Manchester.
Sacred Heart Junior and Infants School, Oldham.
Sacred Heart Primary School, Manchester.
Sacred Heart R.C. Primary School, Warrington.
Sacred Heart R.C. Primary School, Wigan.
Sacred Heart School, St. Silas's Road, Blackburn.
Sale Urban Road County Primary School, Sale,Cheshire.
Saxon Nook County Primary School, Middleton, Rochdale.
Seymour Road Junior School, Manchester
South Failsworth County Junior School, Failsworth,
    Lancashire.
Stamford Park Junior School, Hale, Altrincham, Trafford.
Standish C. of E. Junior School, Standish, Wigan, Lancashire.
Stanley Grove Junior School, Manchester.
Stansfield Hall County Primary School, Littleborough,
    Manchester.
Stansfield Road Junior School, Failsworth, Lancashire.
Stretford King's Road Primary School, Trafford.
Sudell County Primary School, Darwen, Lancashire.
Sunning Hill County Primary School, Bolton.

Tottington Primary School, Bury.
Trafford Park County Primary School, Manchester.
Trafford Road Junior School, Salford.
Turton Belmont County Primary School, Bolton.

Upton Priory School, Macclesfield, Cheshire.

Vernon County Junior School, Poynton, Stockport.

Wargrave C. of E. Junior School, Newton-le-Willows.
Webster Junior School, Manchester.
Whitehill County Primary School, Heaton Norris, Stockport.
Whittle-le-Woods C. of E. School, Chorley.
Winsford C. of E. Primary School, Winsford, Cheshire.
Worsley Hulton Peel Hall County Junior School, Worsley.

# Appendix 2-A

*Summaries of Numbers of Schools, Classes and Children
Tested and Selected for Intensive Study Year 1975—6*

**Tables 1 and 2** *Children in categories of reading
attainment (Southgate Group Reading Test 2)*

*Table 1 Numbers of 1st year juniors*

| Reading Level | Original Testing | Final Selection |
|---|---|---|
| Above Average | 247 | 196 |
| Average | 289 | 251 |
| Below Average | 207* | 140 |
| Total Numbers of Children | 743 | 587 |

*Table 2 Numbers of 2nd year juniors*

| Reading Level | Original Testing | Final Selection |
|---|---|---|
| Above Average | 279 | 223 |
| Average | 223 | 184 |
| Below Average | 285 | 133 |
| Total Numbers of Children | 787 | 540 |

*Table 3 Summary of numbers of children
tested and selected*

| Numbers of Children | Original Testing | Final Selection |
|---|---|---|
| Schools | 14 | 12 |
| Classes | 53 | 35 |
| 1st Yr. Jun. | 743 | 587 |
| 2nd Yr. Jun. | 787 | 540 |
| Total Children | 1,530 | 1,127 |

(*N.B. This figure is an underestimate of the total number
of 1st year juniors at a below average level, as certain of
the children who had barely begun to read, were, after
discussion with their teachers, not asked to take the test.)

## Appendix 2-B

### Classes selected for Intensive Study Year
### Children in 3 Categories of Reading Attainment

*Table 4 Test used: Southgate Group Reading Test 2*
Categories:  AA – Above Average Reading Attainment
A – Average Reading Attainment
BA – Below Average Reading Attainment

| School | No. of classes | 1st Year Jun. | | | 2nd Year Jun. | | |
|---|---|---|---|---|---|---|---|
| | | AA | A | BA | AA | A | BA |
| 1/Z | 2 | 21 | 15 | 1 | 18 | 12 | 9 |
| 2/Z | 3 | 16 | 18 | 1 | 17 | 19 | 3 |
| | | 11 | 14 | 19 | | | |
| 3/Z | 2 | 9 | 13 | 4 | 8 | 15 | 8 |
| 4/Z | 2 | 8 | 21 | 9 | 10 | 10 | 12 |
| 5/Y | 4 | 8 | 17 | 5 | 19 | 6 | 10 |
| | | 12 | 15 | 4 | 14 | 12 | 9 |
| 6/Y | 3 | 11 | 19 | 6 | 5 | 11 | 9 |
| | | 9 | 13 | 13 | | | |
| 7/Y | 4 | 23 | 8 | 3 | 25 | 10 | 2 |
| | | 23 | 9 | 2 | 24 | 8 | 5 |
| 8/Y | 2 | 10 | 10 | 5 | 20 | 6 | 1 |
| 9/X | 2 | 7 | 15 | 13 | 2 | 5 | 11 |
| 10/W | 5 | 4 | 15 | 7 | 16 | 17 | 6 |
| | | 7 | 14 | 5 | 14 | 6 | 16 |
| | | | | | 18 | 12 | 10 |
| 11/W | 4 | 6 | 9 | 12 | 8 | 17 | 10 |
| | | 3 | 13 | 14 | 5 | 18 | 12 |
| 12/W | 2 | 4 | 5 | 23 | | | |
| | | 4 | 8 | 3 | | | |
| Totals | 35 | 196 | 251 | 140 | 223 | 184 | 133 |
| | | | 587 | | | 540 | |

## Appendix 9-A
### *Publications Referring to the Grading of Books*

ATKINSON, E. J. and GAINS, C. W. (1973)
*An A−Z List of Reading and Subject Books*
National Association for Remedial Education
(Obtainable from Mr. F. Brookman, 9 Cranleigh Rise, Eaton,
Norwich, NOR 54D)

GOODACRE, E. J. (1972)
*Hearing Children Read*
(including a list of reading schemes and other materials)
University of Reading: Centre for the Teaching of Reading

LAWSON, K. S. (1968) (revised edition 1971)
*Children's Reading*
University of Leeds: Institute of Education

MOON, C. (1973)
*Individualized Reading*
(Comparative Lists of Selected Books for Young Readers)
University of Reading: Centre for the Teaching of Reading

PASCOE, T. W. (ed.) (1962)
*A Second Survey of Books for Backward Readers*
London: University of London Press

PURTON, R. W. (1970)
*Surrounded by Books*
London: Ward Lock Educational

WEST BROMWICH CHILD PSYCHOLOGY SERVICE (1973)
*Reading Schemes for Slow Learners*
West Bromwich Education Committee

A discussion of readability and details of certain readability formulae
can be found in:

GILLILAND, J. (1972)
*Readability*
London: University of London Press

# Appendix 10-A

*Teachers Log Sheet and Related Notes*

**Schools Council Project: Extending Beginning Reading**     **EBR/183**

**Teacher Log**

Name ....................  ......  ........

Date .......  School.............................................

| Details of Activities (in chronological order) | Category | Group size | Minutes |
|---|---|---|---|
| Geoffrey Lavell — The Ring | | 1 | 4 |
| Andrew Partridge - Jemima and The Welsh Rabbit | | 1 | 3 |
| Chris Wright — Bri's accident | | 1 | 3 |
| Julia Prentice — The Pop Trolley | | 1 | 3 |
| Debbie Ellis - Bonus was a Warrior | | 1 | 3 |
| Nicola Gayton - Malay Pirate | | 1 | 3 |
| Tracey Green - The Strange House | | 1 | 4 |
| Recording Growth spring Flowers. | | 0 | 30 |
| Children requesting words | | 10 | 5 |
| Handwriting practice | | 0 | 30 |
| Phonic Work. | | 0 | 30 |

## Notes on the Completion of Form EBR/183: Teacher Log

*General Notes*
1. A new log sheet should be started for every teaching day during the weeks which are designated 'Intensive Study Weeks'.
2. If a single day's record occupies more than one sheet, it is probable that too much detail is being included.
3. Only those activities relating to reading, writing, spelling or any other language work should be included.

*Notes on Completion of Columns*

*Column 1 – Description*
Give brief (one-line) details of the activity. (See attached sample log)

*Column 2 – Category*
Leave blank

*Column 3 – Group Size*
Indicate, in the following manner, the size of the group to which you were directing your attention.
    (a) An individual child or a number of children.
        State the number of individual children with whom you worked, e.g. 6 signifies that you gave some attention to 6 individual children.
    (b) A group of children.
        Give the number in the group with whom you worked and draw a circle round the number; e.g., ⑤ indicates that your attention was directed towards a group of 5 children.
    (c) More than one group of children.
        Enter each group on a separate line, as explained in (b) above. If the activity is the same for each group, the description need not be repeated.
    (d) The entire class.
        Draw a circle with nothing inside it, i.e. ◯
    (e) Non-child oriented activity.
        Enter an 'X' in the column.
        Examples of teacher activity, relating to reading and language work, but which would be non-child orientated, might be preparing reading apparatus or charts, marking written work, re-organizing library books etc.

*Column 4 – Minutes*
Enter the approximate number of minutes spent on each activity.

# Appendix 10-B
## Teacher Observation Schedule

**Schools Council Project: Extending Beginning Reading**

30 minute observation period — Recorded at 30 second interval

**Teacher**

**Teacher Initiation**

1. Gives direct reading instruction — O    O O O
2. Recounts or reads from book — O O    O O O
3. Explains or expands book content — O    O
4. Organises, supervises reading activity — O    O    O

**Task Supervision**

5. Hears oral reading — O O O    O O O    O O    O    O O
6. Supplies word/spelling — O    O
7. Directs copying or literal recall
8. Requires pupils' ideas on reading activities — O    O O    O
9. Comments on reading or allied work — O    O

**ATTENTION SWITCH** — /    /    / / / /    /    / / / /    /    / /

**Materials**

1. Basic reading scheme
2. Supplementary reading scheme
3. Reading Material (fiction)
4. Reading Material (information)
5. English work — book reading lab. — /    / / / / / / / / / / / / / / / / /    / / / / / /
6. Dictionary or word list
7. Word game
8. Workcard or sheet
9. Exercise book
10. Paper or rough book
11. Blackboard

## Teacher Observation Key to Items: Teacher Schedule

*General guidance*

The categories (1–9 Teachers' sheet) aim to identify the following broad aspects of behaviour:–

1. *Imparting* information, *initiating* skills, where teacher is concerned in transmission of skills or content.
   (Categories T1, 2, 3)
2. *Organizing and directing* pupils engaged on or about to be engaged on a task, including advice on how to set about task.
3. *Incidental instruction.* Differs from 1 in that teacher is concerned with helping pupil occupied on task, and usually involves discussion with pupil.
   (Categories 5, 6, 7, 8, 9)

*Key to Individual Categories*

1. *Gives direct instruction in reading or allied skill*:
   Teacher gives instruction or information directly related to reading or writing. This may include introduction to a new skill, or extended clarification of a previously introduced skill. It does *not* include, e.g. supplying the meaning of a single word or phrase, or instruction on how to set about a task. Change or development in cognitive skills is implied.
   *Examples*
   'We are going to learn about the sound which 'oa' can make in words.
   'When you write a story, you need an exciting beginning. We are going to find out some good ways of beginning stories'.
   'Sometimes we can find out what a book is about by looking at the index. We do this by . . . ' etc.

2. *Recounts or reads from book or passage*:
   Teacher reads aloud or recounts directly from text without elaboration. This does *not* include incidental reading out of instructions or items from work-books etc., (which would come under 4).
   *Examples*
   Teacher reads story to class
   Teacher reads paragraph from history book prior to clarification.
   Teacher reads child's written work out to class.

3. *Explains or expands on content of book or passage*:
   Teacher classifies, analyses or infers from content of text. With a whole class, this would usually accompany 2. May however, include clarification of text with individual pupils. Does not include definitions of single words out of context.
   *Examples*
   'We'll go over that bit to make sure you understand it'.
   'I think that means that the monsters gradually died out because they couldn't get enough food'.

4. *Organizes, supervises reading activity*
   A broad category. Teacher sets children to work on tasks, and explains what is required. It may include incidental clarification of

texts as part of ongoing activity. It does *not* include giving out books, pencils etc.
*Example*
'Now, you are going to do me a snow-picture.'

5. *Hears oral reading*
This applies if teacher is listening to oral reading without comment when signal goes. It covers the activity known as 'Hearing children read' and does not apply to isolated sentences read out by pupil. It may include children reading out their own writing in groups or class context.

6. *Supplies word or spelling:*
Teacher supplies spelling or meaning of isolated words requested by children.
*Example*
Putting word in child's vocabulary book.

7. *Direct copying or literal recall:*
Teacher guides on reading or writing tasks involving literal recall, copying or a selection of facts immediately available to them in text. Questions likely to be closed.
*Examples*
'Put the story in your own words'.
'Can you remember how she arrived? Think back'.
A series of questions which appear to be open-ended may be used by the teacher to reach a preconceived conclusion involving literal recall. This is difficult to categorize, and can only be judged by considering if the pupils' own ideas are accepted during the exchange (in which case it would be Category 8).

8. *Requires pupils' ideas on reading activities:*
Teacher guides or questions pupils, seeking a contribution which reveals comprehension at a higher level than literal recall.
*Examples*
'What do you think might happen next in the story?'
'I think it's interesting to add details about the peculiarities of cats'.

9. *Comments on reading or allied work:*
Includes positive or negative comment, oral or written, or in the form of marks, i.e. provides feed-back on task.
*Example*
'Well done, but I think you could have done a little more on the bit about the garden'.

*Materials*
1. *Basic reading scheme.* Graded scheme used for instructional purposes.
2. *Supplementary reading scheme.* May be supplementary readers of a graded scheme, or books introduced by teacher for consolidation of skills.
3. *Reading material (fiction).* Stories, poems etc. May be library books, or class books not within a graded scheme.
4. *Reading material (information).* Reference books, often library books, used for gaining information, (e.g. topic work). Books attached to subject areas, e.g. maths, history, geography.

5. *English work-book, reading laboratory.* Books requiring pupils to carry out stated tasks. e.g. English Today, S.R.A. Workshop.
6. *Dictionary or word list.* Word list may include pupils' vocabulary books.
7. *Word game.* e.g. Stott's reading kit, Scrabble.
8. *Workcard or sheet.* May include commercial work-cards or teacher-prepared.

## CLASSROOM OBSERVATION SCHEDULE
## TEACHER OBSERVATION – INSTRUCTIONS

The grid is to be marked at 30-second intervals, in conjunction with taped signals. Each sheet covers a 30-minute observation period, although 20 minutes will be adequate for a complete observation. Begin recording with the sheet opened out. Fill in the details at the top of the sheet *before* beginning observation. A brief description of lesson content, titles of books used, etc. should be completed on the reverse side after the observation.

*On each signal, observer should proceed as follows, in the order given.*
1. If teacher has transferred attention to another pupil, or from individual to class, insert stroke (1) in ATTENTION SWITCH square.
2. Select appropriate category from 1–9, if relevant, and record, using one of the following symbols:—

Individual pupil contact                          1
Whole class contact                               0
Contact with groups                               2–9 (according to number in group)
Contact with individual
child within a class teaching
context.                          $\bigcirc\!\!\!/$
Contact with individual child
within a group context.           // Number in group.

3. Insert $V$ in relevant MATERIALS category. If no materials are in use, insert $\sqrt{}$ in empty column below 11.
4. Teacher instructing or organising in other fields than reading or writing, i.e. any other *work activity* not involving written materials. Insert 0 in empty column above ATTENTION SWITCH. Do not mark materials column.
   *If books are involved,* columns should be filled in whatever the subject area, as under 1–3½.
5. *Non-teaching activity.*
   If teacher is organising (not directly connected with content), disciplining, out of room, marking books, etc., insert a vertical wavy line $\xi$ through categories 1–9. Do not mark materials column.
6. If *lesson ends* within 20-minute period insert horizontal line (——) in ATTENTION SWITCH square, plus appropriate letter for new lesson.
   viz. English – E (including oral language, reading, writing.)
       Maths – M
       Art – A
       Other subjects – O

*CHILD OBSERVATION*
*RECORD FORM*

# Child | Schools Council Project: Extending Beginning Reading

30 minute observation period – Recorded at 30 second intervals

**Child's Activity**

- Listens to teacher (or media) reading/ instruction in reading
- Listens to another child reading
- Reads assigned book
- Reads self selected book
- Writes + book
- Writes – book
- Other activity – work
- Asks questions on reading etc
- Answers questions on reading etc
- Volunteers answer
- Spontaneous contribution on reading etc.
- Non-orientated activity

**Materials**

- Basic reading scheme
- Supplementary reading scheme
- Reading material (fiction)
- Reading material (information)
- English work-book/grammar/rdg. lab.
- Dictionary/word list
- Word game
- Workcard or sheet
- Exercise book
- Paper or rough book
- Blackboard

*Do not write any extraneous information on grid itself.* Columns 1–9 are *mutually exclusive,* and should therefore only need one mark per signal. In exceptional cases, teacher may be carrying on two activities simultaneously: even so, she is usually doing one thing on actual signal.


## Key to Items (Child Schedule)

1. *Listens to teacher* (or media) reading or giving instruction in reading.
   Includes listening as one of class, or to teacher individually. 'Media' signifies television, radio or tape-recorded instruction.
2. *Listens to another child reading*
3. *Reads assigned book*
   Chosen by teacher for specific activity. Name on reverse side of sheet.
4. *Reads self-selected book*
   Library or other reading material chosen by child. Name on reverse side of sheet.
5. *Writes + book*
   Child engaged in writing activity while referring to printed question or information. Name text on reverse side of sheet.
6. *Writes − book*
   Child engaged in writing activity without reference to text.
7. *Other activity − work*
   Includes any task where reading or writing of words is not involved e.g. mathematics, art, P.E. etc.
8. *Asks questions on reading etc.*
   Child asks teacher or other teacher about reading or writing activities.
9. *Answers questions on reading etc. −* as in 8
   Neither 8 or 9 includes putting up a hand to ask or answer question. This would come under 10.
10. *Volunteers answer*
    Child raises hand to replay to question connected with reading or writing.
11. *Spontaneous contribution on reading etc.*
    Child makes unsolicited verbal contribution on reading or writing activity to teacher or other children.
12. *Non-oriented activity*
    Child is disengaged from work. Do not include very short periods of non-activity where child is apparently thinking. Include daydreaming, chatting to other children if not related to task. Wandering about room, or carrying out activities like pencil-sharpening.


## Materials

As in Teacher Schedule.

## Classroom Observation Schedule

*Child Observation — Instructions*
The child schedule is to be marked as the Teacher's, with the following variations —

One child will be observed for 20 minute period.

Categories will be marked on signals, by inserting tick ($\sqrt{}$) in appropriate square.

If teacher is making direct contact with observed child on signal insert $\sqrt{}^{T}$ in appropriate square.

If child is waiting for teacher's attention insert $\sqrt{}^{T}$ in category, non-oriented activity. (No. 12)

If child is making individual contact with another child insert $\sqrt{}^{C}$ in appropriate category.

## Appendix 12-A

### Examples of Children's Records of Books Read
### In One School Year

*Example 1      1st Year Boy — Average Reading Ability*

| Books I Have Read By Myself | (Date Completed) |
|---|---|
| 1. *Rumplestiltskin* (Ladybird) | Oct. 21st |
| 2. *No Roses for Harry* (Picture Puffin) | Oct 21st |
| 3. *Lost At The Fair* | Oct. 23rd |
| 4. *Poor Tired Tim* | Oct. 23rd |
| 5. *Conkers* | Oct. 23rd |
| 6. *A Home For The Swallows* | Oct. 23rd |
| 7. *Harold and the Purple Crayon* | Oct. 24th |
| 8. *The Last Puppy* | Oct. 24th |
| 9. *The Three Billy-Goats Gruff* | Oct. 24th |
| 10. *Puss in Boots* | Oct. 24th |
| 11. *Starters Maths — Toyshop Maths* | Nov. 3rd |
| 12. *Butterflies* | Nov. 3rd |
| 13. *A Lion in the Meadow* | Nov. 4th |
| 14. *Dinosaurs* | Nov. 4th |
| 15. *The Very Best of Friends* | Nov. 4th |
| 16. *Fishing* | Nov. 6th |
| 17. *The New Baby* | Nov. 6th |
| 18. *Heidi* | Nov. 6th |
| 19. *The Look-Out Gang* | Nov. 6th |
| 20. *The Sea-Horses of the Islands* | Nov. 13th |
| 21. *The Ice King's Daughter* | Nov. 21st |
| 22. *The Storm* | Nov. 21st |
| 23. *Smoke and Fluff* | Nov. 21st |
| 24. *The Island of the Marc (?) People* | Nov. 26th |

| | | |
|---|---|---|
| 25. | *The Princess Who Wanted the Moon* | Nov. 26th |
| 26. | *Roderick The Red* | Nov. 26th |
| 27. | *The Adventure of Walter Worm* | Nov. 28th |
| 28. | *The Adventure of Willie Worm* | Nov. 28th |
| 29. | *The Little Red Hen* | Dec. 2nd |
| 30. | *Baby Moses* | Dec. 3rd |
| 31. | *Downy Duckling* | Dec. 3rd |
| 32. | *Prickly Pie* | Dec. 10th |
| 33. | *The Policeman* | Dec. 11th |
| 34. | *Topsy and Tim's Thursday Book* | Dec. 11th |
| 35. | *Moon, Sun, Stars* | Dec. 11th |
| 36. | *Greg and the Black . . . (?)* | Dec. 16th |
| 37. | *The Horses of the North Wind* | Dec. 17th |
| 38. | *The Fireman* | Jan. 11th |
| 39. | *The Big Blue Diesel* | Jan. 14th |
| 40. | *Annancy Tale* | Jan. 28th |
| 41. | *Roderick The Red* | Jan. 28th |
| 42. | *On The Land* | Jan. 28th |
| 43. | *The Blue Pirate* | Jan. 28th |
| 44. | *The Three Pirates Meem (?)* | Jan. 28th |
| 45. | *The Look-Out Gang* | Jan. 28th |
| 46. | *Time and Clocks* | Jan. 28th |
| 47. | *The Dragon Princess* | Feb. 2nd |
| 48. | *Annancy Stories* | Feb. 18th |
| 49. | *The Emperor's New Clothes* | Feb. 18th |
| 50. | *Bobby Brewster's Bicycle* | March 3rd |
| 51. | *Clever Folk* | March 11th |
| 52. | *Garden Birds* | March 25th |
| 53. | *Dick Whittington and His Cat* | March 30th |
| 54. | *Man Finds Treasure* | March 30th |
| 55. | *Man Needs The Sun* | March 30th |
| 56. | *The Faithful Beasts* | March 30th |
| 57. | *Man Makes Towns* | April 2nd |
| 58. | *Michael and the Music Makers* | April 5th |
| 59. | *The Great Alexander* | April 28th |
| 60. | *Rob Robin* | April 30th |
| 61. | *The Magic Finger* | May 5th |
| 62. | *The House at Pooh Corner* | |
| 63. | *Chitty Chitty Bang Bang* | |
| 64. | *Nobody Plays with A . . . (?)* | |
| 65. | *Marm* | July 5th |
| 66. | *Mrs. Pepper's Outing* | July 9th |
| 67. | *Cub Away (?)* | July 16th |

*Example 2 – 1st Year Girl – Average Reading Ability*

| Books I Have Read By Myself | (Date Completed) |
|---|---|
| 1. *The Midnight Party* | Nov. 11th |
| 2. *I Didn't Invite You to My Party* | Feb. 17th |
| 3. *Michael and the Deer* | Feb. 20th |
| 4. *The Midnight Party* | March 9th |

5. *Quicksilver*        March 16th
6. *Witchers and Wishes*        June 14th
7. *John's Day At The Sea*        June 29th
8. *The Children In The Bush*        July 5th

*Example 3 – 2nd Year Boy – Above Average Reading Ability*

| *Books I Have Consulted* | *(Date Completed)* |
|---|---|
| 1. *Plants and How They Grow* | Oct. 21st |
| 2. *Farming – Sheep Dogs* | Oct. 23rd |
| 3. *Middle Ages* | Nov. 26th |
| 4. *William The Conqueror* | Nov. 26th |
| 5. *Scott* | Jan. 5th |
| 6. *Explorers* | Jan. 5th |
| 7. *Scott* | Jan. 6th |
| 8. *Great Explorers* | Jan. 6th |
| 9. *Scott* | Jan. 8th |
| 10. *Captain Scott* | Jan. 8th |
| 11. *The Airline Pilot* | Jan. 25th |
| 12. *The Airline Pilot* | Jan. 26th |
| 13. *The Airline Crew* | Feb. 4th |
| 14. *The First Living Things* | Feb. 5th |
| 15. *Prehistoric Animals* | Feb. 5th |
| 16. *The Middle Ages* | Feb. 17th |
| 17. *The Middle Ages* | Feb. 18th |
| 18. *Festivals and Celebrations* | March 3rd |
| 19. *Middle Ages* | March 9th |
| 20. *Middle Ages* | March 10th |
| 21. *Castles* | March 10th |
| 22. *Castles of Britain* | March 10th |
| 23. *The Middle Ages* | March 15th |
| 24. *Castles of Britain* | March 17th |
| 25. *Castles of Britain* | March 18th |
| 26. *Barons, Serfs and King* | March 18th |
| 27. *How Babies Are Born* | May 7th |

# Appendix 15-A

## The first 200 of 'Key Words to Literacy
(McNally and Murray 1962)
(In the order in which they were presented in the test.)

| | | | | |
|---|---|---|---|---|
| a | have | came | made | some |
| and | him | can | make | their |
| he | his | come | me | them |
| I | not | could | more | then |
| in | on | did | much | there |
| is | one | do | must | this |
| it | said | do | must | this |
| of | so | first | no | when |
| that | they | from | new | up |
| the | we | get | now | want |
| | | | | |
| to | with | go | off | well |
| was | you | has | only | went |
| all | about | her | or | were |
| as | an | here | oar | what |
| at | back | if | other | where |
| be | been | into | out | which |
| but | before | just | over | who |
| are | big | like | right | will |
| for | by | little | see | your |
| had | call | look | she | old |
| | | | | |
| after | every | house | own | than |
| again | fast | how | play | these |
| always | Father | jump | put | thing |
| am | fell | keep | ran | think |
| ask | find | know | read | three |
| another | five | last | red | time |
| any | fly | left | room | too |
| away | four | let | round | tree |
| bed | found | live | run | under |
| because | gave | long | sat | us |
| | | | | |
| best | girl | man | saw | very |
| bird | give | many | say | walk |
| black | going | may | school | white |
| blue | good | men | should | why |
| boy | got | Mother | sing | wish |
| bring | green | Mr. | sit | work |
| day | hand | never | soon | woman |
| dog | head | next | stop | would |
| don't | help | once | take | yes |
| eat | home | open | tell | year |

# Appendix 15-B

*New Diagnostic Phonic Test*
*Mean and Median Raw Scores (Feb. 1976)*

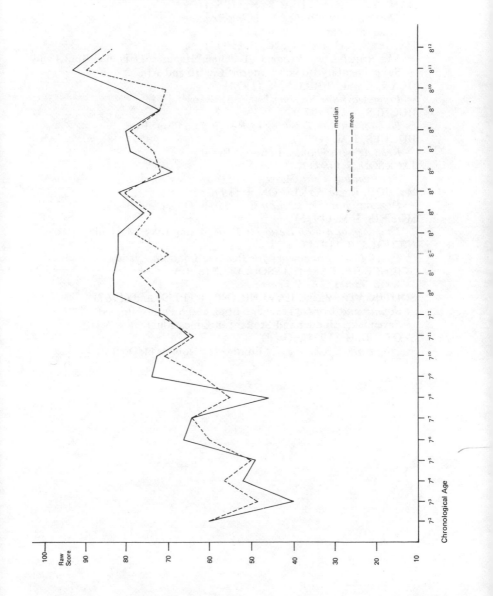

## Appendix 15-C

### *A List of Publications on Phonics*

DANIELS, J. C. and DIACK, H. (1957)
*The Phonic Method of Teaching Reading*
London: Chatto and Windus
DANIELS, J. C. and DIACK, H. (1957)
*The Royal Road Readers* (Teachers' Handbook: Pupils' Books and
Supplementary Books) London: Chatto and Windus
DEAN, J. and NICHOLS, R. (1974)
*Framework for Reading* London: Evans
HUGHES, J. M. (1972)
*Phonics and the Teaching of Reading* London: Evans
HUGHES, J. M. (1973)
*Reading with Phonics* London: Evans
JACKSON, S. (1971)
*Get Reading Right* Glasgow: Gibson
McLEOD, J. and ATKINSON, J. (1972)
*Domain Phonic Workshop* Edinburgh: Oliver and Boyd
MORRIS, J. M. (1975)
*Language in Action Resource Book* Basingstoke: Macmillan
NICHOLS, R. (1974)
*Check Lists: Framework for Reading* London: Evans
SCIENCE RESEARCH ASSOCIATES (S.R.A.)
*Word Games – 6–9 Years*
SOUTHGATE, V. and HAVENHAND, J. (1959) and (1967)
*Sounds and Words* (Teacher's Book and 6 Pupils' Books)
Sevenoaks: Hodder and Stoughton Educational
STOTT, D. H. (1971 revised)
*Programmed Reading Kit* Edinburgh: Holmes McDougall

## Appendix 16-A

### *Classification and Analysis of Miscues (Based on Goodman 1972) – As used in this Research Project*

The following questions must be answered for *each miscue* (i.e. refusals, substititions, omissions, insertions, reversals. Self-corrections are analysed as miscues, although compensation is given as described)

### *1. GRAPHO-PHONEMIC LEVEL*

| | |
|---|---|
| How far does the actual response look/sound like the expected response? | ┌YES: Similar to a high degree<br>├PARTIAL: Similar to some degree<br>└NO: No similarity |

### *2. GRAMMATICAL LEVEL*

| | |
|---|---|
| Does the actual response serve the same grammatical function as the expected response (within the sentence)? | ┌YES: the grammatical functions are identical<br>├PARTIAL: the response fits grammatically with the preceding part of the sentence only<br>└NO: the response does not fit grammatically |

### *3. SEMANTIC LEVEL*

| | |
|---|---|
| Does the response still make good sense? | ┌YES: the response makes good sense in relation to preceding and succeeding text<br>└PARTIAL: the response only makes sense in relation to preceding text<br>NO: response distorts sense of text |

### *4. SELF-CORRECTION*

| | |
|---|---|
| Was the miscue self-corrected? | ┌YES: successful correction<br>└NO: no self-correction or unsuccessful attempt |

One final question should be asked about all miscues, namely: 'Does the miscue result in a change of meaning *which will impede the reader's understanding of the total passage*?

Goodman's manual was used to transfer the coded miscues to grids showing grapho-phonemic, grammatical and comprehension strengths. The relationships between the three levels are complex and the procedure is not simple, so that a simplified method is shown on p. 277. It must be remembered that all calculations are on *miscues,* and that a child whose overall pattern is worked out on the basis of, say, 8 miscues will not be comparable to one whose pattern derives from analysis of 48 miscues. For this reason, the final pattern of strengths should be looked at in relation to the total miscues. Although quantitative results are quoted in this report, it is likely that the practising teacher will gain more through looking at the evidence qualitatively, as has been done in the two children's profiles.

## Appendix 16-B

### *Spache Readability Formula*

To calculate the grade level of any reading materials undertake the following steps:-
1.  Select 100 word samples for analysis.
2.  Determine average sentence length in words (l) of each sample.
3.  Count number of words outside the Dale 'Easy Word List' of 769 words (w) (for guidance on word counts, see below).
4.  Use the following formula:—
    Grade Level = 0.141(l) + 0.086(w) + 0.839
5.  It is usual to take at least three sample passages (beginning, middle, end of book). Average these results for a more reliable estimate of the reading difficulty.
6.  To convert the reading grade level to an approximate reading age equivalent — add 5.

Stone argued that the accuracy of the Spache Formula could be increased by revising the Dale list. It is therefore suggested that the Clarence Stone list of 769 words be used instead of the original Dale list. This list, a copy of which is attached, yields a lower rating than the original Dale list.

**Guide for use in word count**
1.  Count all letters as familiar — A, B, C.
2.  Count regular verb forms (-ing, -ed, -es) as familiar. Count irregular verbs as unfamiliar.
3.  Count plurals and possessive endings of nouns as familiar.
4.  Count adjectival or adverbial endings (-ly, -er, -est) as unfamiliar. (This differs from the Dale—Chall procedure but is supported by the fact that such endings do not appear except at higher levels in primary-grade material.)
5.  Count first names as familiar.
6.  Count an unfamilar word once only, even though it appears again or with variable endings later in the sample. (This rule was adopted to prevent a single hard word from distorting the estimation of grade level in primary-grade materials, which tend to be highly repetitive.)

7. Count a group of words consisting of repetition of a single word (as oh, oh, oh; look, look, look) as a single sentence regardless of punctuation.

# Appendix 16-C

## *Clarence R. Stone's Revision of the Dale List of 769 Easy Words*

| | | | | |
|---|---|---|---|---|
| a | bag | blue | car | cry |
| about | bake | board | care | cup |
| across | baker | boat | careful | cut |
| afraid | ball | book | carry | |
| after | balloon | both | cat | dance |
| afternoon | band | bottom | catch | dark |
| again | bark | bow | caught | day |
| air | bang | howl | cent | dear |
| airplane | barn | bow-wow | chair | deep |
| all | barnyard | box | chick | deer |
| almost | basket | boy | chicken | did |
| alone | bath | branch | child | dig |
| along | be | bread | children | dinner |
| already | bear | break | circus | dish |
| also | beautiful | breakfast | Christmas | do |
| always | become | bright | city | does |
| am | because | bring | clap | dog |
| an | bed | brought | clean | doll |
| and | bedroom | bring | climb | done |
| animal | bee | brown | close | don't |
| another | been | bug | clothes | door |
| answer | before | build | clown | down |
| any | began | building | cluck | draw |
| anyone | begin | bump | coat | dress |
| anything | behind | bunny | cock-a-doodle-do | drink |
| apple | being | bus | | drive |
| are | believe | busy | cold | drop |
| arm | bell | but | colour | dry |
| around | belong | butter | come | duck |
| arrow | beside | buy | coming | |
| as | best | buzz | cook | each |
| ask | better | by | cooky | ear |
| asleep | between | | corn | early |
| at | big | cabbage | corner | east |
| ate | bigger | cage | could | eat |
| away | bill | cake | count | egg |
| automobile | bird | calf | country | else |
| | birthday | call | cover | elephant |
| baa | bit | came | cow | end |
| baby | black | can | cried | engine |
| back | blew | candy | cross | enough |
| bad | blow | cap | crumb | even |

| | | | | |
|---|---|---|---|---|
| ever | fun | her | lady | milkman |
| every | funny | here | laid | mill |
| everything | | herself | lamb | minute |
| eye | game | hid | land | miss |
| | garden | hide | large | Miss |
| face | gate | high | last | money |
| fail | gave | hill | late | monkey |
| family | get | him | laugh | moo |
| far | girl | himself | lay | more |
| farm | give | hit | learn | morning |
| farmer | glad | hold | leaves | most |
| fast | go | hole | left | mother |
| fat | goat | home | leg | mouse |
| father | God | honey | let's | mouth |
| feather | going | hop | letter | move |
| feed | gold | horn | lie | Mr. |
| feel | gone | horse | light | Mrs. |
| feet | good | hot | like | music |
| fell | good-bye | house | line | must |
| felt | got | how | lion | my |
| fence | grandfather | hungry | listen | |
| few | grandmother | hunt | little | nail |
| field | grass | hurry | live | name |
| fill | gray | hurt | log | near |
| find | great | | long | neck |
| fine | green | I | look | need |
| finish | grew | ice | lost | nest |
| fire | ground | if | lot | never |
| first | grow | I'll | loud | new |
| fish | guess | in | love | next |
| fit | | Indian | lunch | nice |
| five | had | inside | | night |
| flag | hair | into | made | no |
| flew | hall | is | mail | noise |
| floor | hand | it | make | north |
| flower | happen | its | man | nose |
| fly | happy | | many | not |
| follow | hard | jar | march | note |
| food | has | joke | matter | nothing |
| foot | hat | jump | may | now |
| for | have | just | me | nut |
| found | hay | | meat | |
| four | he | keep | meet | of |
| fox | head | kept | men | off |
| fresh | hear | kill | meow | often |
| friend | heard | kind | met | oh |
| frog | heavy | kitchen | mew | old |
| from | held | kitten | mice | on |
| front | hello | knew | might | once |
| fruit | help | knock | mile | one |
| full | hen | know | milk | only |

| | | | | |
|---|---|---|---|---|
| open | quick | seven | table | tried |
| or | quiet | shake | tail | trunk |
| orange | quite | shall | take | try |
| other | | she | talk | turkey |
| our | rabbit | shell | tall | turn |
| out | race | sheep | tap | turtle |
| outside | rain | shine | teach | two |
| over | rake | shoe | teacher | |
| own | ran | shop | teeth | uncle |
| | read | sky | tell | under |
| paint | ready | sled | ten | umbrella |
| pan | real | sleep | tent | until |
| paper | red | sleepy | than | up |
| park | rest | slide | thank | upon |
| part | ride | slow | that | us |
| party | right | small | the | use |
| pat | ring | smell | their | |
| paw | river | smile | them | vegetable |
| pay | road | smoke | then | very |
| peanut | roar | sniff | there | visit |
| peep | robin | snow | these | voice |
| | rock | so | they | |
| pet | rode | soft | thin | wagon |
| pick | roll | sold | thing | wait |
| picnic | roof | some | think | wake |
| picture | root | something | this | walk |
| pie | rope | sometime | those | want |
| piece | round | song | though | war |
| pig | row | soon | thought | warm |
| pink | rub | sound | three | was |
| place | run | soup | threw | wash |
| plan | | splash | throw | watch |
| plant | said | spot | ticket | water |
| play | same | spring | tie | wave |
| please | sand | squirrel | tiger | way |
| pocket | sang | stand | time | we |
| point | sat | star | tired | wear |
| policeman | save | start | to | wee |
| pond | saw | station | today | weed |
| pony | say | stay | too | weak |
| pop | school | step | together | well |
| poor | sea | stick | told | went |
| post | seat | still | tomorrow | were |
| present | see | stone | too | west |
| press | seed | sure | took | wet |
| pretty | seem | surprise | top | what |
| puff | seen | swam | town | wheat |
| pull | sell | sweet | toy | wheel |
| push | send | supper | train | when |
| put | sent | swim | tree | where |
| puppy | set | swing | trick | which |

| | | | | |
|---|---|---|---|---|
| while | win | without | work | year |
| white | wind | woman | world | yellow |
| who | window | wonder | worm | yes |
| why | wing | wood | would | you |
| wide | winter | woke | write | your |
| wild | wish | wolf | | |
| will | with | word | yard | zoo |

# References

ATKINSON, E. J. and GAINS, C. W. (1973) *An A—Z List of Reading and Subject Books* The National Association for Remedial Education
BAMMAN, H. and DAWSON, M. (1963) *Fundamentals of Basic Reading Instruction* David McKay Co. Inc.
BARR, R. (1972) 'The influence of instructional conditions on word-recognition error.' *Reading Research Quarterly,* VII 3
BEALING, D. (1973) 'Issues in classroom observational research'. *Research in Education,* 9, 70—82.
BESWICK, N. W. (1972) *School Resource Centres* (Schools Council Working Paper 43) London: Evans Methuen
BESWICK, N. W. (1975) *Organizing Resources: Six Case-Studies* (The final report of the Schools Council Resource Centre Project) London: Heinemann Educational Books
BETTS, E. A. (1946 and 1957) *A Foundation of Reading Instruction* New York: American Book Co.
BIEMILLER, A. (1970) 'The development of the use of graphic and contextual information as children learn to read.' *Reading Research Quarterly VI* 1.
BOARD OF EDUCATION (1931, reprinted 1952) *Report of the Consultative Committee on the Primary School* London: H.M.S.O.
BOND, M. (1959) *More About Paddington* London: William Collins
BORMUTH, J. R. (1966) 'Readability: a new approach.' *Reading Research Quarterly 1,* 79—132
BOYCE, E. R. (1959) *The Gay Way Series* London: Macmillan
BOYDELL, D. (1974) 'Teacher—pupil contact in junior classrooms.' *British Journal of Educational Psychology,* 44, 313—318
BOYDELL, D. (1975) 'Pupil behaviour in junior classrooms.' *British Journal of Educational Psychology,* 45, 122—129
BRADBURNE, E. S. (1965) *Through The Rainbow* Huddersfield: Schofield and Sims
BRIMER, A. (1972) *Wide-Span Reading Test* London: Nelson
BRITTON, J. N. (1977) 'Language and the nature of learning: an individual perspective.' In SQUIRE, J. R. (Ed.) *The Teaching of English* Chicago: University of Chicago Press
BURKE, C. and GOODMAN, K. S. (1970) 'When a child reads: a psycholinguistic analysis.' *Elementary English* 47, 1
BURT, C. (1954) *The Burt (Re-arranged) Word Reading Test* London: University of London Press
CARVER, C. and STOWASSER, C. H. (1963) *Oxford Colour Readers* Oxford: Oxford University Press

CHALL, J. (1977) *Reading 1967–1977: A Decade of Change and Promise* Bloomington, Indiana, USA; The Phi Delta Kappa Educational Foundation

CHOMSKY, C. (1972) 'Stages in language development and reading exposure.' *Harvard Educational Review* 42, 1–33

CHRISTENSON, A. (1969) 'Oral Reading errors at independent, instructional and frustration reading levels.' In FIGUREL, J. A. (Ed.) *Reading and Realism* Newark, Delaware, USA: International Reading Association

CLARK, M. M. (1976) *Young Fluent Readers: What Can They Teach Us?* London: Heinemann Educational Books

CLAY, M. (1968) 'A syntactic analysis of reading errors.' *Journal of Verbal Learning and Verbal Behaviour*, 7, 434–438

CLAY, M. and IMLACH, R. H. (1971) 'Juncture, pitch and stress as reading behaviour variables.' *Journal of Verbal Learning and Verbal Behaviour*, 10, 133–139

CLYMER, T. (1963), 'The utility of phonic generalizations.' *The Reading Teacher 16*, 4, 252–258

CLYMER, T. (1968) 'What is "reading"?: some current concepts.' In ROBINSON, H. M. (Ed.) *Innovation and Change in Reading Instruction.* The 67th Yearbook of the National Society for the Study of Education, Part 2. Chicago: University Press

COX, C. B. and DYSON, A. E. (Eds.) (1969) *Fight for Education: A Black Paper* London: The Critical Quarterly Society

DANIELS, J. C. and DIACK, H. (1957) *The Royal Road Readers* London: Chatto and Windus

DAVIS, F. B. (Ed.) (1971) *The Literature of Research in Reading with Emphasis on Models* Final Report, US Department of Health, Education and Welfare

DAVIS, W. Q. (1970) 'Functional use of standardized reading tests.' In DE BOER, D. L. (Ed.) *Reading Diagnosis and Evaluation* pp. 78–85; Newark, Delaware, USA: International Reading Association

DEPARTMENT OF EDUCATION AND SCIENCE (1967) *Children and their Primary Schools* (The Plowden Report) Volume 1 – The Report London: H.M.S.O.

DEPARTMENT OF EDUCATION AND SCIENCE (1975) *A Language for Life* (The Bullock Report) London: H.M.S.O.

DOLAN, T., HARRISON, C. and GARDNER, K. (1979) 'The Incidence and Context of Reading in the Classroom.' In LUNZER, E. and GARDNER, K. (Eds.) *The Effective Use of Reading* London: Heinemann Educational Books for the Schools Council

DOLCH, E. W. (1945) 'Basic sight vocabulary of 220 words.' *A Manual for Remedial Reading* Champaign, Illinois: Garrard Press

DOWNING, J. (Ed.) (1966) *The First International Reading Symposium – Oxford 1964* London: Cassell

DUKER, S. (1971) *Individualized Reading* Springfield, Illinois: Charles C. Thomas

FLANDERS, N. A. (1964) 'Some relationships among teacher influence, pupil attitudes and achievements'. In BIDDLE, B. J. and ELENA, W. J. (Eds.) *Contemporary Research on Teacher Effectiveness* New York. Holt, Rinehart and Winston

FLANDERS, N. A. (1970) *Analysing Teaching Behaviour* Reading: Massachusetts: Addison-Wesley

FLOWERDEW, P. and RIDOUT, R. (1954) *Reading To Some Purpose* Edinburgh: Oliver and Boyd

FRIES, C. C. (1952) *The Structure of English* New York: Harcourt Brace

GAGG, J. C. (1956) *Using Your Reading* Leeds: Arnold

GARNER, J. and BING, M. (1973) 'Inequality of teacher-pupil contact'. *British Journal of Educational Psychology, 43,* 234–243

GIBSON, E. J. and LEVIN, H. (1975) *The Psychology of Reading* Cambridge, Massachusetts: The M.I.T. Press

GILLILAND, J. (1972) *Readability* London: University of London Press

GOLINKOFF, R. (1975) 'A comparison of reading comprehension processes in good and poor comprehenders.' *Reading Research Quarterly, XI, 4,* 623–659

GOODACRE, E. J. (1967) *Reading in Infant Classes* Slough: National Foundation for Educational Research in England and Wales

GOODACRE, E. J. (1969) 'Published reading schemes'. *Educational Research 12,* 1, 30–35

GOODACRE, E. J. (1972) *Hearing Children Read* (including a list of reading schemes and other materials) University of Reading: Centre for the Teaching of Reading

GOODACRE, E. J. (1972) 'Reading Research in England and Wales.' In SOUTHGATE, V. *Literacy at All Levels,* pp. 198–204, London: Ward Lock Educational

GOODMAN, K. S. (1965) 'A linguistic study of cues and miscues in reading *Elementary English,* 42, 639–643

GOODMAN, K. S. (1968) 'Analysis of oral reading miscues: applied psycholinguistics'. *Reading Research Quarterly, 1,* 3

GOODMAN, K. S. (1974) 'Effective teachers of reading know language and children.' In TIEDT, I. M. (Ed.) *What's New in Reading* Urbana, Illinois, USA: National Council of Teachers of English

GOODMAN, K. S. (1977) 'Reading: the key is in children's language.' In REID, J. F. and DONALDSON, H. (Eds.) (2nd Ed. 1977) *Reading: Problems and Practices* London: Ward Lock Educational

GOODMAN, K. S. and GOODMAN, Y. (1977) 'Learning about psycholinguistic processes by analyzing oral reading.' *Harvard Educational Review,* 47, 3, 317–333

GOODMAN, K. S., GOODMAN, Y. and BURKE, C. (1978) 'Reading for life: the psycholinguistic base.' In HUNTER-GRUNDIN, E. and GRUNDIN, H. U. (Eds.) *Reading: Implementing the Bullock Report* London: Ward Lock Educational

GOODMAN, Y. (1967) 'A psycholinguistic description of observed oral reading phenomena in selected young beginning readers'. (Unpublished doctoral dissertation) Wayne State University, USA

GOODMAN, Y.M. and BURKE, C.L. (1972) *Reading Miscue Inventory Manual: Procedure for Diagnosis and Evaluation* New York: Macmillan

GRASSAM, E.H. (1922, revised 1957) *The Beacon Readers* London: Ginn

GRASSAM, E.H. (1966) *Six Phonic Workbooks* London: Ginn

GRAY, W.S. (1937) 'The nature and types of reading'. In *The Teaching of Reading: A Second Report* 36th Yearbook of the National Society for the Study of Education, Part 1. Chicago: The University of Chicago Press

GRAY, W.S. (1949) 'Basic competencies in efficient reading'. In National Council of Teachers of English, Committee on Reading at the Secondary School and College Levels *Reading in an Age of Mass Communication* New York: Appleton-Century-Crofts

GRAY, W.S., MONROE, M., ARTLEY, A.S., ARBUTHNOT, M.H. (1956) *The Happy Trio Reading Scheme* Exeter: Wheaton

GURNEY, R. (1976) *Language, Learning and Remedial Teaching* Leeds: Arnold

HAFNER, L. (1966) 'The Cloze Procedure *Journal of Reading,* 9, 415–21

HARRIS, A.J. and SIPAY, E.R. (1975) (6th Edn.) *How to Increase Reading Ability* New York: David McKay

HARRISON, C. (1977) 'Assessing the readability of school texts.' In GILLILAND, J. (Ed.) *Reading: Research and Classroom Practice* London: Ward Lock Educational

HILSUM, S. (1972) *The Teacher at Work* Slough: National Foundation for Educational Research

HILSUM, S. and CANE, B. (1971) *The Teacher's Day* Slough: National Foundation for Educational Research

HOOD, J. (1975) 'Qualitative analysis of oral reading errors: the interjudge reliability of scores *Reading Research Quarterly, XI,* 4, 577–598

HUEY, E.B. (1913) *The Psychology and Pedagogy of Reading* New York: Macmillan

JENKINSON, M.D. (1969) 'Sources of knowledge for theories of reading'. *Journal of Reading Behaviour I,* i, 11-29

JOHNSON, M.S. and KRESS, R.A. (1971) 'Individual Reading Inventories'. In DECHANTE (Ed.) *Detection and Correction of Reading Difficulties* New York: Appleton-Century-Crofts

JOHNSON, R.W. (1976) 'Books in schools – curriculum problems'. In CASHDAN, A. (Ed.) *The Content of Reading* London: Ward Lock Educational

KAMM, A. and TAYLOR, B. (1966) *Books and The Teacher* London: University of London Press

KEIR, G. (1949) *Adventures in Reading* Oxford: Oxford University Press

KEIR, G. (1953) *More Adventures in Reading* Oxford: Oxford University Press

KERFOOT, J.B. (1916) *How to Read* London: Constable

KETTLES, P. and MACDONALD, R.A.D. (1949, revised 1963) *Vanguard Readers* Edinburgh: McDougall

KLARE, G.R. (1963) *The Measurement of Readability* Iowa: Iowa State University Press

KOUNIN, J.B., FRIESEN, W. and NORTON, A. (1966) 'Managing emotionally disturbed children in regular classrooms'. *Journal of Educational Psychology,* 57, 1-13

LEVIN, H. and WILLIAMS, J. (Eds.) (1970) *Basic Studies on Reading*

REFERENCES 357

New York: Basic Books

LEVITT, E. (1970) 'The effect of context on the reading of mentally retarded and normal children at the first grade level'. *Journal of Special Education 4*, 4, 425–429

LUNZER, E. and GARDNER, K. (Eds.) (1979) *The Effective Use of Reading* London: Heinemann Educational Books for the Schools Council

MACKINNON, A.R. (1959) *How Do Children Learn to Read?* Toronto: Copp. Clark

McCRACKEN, R.A. (1969) 'The Informal Reading Inventory as a means of improving reading instruction'. In BARRETT, T.C. (Ed.) *The Evaluation of Children's Reading Achievement* (Perspectives in Reading No. 8) Newark, Delaware: International Reading Association

McCULLAGH, S. K. (1959) *Griffin Pirate Series* Leeds: Arnold

McCULLAGH, S. K. (1963) *Dragon Pirate Series* Leeds: Arnold

McKEE, P., HARRISON, M. L., McCOWEN, A., LEHR, E. (1956) *The McKee Readers* London: Nelson

McKENZIE, M. and WARLOW, A. (1977) *Reading Matters: Selecting and Using Books in the Classroom* London: Hodder and Stoughton

McLAUGHLIN, H. (1969) 'Smog grading – a new readability formula'. *Journal of Reading, 22*, 112–118

McNALLY, J. and MURRAY, W. (1962) *Key Words to Literacy* London: The Schoolmaster Publishing Co.

MELNIK, A. and MERRITT, J. (1972) *Reading: Today and Tomorrow* London: University of London Press in association with the Open University

MERRIT, J. (1969) 'Reading skills re-examined'. *Special Education* 58, 1, 18–22.

MERRITT, J. (1972) 'The intermediate skills'. In MORRIS, J. (Ed.) *The First R.* London: Ward Lock Educational

MINISTRY OF EDUCATION (1950) *Reading Ability: Some Suggestions for Helping the Backward* (Pamphlet No. 18) London: H.M.S.O.

MINISTRY OF EDUCATION (1959) *Primary Education* London: H.M.S.O.

MOON, C. (1973) *Individualized Reading* (Comparative lists of selected books for young readers) University of Reading: Centre for the Teaching of Reading

MORRIS, J. M. (1959) *Reading in the Primary School* London: Newnes

MORRIS, J. M. (1966) *Standards and Progress in Reading* Slough: National Foundation for Educational Research

MORRIS, J. M. (1967) 'Reading: the first "R", yesterday, today and tomorrow.' In BROWN, A. L. (Ed.) *Reading: Current Research and Practice* Edinburgh: Chambers

MORRIS, R. (1963) *Success and Failure in Learning to Read* London: Oldbourne

MORRISON, A. and McINTYRE, D. (1969) *Teachers and Teaching* London: Penguin Education

MOXON, C. A. V. (1962) *A Remedial Reading Method* London: Methuen

MOYLE, D. (1971) 'Readability: the use of Cloze procedure.' in MERRITT, J. E. (Ed.) *Reading and the Curriculum* London: Ward

Lock Educational

MOYLE, D. (1972) 'The development of the skills of literacy.' In SOUTHGATE, V. (Ed.) *Literacy at All Levels* London: Ward Lock Educational

MURRAY, W. (1964) *Key Words Reading Scheme* Loughborough: Wills and Hepworth

NEALE, M. D. (1958) *Analysis of Reading Ability* London: Macmillan

O'DONNELL, M. and MUNRO, R. (1949) *Janet and John* Welwyn: Nisbet

O'DONNELL, M. and MUNRO, R. (1956) *High on a Hill, Days in the Sun, The Five-and-a-Half Club* London: Nisbet

OSBORNE, C. H. C. (Ed.) (1962) (3rd impression 1970) *Using Books in the Primary School* London: School Library Press

PARKER, D. H. and SCANNELL, G. (1963) *S.R.A. Reading Laboratories* Chicago: Science Research Associates

PASCOE, T. W. (Ed.) (1956) *A Survey of Books for Backward Readers* London: University of London Press

PASCOE, T. W. (Ed.) (1962) *A Second Survey of Books for Backward Readers* London: University of London Press

POWELL, W. R. (1970) 'Re-appraising the criteria for interpreting informal inventories.' In DE BOER, D. L. *Reading Diagnosis and Evaluation* Newark, Delaware: International Reading Association

POWELL, W. R. (1973) 'Acquisition of a reading repertoire.' *Literary Trends.* October 1973

PRATT, F. (1939) *Secret and Urgent* Indianapolis: Bobbs-Merrill

PUGH, A. K. (1975) 'The development of silent reading'. In LATHAM, W. (Ed.) *The Road to Effective Reading* London: Ward Lock Educational

PUGH, A. K. (1978) *Silent Reading* London: Heinemann Educational Books

PUMFREY, P. D. (1976) *Reading: Tests and Assessment Techniques* London: Hodder and Stoughton

PUMFREY, P. D. (1977) *Measuring Reading Abilities: Concepts, Sources and Applications*

PURTON, R. W. (1970) *Surrounded by Books* London: Ward Lock Educational

RABAN, B. (1973) *Reading Skill Acquisition: Comparative Lists of Reading Games and Support Materials* University of Reading: Centre for the Teaching of Reading

RAVEN, J. C. (1949) *The Coloured Progressive Matrices* London: H. K. Lewis

RAVEN, J. C. (1951) *The Crichton Vocabulary Scale* London: H. K. Lewis

REID, J. (1958) 'A study of thirteen beginners in reading.' *Acta Psychologica* 14, 295–313

REID, J. (1966) 'Learning to think about reading.' *Educational Research 8*, 56–62

REIS, M. (1962) *Fun With Phonics* Cambridge: Cambridge Art Publishers

RESNICK, D. P. and RESNICK, L. B. (1977) 'The nature of literacy: an historical exploration.' *Harvard Educational Review 47*, 3, pp. 370–385

RESNICK, L. B. (1972) 'Teacher behaviour in the informal classroom'. *Journal of Curriculum Studies, 4,* 99–109

RIDOUT, R. and AINSWORTH, R. (1956) *Look Ahead Readers* London: Heinemann Educational Books

ROBINSON, H. A. (1977) 'Comprehension: an elusive concept.' In GILLILAND, H. (Ed.) *Reading: Research and Classroom Practice* pp. 58–64 London: Ward Lock Educational

ROBINSON, H. A. (1966) 'The major aspects of reading.' In ROBINSON, H. A. (Ed.) *Reading: Seventy-five Years of Progress* Supplementary Educational Monographs No. 96 Chicago: University of Chicago Press

ROBINSON, H. and WEINTRAUB, S. (1973) 'Research related to children's interests and to developmental values of reading.' *Library Trends* Oct. 1973

ROSEN, C. and ROSEN, H. (1973) *The Language of Primary School Children* London: Penguin Books

ROSENSHINE, B. (1971) 'Teaching behaviours related to pupil achievement: a review of research.' In WESTBURY, I. and BELLACK, A. A. (Eds.) *Research into Classroom Processes* Columbia: Teachers' College

SCHONELL, F. J. (1938) *The Happy Venture Readers* Edinburgh: Oliver and Boyd

SCHONELL, F. J. and SERGEANT, I. (1938) *The Happy Venture Readers* Edinburgh: Oliver and Boyd

SCHONELL, F. J. (1948) *Graded Word Reading Test* London: Oliver and Boyd

SCHONELL, F. J. and FLOWERDEW, P. (1953) *The Wide Range Readers* Edinburgh: Oliver and Boyd

SCHOOL LIBRARY ASSOCIATION (1966) *The Library in the Primary School* London: School Library Association

SIMON, A. and BOYER, E. G. (1970) *Mirrors for Behavior II: An Anthology of Classroom Observation Instruments* Philadelphia: Research for Better Schools, Inc.

SMITH, E. B., GOODMAN, K. S. and MEREDITH, R. (1976, 2nd Edn) *Language and Thinking in School* New York: Holt, Rinehart and Winston

SMITH, F. (1971) *Understanding Reading* New York: Holt, Rinehart and Winston

SMITH, F. (1977) *Harvard Educational Review,* 47, 3, 386–395

SMITH, F. (1978) *Reading* Cambridge: Cambridge University Press

SOUTHGATE, V. (1962) *Southgate Group Reading Test 2* Sevenoaks: Hodder and Stoughton Educational

SOUTHGATE, V. (1968) 'Formulae for Beginning Reading Tuition'. *Educational Research, 11,* 1, 23–30

SOUTHGATE, V. (1973) 'The language arts in informal British Primary schools'. *The Reading Teacher,* 26, 4, 367–373

SOUTHGATE, V. (1975) 'Planning for reading progress in informal primary schools'. In MOYLE, D. (Ed.) *Reading: What of the Future* London: Ward Lock Educational

SOUTHGATE, V. and HAVENHAND, J. (1959) *Sounds and Words* London: University of London Press

SOUTHGATE, V. and LEWIS, D. Y. (1973) 'How Important Is The Infant Reading Scheme.' *Reading, 7,* 2, June 1973

SPACHE, G. (1953) 'A new redability formula for primary grade reading materials'. *Elementary School Journal, 53,* pp. 410–413

SPACHE, G. (1966) *Good Reading for Poor Readers* Champaign, Illinois: Garrard

SPACHE, G. D. and SPACHE, E. B. (1969, 2nd Edn.) *Reading in the Elementary School* Boston: Allyn and Bacon

STAUFFER, R. G. (1975) *Directing The Reading–Thinking Process* New York: Harper and Row

START, K. B. and WELLS, B. K. (1972) *The Trend of Reading Standards* Slough: National Foundation for Educational Research

STONE, C. (1956) 'Measuring difficulty of primary reading material: a constructive criticism of Spache's measure'. *Elementary School Journal, 57,* pp. 36–41

STOTT, D. H. (1962) *Programmed Reading Kit* Glasgow: Holmes

STRANG, R. (1965) 'The reading process and its ramifications.' In *Invitational Addresses – 1965* Newark, Delaware, USA: International Reading Association

STRANG, R. *et al.* (1967) *The Improvement of Reading* New York: McGraw-Hill

STRANG, R. (1969) (2nd Ed.) *Diagnostic Teaching of Reading* New York: McGraw-Hill

STRANG, R. (1972) 'Informal Reading Inventories'. In MELNIK, A. and MERRITT, J. (Eds.) *The Reading Curriculum* London: Hodder and Stoughton Educational

TANSLEY, A. E. (1960) *Racing to Read* Leeds: Arnold

TANSLEY, A. E. (1961) *Sound Sense* Leeds: Arnold

TAYLOR, B. (1958) *The Dolphin Books* London: University of London Press

TAYLOR, J. and INGLEBY, T. (1961) *Reading With Rhythm* London: Longman

TAYLOR, W. L. (1953) 'Cloze Procedure: a new tool for measuring readability'. *Journalism Quarterly, 30,* 415–33

THORNDIKE, Robert, L. (1973) *Reading Comprehension Education in Fifteen Countries* (International Studies in Evaluation III) New York: John Wiley

VERNON, P. E. (1969) *Intelligence and Cultural Environment* London: Methuen

WAITE, C. and COLEBOURN, R. (Eds.) (1975) *Not By Books Alone* Oxford: School Library Association

WALKER, C. (1974) *Reading Development and Extension* London: Ward Lock Educational

WEBER, R. M. (1968) 'First graders' use of grammatical content in reading'. In LEVIN, H. and WILLIAMS, J. *Basic Studies in Reading* New York: Harper and Row

WEBER, R.M. (1970) 'A linguistic analysis of first grade reading errors'. *Reading Research Quarterly, V,* 427–451

WEBSTER, J. (1965) *Practical Reading: Some New Remedial Tech-*

*niques* London: Evans

WEST BROMWICH CHILD PSYCHOLOGY SERVICE (1973) *Reading Schemes for Slow Learners* West Bromwich Educational Committee

WHITEHEAD, F., CAPEY, A. C. and MADDREN, W. (1975) *Children's Reading Interests* (An interim report for the Schools Council Research Project into Children's Reading Habits, 10–15) London: Evans and Methuen Educational

WHITEHEAD, F., CAPEY, A. C., MADDREN, W. and WELLINGS, A. (1977) *Children and their Books* London: Macmillan Educational

WIJK, A. (1966) *Rules of Pronunciation for the English Language* Oxford: Oxford University Press

# Index